D1559705

Folk Literature of the
Chorote Indians

UCLA LATIN AMERICAN STUDIES

Volume 60

A Book on Lore

Series Editor
Johannes Wilbert

FOLK LITERATURE OF SOUTH AMERICAN INDIANS

Folk Literature of the Warao Indians: Narrative Material and Motif Content. Edited by Johannes Wilbert. UCLA Latin American Studies, Vol. 15. Los Angeles: Latin American Center Publications, University of California, 1970.

Folk Literature of the Selknam Indians: Martin Gusinde's Collection of Selknam Narratives. Edited by Johannes Wilbert. UCLA Latin American Studies, Vol. 32. Los Angeles: UCLA Latin American Center Publications, University of California, 1975.

Folk Literature of the Yamana Indians: Martin Gusinde's Collection of Yamana Narratives. Edited by Johannes Wilbert. UCLA Latin American Studies, Vol. 40. Berkeley and Los Angeles: University of California Press, 1977.

Folk Literature of the Gê Indians, Volume One. Edited by Johannes Wilbert, with Karin Simoneau. UCLA Latin American Studies, Vol. 44. Los Angeles: UCLA Latin American Center Publications, University of California, 1978.

Folk Literature of the Mataco Indians. Edited by Johannes Wilbert and Karin Simoneau. UCLA Latin American Studies, Vol. 52. Los Angeles: UCLA Latin American Center Publications, University of California, 1982.

Folk Literature of the Toba Indians, Volume One. Edited by Johannes Wilbert and Karin Simoneau. UCLA Latin American Studies, Vol. 54. Los Angeles: UCLA Latin American Center Publications, University of California, 1982.

Folk Literature of the Bororo Indians. Edited by Johannes Wilbert and Karin Simoneau. UCLA Latin American Studies, Vol. 57. Los Angeles: UCLA Latin American Center Publications, University of California, 1983.

Folk Literature of the Gê Indians, Volume Two. Edited by Johannes Wilbert and Karin Simoneau. UCLA Latin American Studies, Vol. 58. Los Angeles: UCLA Latin American Center Publications, University of California, 1984.

Folk Literature of the Tehuelche Indians. Edited by Johannes Wilbert and Karin Simoneau. UCLA Latin American Studies, Vol. 59. Los Angeles: UCLA Latin American Center Publications, University of California, 1984.

FOLK LITERATURE
of the CHOROTE INDIANS

JOHANNES WILBERT

and

KARIN SIMONEAU

Editors

CONTRIBUTING AUTHORS

Edgardo J. Cordeu
Celia O. Mashnshnek
Erland von Nordenskiöld
Alejandra Siffredi
María Alejandra Verna

UCLA LATIN AMERICAN CENTER PUBLICATIONS
University of California, Los Angeles

Library of Congress Cataloging in Publication Data

Main entry under title:

Folk literature of the Chorote Indians.

(Folk literature of South American Indians) (UCLA Latin American studies ; v. 60)
Bibliography: p.
Includes index.
1. Choroti Indians—Legends. 2. Choroti Indians—Religion and mythology. 3. Indians of South America—Legends. 4. Indians of South America—Religion and mythology. I. Wilbert, Johannes. II. Simoneau, Karin. III. Cordeu, Edgardo J. IV. Series. V. Series: UCLA Latin American studies ; v. 60.

F3320.2.C5F66 1985   398.2'08998   85-9961
ISBN 0-87903-060-7

Grateful acknowledgment is made to the following for permission to translate and print:

Carlos J. Gradin, Editor, *Relaciones* de la Sociedad Argentina de Antropología (Buenos Aires, Argentina), for Celia O. Mashnshnek (1972, 1973*b*).

Preface

Folk Literature of the Chorote Indians is the tenth volume in the series of South American Indian folk literature which UCLA Latin American Center Publications and/or the University of California Press have been issuing since 1970. Previous volumes were dedicated to the oral lore of the Selknam and Yamana of Tierra del Fuego, the Tehuelche of Patagonia, the Mataco and Toba Indians of the Gran Chaco, the Bororo of Mato Grosso, the Gê Indians of Central Brazil, and the Warao of the Orinoco Delta. Thus, the Folk Literature of South American Indians series concentrates on the so-called marginal societies of the subcontinent and is scheduled to include future collections of the Halakwulup of Tierra del Fuego; the Mokovi, Lengua, Nivakle, Kaduveo, Chamacoco, and Ayoreo of the Gran Chaco; the Yanoama of Amazonia; the Guahiboan tribes of Colombia; the Goajiro of Colombia and Venezuela; and possibly others. A comprehensive motif dictionary including an analysis of motif indexing will conclude the series.

Folk Literature of the Chorote Indians was made possible through the active collaboration of the contributing authors. Principal among them is Alejandra Siffredi (1982), who contributed eighty-one unpublished narratives to the present collection; Celia O. Mashnshnek (1972, 1973b) collected thirty-three; María Alejandra Verna (ms.) transcribed twenty-six heretofore unpublished texts from the archives of the Centro Argentino de Etnología Americana; Edgardo J. Cordeu contributed eight unpublished narratives included in Siffredi's doctoral dissertation; and two short texts were taken from Erland von Nordenskiöld's book (1926).

The editors of *Folk Literature of the Chorote Indians* are deeply grateful to the contributing authors, to translators Sally Sizemore and Bruce Williams who provided the first draft of the Spanish-English translation, and to Michael Paolisso for word processing. Colleen Trujillo, Production Manager, UCLA Latin American Center Publications, and her staff assistant, Jocelyne Bauduy, produced the book. Very special thanks are due to Yehuda Afek, who designed the computer program which generated the indexes of the book and which will produce the apparatus of all future volumes in the series, including the final comprehensive *Motif Dictionary of South American Indian Narratives.*

Chancellor Charles E. Young and Dr. Franklin D. Murphy have taken an active interest in the UCLA project of South American Indian lore. Financial aid for research and publication was generously provided by The UCLA Foundation and the Ahmanson Foundation.

Contents

CONTRIBUTING AUTHORS AND NARRATIVES   xvii

EDITORS' NOTE   xxi

INTRODUCTION   1
  Johannes Wilbert

THE NARRATIVES

1. The paths of Sun and Moon, *p. 17*
   Siffredi
2. The contests of Sun (Kilát) and Moon (Wuéla), *p. 17*
   Mashnshnek
3. Moon's wives turn into stars, *p. 18*
   Siffredi
4. A lunar eclipse caused by Tséxmataki, *p. 19*
   Verna
5. The origin of a five-star constellation, *p. 19*
   Siffredi
6. Children transformed into stars, *p. 21*
   Verna
7. Birds of the sky and the earth, *p. 21*
   Siffredi
8. Moon creates the earth, *p. 23*
   Siffredi
9. The star and the origin of man, *p. 25*
   Mashnshnek
10. A star made pregnant by the earth, *p. 26*
    Mashnshnek
11. The celestial couple, *p. 27*
    Siffredi

12. The origin of women, *p. 29*
    Mashnshnek

13. The origin of women and of death, *p. 31*
    Siffredi

14. Kíxwet and the origin of women, *p. 33*
    Siffredi

15. Kíxwet and the women from the sky, *p. 36*
    Siffredi

16. The great flood, *p. 38*
    Verna

17. The destruction of mankind by subterranean water, *p. 38*
    Verna

18. The destruction of the world, *p. 39*
    Verna

19. The world-fire, *p. 40*
    Nordenskiöld

20. The origin of animals, *p. 41*
    Mashnshnek

21. The destruction by fire, *p. 42*
    Siffredi

22. The destruction by fire, *p. 45*
    Siffredi

23. The destruction by fire, *p. 46*
    Cordeu

24. The great fire, *p. 47*
    Siffredi

25. The origin of trees, *p. 49*
    Mashnshnek

26. The origin of the green algarrobo tree, *p. 49*
    Mashnshnek

27. Fox brings and scatters algarrobo trees, *p. 50*
    Siffredi

28. The folly and power of Kíxwet, *p. 51*
    Siffredi

29. Fox changes the habitat and the properties of the chaguar, *p. 52*
    Siffredi

30. The origin of Sachasandia, *p. 53*
    Siffredi

31. The origin of bitter manioc, *p. 54*
    Siffredi

32. Moon shows Armadillo the properties of his plants, *p. 55*
    Siffredi

33. Armadillo and the leisurely way of planting, *p. 56*
    Siffredi

34. Fox causes sowing and harvesting to be no longer simultaneous,
    p. 60
    Siffredi

35. Armadillo and his fields, *p. 61*
    Mashnshnek

36. Fox and Armadillo sow, *p. 62*
    Mashnshnek

37. Moon reveals the plant cycle to a shaman, *p. 63*
    Siffredi

38. The origin of cultivated plants and of batrachians, *p. 65*
    Siffredi

39. Kíxwet-Aséta: The magic pregnancy and the introduction of
    food fish, *p. 67*
    Siffredi

40. Séta's son teaches man to eat fish, *p. 70*
    Mashnshnek

41. The origin of fish, *p. 71*
    Cordeu

42. Kíxwet introduces fish and creates the river, *p. 76*
    Siffredi

43. Kisbar introduces fishing, *p. 80*
    Verna

44. Fox discovers a trough full of fish, *p. 81*
    Siffredi

45. Fox discovers a container of food, *p. 84*
    Siffredi

46. Fox, releasing the waters, causes the great flood, *p. 87*
    Verna

47. Fox causes the great flood, *p. 89*
     Mashnshnek

48. Fox discovers the container of food, *p. 90*
     Siffredi

49. Fox releases the waters, causing the great flood, *p. 92*
     Verna

50. The origin of fire, *p. 92*
     Mashnshnek

51. The origin of fire, *p. 93*
     Siffredi

52. The origin of fire, *p. 94*
     Siffredi

53. The origin of fire, *p. 97*
     Cordeu

54. How the hawk stole fire, *p. 99*
     Mashnshnek

55. Why the Indians are poor, *p. 99*
     Mashnshnek

56. Moon teaches the people to construct houses, *p. 100*
     Mashnshnek

57. Fox seduces the king vulture's daughter, *p. 101*
     Siffredi

58. The origin of chicha and of shamanism, *p. 102*
     Siffredi

59. The origin of honey-chicha, *p. 106*
     Siffredi

60. The origin of honey, *p. 107*
     Siffredi

61. Tséxmataki, the cannibal, and the origin of tobacco, *p. 110*
     Siffredi

62. Tséxmataki, the cannibal, goes to the sky: The origin of
         tobacco, *p. 111*
     Siffredi

63. The origin of green tobacco, *p. 114*
     Mashnshnek

64. Tséxmataki, the cannibal, and the origin of shamanic helpers,
    p. 116
    Siffredi
65. The death of Tséxmataki, and the origin of green tobacco, *p. 121*
    Verna
66. The death of Tséxmataki, and the origin of green tobacco, *p. 123*
    Verna
67. The man who turned into Tséxmataki: The origin of birds and
    wild animals, *p. 124*
    Siffredi
68. The hunters in the sky: The origin of certain animals, *p. 128*
    Verna
69. The origin of wild animals, *p. 129*
    Siffredi
70. The origin of peccaries and other wild animals, *p. 138*
    Cordeu
71. The sparrow hawk gives names and habits to the animals, *p. 143*
    Mashnshnek
72. The sun and the origin of some domesticated animals, *p. 146*
    Verna
73. The origin of chickens, *p. 147*
    Verna
74. The origin of felines, *p. 148*
    Verna
75. The chief of the anteaters, *p. 148*
    Siffredi
76. The chiefs of the iguanas, *p. 149*
    Siffredi
77. The chief of the peccaries, *p. 150*
    Siffredi
78. The chief of the peccaries, *p. 152*
    Siffredi
79. How the tapir got a prominent nose, *p. 153*
    Siffredi
80. How armadillos got their distinctive features, *p. 154*
    Siffredi

81. The origin of the capybara, *p. 155*
Siffredi

82. The chief of tapirs, *p. 157*
Siffredi

83. The mistresses of doves, *p. 158*
Siffredi

84. The chief of batrachians, *p. 160*
Siffredi

85. The origin of wild pigs, *p. 161*
Mashnshnek

86. The chief of pumas, *p. 161*
Siffredi

87. How an old husband turned into a bird, *p. 162*
Siffredi

88. The constellations and the origin of birds, *p. 163*
Mashnshnek

89. Killing the sharpened-leg cannibal: The origin of Kiésta, *p. 164*
Siffredi

90. The origin of the mockingbird, *p. 168*
Mashnshnek

91. The origin of the black vulture, *p. 172*
Mashnshnek

92. Killing the blind man who ate children: The origin of Atá, *p. 174*
Siffredi

93. Killing Atá, the old man who ate children, *p. 176*
Siffredi

94. The origin of pottery and of the ovenbird, *p. 178*
Siffredi

95. Killing the hidden murderer: The origin of Sáti, *p. 180*
Siffredi

96. Origin of the ovenbird, *p. 181*
Mashnshnek

97. The origin of the burrowing owl, *p. 182*
Mashnshnek

98. Killing the hidden murderer: The origin of Kioí, *p. 183*
Siffredi

99. The origin of parrots and herons, *p. 185*
    Mashnshnek

100. Killing Sákiti, the man-eating celestial bird: The origin of the
     color of birds, *p. 187*
     Siffredi

101. Killing Sákiti, the man-eating celestial eagle: The origin of the
     color of birds, *p. 197*
     Siffredi

102. Confrontation with Sákiti, *p. 199*
     Siffredi

103. Confrontation with Sákiti, *p. 200*
     Siffredi

104. Confrontation with Kiliéni Thlásini, *p. 201*
     Siffredi

105. The origin of snakes, *p. 203*
     Mashnshnek

106. Killing the woman impregnated by a snakeskin: The origin of
     the vampire and of snakes, *p. 205*
     Siffredi

107. Killing the man-eating water snake: The discovery of aquatic
     animals and the origin of the drying up of lakes, *p. 209*
     Siffredi

108. Killing the mother of the man-eating water snakes and the
     mother of the alligators: Origin of the drying up of lakes
     and of dangerous storms, *p. 211*
     Cordeu

109. The man who was swallowed by the big snake, *p. 216*
     Verna

110. The Indian swallowed by a snake, *p. 217*
     Nordenskiöld

111. The man-eating wasps, *p. 217*
     Verna

112. The headhunter, *p. 218*
     Verna

113. Killing the bird catcher's wife who was possessed by Tséxmataki,
     p. 219
     Siffredi

114. Killing the bird catcher's wife who was possessed by Tséxmataki, *p. 221*
     Cordeu
115. The bird-men ascend to heaven on a chain of arrows, *p. 225*
     Cordeu
116. The sexual excesses of Kíxwet, *p. 227*
     Siffredi
117. The sexual excesses of Kíxwet, *p. 228*
     Siffredi
118. Kíswet deflowers girls, *p. 230*
     Mashnshnek
119. Kiswét turns into a gaucho, *p. 232*
     Verna
120. Confrontation with Kíxwet, *p. 233*
     Siffredi
121. Misdeeds, deaths, resurrections, and transformations of Kíxwet, *p. 234*
     Cordeu
122. Kíxwet kills the club murderer, *p. 237*
     Siffredi
123. The giant Kíswet searches for his family, *p. 238*
     Mashnshnek
124. Killing the Thlimnál i-wós cannibals, *p. 239*
     Siffredi
125. Pasá, the *yulo* bird, destroys the bird snatchers, *p. 242*
     Siffredi
126. Confrontation with Siéhnam, the deer, *p. 243*
     Siffredi
127. Confrontation with the deer-man, *p. 243*
     Siffredi
128. Confrontation with the jaguar-man, *p. 244*
     Siffredi
129. The woman married to the jaguar, *p. 246*
     Mashnshnek
130. The woman who was married to Aiés (the jaguar), *p. 247*
     Verna

131. The woman who married Aiés (the jaguar), *p. 248*
     Verna
132. War between the Chorote and the Sirakua, *p. 248*
     Verna
133. The land of plenty, *p. 250*
     Siffredi
134. The man who turned himself into a rhea, *p. 253*
     Verna
135. A celestial puma hunt, *p. 254*
     Verna
136. The star-woman, *p. 254*
     Mashnshnek
137. Katés, the morning star, *p. 257*
     Siffredi
138. Star-Woman marries a man, *p. 263*
     Verna
139. Katés, the morning star woman, *p. 265*
     Siffredi
140. Star-Woman marries a man, *p. 267*
     Verna
141. Moon remakes an ugly man, *p. 268*
     Siffredi
142. Moon remakes an ugly man, *p. 269*
     Siffredi
143. Moon grants strength to a man, *p. 270*
     Mashnshnek
144. Fox deceives Bee and has his bodily orifices stopped up, *p. 271*
     Siffredi
145. Fox makes fun of the women who grind algarrobo, *p. 273*
     Siffredi
146. The fox and the cariama, *p. 274*
     Mashnshnek
147. The fox and the jaguar, *p. 274*
     Mashnshnek
148. The fox and the iguana, *p. 277*
     Mashnshnek

149. Fox, the stupid imitator of the maize parrots, *p. 279*
    Siffredi
150. Fox and the lamb, *p. 279*
    Verna

THE MOTIF INDICES

Motif Distribution by Narrative   283
Topical Motif Index   289
Alphabetical Motif Index   329
Motif Distribution by Motif Group   387

Glossary   393
Bibliography   397

Contributing Authors and Narratives

EDGARDO J. CORDEU, Argentine anthropologist, holds a doctorate from the Universidad de Buenos Aires. He is professor of anthropology at the same university and a researcher at the Instituto Nacional de Antropología. One of Argentina's foremost scholars in his field of specialty, Cordeu has made substantial contributions to Gran Chaco anthropology. His monographic studies of the Toba of Miraflores (1967, 1969) investigate the cultural configuration of this community, placing special emphasis on the dynamics of culture change. More recently, Cordeu has turned to topics of religion and mythology of several Chaco societies (1973a, 1973b, 1980, 1984). His treatise on Toba cosmogony and folklore (1969–1970) is the most scholarly contribution on the subject to date, and his essay on Chamacoco cosmology (1984) represents a major contribution.

In 1969 Cordeu participated in an ethnographic survey of the central Chaco conducted by the Instituto de Antropología of the Universidad de Buenos Aires, under the direction of the late Marcelo Bórmida. On this occasion Cordeu collected eight Chorote narratives which were included in Alejandra Siffredi's doctoral dissertation and from which manuscript they were translated for inclusion in the present collection: narratives 23, 41, 53, 70, 108, 114, 115, 121 (Siffredi ms).

CELIA O. MASHNSHNEK, Argentine anthropologist, received her Licenciatura in anthropology from the Universidad de Buenos Aires, where she is presently working on her doctoral degree. She has taught as a professor of anthropology at the same university, and pursues the career of scientific investigator sponsored by the Consejo Nacional de Investigaciones Científicas y Técnicas.

As a student and collaborator of the late Marcelo Bórmida, Mashnshnek participated actively in the work of the modern Escuela de Etnología Americana and distinguished herself as a fieldworker among tribes of the central Chaco (Chorote, Mataco, Pilagá, Nivakle) and the northern Chaco (Ayoreo). Her personal bibliography includes important articles on mythology (1972, 1973a, 1975), cosmology (1976), life cycle and economy (1973b, 1974, 1978) of these Chaco societies.

For the present volume, Celia Mashnshnek has contributed a collection of thirty-three narratives: 2, 9, 10, 12, 20, 25, 26, 35, 36, 40, 47, 50, 54, 55, 56, 63, 71, 85, 88, 90, 91, 96, 97, 99, 105, 118, 123, 129, 136, 143, 146, 147, 148 (Mashnshnek 1972, 1973*b*).

ERLAND VON NORDENSKIÖLD (1877–1932), from Tveta, Sweden, established himself as one of the foremost scholars of South American ethnography and culture history of his time. In 1924 he became a professor of anthropology at the University of Göteborg and served as intendant of the Göteborg Museum (Wassén 1966–1967). Although concentrating on material culture and acculturative culture change, he occasionally also collected narratives of the different Indian tribes he visited. The present corpus contains two narratives which the distinguished scholar collected during the Swedish Chaco-Cordillera expedition to Argentina and Bolivia in 1901–1902: narratives 19, 110 (Nordenskiöld 1926).

ALEJANDRA SIFFREDI, Argentine anthropologist, holds a doctorate from the Universidad de Buenos Aires. She is professor of American ethnography and director of the Centro de Estudios de Antropologías Especiales at the same university. Since 1970 and in the capacity of an investigator of the Consejo Nacional de Investigaciones Científicas y Técnicas of Argentina, Siffredi has concentrated on the reconstruction of Chorote culture and cosmology. She analyzed the mythology of these Indians and its relationship to tribal social structure (1973), examined methodological and theoretical problems related to forms of mythical expression (1976; Cordeu and Siffredi 1979), and designed a model of reciprocity that governs the distribution of wealth and services (1979). Her reconstruction of Chorote cosmology evolves around the categories of mythical time and space, within the theoretical framework of symbolic anthropology (1983, 1984). For inclusion in the present corpus, she selected eighty-one narratives: 1, 3, 5, 7, 8, 11, 13, 14, 15, 21, 22, 24, 27, 28, 29, 30, 31, 32, 33, 34, 37, 38, 39, 42, 44, 45, 48, 51, 52, 57, 58, 59, 60, 61, 62, 64, 67, 69, 75, 76, 77, 78, 79, 80, 81, 82, 83, 84, 86, 87, 89, 92, 93, 94, 95, 98, 100, 101, 102, 103, 104, 106, 107, 113, 116, 117, 120, 122, 124, 125, 126, 127, 128, 133, 137, 139, 141, 142, 144, 145, 149 (Siffredi 1982).

MARÍA ALEJANDRA VERNA, Argentine anthropologist, received her Licenciatura in anthropology from the Universidad de Buenos Aires and is a member of the Centro Argentino de Etnología Americana. She has carried out fieldwork among the Toba of the Chaco province, in Jujuy, and among the Ese'ejja of Bolivia. Her publications reflect a special interest in shamanism, cosmology, and mythology of the societies she has visited. Quite recently Verna's scholarly standing has been recognized by the Consejo Nacional de Investigaciones Científicas y Técnicas, which awarded her a grant to conduct anthropological studies among the Chorote of the central Chaco and the Ese'ejja of western Amazonia. For the present volume she has contributed twenty-six narratives: 4, 6, 16, 17, 18, 43, 46, 49, 65, 66, 68, 72, 73, 74, 109, 111, 112, 119, 130, 131, 132, 134, 135, 138, 140, 150 (Verna ms).

Editors' Note

Folk Literature of the Chorote Indians comprises 150 narratives which, except for two narratives in Swedish, were translated from Spanish. The Spanish-English translations were edited and subsequently forwarded to the contributing authors for verification of accuracy. Of the total of 150 narratives contained in the present volume, 115 (77%) are published here for the first time.

Technical nomenclature of plants and animals in the text is given by the contributing authors. Additional information can be found in the glossary. Footnotes, if not explicitly identified [eds.], were supplied by the contributing authors. Inconsistencies in the spelling of informants' and other personal names are intentional.

The motif index is as comprehensive as practically possible. Identification of motifs is according to Thompson's *Motif Index of Folk Literature* (1955-1958). Thompson motifs that required amplification according to Chorote narrative context are identified with a plus sign. In all such cases Thompson's motif wording is juxtaposed with the editors' rendering to facilitate instant comparison and appreciation of the changes made.

All motif listings and indexes of the book are computer generated.

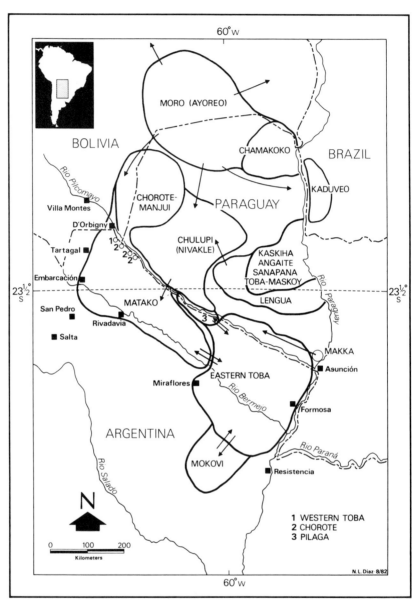

Approximate present distribution areas of the Chorote Indians and of other tribes of the Gran Chaco. Map by Niels Fock and Alfredo Tomasini. Arrows indicate directions of population movements.

Introduction

HISTORY OF CHOROTE FOLK LITERATURE STUDIES

The Chorote are a society of Gran Chaco Indians who inhabit the vicinity of the three-corner area of Argentina, Paraguay, and Bolivia (see map).[1] Referring to themselves generically as Yoxwáha, one distinguishes a southern and a northern branch of modern Chorote and at least three tribal subdivisions.[2] The southern Chorote, or Yoxwáha proper,[3] of Argentina, are concentrated along the right bank of the upper Pilcomayo and near the town of Tartagal, one hundred miles inland from that section of the river (Siffredi 1973:71–72; 1982:11–15). A splinter group of Yoxwáha proper can be found on the left bank of the Pilcomayo northeast of Colonia Pedro P. Peña (Chase-Sardi 1972:91).

The northern Chorote, comprising the Yowúxua and the (northernmost) Xuikína-wó,[4] inhabit the arid hinterlands of the upper Pilcomayo and places near the western border of Paraguay. A small group of Yowúxua has been located near Galpón on the north shore of the Pilcomayo (Chase-Sardi 1972:29–30, 92, 100, map). Chervin (1908) suggested that nomadic Chorote groups were also found along the left bank of the Bolivian Pilcomayo, but nothing has been heard of them in more recent times (Key and Key 1967:126). Although suspicious of each other and prone to mutual enmity, modern representatives of the southern (Yoxwáha proper) and northern (Yowúxua) Chorote reside together in several, albeit segregated, Pilcomayo settlements. In others, they coexist with members of the Mataco, Nivakle, and Toba tribes.

For these and sundry other reasons, good partial or aggregate data on Chorote demography are difficult to find. The Argentine Indian census of 1967–68 registers a total of 1,212 inhabitants for the mixed

---

[1]Special thanks to Alejandra Siffredi for providing a copy of her doctoral dissertation which facilitated writing the introduction.
[2]The designation "Chorote" or "Choroti," by which these Indians have become known in the ethnographic literature, originated with the Tupian-speaking Chiriguano, their neighbors to the north (Nordenskiöld 1912:25).
[3]Known also by their Nivakle name, Eklenxúi (Eklenjuy).
[4]Jointly known also by their Nivakle name, Manxuí (Manjuy).

1

and unmixed Pilcomayo and Tartagal settlements in question, a figure which Siffredi (1982:43) adjusts to 800 to account for their Chorote contingents. This number is close to Bartolomé's (1972:430–431) figure of approximately 700 Argentine Chorote. For the Paraguayan Chorote, Chase-Sardi (1972:29) records a partial figure of 700 individuals, while Bejarano (1977) estimates them to comprise a total of 2,000 members. Given the preliminary nature of these data and conscious of the complete lack of information for possible (though unlikely) Bolivian groups, a global total of 2,500 Chorote, as suggested by Hunt (1915:170), may not be too far off the mark.

The Chorote speak a language of the Matacoan linguistic family (Loukotka 1968:54), considered by Brinton (1891) and Hunt (1915) to be of great antiquity in the Gran Chaco. Ethnohistorical evidence suggests that the Chorote came to occupy their present habitat as a consequence of a general population displacement occasioned by the intrusion of the Chiriguano into the region northwest of the Gran Chaco (Canals Frau 1953:318, 333; Susnik 1972:98). Considerable readjustments of traditional tribal territories were also caused by military expeditions against the independent Indians of the general region. In early periods, people ancestral to the present-day Chorote occasionally appeared in the literature under designations such as Paloma, Xolota, and Abucheta. But in the account of Lozano's (1941:218–219) punitive expedition of 1673, out of Tarija, the Chorote emerge unequivocally identified by that name. At the time, they inhabited the headwaters of the Bermejo river. But under the pressure of this foray and subsequently, as a result of interethnic feuding between the Chorote on the one hand and the Toba and Mocovi on the other, the bulk of the former migrated during the seventeenth and eighteenth centuries northward to the Pilcomayo, where they occupied the general region of their present habitat. By 1845, no Chorote had apparently remained on the upper Bermejo, but were mentioned instead as among the "unpacified" Indians of the upper Pilcomayo, fiercely poised against any intruder, Indian and non-Indian alike (Nivel 1845). These included also the Franciscan missionaries who, beginning in 1863, made their first attempts at proselytizing the Chorote. In spite of some sporadic contact, their plans did not materialize (Comajuncosa and Corrado 1884:410, 422–423).

Scholarly efforts at befriending the Indians of the upper Pilcomayo fared rather worse than better. The scientific expedition in 1882 by naturalist Jules N. Crevaux resulted in calamity after ". . . Chorotes and Toba tribes had in a most friendly and peaceful manner carried on barter with the Crevaux expedition until, at a preconcerted sign, they took out their clubs and began the massacre, which ended in the annihilation of the expedition" (von Rosen 1904:11). A second exploration of Chorote territory took place one year later under Campos-Thouar. He also failed to enter into friendly contact with the Chorote, and saw, instead, his two Indian guides killed for having led him into their land. Reports von Rosen (1904:3) at the beginning of the twentieth century, ". . . the Chorotes Indians . . . are practically unaffected by any civilization." And little had been learned until that time from soldiers, missionaries, or scholars of their way of life.

Initial scholarly success came only during the first half of the twentieth century, after the Chorote and other Indian groups of the lower Pilcomayo had struck a more enduring modus vivendi with the encroaching frontier. Young tribal men had begun a seasonal pattern of wage labor as ranch hands or workers on sugar plantations, whence they returned to their villages with goods and customs of the outside world, triggering the processes of progressive acculturation. Among the first scholars to take advantage of the improved rapport were von Rosen (1904), Nordenskiöld (1912), Hunt (1915), and Karsten (1932), who visited the "tame Chorote," as the Bolivians had come to refer to the upper Pilcomayo groups, and produced extensive ethnographic and linguistic accounts of Chorote culture. Included in these were also the first two short narratives published by Nordenskiöld (1926:24–25, 88) which marked the beginning of the study of Chorote folk literature.

Following the Chaco war (1932–1935), the Yoxwáha proper abandoned their settlements on the left bank of the Pilcomayo to establish themselves in the nowadays partially mixed villages of La Merced, La Gracia, La Paz, and La Bolsa, on the right bank of the river. Here they soon came under the influence of the Anglican and Pentecostal missionaries and, beginning in 1969, became accessible to intensive anthropological inquiry.

Not so the northern Chorote of Paraguay, who until quite recently were described as roaming their territory, little "contacted by missionaries, unacculturated, unstudied, and unharmed" (Smith ms). Also on the map of Chase-Sardi (1972) are the Yowúxua of the northern Chorote, described as independent and evasive, and the Xuikína-wó, persisting in an attitude of hostile defense. Fortunately, thanks to Siffredi's work, we have not remained entirely ignorant of Yowúxua ideology.

The year 1969 marks the turning point in the study of Chorote folk literature. Except for Nordenskiöld's brief texts, the entire corpus of narratives presented here was recorded between 1969 and 1977 among the Yoxwáha proper and the Yowúxua of La Merced, La Gracia, La Paz, and La Bolsa. The first exploration took place during the months of May and June 1969, when Marcelo Bórmida led an expedition of ethnologists to initiate a study of the Argentine Chorote with special emphasis on their oral literature. This was the year when Bórmida had formulated his sociological approach to mythography and when he was expressing his views on the role of myth in primitive society (Bórmida 1969–1970*a*). He had also addressed the problems of text collecting and was in a position to provide his colleagues and students with a heuristic guide to the study of mythography (Bórmida 1969–1970*b*). The thoroughness of this methodological and theoretical preparation characterizes the work of Bórmida's mythographic school and explains the high standards of field methodology and data analysis adopted by his followers.

One of the original fieldworkers of 1969 was contributing author Edgardo Cordeu who, with the assistance of a blind seventy-five-year-old tribal elder, Centawó (Sentawó), recorded eight richly detailed narratives in the Yowúxua dialect of Chorote. Other members of the expedition collected an additional eleven narratives from the same informant.

Thus, Centawó contributed also to Celia Mashnshnek's collection, which was started in 1969 and supplemented in 1971 by narratives she recorded during her expedition to La Merced and La Bolsa. Centawó had passed away in the meantime, but otherwise Mashnshnek engaged the same informants who had collaborated with the first group of fieldworkers two years earlier. Their names appear at the end of each story they told, as Alipa, Cepillo, Esteban Mariano, Petiso, and Simplicios. They are also the storytellers of the collection which María Alejandra Verna transcribed from recordings made in 1969 and which are preserved in the archives of the Centro Argentino de Etnología Americana, Buenos Aires. Altogether, this group of informants provided sixty-one narratives (41 percent) to the corpus at hand. Mashnshnek collected an additional six stories from newly recruited informants whose names are given as Espinosa, Oliveira, and Talimpí.

To conduct a comprehensive study of Chorote cosmology, Alejandra Siffredi, in 1970, 1972, and 1977, spent a total of six months among the Indians of La Merced, La Gracia, and La Paz. In selecting her informants, she engaged only Chorote who identified themselves as Yowúxua, or northern Chorote. The eighty-one narratives contributed to the present corpus were collected with the assistance of nine informants between the ages of 50 and 75. Introducing them in terms of relative importance to her study, Siffredi (1982:87–89) furnished this additional information.

Kasókchi ilánek, from La Paz, was 65 years of age in 1972. Siffredi ranks him highest among her informants, mainly because of his exceptional knowledge of mythical lore. He was an excellent and lively narrator and rendered his stories accompanied by imitations of animal manners and voices. Patient, retentive of memory, and intelligent, he contributed twenty-one narratives to Siffredi's collection and facilitated her access to Chorote cosmology.

Aió, from La Paz, was 70 years of age in 1977. He was keen-witted, of great analytical abilities, indefatigable as an informant, and endowed with a great sense of humor. Aió was a shaman, and his knowledge of shamanic practice, shamanic mythology, and ethnozoology made him a particularly qualified resource person for the analytical study of myth.

Kíki, a woman from La Merced, was 75 years old in 1970. She was well versed in narrative art and told fourteen of the tales in the volume. As a blind person, she lived almost exclusively within the traditional past of her culture.

Axués pa, nicknamed the Bishop, from La Merced, was a man of 70 years in 1970. He was a shaman of considerable prestige and contributor of five narratives.

Máki, a woman from La Paz, was 50 years old in 1972 and the youngest of Siffredi's narrators. She was the daughter of a Nivakle father and a Yowúxua mother, and narrated six of the stories in the present volume. Although she enjoyed considerable prestige among the people, she was not particularly gifted as a storyteller.

Póm ilánek, from La Paz, was about 60 years of age in 1977. Like Máki, he was of mixed parentage and descended from a Tapiete father and a Yowúxua mother. Although a distinguished shaman, he was not particularly knowledgeable in the mythical tradition of his people. Two narratives of the corpus were recorded from him.

Domingo, from La Paz, was 60 years old in 1972. He was a shaman and only one tale is attributed to him. No additional information is available for Alenta, who also narrated one story. All told, however, Siffredi's corpus of northern Chorote narratives comprises more than half (54 percent) of the stories assembled in the volume at hand.

According to information supplied by the Argentine authors, the narratives were magnetophonically recorded in the native language. Interrupting the storyteller at short intervals, translators were employed to render literal translations of the segments into Spanish. This kept text omissions to a minimum and avoided alterations and arbitrary summary formulation of passages by the translator. The authors corrected only the grammar of the translations rendered in hinterland Spanish; confused sentences were omitted and so were repetitions that did not essentially pertain to the contextual meaning.

Siffredi mentions three translators who assisted in establishing the narratives in this volume. Tito Martínez, who was 25 years old in 1969, lived in La Merced. Identifying himself as a Yoxwáha, he was the translator of the narratives recorded by contributing author Cordeu with the help of Centawó. Tito's knowledge of Spanish was quite remarkable. Although not specifically mentioned by other contributing authors, it is likely that his skills were also employed in recording other texts collected by the members of the 1969 expedition and subsequent ones.

Felipe González, alias Kalís, from La Paz, was 27 years old in 1972 and collaborated with contributing author Siffredi as principal translator. He had received formal education at the Bible school of Embarcación, and qualified as native pastor of the Anglican Mission of La Paz. Much of the success of Siffredi's work with northern Chorote is attributed to his spontaneous and generous cooperation.

Of the older generation, Juan Lescano, alias Nókona, Yarará, 58 years of age in 1970 and from La Merced, knew enough Spanish to function as a translator. He was the chief of the village, son of Yoxwáha parents, and capable of conversing in three Chorotean dialects.

Thus, it would appear that the degree of trustworthiness of the collection of Chorote folk literature here assembled is very high indeed. Except for the two Nordenskiöld fragments, all the narratives included in the volume have been identified by the names of their native informants. In addition, the tellers of the majority of the texts are known through short biographies identifying them by sex, age, place of residence, biological origin, and qualification. Undoubtedly, therefore, the identity of the informants as Chorote Indians is clearly established.

Furthermore, as becomes apparent in the preceding account of the history of Chorote folk literature studies, the narratives of this volume have been collected in a genuine cultural context. Considering the late hour in which story recording among the Chorote finally got under way, it was extremely propitious that this work has been accomplished by scholars prepared for the task and for whom the recording of narratives represented the main objective rather than a side issue of their fieldwork, as is most often the case. Finally, portable electronic recording equipment had come of age by the time fieldwork was begun, so that the texts in their original form and in translation could be recorded with utmost efficiency and archived for multiple future analyses.

THE NARRATIVES

The corpus of Chorote narratives opens by introducing Sun and Moon as masculine personages. Their initial exploits take place at a time prior to the creation of the earth and in a preexisting universe the origin of which remains unexplained. Peculiarly enough, the two celestial heroes are of different but equal strengths and not, as is common in South American mythology, of uneven status. Though the two are contentious in disposition, their exploits establish their contrasting natures, and the contest they engage in ends in a draw.

Both celestial personages are creators. Sun creates the (Old World) domesticated animals like horses, cattle, and goats, which have become all-important in the post-contact Chorote economy. Moon shapes the earth out of amorphous dust and plants it with different kinds of cultigens; " . . . he produced many plants, . . . regulated the trees and gave away seeds." Witness to his act of creation was Moon's beautiful wife, Katés, the Morning Star, and it is interesting to observe how Chorote mythology transfers some of the antagonism that characterizes the equally nonegalitarian twin heroes of other South American mythologies to the celestial couple of Moon and Venus. She is the mistrusting and ignorant partner apt to stifle the creative imagination of her spouse.

Sun and Moon have forever left the earth to assume their respective places in the sky. Occasionally they fall victims either to attacks of the sky people (on Sun) or of the cannibalistic Tséxmataki (on Moon). Sun eclipses as a consequence of being disemboweled but revives (Mashnshnek 1972:112). Moon diminishes while being devoured but gradually regenerates again.

Constellations of stars are believed to be children who in primordial times went to the sky because of maternal neglect. Planets appear to be women who, like Morning Star, may descend to earth and become the consorts of men. Venus is the Star Woman who takes pity on a rejected man. She appears in several beautiful text versions of the collection which resemble in form and content the celestial bride tales of other Chaco mythologies, as well as their counterparts in the Gê tradition of eastern Brazil. While associated with her terrestrial companion, the Morning Star of Chorote mythology repeatedly demonstrates her power to destroy human adversaries and their fields. But her benevolent role as a preserver of life, whose breath and saliva revive the dead and invigorate the desiccated crops, distinguishes her as Moon's spouse. Once Moon had created the earth by compacting the dust with his spittle, Morning Star descended on a rope from the sky. She fertilized herself by placing earth in her vagina and in successive pregnancies gave birth to a son and a daughter. From this primeval human pair and from additional children born of the Morning Star, humanity of a mythical age descended. In another context the Star creator, rather than forming the first humans in her womb, does so by modeling them out of clay. She goes on to produce and vivify such handmade images in different places on earth and gives origin to the various tribes of mankind.

Chorote mythology distinguishes between two epochs of the world: a mythical age and a modern one. Recognizable in the mythical age is a period of harmonious undifferentiated origins and a period of disjunctive entropy. The modern age is subdivided into a period of remote past and a period of recent past (Siffredi 1982:99). The two great epochs of the world are apparently separated by the cosmic cataclysms of the World Deluge and the Great Fire.

Out of the misty dawn of the edenic age of origin emerges the faint image of a Supreme Being and his wife, whom the Chorote refer to as Kihíl Wehé, or "Little Old People." The Ancient Old Man endowed humans with three different souls: the nucleus soul, the image soul, and the shadow soul. This gift enabled humans to have offspring and to lead personal lives. A Prime Mover, the Ancient One is old but not aging. He provided for all of mankind's needs without ever moving from his seat in heaven. The Ancient Man taught the male how to hunt and the Ancient Woman instructed the female how to gather fruit. Both men and women, when embarking on their specific activities, remember the Ancient Couple in their prayers and speak their names. It is through the dreams of shamans that the Chorote know of the existence of the "Little Old People," but nobody could actually approach them in their otioseness. While the belief in multiple souls of living beings, particularly in humans, is not altogether rare in American Indian mythology, the notion of a Supreme Being certainly is, and each new appearance of a tribal High God is bound to rouse the interest of scholars in the study of religion (Haekel 1959; Mashnshnek 1972:121).

In addition to myths that explain the origin of mankind through the act of a potter-creator, there are those in Chorote mythology that tell of a generation of humans composed of men who roamed the earth and of women who joined them by descending on a rope or ladder from their place of origin in the sky. This seems to have occurred toward the end of the mythical epoch when the age of edenic harmony came to an end and that of entropic disjunction began. Animals and humans no longer remained undifferentiated as at the beginning of the myths of the origin of women. Eventually they metamorphized from animals into men and women, whose children populated the earth. Had the strong animal-people rather than the weak ones copulated first, humans would be robust and immortal.

Chorote cosmogony records two major cataclysms that destroyed all life and almost all of mankind in the world: the Deluge and the Great Fire. Of the former there are two kinds, a universal and a regional flood. The destructive world catastrophe appears to have been of chthonic origin. The land sank and groundwater swelled up to cover the earth.

No particular reason is given for the universal flood, and mankind survives either because a number of individuals were rescued by an avian creature or because a family, whose head had been forewarned of the impending disaster, escaped by taking refuge under a big tree. In contradistinction to the destructive powers of the telluric waters, the rain is endowed with regenerative properties and facilitates the reemergence of life.

The regional flood, of apparently more recent occurrence than the world deluge, was caused by Kiswet in one case, but more typically by Fox, the trickster of Gran Chaco fame. His act of disobedience causes the lagoon or the bottle tree, in which the water had been originally contained, to overflow. The resulting flood gave origin to the rivers.

Like the world Deluge, the Great Fire ravaged the land for no explicit reason. A good number of people escaped the conflagration by taking refuge in a hole they dug in the earth. However, upon emerging and looking out across the desolated earth, most of the survivors changed into animals. Those that survived in human form were often consanguineally related men and women who through their incestuous unions became the ancestors of the present-day Indians. In search of food and company, the survivors roamed the world and discovered other peoples of terrestrial, subterranean, and overseas (European) origin.

The acquisition of fire appears to have been as epochal an event in Chorote mythology as the two cataclysms of Flood and Fire. It required the intervention by none other than Carancho, the culture hero of Chaco mythology, to accomplish the feat. Originally fire was owned by only a few animals such as Anaconda, Rabbit, Partridge, Woodpecker, and Sparrow Hawk. Carancho stole it from them during a particularly cold spell of winter. Since then, people have been able to keep warm and to make use of fire in honey collecting. Honey was unknown to the Chorote of old until a shaman pointed it out to them and taught them how to go about gathering it with the aid of fire. The man who recognized tobacco growing from the ashes of a devastating ogre was also a shaman; he initiated the use of the drug.

This mythologem of the origin of plants from the body of a slain person is of wide-flung distribution on the subcontinent (Zerries 1969). In the context of the present collection it introduces Tséxmataki, the cannibalistic dema-deity of Chorote mythology (Siffredi 1982:147–177). She is the insatiable devourer from the world below who cannibalizes the Moon and humanity alike. Taking her origin in remote mythical times she was killed by a shamanic hero but survived to the present day in the form of the tobacco plant. The perpetual craving for nicotine tobacco which habituated persons experience is a demonstration of the power the terrible ogress continues to wield over man. In one particular version of the myth (no. 67) an old man, outraged over having been abandoned by his family, turns into a Tséxmataki person and terrorizes the people just like the underworld protagonist.

Fleeing the destruction of his land and plants, Moon left the earth on the occasion of the Great Fire to cultivate the sky world. He also sent rain and seeds from there to replant the forests and to restock the fields. This specific mention of Moon as the lord of vegetation suggests him as the benefactor who replanted the earth after the deluge as well. Moon's identification as a male lunar deity who, subject to waxing and waning himself, creates and recreates the universe is particularly unambiguous in Chorote mythology. As a personage of exceptional sexual prowess, he symbolizes the fertility of the forest, the garden, and the home, and teaches mankind the advantages of horticulture and construction of the family house. Disadvantaged humans are believed to have been assisted by Moon or to have visited his celestial world to seek his help. Myth tells of a man who, to overcome his enemies, received from Moon power over the life and death of his tormentors.

Another ancestral Chorote of the modern world age who visited Moon in his celestial world was a shaman. Welcoming him, Moon let his human visitor taste a variety of wild and cultivated fruits which instantaneously grew whole again. In this fashion, the shaman learned the secret of the regenerative potential of plant life and understood why Moon instructed him to save some seeds for annual planting. Identified as the armadillo, the shaman married the oldest daughter of Moon and was instructed by his father-in-law in his special art of maize cultivation, that is, harvesting almost immediately after sowing the seed. Fox, the Trickster, married Moon's younger daughter. Failing to grasp the generative power of the seed or impatient with the idea of deferred gratification, he eats rather than plants the seed. His fields turn into uncleared brushland and the Chorote, following Fox's instead of Armadillo's practice, lose Moon's secret of instantaneous harvesting and must contend now with an extended waiting period between sowing and harvesting. An example of the hardship Indians endure for lack of garden products is given in the case of Pigeon who, when still living in the sky, was owner of many cultigens. Once on earth, she lacked all these foods and her call gives mournful evidence of her gnawing pangs of hunger. Some Chorote (La Merced) credit Pigeon with having brought the first seeds of maize from the sky.

Bitter manioc, on the other hand, is not considered of celestial origin. Instead, its usefulness as a food crop was revealed to the Indians by Thlamó, a chthonic personage of the underworld. He instructed a shaman to fetch it from people to the east, and it is through them that the Chorote learned how to cultivate and eat this poisonous plant. Thlamó is also the bringer of the seed of *sachasandia*, a tree whose fruit is as dangerous for human consumption as bitter manioc. The seed of the carob tree came from an equally ambiguous personage, namely Fox, the Trickster. He stole it from certain villagers to the north and raised the first specimen of this all-important Chorote land food source.

The practice of fishing and the introduction of fish as food is ascribed by some Chorote to the son of a beautiful Indian woman and the white-brisked hairy armadillo known in the Gran Chaco as *gualacate*. As among other tribes of the general region, the fish were originally contained in the magic bottle tree. Armadillo's son caught them there for the first time with a dip net of his manufacture and taught the Indians how to dress and prepare fish for consumption. Another personage credited with the introduction of fishing is Kisbar, the son of the owner of the bottle tree which contained the fish. Having been born in the hand of his father, the son went in search of a foster mother and found acceptance by a young woman once he was big enough to aid her in food gathering and especially after he provided her with the first fish. Not only did the boy introduce his mother's folk to the new food, but he also taught the men how to fashion dip nets with which to catch the fish.

In addition to Kisbar and the *gualacate* armadillo, Chorote myth mentions several other Owners of the River (or lagoon) and Masters of Fish. Shiushikanakí is one such personage, with a body half-man (or woman) and half-fish (Mashnshnek 1972:120–121; 1973b:59). He has ordained the proper conduct of fishermen which prohibits, among other things, the waste of fish food. Also mentioned as the Owner of the Lagoon is the jabiru stork.

In primordial times Kisbar lived in the middle of the "river," a body of standing water which began to flow only after his son had found acceptance by a human family and especially after Fox, or Kíxwet, intervened and released the water from its original reservoir. This is a common trickster story in the Gran Chaco, which describes the origin of the rivers—and of river fishing—as the result of a taboo violation on the part of the trickster. Less frequently heard is the additional Chorote motif that, in the context of the Father of Fish, ascribes the creation of the river and the practice of weir fishing to the intervention of Carancho, the culture hero.

The Ancient Old Man had taught humans how to hunt, but it was Jaguar who taught them how to stalk their prey. Animals seem to have originated in heaven, where according to one tradition they were created by Sun.

Birds which nowadays inhabit the terrestrial plain are the descendants of those that, unlike some of their companions, remained on earth after a longer or shorter visit from heaven. Couched in a dramatic series of battle stories with ogres are the etiologies of several specific birds that result from these confrontations. One such story relates the origin of the mockingbird, who used to be a handsome but very angry young man. In a contest he loses one leg and sharpens his shin bone. Having been abandoned by his people, Sharpened Leg takes revenge by spearing them with his peculiar weapon. As elsewhere in North and South America, he is eventually killed by the culture hero. The monster is burned and his ashes turn into the mockingbird. Carancho is also called upon to rescue the people from a cannibal ogre who kills and devours children. The hero disarms the ogre, kills and burns him, and from the ashes rises the vulture. The ovenbird originated from an industrious woman who introduced the art of pottery making. Being rejected and mocked by her fellow women, she leaves them and turns into this kind of bird. Another story relates that the ovenbird used to be an ogress who killed unsuspecting passersby by dropping a heavy oven on them. Carancho outsmarts and burns her, and watches the bird come out of the ashes. A similar fate brought about the transformation of the burrowing owl, who used to be a man. With his song he attracted any number of people to his burrow, where they died. Carancho set fire to the man's trap and saw him transform into a burrowing owl. Thus, Carancho "simply burns what is dangerous until only ashes remain," and cremation becomes the modality of creation of new life forms. In a less dramatic way, parrots and herons were transformed from bathing boys.

The origin of the color of birds is told in the context of a story of a battle between a gigantic celestial form of harpy eagle and Carancho, the hero hawk. The body of the overpowered harpy is punctured and the splattering blood colors the plumage of the birds.

At a time when as yet there were no animals on earth, a star took pity on human hunters and sent the animals down to earth. At possibly a different mythological time, terrestrial animals originated on earth by adopting their forms from undifferentiated animal-people that had survived the Great Fire. As in the case of the origin of bird life, the origin of animals in Chorote mythology is closely associated with the great transformer fire. At one time, for instance, Sparrow Hawk created wild animals by pushing people into a pit of live coals. There are also the animals that arose from the ashes of the cremated ogre Tséxmataki, some of which became shamanic tutelary spirits. The sparrow hawk is involved in a number of etiological stories, and it will be recalled that he was mentioned among the original owners of fire who taught Carancho the art of fire making and the proper way to take care of the element. The sparrow hawk transformed people into animals and ordained their identity.

Snakes were born of a girl who became impregnated by a snakeskin. The young snakes inside her womb castrate men who attempt to have intercourse with her. Carancho lures the young woman into a firetrap and burns her. She rises from the ashes as the vampire bat and her brood takes refuge in a lagoon where they are given their names by the hawk hero. Lagoons are inhabited by man-swallowing anacondas, the giant Mother of Snakes, and the Mother of Caimans. Upon escaping from inside the anaconda who had devoured them, two men see the lagoon dry up, revealing all the water creatures. The people eat the dead snake but when they pursue the Mother of Caimans they all die. Other stories tell of man-eating wasps, head trophy taking men, and a crazed woman possessed by the cannibal spirit Tséxmataki. Only after she reveals her vital spot can the otherwise invulnerable ogress be killed. At a time when all birds were men, Tséxmataki pursued them up to the sky on a rope. The parrot, however, cut the rope before the ogress could reach the upper world and she fell back to earth.

Another terrible and devastating creature of Chorote mythology is Kíxwet, a giant of uncommon sexual prowess. In primordial times when there were only men on earth, he was the one who schemed to lure the sky women into leaving their home to join the lonely men below. He designed the strategy that served to trap the women on earth. Being without a woman himself, he engendered a son in his hand and set out to find a foster mother for him. This he accomplished by having the boy regale a girl with a new kind of food, that is, fish. Tracing the course of the riverbed with his staff, he created the Pilcomayo and introduced river fishing.

Kíxwet's sexual voracity is expressed through the image of his penis which, on account of its extraordinary length, he carries around his waist like a belt. Relentlessly pursuing young women, he adopts any number of different forms to approach his unsuspecting victims and copulate with them. Even his clothes, when donned by women, have the power to impregnate. Kíxwet not only deflowers and kills young women, but also disregards any social norms, violating even his own sister-in-law and his niece. Thus, his physical strength as a giant, his irresistible drive, his ability of transformation, and his agility as a cunning schemer characterize Kíxwet as a major figure of Chorote mythology, signaling like none other the violent underside of sexuality. To accomplish his goals, Kíxwet overrides all personal and social norms and rights. In the process, he may coincidentally benefit mankind by overcoming a devastating monster or by creating a new source of food. But behind the prima facie appearance of Kíxwet as a benefactor, one can hardly fail to recognize the ulterior significance of theophanic imagery that presents a creator who, with his staff, brings forth the river and the fish that serve as food. According to Chorote mythology, Kíxwet's power is to remain in this world forever; people have shot, clubbed, and cremated him to no avail. Not only has he come back after each futile attempt on his life, but he has also renewed himself manifold from each of his severed body parts.

Other devastating personages of Chorote mythology include the pair of male and female Guardians of the Forest who devour people and who had to be destroyed by Carancho. Then there is the deer monster who impales sleeping people with his antlers and bites their throats. He was stopped by a resourceful shaman. A similar tactic of killing people was adopted by the jaguar until he too was overcome by shamanic intervention. The jaguar is pictured in several instances as the reluctant husband of a girl who bears him a son. But the union is mostly short-lived and ends in disaster. Finally, there is the tribe of night people whose bodies are covered with hair and whose excellent eyesight permits them to hunt by night. The corpus of narratives includes a battle story of how the Chorote ancestors traveled to finish off this tribe of supernatural beings. Other journeys are taken by a man to the land of plenty whence he invariably returns laden with gifts of food.

The collection ends with a group of tales about Fox, the randomly nasty trickster, who shares certain characteristics with Kíxwet but who is a chief character of Chorote mythology in his own right. As in other Chaco traditions he is lewd, cruel, cunning, boastful, and self-seeking. His adventures usually end badly for him and he is as often victimized as he tricks and ridicules others. The trickster in Chorote mythology and other principal characters have undergone considerable analysis (Cordeu and Siffredi 1978; Siffredi 1982). As a result and thanks to the efforts of the contributing authors of the present volume and their Indian assistants, Chorote mythology emerges as a creative and rich tradition of indigenous lore.

Johannes Wilbert

Los Angeles, California
April 2, 1985

THE NARRATIVES

1. The Paths of Sun and Moon

Moon tried to walk the path of Sun but he almost died of the heat. Then Sun tried the path of Moon and almost died of the cold. Finally Moon and Sun stopped disagreeing: they were testing their strength. Moon's strength is the freezing cold, and Sun's is the fiery heat. Moon has power: his path is snow covered. Sun also has power: his path is very hot. The two were opposites and were always testing each other, but since that time they did not want to quarrel anymore. One could not take the other's place.

Informant: Kasókchi ilánek

Source: Siffredi ms.

Motif content

A733.+.	Sun hot. (A733. Heat and light of the sun.)
A736.11.	Contest between sun and moon.
A750.+.	Moon cold. (A750. Nature and condition of the moon.)
F840.+.	Extraordinary cold path. (F840. Other extraordinary objects and places.)
F840.+.	Extraordinary hot path. (F840. Other extraordinary objects and places.)
H1500.	Tests of endurance.
H1511.	Heat test. Attempt to kill hero by burning him in fire.
H1512.	Cold test.
H1541.	Contest in enduring cold.
H1542.	Contest in enduring heat.

2. The Contests of Sun (Kilát) and Moon (Wuéla)

Moon played a game. One day he wanted to try out Sun's road. He set foot on the path, but could not stand the heat. It was so hot that

Moon turned back, almost dead from the heat. Moon then asked Sun: "Let us see, Sun, come try my path."

Sun tried Moon's road; he walked along the path, but had to turn back because he could not stand the cold. They met each other outside and began to laugh. "Who is the stronger of us?" Sun asked. "It appears we are equal. We almost died from the heat and the cold," he added. "My path is cooler," said Moon. "It is better than yours."

Moon returned to his own path and proceeded along his way.

Informant: Esteban Mariano

Source: Mashnshnek 1972, p. 124.

Motif content

A733.+.	Sun hot. (A733. Heat and light of the sun.)
A736.11.	Contest between sun and moon.
A750.+.	Moon cold. (A750. Nature and condition of the moon.)
F840.+.	Extraordinary cold path. (F840. Other extraordinary objects and places.)
F840.+.	Extraordinary hot path. (F840. Other extraordinary objects and places.)
H1500.	Tests of endurance.
H1511.	Heat test. Attempt to kill hero by burning him in fire.
H1512.	Cold test.
H1541.	Contest in enduring cold.
H1542.	Contest in enduring heat.

3. Moon's Wives Turn into Stars

When Moon went up to the sky, his wife stayed behind. Her sister, a fat woman who turned into a big star, followed him, and she can be seen next to Moon whenever he begins to travel across the sky. As he was very nice and handsome the fat woman did not want to abandon him, so she joined him. Later, while traveling along his path, he met the wife he had lost and rejoined her. This is the star which we see next to Moon when he is already far away, near dawn (Katés Thlét, mother of Katés; Morning Star).

That is why we are fond of playing this game, when we say: "I would like to be like Moon who has two wives. On his way he found another wife. I would like to be as handsome as he, because the women like him and they go after him, unlike our wives who desert us if we leave them. Better to be like Moon: then, even if I went far away, my wife would follow me, and if she did not I would get another one."

We men, both young and old, always laugh at this.

Informant: Aió

Source: Siffredi ms.

Motif content

A740.	Creation of the moon.
A745.	Family of the moon.
A747.	Person transformed to moon.
A761.	Ascent to stars. People or animals ascend to the sky and become stars.
A770.	Origin of particular stars.
D293.+.	Transformation: woman to star. (D293. Transformation: man to star.)
F575.2.	Handsome man.

4. A Lunar Eclipse Caused by Tséxmataki

The creature Tséxmataki started to eat the moon which therefore became small and dim. As she had already eaten her fill elsewhere she was unable to devour it completely, but left it quite diminished. When we saw the moon becoming small like that, we grew very frightened. Since everyone had rifles we started shooting at Tséxmataki so she would not eat the moon. Someone took a mortar and began to pound it, *ta, ta, ta.* Others fired their rifles five times. Thus the moon grew big again, gradually returning to its original size and its place in the sky.

Informant: Petiso

Source: Verna ms.

Motif content

A737.1.	Eclipse caused by monster devouring sun or moon.

5. The Origin of a Five-Star Constellation

There was a woman who was grating bitter manioc. When her two sons and two daughters returned, they said to her: "We are going to move farther away, because something is going to happen." The oldest daughter wanted to be away from home, at a place where there was another house, in order to jump up to the sky with her little sister, whom she was carrying in her arms. They positioned themselves to be able to jump on the roof, and then the younger girl said: "You have to hold me tight!"

When the mother stopped working, she began to ask for her little daughter, the one who was where the other children had taken her. They had the little girl and the mother asked for her. However, the children did not want to part with her; they were already well prepared, so they said to her: "No, we cannot give the little girl to you because we are set to go."

The two girls who were all prepared could not come down because they had already reached the top of the roof. When the mother saw her two daughters, she wanted the younger one down. Yet, the older daughter could not return her to her mother because they were both high up there. And now they went up higher, ascending slowly. Their brothers, realizing that their younger sister was going up, began to cry.

At first the mother heard the little girl crying, but then she could not hear her anymore. She returned to her working place, and when she saw the water that had accumulated from the manioc, she threw it out because she was angry and worried about her little girl.

At night the mother was crying. Then an old man who lived there looked at the sky and saw the two girls. But the little one was now big, the same size as her sister. There they were, next to Katés (Morning Star). Then the two brothers climbed up as well and joined their two sisters and Katés. The four of them kept watching their mother who had remained on earth.

Informant: Póm ilánek

Source: Siffredi ms.

Summary
Four brothers and sisters ascend to sky to form constellation.

Motif content

A761.	Ascent to stars. People or animals ascend to the sky and become stars.
A766.	Origin of constellations.
D293.	Transformation: man to star.
D2135.	Magic air journey.

6. Children Transformed into Stars

There was a woman who had two daughters, one very small and another a bit bigger. The little one was crying. Then the other girl asked her mother: "Mother, do you not hear your daughter crying?" Three times she went and asked her mother. "I am coming right away," the mother would say. Again the girl told her, and the mother replied: "I am going to pick her up." Finally the girl was shouting at her, but the woman did not even turn around. So the older girl picked up her little sister and began to rise upward. Slowly the two rose toward the sky, the older girl holding the little one in her arms.

When the mother realized that her daughters were gone she looked up. Seeing them ascending she started to call: "Come back, come back, my daughters!" But they kept on rising. The woman was left there, crying.

That is why we always see two stars close together in the sky. One is very bright but the other is dim. The big one shines brightly and the other star shines hardly at all. We always see the star that is embracing the little one.

Later two men, who were the girls' brothers, also went up to the sky and became stars. The woman remained here alone because her sons and daughters had flown to the sky.

Informant: Esteban Mariano

Source: Verna ms.

Motif content

A761.	Ascent to stars. People or animals ascend to the sky and become stars.
A766.	Origin of constellations.
D293.	Transformation: man to star.
D2135.	Magic air journey.
P250.1.	Elder children to protect younger.
S12.	Cruel mother.

7. Birds of the Sky and the Earth

There were some birds that came from the sky, and when they had lived down here for some time they did not want to go back. But there were other birds that did not want to be here on earth; they stayed for a while and then went back up. Most of the birds lived next to the ones that did not want to leave the sky.

What happens is that all the celestial birds live in a very lovely place, lovelier than here. The Masters of Birds said to their followers: "It does not matter if you go to live in the land below. We can always send you a little rain so you will be able to live well. Do not worry about returning to the land up here."

So that is why some birds did not want to return anymore and now live on this earth. The Masters of Birds said to those who always came back: "In order to make fewer trips, you will be able to live on the earth below. While you are there you will not suffer, because we can send you some rain, and you will be able to drink the water that falls from the leaves. So you will be able to produce many chicks. It is better that we have two places now!"

The rains that we receive on this earth are not made in the clouds. They come from another sky above the clouds; they come from the lagoons where the Masters of Birds live, from another heaven that is beyond the one we see.

The celestial birds are always fighting; they have enemies that are other birds. They fight among themselves and they club one another. Some want to take the lagoons away from their owners. As they fly around in the air fighting they collide and cause thunder. When Oxuo, the pigeon, makes noise up there he simply says *coo!* He does not have enough strength. There are other birds, like Kaláwon (aquatic bird), that always collide: *bam!* These have a roaring thunder and release much light (lightning) because they are strong.

Informant: Kasókchi ilánek

Source: Siffredi ms.

Summary

Some birds leave sky to settle on earth. Sky-birds send them rain for survival. Former occasionally fight among themselves, causing thunder and lightning.

Motif content

A651.1.	Series of upper worlds.
A1131.3.	Rain from sea in upper world.
A1141.	Origin of lightning.
A1142.	Origin of thunder.
B242.+.	Master of birds. (B242. King of birds.)
B266.	Animals fight.

D2143.1.	Rain produced by magic.
F30.	Inhabitant of upper world visits earth.
F162.6.	Lakes in otherworld.
F167.1.2.	Birds in otherworld.

8. Moon Creates the Earth

Moon is the man who in the beginning made this earth or, rather, this world. There used to be nothing, only some loose dust. It was not easy for him to create the earth. His wife kept negating him whenever she heard her husband say: "How about if I made an earthly surface; it would be useful, and we could live without suffering."

His wife would always answer: "But what is 'earth'?"

"Earth is something we could walk on. And once there is an earth there will be many things."

But his wife was always against it, saying: "No, you will not be able to do it."

He began to mark off an area in the shape of a small square, drawing it with his hand. Then he spat on the square, and the dust stayed there; it settled and did not go away anymore. Also the saliva did not disappear; it too stayed there. Then Moon said to his wife: "Look, I shall be able to make this earth. This is going to be called earth, for it will be useful."

"All right."

It began to grow, more and more. Then it began to look like earth, like powder, but it was very small, not large enough. Moon tried to moisten it, and with his power he got some water and sprinkled it over the surface to see what would happen. When he moistened the dust it settled. At first it was soft to the touch, and he had to wet it a little so that it would stay and become harder. When his wife saw this she said: "Well, now I really believe what you were talking about. What is this going to be?"

"Every year, every day, every night it will keep on growing bigger and bigger, as much as I tell it to!" It was as though he had struck an accord with his wife: "Believe what I am telling you: this earth will keep on increasing, for the benefit of whatever is going to exist."

Moon did not mention what, but he knew that later on there would be people. His wife, on the other hand, did not think that any human beings would exist.

Every year they saw the earth growing bigger and bigger, and Moon's children were now playing on it. They liked it: "Look, it is very firm!"

And Moon named it earth.

When the earth stopped growing Moon's wife was very pleased, and kept saying: "Moon, now I really believe in what you were planning before."

"And why not? For I can make things. I am powerful," said he.

They were very happy that the earth, which Moon had planned, now existed. After some time, when the land was extensive already and still growing, there were also sandy areas where it would be possible to sow, areas that Moon called *hótai*. He said to his wife: "Now I am going to do something else: I have to burn a patch where there is now pasture, so that I can sow there."

His wife said: "What are you going to sow?"

"You will see. You do not know what I am doing, but when these things (plants) appear you will soon be happy, just as you were with the earth that I made."

"All right," she said.

Moon began to burn off the grass, and then he planted a seed.

I do not know where he got it, but since he knows what to do he got a squash seed, not *anco* but squash. After sowing a small seed he sprinkled water over it. We do not know where he got the water; he knows what to do. No sooner had he planted the seed than the bud appeared; it grew into a plant, and a few days later it was already in bloom. A few more days and it bore fruit. It happened very quickly! It grew and grew until a big plant was formed, with much fruit on it. They began to taste the fruit, to eat it, and Moon's wife said to her husband: "This is really good!"

Then he began to plant other kinds of seeds—beans, watermelons— and always one seed of each kind, until all the plants that exist had appeared. Then Moon and his family lived well with all that food. All the plants that exist came about because he had prepared a special field for planting.

Once Moon had finished the world and once all the plants had come to be in the place where he was living he said: "These domestic plants should exist all over the world." He was a powerful man.

And that is how plants came to exist everywhere, only because he said so. That was how Moon's promise turned out, and it has been kept to this day. Of course, the only one who refused him was his wife; there was no one else; they were living alone.

Informant: Aió

Source: Siffredi ms.

Summary

Over wife's objections Moon makes earth, and then field with cultivated plants (origin of such plants).

Motif content

A1.+.	Moon as creator. (A1. Identity of creator.)
A745.	Family of the moon.
A753.	Moon as a person.
A800.	Creation of the earth.
A1425.	Origin of seed.
A2602.	Planting the earth.
A2684.	Origin of cultivated plants.
D489.+.	Small earth made to grow large. (D489. Objects made larger—miscellaneous.)
D631.3.	Size of object changed at will.
D1810.	Magic knowledge.
D2157.2.	Magic quick growth of crops.

9. The Star and the Origin of Man

A star who was a woman fell to earth. There was nothing here, not even people. She came down during the night. Then she created people. She made a man out of earth, fashioned hands for him, a little head, and attached everything together. She then braced him upright with earth, and made the body walk. "How are you?" asked the star. But the clay figure did not answer. He walked a little farther, and she asked him again: "How are you?" But he did not answer. After the man had walked some five hundred meters away from the star, she asked him once more. He still did not respond. The star told him: "Go on, if you want to." The clay figure continued onward and the star repeated her question: "How are you?" Only then did he answer: "Everything is fine." The star called him. "Come back," she said. And he returned.

Afterward the star had to create a woman, for there were no people. She made a woman who emerged from the earth just like the man. She then made them mate; she made them marry. A few days later the woman conceived, and then there existed human beings. Now man had been created.

Later the star went to another place where she repeated everything. She then moved on to yet another place and made people out of the

same earth—she made the Mataco. Then she went on; there she took
some earth and made those who speak Chulupi. She proceeded on, once
again took the same earth and made those who speak Toba. She then
went to another place, took some earth, and made those who speak
Tapiete. Thus she went everywhere; that is why there are now so many
people here. If it had not been for this star who made us all. . . . After
she had finished there now existed the Mataco, the Chorote, the Toba,
and the Tapiete.

Informant: Esteban Mariano

Source: Mashnshnek 1972, pp. 125–126.

Motif content

A762.	Star descends as human being.
A1241.3.	Man made from clay image and vivified.
A1270.	Primeval human pair.
A1275.	Creation of first man's (woman's) mate.
A1280.	First man (woman).
A1611.+.	Origin of the Chorote. (A1611. Origin of particular tribes.)
A1611.+.	Origin of the Mataco. (A1611. Origin of particular tribes.)
A1611.+.	Origin of the Tapiete. (A1611. Origin of particular tribes.)
A1611.+.	Origin of the Toba. (A1611. Origin of particular tribes.)
F30.	Inhabitant of upper world visits earth.

10. A Star Made Pregnant by the Earth

There was nothing on earth, no people. A star, Katés, came down.
She was just like us. She can be seen all alone in the eastern sky. The
star had thought about the fact that there were no people and how alone
she was. So she made a rope to come down to earth. She came down
from the sky. She put earth into her vagina. Thus the star conceived.
A son emerged. He soon grew up and became a young man whose name
was Kialé. The star once again got pregnant from earth, giving birth to
a girl named Kialkí. She grew up right away. The star thought: "Now
they must get married."

The girl soon got pregnant by her brother and gave birth to a daughter.

"We now have many people," the star thought. She continued to get
pregnant. The children grew up and married their siblings. The star
continued to get pregnant and built a house for herself.

Informant: Simplicios

Source: Mashnshnek 1972, p. 127.

Motif content

A762.	Star descends as human being.
A1270.	Primeval human pair.
A1273.1.	Incestuous first parents.
A1280.	First man (woman).
A1282.	The mother of men.
F30.	Inhabitant of upper world visits earth.
F51.	Sky-rope.
T532.+.	Conception from sand in vagina. (T532. Conception from other contacts.)

11. The Celestial Couple

A long, long time ago there was a very old man, yet not so old that he was about to die, who spoke these words: "I am going to give man these three things: a soul kernel, a soul image, and a soul shadow. They will give life to men in the future and will produce offspring, and many people will derive from these three small things. They will have everything."

This was his plan; he had distributed everything, so that everything that men would need would exist in the world. He sent these three things so that people would continue multiplying and growing. Siúna Kihíl (that old man) built things.

That ancient one, whom we have called Kihíl from early on to this day, has very white hair and much power; he always sits in heaven, with bent knees, never looking ahead, just down. He is very quiet; he never moves or looks at things. It seems he is always surrounded by clouds. Kihíl never changes; the appearance he had he will have forever. He has a wife, also old, with this same look.

We call the old man Saká Kihíl (our own old man), Sinnáa (our father), and Ieén (grandfather). Both are called Kihíl Wehé (little old people)[1] because they have an old person's life, and also a young life; they will always be equally old without aging any further.

When the men call a shaman Kihíl, it is because he has many spirit helpers, much ability, and because he cures many illnesses. Naming him thus does not anger the man because Kihíl is a good example.

---

[1] "(. . .) means that the word is almost like the diminutive of the last one because Kihíl Wehé is like an old man (. . .) so that the people will understand that the old man really is not old; he's old and young like a boy (. . .); he has a life like an old man and a very young life also. His wife is Kihíla Wehé also."

Only the shamans know Kihíl through their dreams because their spirits show them his image and the way he used to live before. That is also why they do not know him well and why they do not know what road to take to visit him, where to enter to find him. Only his appearance is known and the fact that he exists. Thanks to dreams, men learned to trust more in Kihíl every day.

The old man dedicated his works to the men and taught them how to hunt. Kihíla did the same with the women and taught them how to gather fruit. The old woman said to them: "In order for women to have power, work, and everything else, we are going to arrange all things well on earth. Look, I shall lead the women who will live with their children, and the men who have souls, thought, and all those things. My future daughters and granddaughters will have to do the same."

If things abound on earth, it is because of them, the Ancient Ones, who never forget mankind just as mankind never forgets to think of them. That is why a man who goes out to hunt always says: "My grandfather, we always look to you."

And the mother teaches her recently married daughter to repeat: "My grandmother, we always look to you." This is done so that she will never be in want of anything.

The shamans always tell the people about the Ancient Ones, saying that they will never be able to see them because only shamans can. The story makes the people take heart; it is as if it gave them energy, strength.

Then the girls say: "I shall always remember my grandmother."

And the young men, when they need something, say: "I am going to speak the name of the Ancient One, and then I shall have it."

The Old Couple did not want to divide things up or differentiate them all at once. That is why they only gave men the promise that they would live on earth, would eat, have thought, a soul, and many things.

Both the Ancient Ones would talk about what they would do so that man would possess a soul image, a soul shadow, a soul nucleus, thought, and discernment, simply by speaking the words: "These men will have . . . ; the women will have. . . ."

They gave humans the most important thing: the possibility to live their lives. And because there were two sexes, the tasks they gave were twofold: some for men, others for women.

When this great plan of the Ancients was changed, rain and fire came, men became animals, the shamans got their spirit helpers, the wild animals got their chiefs; that is, all this took place during the end of primeval time. Since the Old Couple already existed before that time, they are from the very earliest time.

Informant: Aió

Source: Siffredi ms.

Summary

Old man and woman living in the sky give primeval people soul and reasoning power and allocate tasks to men and women.

Motif content

A15.1.1.	Old woman as creator.
A15.3.	Old man as creator.
A21.2.	Old man from sky as creator.
A32.3.	Creator's wife.
A183.	Deity invoked.
A185.3.	Deity teaches mortal.
A185.12.	Deity provides man with soul.
A191.1.	Great age of the gods.
A1131.	Origin of rain.
A1300.	Ordering of human life.
A1414.	Origin of fire.
A1420.2.	Gods teach how to seek and prepare food.
A1458.	Origin of hunting.
A1472.	Beginning of division of labor.
B241.2.+.	Masters of the various kinds of beasts. (B241.2. King of the various kinds of beasts.)
D100.	Transformation: man to animal.
D1711.	Magician.
D2161.	Magic healing power.
F403.2.	Spirits help mortal.
J157.	Wisdom (knowledge) from dream.

12. The Origin of Women

There once existed only men. They used arrows to hunt tuco-tucos, the small animal that lives inside the earth. They hunted them regularly and roasted them. When they had roasted a lot, the men stored them on a platform. This done, they went hunting again. Before departing, they left Elé, the parrot, in charge of the roasted meat.

After the hunters had left, women came down from above. It was about noon when they came and began to take the meat. Elé did not keep quiet about this: "The women have come!" he shouted. Then they went back up.

The hunters then sent Elé away because he was worthless. In his stead they appointed Ajlík, the iguana, to guard the meat. He hid quietly in a tree. At noon the women started to come back down; they were laughing. They were aiming straight for the place where the meat was. They reached the ground and began to pack the roasts in a net bag, filling it completely. Iguana started to throw sticks at the rope from which the women were hanging, cutting it. All the women fell and remained down here. Now there were women on earth.

Okináwo, the sparrow hawk, called out for the hunters to return. The ones who returned first received a good, beautiful woman; those who came later were given an ugly one. Ijlió, the armadillo, came last, and there were no women left. So he began digging where they had fallen, because some of them had gone underground. Since the armadillo had long fingernails, he dug right where one of the women was, putting out her eyes. He said: "It does not matter if she is blind; she will belong to me."

Informant: Petiso

Source: Mashnshnek 1972, p. 126.

Motif content

A651.3.	Worlds above and below.
A1231.+.	First woman descends from sky. (A1231. First man descends from sky.)
A1280.	First man (woman).
A1281.	Condition of first man (woman).
B200.+.	Animals in human form. (B200. Animals with human traits.)
B576.1.1.	Guardian animals evaded.
F30.	Inhabitant of upper world visits earth.
F51.	Sky-rope.
F113.	Land of men.
F167.+.	Women live in the sky. (F167. Inhabitants of otherworld.)
J1144.	Eaters of stolen food detected.
K300.	Thefts and cheats—general.
K437.	Robber overcome.
K730.	Victim trapped.
K963.	Rope cut and victim dropped.
K1622.	Thief climbing rope discovered and rope cut.
R4.	Surprise capture.
S165.	Mutilation: putting out eyes.

13. The Origin of Women and of Death

Out there on the savanna there were people; they were all bachelors, unmarried men. Every morning they would go out on the savanna to catch a lot of tuco-tucos. They would return close to noon, roast the animals, and store them on platforms. They did this every day until the women, who at that time were living in the sky, discovered these stores.

When the young men were out to hunt, the women came from the sky on a rope. Upon arriving, they saw where each man had stored roast tuco-tuco. Since the young men kept their roast on personal platforms, the women each climbed onto one, grabbed the meat, and exclaimed: "This one is going to be my husband!"

Another one would do the same: "This other one is going to be my husband!"

When the men returned everything was gone; the girls had taken all the meat. Then the boys said to Máie, the hare, who at that time could talk: "You stay here and stand guard! Take care of the roast for us."

But since the hare is a sleepyhead, when the women came down he was snoring. He did not wake up for anything, so the girls took the meat again and carried it away. The hare woke up only after they had left. He looked at each platform and there was not even one roast left: "What?"

Then he got up and went off tracking: "Ah, they came again! What misfortune! How could I have slept so heavily that I did not hear anything?"

Then they assigned the task to another boy; they ordered Sén, the hummingbird, to take care of those roasts, and the rest went again to hunt tuco-tucos. While Sén was nibbling on the flower of a tree the women began to come down. Sén had a stick that could cut that rope on which they were descending. He threw it, and it hit the rope and cut it. All the women fell to the ground, and Sén said to them: "You will not return to the sky anymore!"

When they came down, they returned to the platforms with the boys' meat and said: "The owner of this one is going to be my husband."

"The owner of that one will be my husband."

The first one to get the best girl for his wife was Sén, and he took her away from the other girls. Then a messenger went to call the men and said to them: "The women are on the earth now! Come on!"

They went racing back to catch them.

The one to arrive last was Oxuo, the dove, and he was only able to catch a blind girl. The others, who were faster, ran ahead. They knew that each woman wanted one of them so each boy caught the girl who had chosen his platform. There were fifteen girls and there were also exactly fifteen boys; with the blind one they were sixteen, and this one was Oxuo's.

One of the boys had caught one of the best girls, and the others wanted to take her away from him. However, he did not want to let her go. They say he was also a handsome young man. The others asked the girl: "Do you want this young man?"

"Yes, I want him," she said. "I know he brings a lot of meat. I do not want another one. I want the one I chose, the one who caught me!"

So the rest let her be; they could not take her away.

The dove, who arrived last, ended up with the blind girl, and then the others said to him: "You are not going to get ahead of all of us. You are not going to copulate first, because when you make the woman pregnant and she gives birth, the baby will die within two or three days."

But the dove went ahead anyway and was the first to copulate with the woman he had caught. He made her pregnant, and the next day she gave birth. But three or four days later the child died. His friend had warned him not to do it, saying that he should first let those do it who were more powerful, like the hummingbird. If he had paid attention we would have been lucky; our children would never die. If those who were stronger had copulated first, nobody would die. It was because of that one who went ahead of the others.

Only after the dove had copulated with that woman did the others follow suit. They were the ones who had caught the women first. After they gave birth, each man went with his wife and children to live in different places.

Informant: Kíki

Source: Siffredi ms.

Summary

In primeval all-male world women descend from sky on rope in men's absence and steal their food. Men post guards, and hummingbird finally succeeds in cutting sky-rope. Each man catches wife for himself, and eventually children are born.

Motif content

A651.3.	Worlds above and below.
A1231.+.	First woman descends from sky. (A1231. First man descends from sky.)
A1280.	First man (woman).

A1281.	Condition of first man (woman).
A1335.	Origin of death.
A1352.	Origin of sexual intercourse.
B200.+.	Animals in human form. (B200. Animals with human traits.)
B576.1.1.	Guardian animals evaded.
F30.	Inhabitant of upper world visits earth.
F51.	Sky-rope.
F113.	Land of men.
F167.+.	Women live in the sky. (F167. Inhabitants of otherworld.)
J652.	Inattention to warnings.
J1144.	Eaters of stolen food detected.
K300.	Thefts and cheats—general.
K400.	Thief escapes detection.
K437.	Robber overcome.
K730.	Victim trapped.
K963.	Rope cut and victim dropped.
K1622.	Thief climbing rope discovered and rope cut.
N396.	The sleeping guard.
R4.	Surprise capture.
T573.	Short pregnancy.

14. Kíxwet and the Origin of Women

Our ancestors did not know about fishing. They had another practice which was to look for animals of the savanna (tuco-tucos) that live underground and are plentiful. The people liked these tuco-tucos, but they asked Kíxwet: "Why can we not hunt for these animals in peace? Every time we catch tuco-tucos and kill them, we leave them in a safe place. But when we return from the hunt with some more, they have all disappeared."

They would cook and prepare them to be carried home to their families that were far away. The men used to camp alone in places where food could be found. They asked Kíxwet to explain why they always lost their meat. He said: "All right, I am going to tell you next time you go out."

It was customary for each man to take his arrows and hunt tuco-tucos on the savanna before dawn. Depending on their luck, the men would remain there until noon or into the afternoon. But always when they returned, the meat they were going to give to their families had vanished.

They would store it high up like on a platform. Each one of them had such a platform, and there were many people, all young. They were animals but acted like people.

Kíxwet told them: "Next time you go out leave Ele, the parrot, behind. He lives in that green tree, and he will warn us. I am going to go with you; I also want to try to shoot."

Well, they arrived at the spot and Kíxwet said: "Listen, boys, anyone can come along here. There is going to be a message; we are going to receive some kind of message."

But what happened? They waited until the afternoon, and there was no message.

Ele had seen many girls coming down from the sky. They descended on a ladder and began to eat that food. After a little while they began to twist chaguar fibers. Thus they acted like married women, but actually they were not. They were sitting there resting, twisting fibers. Then Ele, since he is a parrot—he is roguish to this day—took a leaf from the tree where he was sitting and threw it down. It landed right on the leg of one of the girls.

She thought: "What is this? Could it be Ele?"

Just then the others looked: "Yes, look, there's Ele. Get down!"

"No, I am not coming down."

"Come down; if you do not, we shall throw something at you."

Then they took a dry black cactus fruit and threw it at him, hitting him in the mouth. That is why Ele has a black beak.

They threw that fruit well inside his mouth. No wonder he could not talk all that time! The girls finished and quietly went back to the sky. Ele could not speak anymore; he was mute because he had the dry fruit sticking in his mouth. Of course he wanted to talk but couldn't; he wanted to shout and warn the men, but he couldn't.

When the hunters came back they asked: "How are you, Ele? What happened around here?"

He wanted to answer, but could not talk. He did not have a voice. That is what happened. Later, the second time, someone else was left as a watchman: Alawó, a black fishing bird. Kíxwet said to the men: "Let us try this, brothers. Maybe he will be clever enough for the job, now that Ele cannot talk anymore. The girls must have injured him. We had better try Alawó, to see what he can do."

Then they went hunting again. They sent Alawó to the top of a charred tree trunk that was of the same black color as he. And that is why the girls did not notice him as he was sitting there quietly. When they came, Alawó said: "Ah! So that is how these girls get here! They are beautiful!"

At that time there were, as yet, not many women in the world, just a few. But now there were going to be more. Alawó thought: "I am going to wait until all of them are down."

When all of them were on the ground, he flew up and cut the ladder[2] from above. Then he yelled out, and those who were on the savanna came running.

"Let's go; he's signaling us!" they said.

Then all the armadillos ran, and all the men (who were animals) ran to look for wives. For those who arrived first there was a good, beautiful girl. But as it happened, Ithlió, the armadillo, came last, and the only girl left was one who had hidden. There he was, searching everywhere. Finally he grabbed her around the eyes and she became blind, but that did not matter to him. "It is better than nothing," he said. "This blind one had better stay with me!"

Eventually all those young people got married.

Informant: Kasókchi ilának

Source: Siffredi ms.

Summary

Primeval hunters repeatedly find their food stolen in their absence. They post guards. First guard is rendered mute by thieves, but second guard sees women descending from sky on ladder to steal meat. He cuts ladder, forcing women to remain on earth as men's wives.

Motif content

A651.3.	Worlds above and below.
A2210.	Animal characteristics: change in ancient animal.
A2213.5.	Animal characteristics from being struck.
A2343.2.1.	Why parrot's beak is black.
B200.+.	Animals in human form. (B200. Animals with human traits.)
B576.1.1.	Guardian animals evaded.
F30.	Inhabitant of upper world visits earth.
F51.	Sky-rope.
F167.+.	Women live in upper world. (F167. Inhabitants of otherworld.)
J1144.	Eaters of stolen food detected.
K300.	Thefts and cheats—general.
K400.	Thief escapes detection.
K437.	Robber overcome.

[2]The ladder was of chaguar fiber and in the form of a spider's web, but elongated rather than round.

K730.	Victim trapped.
K1622.	Thief climbing rope discovered and rope cut.
R4.	Surprise capture.
S165.	Mutilation: putting out eyes.

15. Kíxwet and the Women from the Sky

Kíxwet did other things for certain ancestors who lived in another place. He was walking around and ran into people who were suffering; they had no food. Kíxwet through his thought gave them food, and made a large oven for them. He also thought that the people (the men) needed wives in this world. Thanks to his help they already had them in the place where he had come from, but here they were still without. He thought: "I believe there are still girls in another place."

He knew where these women, who were parakeets, lived. He thought he would have to give them also to the people.

Then he sent Kilílik, a very handsome tiny sparrow hawk, to them. Kíxwet told him to go to the sky where the women were, because he knew that Kilílik was handsome and that the women might desire him. Kilílik went there, apparently to display himself. The parakeets saw him, and he returned to earth. The parakeets said: "Where is he going, that young fellow who loves us so much?"

They did not know where he was going. They thought: "Where is he going? Maybe he lives below."

When Kilílik arrived where Kíxwet was, he told him all that had happened: "Well, I think they will come; we will see."

Just then the parakeets came down along a path they had: it was a tall tree that reached to the sky. After descending they wanted to go back up, but they could not. Kíxwet caused the tree to be cut, so that when the laughing women wanted to return, they had lost the power to fly. They no longer remembered where they had come from. They stayed where they were, content in knowing that they had found Kilílik, who was like a king. He was good to them and they loved him.

Then Kilílik said to them: "Well, I am not alone here."

"Where are the others?" asked the women.

"There they are," said Kíxwet, and he showed them many young men.

"Then we parakeets are going to join each with one of them."

And so they split up, one man to a woman, and in that way all the men got families. Kíxwet was happy again.

"Kilílik did well, and I can go somewhere else," he thought to himself.

After the parakeets had arrived on earth they thought: "Why did we come down? We miss our own country a lot; we never lacked food there."

They were missing their place because they still followed the customs of their former home. For example, their house was in the shape of a nest and too small to live in with their husbands.

So they begged Kíxwet to turn them into people: "It is better that we become people, that we forget the customs we followed as birds; it is better that we change and live like people, like Kíxwet."

And they urged Kíxwet to transform them to people. They wanted to have houses like people. They were looking at Kíxwet, who was a person, and they liked the life of a human. They saw that a person can lift heavy things and speak well, and that when he speaks he has a stronger and more beautiful voice than a parakeet, who talks in a very low voice and says very little. For this reason they begged Kíxwet to change their lives for the lives of persons. Then Kíxwet caused all the parakeets to die and sprinkled a little soil over them. When he threw the soil on them they stood up. "I just woke up, I was asleep," they said.

"No, you were not asleep; I was transforming you," said Kíxwet.

He would sprinkle earth on them and make them rise as humans.

Informant: Kasókchi ilánek

Source: Siffredi ms.

Summary

In all-male primeval world, Kíxwet sends sparrow hawk to sky to lure parakeet women into descending to earth. They do so, and marry men. Eventually they persuade Kíxwet to change them into human form.

Motif content

A651.3.	Worlds above and below.
A1280.	First man (woman).
A1281.	Condition of first man (woman).
B455.4.	Helpful hawk.
D350.+.	Transformation: parakeet to person. (D350. Transformation: bird to person.)
D2060.	Death or bodily injury by magic.
D2105.	Provisions magically furnished.
E3.	Dead animal comes to life.
E50.+.	Resuscitation by sprinkling earth. (E50. Resuscitation by magic.)
F30.	Inhabitant of upper world visits earth.
F54.	Tree to upper world.

F167.1.2.   Birds in otherworld.
F811.   Extraordinary tree.
K700.   Capture by deception.
K730.   Victim trapped.

16. The Great Flood

Long ago there were people. Then came heavy rains which killed all
those people. Afterward the water subsided, and when it was gone other
people arrived, lots of them, from above. When they came, the earth
was completely dry. Then all of us new people appeared here. There
was a man who gave birth to a girl from his hand. He had to marry her
himself. After they got married there began to be people. There were
men and women; all were there.

Informant: Petiso

Source: Verna ms.

Motif content

A1006.   Renewal of world after world calamity.
A1006.1.   New race from single pair (or several) after world calamity.
A1006.2.   New race from incest.
A1010.   Deluge.
A1231.   First man descends from sky.
A1273.1.   Incestuous first parents.
A1280.   First man (woman).
T541.+.   Birth from hand. (T541. Birth from unusual part of
                             person's body.)

17. The Destruction of Mankind by Subterranean Water

There were a lot of people, as many as in Buenos Aires. Suddenly the
earth sank and some water began to seep out like in a dry riverbed, and
then came more and more. The people who were sitting quietly in their
homes wondered: "What is going on? Why is this water coming?" The
trickle of water grew to a torrent. "It will stop," said the people. "There
cannot be much more of it coming." But the flood kept rising, killing
all the people. No one was left.

An animal came from the sky, a very large white creature, like a bird. A boy emerged from the water, and the animal saved him. After pulling him out he took the boy up to the sky. Then he returned and carried off many more boys.

Informant: Simplicios

Source: Verna ms.

Motif content

A1005.	Preservation of life during world calamity.
A1010.	Deluge.
A1020.	Escape from deluge.
B527.	Animal saves man from death by drowning.
F10.	Journey to upper world.

18. The Destruction of the World

The sky began to lower, and the earth was sinking. There was a man with his wife and two children, who dreamed that the sky spoke to him. It said: "Well, you are going to live." Showing him a large tala tree it said to him: "You will be right there. You will collect some firewood and suitable seeds, and then you will go and gather some grass."

Soon there was a sound coming from the earth; it was about to sink. The man heard sounds from above as well, and all the animals began to fall. The sounds from above meant that the sky was about to come down. The man was comfortable under the tree. The sky said to him and his people: "When you hear a tiny red bird singing, dawn will be near."

When it dawned the man went out and saw that everything was reduced to savanna; there were no trees, and the rest of the people were nowhere to be seen. They had sunk into the ground. Those who wanted to look far away became rheas, iguanas, peccaries, or birds.

Around noon it began to rain. When it stopped, the man happily went out to plant. He was the only one left; he was alone with his wife and children. They sowed *bola verde*. Then some short grass shot up. Later came many trees, and there was forest, like today.

Informant: Esteban Mariano

Source: Verna ms.

Motif content

A1005.	Preservation of life during world calamity.
A1006.	Renewal of world after world calamity.
A1060.	Earth-disturbances at end of world.
A1061.1.	Earthquakes at the end of the world.
A1711.	Animals from transformations after deluge or world calamity.
A2602.	Planting the earth.
B34.	Bird of dawn.
D114.3.1.	Transformation: man to peccary.
D150.	Transformation: man to bird.
D197.1.	Transformation: man to iguana.
D1619.+.	Sky speaks. (D1619. Miscellaneous speaking objects.)
D1812.3.3.	Future revealed in dream.
D1814.2.	Advice from dream.
F791.1.	Sky lowers on people.
F942.	Man sinks into earth.
Z356.	Unique survivor.

19. The World-Fire

A long time ago everything was ravaged by a great fire which killed all the Chorote except two, a man and a woman, who saved themselves by hiding in a hole in the ground. When the fire had stopped burning and all the flames were extinguished, the man and the woman dug themselves out of the ground, but they had no fire. The black vulture had carried a firebrand to its nest, which had caught fire. The fire had spread down into the tree, and some of it was still smoldering under the tree stump. The vulture gave the Chorote some of its fire, and since then they have had fire. All Chorote are descended from this man and this woman.

Source: Nordenskiöld 1926, pp. 24–25.

Motif content

A1005.	Preservation of life during world calamity.
A1030.	World-fire.
A1038.	Men hide from world-fire and renew race.
A1414.	Origin of fire.
A1414.6.	Bird as guardian of primordial fire.
A1414.7.1.	Tree as repository of fire.
A1415.0.2.	Original fire property of one person (animal).

A1611.+.   Origin of the Chorote. (A1611. Origin of particular tribes.)
K515.6.   Escape by hiding in the earth.

20. The Origin of Animals

There once was a fire which spread throughout the entire world. It burned all the trees and their roots. No tree remained. There was a man with two daughters. They dug deep into the earth, making a hole. When the man realized that the fire was spreading over the entire world, he gathered firewood, water, and provisions. When the fire passed overhead, he felt it go by. Several days passed. The people who had taken refuge in the hole came out. There were many of them. One person looked off into the distance and was transformed into a rhea. On the entire plain, not a single tree was left. Each person who came out of the hole and looked off into the distance was transformed into a peccary or into a *rosillo* or a *quimilero* pig. Another one came out and turned into a peccary. The women who looked off into the distance became anteaters or jaguars, and rabbits. The man and his two daughters were the last to remain in the ground. They realized what was happening, and when they came out they refrained from looking into the distance so as not to end up as animals. When the man came out of the hole he covered his face with his arms and returned to the hole. When he emerged once again he was a man. This man and his two daughters lay together and had a family. That is why there are people today.

Informant: Espinosa

Source: Mashnshnek 1973, p. 59.

Motif content

A1005.	Preservation of life during world calamity.
A1006.1.	New race from single pair (or several) after world calamity.
A1006.2.	New race from incest.
A1030.	World-fire.
A1038.	Men hide from world-fire and renew race.
A1711.	Animals from transformations after deluge or world calamity.
C332.	Tabu: looking around.
D100.	Transformation: man to animal.
J580.	Wisdom of caution.
J710.	Forethought in provision for food.
K515.6.	Escape by hiding in the earth.
T411.	Father-daughter incest.

21. The Destruction by Fire

There was a village in the forest which burned down. Even the surrounding area was burned. In the center some people survived without being burned. An old man, an ancestor, began to dig a hole to live inside of until the great fire had gone by. When it was over, he dug again to get out. He was coming out very slowly. He was afraid and was looking, wondering what he could do to get out. He stuck out his head, and when he was completely out of the hole he looked searchingly. Everything had been burned, and he could not see anything. He went a distance on all fours but stopped after a while. Then he ran off as if frightened, calling like a cariama bird: the man had changed into a cariama.

Then another old man came out. He lived in an area that had not been burned and where there was a small round thicket. He lived there with his five grandchildren. The old man said to his grandchildren: "I don't know what's going on. But do not look directly at the burned land."

For four months the old man looked all over the scorched area but he did not want his grandchildren to look there. Finally he saw two plants of *bola verde* rising from the burned savanna. One month later he saw that a forest was quickly appearing; it had white algarrobo, *tusca* (scrub wood), *sachanaranja, shiniuk, molle,* palo santo, teasel, and *mistol.*

Then all the people who had remained in the little round thicket went away, saying: "We are going to other places!"

The old man was remembering his children who had gone with other people. So he and his grandchildren went far away, for they realized now that there was going to be a forest again, and that all that was burned would become forest. In the meantime the old man went after his children who had left him, and he said to his grandchildren: "Go look for them until you find water. There is a spring that has a lot of deep water; that is where they will be."

When they reached the place, the old man shouted: "Could my children still be alive? I cannot go there because the water is very wide."

But he told them that from now on they were going to live well, that it was not going to be like before anymore. The children began to cry for their father who had told them this. Then the grandchildren returned together to their grandfather and told him that they had seen their father, but that he could not pass because of the water. The old man told them: "Well, that's all right; we shall just go to live where we lived before."

Then he went alone to where the earth ends to look for other children, to see if they were still alive. But he did not find his married sons and daughters because they were all burned. He only found the ashes of the place where they had lived. Everything had burned there also. After a while he arrived at the place where the earth ends. It has roots hanging down below, and these roots support the earth's surface. There is another earth below this one, and the roots of the earth above cling to the earth below. This earth, called the sky by those who live below, does not fall down because of the roots supporting both the upper and the lower earth.

There are people down there, and when this earth went up in flames the people went below. They speak another language: there are Inxuéinai (Tapiete), Iothlókie (Toba). . . . They were talking among themselves, saying they would like to visit those above to see if they were alive. Then they went out to the end of the earth, and the old man who was an Iowúxua (inland Chorote) accompanied them. They found some Athluthlay (Chulupi), Inxuéinai hitóix (different Tapiete), and Siléwa (Chorote).

To find the Athluthlay they traveled down the Pilcomayo. There the Iowúxua saw that only the old people had remained; there were no children or young people, for they had all gone to the lower earth. He continued looking where the Ioxuáha (riverine Chorote) once lived to see if they were still there, but he did not find them.

"Maybe they went with the others to the earth below."

That old Chorote went all over. Everywhere! That is why he knew all the places where people had lived. Then he went upriver and said: "Other Siléwa were living here, the Noótiniui (northwestern group of the riverine Chorote)."

But the village was destroyed, and only half the people remained. He continued to the north and saw that the same thing had happened to the camp of the Inxuéinai. When he stopped wandering all over he said: "Now all will finish because many died in this region."

When the remaining Noótiniui saw other Siléwa arrive, they said to them: "You must stay; it is beautiful here!" And they gave them a part of their land.

The old Iowúxua who had walked all over said to his children: "Let's go; the *bola verde* tree must be ripening now!"

They went, and arriving at their forest they found ripe *bola verde* fruit. It was the very plant that had had only shoots before, because it had burned. They began to eat, and afterward the old man said to them: "I knew that these fruits were ripening."

They went a distance more and found *mistol* that was ripening. Half of the fruit was on the ground. The old man said: "I said that it was ripening; I already knew it."

Some distance away they found watermelon that was ripening. They went to look for white algarrobo, and from afar they saw that it was ripening. Some fruits were falling to the ground.

The old man said to his children: "Now we will not want for food, because we are going to have every kind of fruit."

They continued to walk toward the village and found white algarrobo.

They continued walking, and the old man's daughters asked him whether there was any sugarcane.

"Yes," said the father, "there it is."

In that same place there was also a palm tree with fallen fruit. They continued, and the old man's children asked him if there was any prickly pear.

"When we pass by this palm grove there will be prickly pear," said the old man. And as they approached the other side they saw that indeed there was; they were ripening already. Continuing on they saw other prickly pears. The old man said: "Everything is ripening now. No food is lacking."

They still went on, and found teasel. The old man's children did not know this plant and asked him: "What does it smell like? How would it be to eat?"

Since the old man said the fruit was tasty, they tried it to find out. The old man said it was very salty, and when they ate it, they found it quite salty and they liked it. They went off again, and further on found *ucle* cactus. The old man's daughter saw that the fruits were split on top because they were ripe. Then they looked for a forked stick to pick them with, saying: "They taste wonderful!"

They continued, and suddenly they arrived at an open area covered with grass. They found tiny prickly pears. The old man's daughters asked him: "What do we do to eat this?"

"You have to cut off a little grass with which to take out the thorns."

They did this and began to eat. They then continued on, and up ahead they found high grass. The old man said to them: "This is very good to put on top of the hut, so that it does not leak inside."

Then they fixed up their huts and stayed in their own country.

Informant: Póm ilánek

Source: Siffredi ms.

Summary

After fire destroys village, old man turns into bird. Seeing that vegetation has started to grow back, another old man and his grandchildren travel around to inform people. They travel to end of earth, meeting people of different tribes. Finally they return home, where they find abundant fruit supply.

Motif content

A651.3.	Worlds above and below.
A840.+.	Earth supported by roots. (A840. Support of the earth.)
A1005.	Preservation of life during world calamity.
A1006.	Renewal of world after world calamity.
A1030.	World-fire.
A1038.	Men hide from world-fire and renew race.
A1620.	Distribution of tribes.
C330.	Tabu: looking in certain direction.
D150.	Transformation: man to bird.
D1810.	Magic knowledge.
F80.	Journey to lower world.
H1371.1.	Quest for the world's end.
H1385.	Quest for lost persons.
J580.	Wisdom of caution.
K515.6.	Escape by hiding in the earth.
R323.+.	Refuge in lower world. (R323. Refuge in upper world.)

22. The Destruction by Fire

In ancient times there was a fire that burned the entire forest. It started in the north, and the people were running away from there. The fire advanced slowly toward this region. Although there was a lot of wind it came slowly, not like the fire of the hearth which catches instantly when lit. That is why those people could flee, pushing, shoving.

When they reached this river (Pilcomayo), they came across it. But there was one young man who alone with his sister stayed over there where the steep riverbanks (the left bank) are. The other continued, crossing over to the other side (the right bank) and pressing on toward the south. The ancients say that the people in this area are the descendants of those who crossed the river at the time of the big fire, when not a single tree remained standing.

The youth who had stayed behind with his sister married her after three days. When the fire was approaching, he dug a hole in the middle of the forest. When the hole was three feet deep, he gathered mud and brought it inside the hole. He got in with his sister and covered the hole tightly. There they stayed. When the fire arrived at the hole the boy realized it because smoke seeped in along the roots of the trees. He immediately grabbed some of the mud and stopped up the chinks through which the smoke entered from above. Soon there was more fire, but before the hole could fill up with smoke he covered everything with mud. The two remained there quietly for five or six days. Then the youth took a stick and pushed it through the top to see if they could go outside yet. He could smell that it was no longer burning and realized that the fire had passed. Then he thought about getting out.

When he came out he still could not see. He crouched down against the earth, supporting his forehead. When he looked toward the forest he saw that not even a single tree had remained; everything was pure savanna. Then he got up and ran off across the plain in the form of a cariama bird. Looking about, he got up and found himself transformed into a cariama. He did not have the body of a man anymore. He was a cariama and stayed that way.

From the hole, his wife, who was his sister, heard him singing like a cariama. She came out also, and when she looked at the scorched plain she turned into an anteater. And they continued like that, the man as a cariama and the woman as an anteater.

Informant: Kíki

Source: Siffredi ms.

Summary

    Man and wife take refuge in earth from fire. Upon emerging they turn into bird and anteater.

Motif content

A1005.+.	Preservation of life during great calamity. (A1005. Preservation of life during world calamity.)
A1030.+.	Great fire. (A1030. World-fire.)
A1611.	Origin of particular tribes.
D100.+.	Transformation: woman to anteater. (D100. Transformation: man to animal.)
D150.	Transformation: man to bird.
K515.6.	Escape by hiding in the earth.
T415.	Brother-sister incest.
T415.5.	Brother-sister marriage.

23. The Destruction by Fire

Our ancestors saw a huge fire that spread all over the world. Those other people, the Tsirakúa (Ayoreo), became afraid and fled quickly to escape the flames. They crossed a great water, called the ocean, and were in the middle of it when they found a dry place. There they were able to stay awhile. An old Ayoreo said to them: "Let's see if you remember the salt that I put there, that I hid in the ground."

The men began to dig for the salt and found it. Then they left and came to another dry spot. The old man said to them: "Let's see if you remember the swamp. There is some more salt which I hid last year."

The fire had stopped on the other side of the ocean. The Ayoreo who had been able to cross to the other side found the salt. Those who stayed behind were overtaken by the fire and perished.

When the fire stopped, there was not one plant or tree left; everything was burned and the land was flat. The fire also burned the roots of the trees. Therefore our ancestors began to search for iguanas. They saw that there were embers underground. They found the embers of the fire that had destroyed the people, but they could not make a fire because there was no firewood.

Eventually the plant called *bola verde* came out. It began to bud, and when it was big, birds came to perch on it. Where were the birds getting seeds from? Because they defecated, plants and trees of all kinds appeared. They began to sprout, and a forest appeared, one like those we see today.

Informant: Centawó

Source: Cordeu ms.

Motif content

A1005.	Preservation of life during world calamity.
A1006.	Renewal of world after world calamity.
A1030.	World-fire.
A2602.	Planting the earth.
R316.1.	Refuge on island.

24. The Great Fire

When Moon was on earth our ancestors were also suffering, but since he was living here the suffering was less. If anyone needed help he went to ask Moon who produced many plants. It was he who regulated the trees and gave away seeds. The people lived peacefully and worked just like we do.

But then the great fire came from the north, burning the entire earth. Some of our ancestors tried to dig holes and turned into vizcachas, iguanas, and all the animals that live in the ground. Other people dug into the ground to hide but died because the earth got very hot. All the rivers, too, had become very hot and nobody could drink the water, which was steaming. The people suffered great hardship. Some went far away and would have continued traveling had they not reached the end of the earth where the ocean is and where there is no forest. They are the ones who later obtained many things: they have spiritual money and live in wealth (an allusion to the whites).

In a certain place in the forest we always see a quebracho tree, which also burned on that occasion. Moon, who previously had made the earth, the plants, and the trees, escaped to the sky by means of that tree. When the fire came he went to the sky, for he did not want to see all his fields, all the brush forest, and the entire earth where we live burned. So he went to live up there and created the earth up high, the sky. As he is powerful he can do anything he pleases.

Later, Moon sent a heavy rain to fall on the earth. The burned quebracho tree, the only one left after the fire, began to sprout buds and was reborn. Moon also sent seeds from the sky, and the trees (wild plants) and the fenced-in plants (cultivated plants) reappeared.

Informant: Aió

Source: Siffredi ms.

Motif content

A1.+.	Moon as creator. (A1. Identity of creator.)
A81.	Creator goes to sky.
A701.	Creation of the sky.
A740.	Creation of the moon.
A753.	Moon as a person.
A800.	Creation of the earth.
A1006.	Renewal of world after world calamity.
A1029.1.+.	Marvelous tree survives world-fire. (A1029.1. Marvelous tree survives deluge.)
A1030.	World-fire.
A1425.	Origin of seed.
A1614.9.	Origin of white man.
A2600.	Origin of plants.
A2602.	Planting the earth.
A2681.	Origin of trees.
A2684.	Origin of cultivated plants.
D100.	Transformation: man to animal.
D2143.1.	Rain produced by magic.
F54.	Tree to upper world.

K515.6. Escape by hiding in the earth.
N818.1.+. Moon as helper. (N818.1. Sun as helper.)
R323. Refuge in upper world.

25. The Origin of Trees

After the great world-fire there was only the empty plain, there were no trees. The first tree to emerge, because its roots had not been completely burned, was the *bola verde*. It grew alone. The following year other trees sprang up, and finally all the trees that exist today emerged.

Informant: Espinosa

Source: Mashnshnek 1973, p. 60.

Motif content

A1006. Renewal of world after world calamity.
A1030. World-fire.
A2681. Origin of trees.

26. The Origin of the Green Algarrobo Tree

The armadillo climbed a tree to pull off some branches. The fox decided to shake him down. The armadillo, upon falling, broke his ribs, so the fox tied him up with string. That is why he now has little knots on his shell.

Then the two went to the village. There the people refused to give the fox algarrobo seeds and only gave him algarrobo *añapa*.

The armadillo called the fox over to eat *añapa*. They ate, and the fox opened his mouth and put algarrobo seeds on his tooth. The fox said he had a toothache. They returned home to the fox's wife. They went out to plant. The fox took out the seed, and a little tree sprang up. He pulled it up with his own hands and planted it elsewhere. In a dry trunk he placed some soil, and the plant grew bigger. The others realized that the fox had stolen the seeds. They went to the soldiers (who were vizcachas) to prevent their plants from getting away from them. The vizcachas saw the plant; the tree was already developed. They tried to dig it out but were unable to budge it. The tree grew. Fruits were already falling from it. The fox lay down under the tree, refusing to share the algarrobo fruit with anyone. Whenever he ate some, he saved the seeds and planted them at the edge of a marsh, where they subsequently grew. That is why we always find green algarrobo in marshes.

Informant: Olivera

Source: Mashnshnek 1973, p. 60.

Motif content

A1423.0.1.	Hoarded plants released.
A1425.0.1.	Hoarded seeds.
A1429.	Aquisition of food supply—miscellaneous.
A2210.	Animal characteristics: change in ancient animal.
A2312.+.	Origin of knots on armadillo's shell. (A2312. Origin of animal shell.)
A2681.+.	Origin of algarrobo tree. (A2681. Origin of trees.)
D2157.4.	Miraculous speedy growth of a tree.
F811.	Extraordinary tree.
J1117.+.	Fox as trickster. (J1117. Animal as trickster.)
K341.2.2.	Thief shams sickness and steals.

27. Fox Brings and Scatters Algarrobo Trees

There was a man whose several sisters lived in another place. They say that in that place, toward the north, there were many white algarrobo trees while here, in those days long ago, there were none. The people never tasted algarrobo flour, because they were not familiar with the tree.

Suddenly the man who was dying of hunger thought: "I would like to eat algarrobo flour!"

Fox, who was close by, said to himself: "I will follow behind him."

When they were halfway there, the man noticed Fox and said: "What are you coming for?"

"I came to accompany you; that's all," said Fox.

But they say that he was hungry, too. They went to find the place.

When the man got close to where his sisters lived, Fox saw the algarrobo, seized one or two pods, and began to taste them: "How delicious! What am I going to do with this?"

While he was eating he noticed the seeds, saved them, and took them home. Upon his return he began to sow the seeds. One plant was all he got, but he cared for it and cared for it until finally it grew into a tree that bore fruit. He tasted one and, finding it delicious, let all the fruit fall to have more seeds. He planted them all over.

For this reason people say: "Who was the one who gave us food?"

It was Fox who brought a good tree from elsewhere for us to eat: algarrobo. We give Fox thanks for what he did.

Informant: Máki

Source: Siffredi ms.

Motif content

A1429.	Aquisition of food supply—miscellaneous.
A2681.+.	Origin of algarrobo tree. (A2681. Origin of trees.)
B435.1.	Helpful fox.
B531.	Animals provide food for men.

28. The Folly and Power of Kíxwet

Because of all the evil things Kíxwet kept doing, one day his family deserted him. When he returned from searching for honey and saw the abandoned camp, he burst into tears, realizing that his brother would now copulate with his wife. Of course, Kíxwet had slept with his brother's wife! So he said: "I'm sure he's going to get even!"

Seeing some feces there he inquired: "Where did my wife go?"

The excrement told him nothing, but jumped from one side to another, making noises. Kíxwet became angry, picked it up, and threw it against a tree. The excrement came back and hit him hard in the face. Kíxwet began crying like a woman. He cried and cried!

Later he saw that they had left an old sandal lying about, and he asked it: "Where did my wife go?"

But the sandal did not want to tell him either. It only kept standing up and falling back to the ground. Kíxwet left along a path and found Hónikiu, the cariama bird. He asked it what he had asked the others, and the bird said to him: "She went that way, but she has copulated with your brother already, so it's too late."

"I don't care," Kíxwet lied. "I told her to be with him!"

When Kíxwet caught up with his family, the brothers began to fight with clubs. How they were fighting! Finally Kíxwet's brother won, and he grabbed an ax and began to hack at Kíxwet's belly. Some of his intestines burst out, and from them Kíxwet was formed again. The brother angrily grabbed another piece of gut and flung it up into the treetops, where it turned into lianas. Kíxwet is a living man; no matter how many times they killed him he always returned to life.

Informant: Kasókchi ilánek

Source: Siffredi ms.

Motif content

A2610.	Creation of plants by transformation.
A2611.0.5.	Parts of human or animal body transformed into plants.
A2680.+.	Origin of lianas. (A2680. Origin of other plant forms.)
D437.+.	Transformation: intestines to person. (D437. Transformation: part of animal or person to person.)
D457.+.	Transformation: intestines to lianas. (D457. Transformed parts of person or animal to object.)
D1002.	Magic excrements.
D1065.5.	Magic sandals.
D1600.	Automatic object.
D1602.	Self-returning magic object.
D1643.	Object travels by itself.
E1.	Person comes to life.
E780.	Vital bodily members.
F559.3.	Extraordinary excrement.
H1385.3.	Quest for vanished wife (mistress).
J640.	Avoidance of others' power.
K2211.	Treacherous brother.
Q242.3.	Punishment for man who makes advances to sister-in-law.
Q450.	Cruel punishments.
Q580.	Punishment fitted to crime.
T410.	Incest.
T425.	Brother-in-law seduces (seeks to seduce) sister-in-law.

29. Fox Changes the Habitat and the Properties of the Chaguar

Long ago it was easy to collect chaguar. It hung from trees and was easy to remove. But it was Fox who said: "Well, now I am going to find out if women are capable of gathering chaguar. I am going to move it to another place."

So he planted it in the earth and put thorns on it.

Previously it was not like that. It was easy for the women to gather chaguar and work it. But since Fox changed its place and form, giving it thorns, when we collect chaguar now it hurts us badly.

It didn't use to be like this, never, never; the women of long ago did not have this problem. Collecting chaguar and removing the fibers was quicker when it had no thorns.

Informant: Máki

Source: Siffredi ms.

Motif content

A1101.1.	Golden age.
A2752.	Thorns on plants.
A2770.+.	Why chaguar is rooted in the ground. (A2770. Other plant characteristics.)
J1117.+.	Fox as trickster. (J1117. Animal as trickster.)

30. The Origin of Sachasandia

In former times there was no *sachasandia*. It was Thlamó (god of the underworld) who gave the seeds to a shaman who lived at the time of our parents. Before letting the shaman plant them, Thlamó said: "Explain well to the people that when the seeds I gave bring fruit, you must cook them repeatedly."

In time there grew a beautiful tree. But the bad thing in the *sachasandia*, something like poison, comes from Thlamó. Therefore, when the shaman who made it grow saw his wife gathering fruit, he told her: "*Sachasandia* takes a long time to cook. You boil it once and throw out the water; then you add more water and continue boiling it. Repeat this several times until you see the poison come out."

When a boy wanted to eat *sachasandia* before the water had been changed several times, the shaman said to him: "No, son! You should wait until your mother takes the poison out of it. Do not think that you will be able to eat it soon; it takes a long time, from what Thlamó told me."

Then he explained to the people: "I can only repeat to you what Thlamó told me: 'Explain to them that if they want to eat *sachasandia*, he who is not afraid will be able to eat it although it is not ready. He who does not have the patience to wait, and feels afraid, will not be able to eat it.'"

That's why *sachasandia* continues to be bad to this day. It is dangerous for children to eat it before it is ready. Many people die from *sachasandia*. That power of *sachasandia* continues today. Thlamó makes it dangerous to eat; it kills people.

Informant: Máki

Source: Siffredi ms.

Motif content

A182.3.5.	God advises mortal.
A300.	God of the underworld.
A2600.+.	Origin of *sachasandia*. (A2600. Origin of plants.)
A2692.+.	Why *sachasandia* is poisonous. (A2692. Origin of poisonous plants.)
J1050.	Attention to warnings.
N817.0.1.	God as helper.

31. The Origin of Bitter Manioc

Before, we did not know bitter manioc which, like *sachasandia*, is dangerous. Thlamó told a shaman named Wélaik that he could plant it. In those days the plant did not grow here but far away toward the east. Those who were planters did not know bitter manioc. Thlamó chose Wélaik, who lived here, to bring it from the east. Then little by little he returned until bitter manioc came to this region.

This plant is not like *sachasandia*, which they planted right here, and which we suddenly realized existed. Bitter manioc is from far away and was unknown to us. But the shaman, whom Thlamó sent, went to the east and asked those who had manioc what he could do to obtain it.

The people taught him how to plant it, make it grow, and prepare it. They told him that if he did not learn to prepare it properly, it could kill people.

Informant: Máki

Source: Siffredi ms.

Motif content

A300.	God of the underworld.
A1423.4.	Acquisition of manioc.
N817.0.1.	God as helper.

32. Moon Shows Armadillo the Properties of His Plants

In those days our ancestors were still suffering. They did not know what to do and were starving.

Then one of them, Ithlió, the armadillo, thought of asking Moon for help. "I should go and visit Moon," he said.

He was the first man to visit him. He got there, and Moon's children told their father: "Father, there's a man coming. Who could it be?"

"I recognize him from a distance; it is Armadillo. Come over here," he said. "I know that you are looking for something."

"Yes, I am hungry."

Moon called his son: "Bring some watermelon for this man."

When he brought it the man took only a small piece, and had no sooner tasted it than he was full. "I am full, so I shall not eat any more."

"All right, but put back that little piece (the rind) so that the watermelon will be whole again."

Sure enough. As Moon put the rind next to the fruit he asked the man to look behind him. When he turned around once more, the watermelon had become whole again.

"Look," said Moon, "what I said has come to pass. Although the plant dies it will always reappear. If you like these seeds and want to have them you can take them with you."

Said Armadillo: "I shall take them, for I would like to have them, too."

Informant: Aió

Source: Siffredi ms.

Motif content

A182.3.5.	God advises mortal.
A745.	Family of the moon.
A2687.+.	Origin of watermelon. (A2687. Origin of fruits.)
D1349.1.6.	Tiny amount of food magically satisfies.
D2150.+.	Partially eaten fruit made whole again. (D2150. Miscellaneous magic manifestations.)
F16.	Visit to land of moon.
N818.1.+.	Moon as helper. (N818.1. Sun as helper.)

33. Armadillo and the Leisurely Way of Planting

Moon's eldest daughter liked Armadillo and said to her father: "Look, father, I would like to marry Armadillo. He is handsome."

This was her idea, and she asked her father's permission to woo Armadillo. But the former said to her: "No, leave the poor man alone; he came here to eat and nothing else."

But the girl kept begging and begging, until finally her father said: "All right, I can't deny any of you anything, but you must take good care of him."

Thus they got married. Instead of going to Moon just for help (food) Armadillo managed to sleep with a girl.[3] Afterward Moon said to his daughter: "Let us see if the man who is with me and who is now your husband likes to plant. If he does I shall give him seed."

The girl said to the man: "My father says that if you want to learn how to plant he will give you seed."

"All right."

Then Moon gave his daughter two small kernels of corn. As soon as he had put them in the bag it was full of seeds, as though they had multiplied there.

Then he said to his daughter: "Take this to him and tell him to plant it over there."

Armadillo went straight to the place indicated, where he was supposed to plant,[4] though he did not know what to do. Moon explained to him: "This is how you do it: dig little holes and put the seeds in them. But do not look back until there are no seeds left; only then may you look back."

Armadillo did exactly as he had been told, planting the seeds until around noon when they were all gone; then he turned around and looked: "Oh, the maize is already in bloom and has kernels, too! How nice! And how quick!" he said. Armadillo was very pleased, for he had never thought of carrying out such a task.

"Well, then I shall go back and take an ear of corn with me," he said.

He took one to show to his wife[5] and said to her: "This ear which was out in the field, does it by any chance belong to your father?"

---

[3]Among the Chorote postmarital residence tends to be uxorilocal, and the son-in-law has to carry out a series of tasks for his parents-in-law, as the story shows.

[4]An allusion to the practice of marking off the fields on the surrounding trees, a task reserved for the old men.

[5]In the agricultural cycle the first crop harvested is maize. Its ripeness is symbolized by the husband bringing his wife an ear of corn.

The girl took the ear and showed it to her father: "Look, my husband thinks that this is your ear of corn which was left out there."

But Moon said: "No, I do not have anything now. My maize is all gone, so it must be from his crop. Let us go and see!"

The parents-in-law were very pleased, and when they went to take a look they were even more pleased, for many plants had come up with their ears.

This was the first planting lesson, with Armadillo as the planter. He worked better, but after him another man came to visit Moon: the Fox. He came, and on his way back he passed by Armadillo's field and stole some ears. Immediately the ears and the stalks disappeared. The stalks turned into brushwood and all the other shrubs. Because of what Fox had done all arable land disappeared.

The following day Fox returned, and Moon said to him: "I do not know what you did, maybe you stole something. . . ."

The other denied it: "No, I did not."

Moon's youngest daughter wanted to court the man whose name was Wóiki (Fox), for she liked him, and at last her father gave her to him, trusting him. The next morning Moon asked his daughter whether her husband wanted to plant, for he could give maize seeds to him, too.

The girl said to Fox: "If you want to plant, my father can give you seeds."

"All right, I shall plant."

Then Moon gave his daughter two seeds, just as he had first given two to his eldest daughter for Armadillo. Once more they multiplied until there were many. As the other field had disappeared and since Moon was the owner of the earth, he showed Fox another field, saying: "Go to that land and plant there."

Fox got ready and went off with the seeds. But he was very mischievous. When he began to dig, instead of putting the seeds in the little holes he only put his hand down. This way he pretended that he was throwing in the seeds. But instead he put them into his mouth and ate them. He ate and ate, not putting a single seed in any of the small holes that he dug. Moon already knew that his daughter's husband had been squandering the seeds, yet he did not want to say anything before Fox had returned from the field. He came back very late, and his father-in-law asked him: "How is it going? Did you plant?"

"Yes, I did."

"And why do you come so late?"

"Well, I planted so much that I was not able to finish earlier."

"All right, I am going to take a look."

Moon went and looked at the field: there was nothing to be seen, only
holes. He said: "What is this?"

He began to poke around in the holes but found nothing.

"I think Fox has been eating my seeds. Yes, that is how it is."

He went back home and asked: "Fox, what did you do with the seeds
that I gave you today?"

"Well, I planted. . . ."

"No, I do not believe you did. I think you ate them. For what you
have done you must leave my daughter; I am going to take her away
from you. I do not like you anymore and you have to leave, for you are
a real rascal. Look, the land is turning into brushwood! I did not want
that kind of uncultivated land."

From there came the trees we always see, because of Fox's tricks.
Instead of the good plants (cultivated plants) which used to be the only
ones around, shrubs and trees began to grow. In the beginning when
Moon made the earth it was all arable, but because of Fox's mischief it
turned into the high and low unbroken forest and the scrubwoods that
we see today.

Armadillo was the best planter, and we would have been like him had
we followed his example and not paid attention to Fox's nonsense,
saying that the seeds were no good; he always ate them. Armadillo, on
the other hand, took good care of the seeds and his plants turned out
best, for he was the first to visit the owner of seeds and did everything
the latter told him. Therefore the plants kept coming out of the ground
as soon as Armadillo put the seeds in. And that is how it would have
been today if we had not followed the bad example of Fox. But none
of our immediate ancestors did as Armadillo, so that none of us present-
day people know how to plant as he and Moon did. Things are really
hard for us. When we plant, crops take very long to mature, or they
turn out badly.[6]

When Moon drove Fox away because he was annoyed that the latter
was eating the seeds, Fox was reluctant to go, for he wanted to sleep
with Moon's daughter. He pretended that his feet hurt, and Moon said
to him: "Look, Fox, be gone at once."

"No," said Fox. "Let me stay a while longer. My feet hurt very much,
and I cannot walk."

[6]The epochs of Chorote mythical time are markedly qualitative. They always express
a sense of different ways of being, based on the nature of the ties established between
the subjects and the gods. In this case the distant ancestors place themselves on the
highest level, through Moon's revelation of an abundant vegetal order. The close ancestors, on the other hand, expressly tie themselves to Fox's harmful actions which per-
manently alter that order, affecting even the people of today.

But it was a lie. He wanted to have intercourse with the girl, and kept looking at her. . . . In those days everyone went naked, and Fox could see her parts. As it was the last day that he was going to be with her he thought: "Why is he throwing me out? With whom am I going to have relations now?"

His penis became erect, and when he had to turn away because his father-in-law was anxious to get rid of him they said: "Look at Fox; he has an erection!"

All of Moon's family got up, each grabbing a stick and hitting him. As they were beating him Fox kept shouting: "Chajajaja!" which is how the fox howls to this day. They killed Fox for what he had done and because of all his mischief. Of course, as always, he revived at once and went away.

Informant: Aió

Source: Siffredi ms.

Summary

Moon's oldest daughter marries Armadillo who is given seeds and goes out to plant, scrupulously following Moon's instructions. Maize grows at once. Youngest daughter marries Fox who is also given seeds; he eats them, however, causing field to turn into brushwood. (Origin of brushwood.) Fox is killed by Moon's relatives, but revives.

Motif content

A185.3.	Deity teaches mortal.
A745.	Family of the moon.
A1101.1.	Golden age.
A1346.	Man to earn bread by sweat of his brow.
A1441.	Acquisition of agriculture.
A1441.4.	Origin of sowing and planting.
A2426.1.+.	Cry of fox. (A2426.1. Cries of mammals.)
A2631.	Origin of plant as punishment.
A2680.+.	Origin of brushwood. (A2680. Origin of other plant forms.)
A2700.	Origin of plant characteristics.
C331.	Tabu: looking back.
D451.+.	Transformation: maize to brushwood. (D451. Transformation of vegetable form.)
D1810.0.1.	Omniscience of a god.
D2081.	Land made magically sterile.
D2106.	Magic multiplication of objects.
D2157.2.	Magic quick growth of crops.
E1.	Person comes to life.

E151.	Repeated resuscitation.
J1117.+.	Fox as trickster. (J1117. Animal as trickster.)
J2400.	Foolish imitation.
Q212.	Theft punished.
Q422.0.1.	Punishment: beating to death.
Q432.	Punishment: ejectment.
Q550.	Miraculous punishments.
Q552.3.4.	Food magically disappears.
Q595.	Loss or destruction of property as punishment.
T55.	Girl as wooer.
T111.1.2.	Man marries the daughter of a god.
T131.1.2.	Father's consent to son's (daughter's) marriage necessary.

34. Fox Causes Sowing and Harvesting to Be No Longer Simultaneous

When another sowing season came around, Armadillo, who had saved some seeds, thought of sowing again. When Fox saw that his friend was carrying seeds in a bag, he said: "I am going to follow him. I am going to sow next to my friend, because at the last *nahkáp*[7] he harvested a lot. I would like to have things grow for me the way they do for him. I am very hungry! I would like to marry a girl, but first I must produce much fruit. Then I shall have a wife like he does."

He followed Armadillo, watching him from afar.

"Fox, what did you come here for?" said Armadillo.

"For nothing!" said Fox. "I came because I want to accompany you, and I also want to sow."

"And why?"

"Well, I like you. I miss you a lot when you go to the garden."

"Well, follow me, then."

And so they went. Armadillo was going to sow in a certain place, and told Fox: "Friend, here is where I am going to sow. You put your seed over there, and I put my seed right here. That's how the two of us will sow."

"Very well," said Fox.

As it was with Armadillo, no sooner had he sown and covered the seeds with earth than he would look behind him, and there would be

---

[7]*Nahkáp* designates the year and the season that coincide with the ripening of wild fruit and with the harvest of rapidly growing cultivated vegetables. It extends over the months of November and December (Siffredi 1973).

plants already. But he also saw how Fox was sowing, poking the earth with a digging stick and pretending to be putting in seeds. He was not throwing them in at all, but eating them. Thus he continued. A little later Armadillo asked him: "What is wrong, my friend, your seeds do not grow?"

"No, they have no buds yet. They will soon, however."

But the earth contained no seeds. Fox only said it did, but actually he had eaten them all up. That is why at noon he had a stomachache; he had indigestion. He said: "Friend, I am going to sleep!"

"All right, sleep right there." Armadillo kept on working, working, sowing. After a little while he said: "Fox, my friend, why are you snoring? Are you asleep? Are you weak?"

"I do not know."

"It seems to me you have indigestion!"

"No, I do not have indigestion. I think I am just ill. I do not know what I have. . . ."

But he had indigestion. A rogue, that is what Fox is! He did many bad things, and the old ones say that Fox is the one we are imitating. That is why there is always a place where we sow and things grow and another where they don't. If we had continued Armadillo's practices, we would have easy harvests immediately after sowing.

Informant: Kasókchi ilánek

Source: Siffredi ms.

Summary

Armadillo, who sows and harvests almost simultaneously, is accompanied by Fox, who eats his seeds instead of sowing. Chorote adopt Fox's way instead of Armadillo's; hence long time span between sowing and harvesting.

Motif content

A1346.	Man to earn bread by sweat of his brow.
A2700.	Origin of plant characteristics.
D2157.2.	Magic quick growth of crops.
J1117.+.	Fox as trickster. (J1117. Animal as trickster.)
J2400.	Foolish imitation.

35. Armadillo and His Fields

There once was a man named Ijlió, Armadillo. He liked to sow. He sowed lots of different seeds in a field. When he turned around to look, the plants had already grown. His mother-in-law came and began choosing watermelons, maize, everything. She got lost amid the plants. Armadillo went home and did not know that his mother-in-law had gotten lost.

On the way he met Fox (Wóiki). He saw the blossom on a plant. Fox ordered him to climb up, but Armadillo fell to the ground and got sick. This is why he has marks on his shell. Fox went to Armadillo's house in search of the latter's wife. He took her away and slept with her. She smelled an odor: "What has happened here?" she asked. "Where does this smell come from? I do not think this is my husband. I think it is someone else, Fox."

Dawn came. Fox wanted to plant seeds and left to do so. He gathered some maize seeds and placed them in a hole, and he also ate them. Many days later he went out to see the plants. There were none. No plants had come out since he had eaten the seeds and had given himself a stomachache.

Informant: Cepillo

Source: Mashnshnek 1972, pp. 142–143.

Motif content

A2210.	Animal characteristics: change in ancient animal.
A2214.	Animal characteristics from dropping ancient animal from air.
A2412.1.+.	Markings of armadillo. (A2412.1. Markings of mammals.)
D2157.2.	Magic quick growth of crops.
H30.+.	Recognition by smell. (H30. Recognition through personal peculiarities.)
J1117.+.	Fox as trickster. (J1117. Animal as trickster.)
J1700.	Fools.
K1311.	Seduction by masking as woman's husband.

36. Fox and Armadillo Sow

The fox and the armadillo got married to a couple of women. "Let us sow since we now have wives," they decided. They went out to sow. The armadillo sowed corn. When he turned around, the corncobs had already emerged. The fox wanted to do likewise. He wanted to sow, but instead of scattering the seeds, he ate them. He did not sow his grain.

Informant: Talimpí

Source: Mashnshnek 1973, p. 61.

Motif content

D2157.2.	Magic quick growth of crops.
J1700.	Fools.

37. Moon Reveals the Plant Cycle to a Shaman

A recent ancestor went to visit Moon. He was the first shaman. It was he who informed the shamans that they have to find a way of reaching the place where Moon lives to this very day.[8]

When the ancestral shaman got there Moon's children saw him while they were playing outside. They ran home to tell their father: "Someone is coming to visit."

"All right, we must welcome him," said Moon.

The children had to take him to the house. Then Moon said to his wife: "Just what I wanted, someone to visit me. That is what I wished for, and it makes me very happy. Now we must give our newly arrived son something to eat."

When his wife brought some fruit he said to the shaman: "You came to ask for my help. Well, this is the fruit of my work."

And he showed him first a squash: "Eat this, but do not throw away the rind."

When the shaman had finished eating he handed Moon the rind. Moon asked him to turn around. The shaman looked back, and when he turned around once more, the squash was whole again. For the fruit may come to an end, but Moon can always make it whole again.

"This is what I do," repeated the Moon. "Now try this watermelon, but do not throw away the rind."

The man tasted it, putting aside the rind, and when he looked again, there it was, whole once more. Thus Moon kept showing him different fruits: melon, *anco* squash, and others.

Then Moon said: "This means that when you are on earth you, like everybody else, will suffer for a while, for you will not have any crops, but I'll be able to help you from up here. When one crop is exhausted there has to be another the following year. You see, since you have come to see me I shall have to help you. When the crop has been eaten

---

[8]After Moon's ascent to the sky communication with him, which in primordial times was available to everybody, is restricted almost exclusively to those shamans who receive the god's revelation.

maybe some neighbor will say that it is gone for good. But that is not how it shall be. A similar crop will come up and return year after year."

This was what Moon wanted to tell the shaman. He had a plan for him that had to be followed, and thus he explained: "The rind will not become a whole fruit again at once; it will take a year. But you will have a crop. And even if you throw away the rind, the fruit will return the following year. Each year I will look after the plants and the water."[9]

Moon wanted to show the shaman that what he was doing in the sky was also going to happen on earth, though over a much longer time, and that even if they threw away the rind the fruit would return.

Then Moon made the man taste beans. But since he did not like them he refused. However, Moon insisted: "Eat. It is very good and very nutritious. You must take good care of the seeds of all these fruits that I make you try. If you guard them well, the crops will grow more bountiful every time, and there will be different kinds of plants. This is my work, and it is good. I do not do anything bad. I send food to every place on earth because I am a very good man. Now you know me, so that if any calamities should happen down there you can come and tell me."

Moon also showed him *kixét*, cacti, and other wild fruits: "Eat a piece of this fruit and leave another piece there."

No sooner had he turned around than it was whole once more. Then Moon said to him: "You will be able to harvest these fruits as well, not at once like here but on a yearly basis. You will not have to keep the seeds of those, for I am going to send them to you."

Informant: Aió

Source: Siffredi ms.

Summary

Shaman visits Moon in sky. Latter lets him taste several kinds of wild and cultivated fruit which at once miraculously grow whole again, symbolizing periodic renewal of plant life. He also instructs shaman to keep seeds for annual planting.

Motif content

A182.3.5.	God advises mortal.
A185.3.	Deity teaches mortal.
A745.	Family of the moon.
A753.2.	Moon has house.

[9]In fact, the Chorote believe that Moon protects the crops, sends rain, and in general renews all plant life. These beliefs are based on mythical as well as shamanic sources.

A1441.4.   Origin of sowing and planting.
A1654.   Origin of priesthood (shamanism, etc.).
A2602.   Planting the earth.
A2684.   Origin of cultivated plants.
A2700.+.   Origin of seasonal plant cycle. (A2700. Origin of plant
                      characteristics.)
D2143.1.   Rain produced by magic.
D2150.+.   Partially eaten fruit made whole again. (D2150.
                      Miscellaneous magic manifestations.)
F10.   Journey to upper world.
F12.   Journey to see deity.
F16.   Visit to land of moon.
F166.11.   Abundant food in otherworld.
N818.1.+.   Moon as helper. (N818.1. Sun as helper.)

38. The Origin of Cultivated Plants and of Batrachians

One morning, when the time of *kílaship*[10] was near, Oxuo, the pigeon, began to chat with his wife: "What am I going to do? What will our children eat when the season comes in which people sow and harvest? I am going over there!" He pointed to the north and to the west, toward Bolivia. Over there, he thought, people had had a great harvest, and the empty fields would be strewn with rejected seeds.[11]

He went there and gathered bean seeds, squash seeds, corn seeds, pumpkin seeds, and seeds of several other plants. He filled his belly, which he called his bag, and when it grew late, he said: "Now I am leaving. I am going home." He flew back and descended. Finding a place where there was water he drank, for he was tired. At first he only put his beak into the water, but then he immersed his head until the water reached his eyes. "I was thirsty!" he said. "I almost died of thirst."

He set off again and got to where his wife was. There he took all kinds of seeds from his bag, and at the next *kílaship* he was able to sow

[10]The season called *kílaship* (derived from *kílaik* = quebracho) covers approximately January and February, corresponding to the second part of the rainy season. During this time vegetables with a long growing period are sown (Siffredi 1973:78–79). In primordial times, on the other hand, sowing and harvesting took place at the same time, as the myth explains.

[11]The myth alludes to the agricultural production of two groups: the Chiriguano-Chané (Iñóna), Amazonian horticulturalists located northwest of the Chorote, and the Tapiete (Inxuéinak), a Chaco tribe strongly influenced by the former and located to the north of the Chorote. The latter maintained relations of regulated interchange with both groups, as analyzed in Siffredi (1975, 3, 1:41–70).

and produce food for his children. He is the only one who traveled far
away to bring seeds.

When Pigeon had brought the seeds he realized that if they ate them
all they would be without any for the next season, so he said: "I had
better sow!"

He prepared a beautiful patch in a pasture with sandy soil. But the
following day many people came and carried off what he had sown:
melons, watermelons. . . . When he saw this, he said to his wife: "Could
you gather what's left? We shall put everything together in an elevated
granary."

When Ithlió, the armadillo, heard this he said to himself: "I ought
to take some seeds for myself, because if I do not I shall be left without
seeds and without food."

He went off, because they had the same customs then as we have now.
We sow, and when the plants bear fruit we harvest them. Then we plant
something else in order to have food in the future. Therefore, when
Armadillo realized that Pigeon had already sown other plants, he went
and poked around in his field. He dug out the new seeds until he had
gathered a good many. Now, finally, he had seeds, too.

But Armadillo was different from the others. Whenever he was finished sowing he would look behind him, and there would already be
watermelons and whatever else he had sown. They grew pretty quickly!
Before he would run out of seeds, suddenly Armadillo's plants would
have fruit. If he sowed corn seeds it was the same. When he turned
around the plants would already be large and quite edible. That is how
it was with him, and that is why the old ones say: "If Armadillo had
passed this practice on to us, it would be easy for us to plant and harvest."

When Armadillo reaped a big harvest, some boys wanted to go to his
field. Wandering around in there, one of them could not find the end
of the field. He became totally lost and failed to return in the afternoon.
Then Armadillo thought: "Ah, those boys have been stealing from me!
I shall let it rain hard tonight so they will get soaked inside my garden.
They are at fault. They went there without my permission. They may
even be eating my melons!"

He made it rain hard that night. It rained, leaving many puddles
beneath the plants. The boys were freezing, crying and crying until
they changed into various kinds of batrachians. The boys were heard
crying. Some were smaller and became frogs; others were a little bigger
and became toads; and yet other, bigger ones became bullfrogs. They
stayed like that. Armadillo caused the rain to make the boys suffer for
playing around in his garden. The boys got lost and turned into different

batrachians. These are the ones you can hear when it rains. Hearing them we say: "Those were the boys that turned into frogs when they were cold and unable to leave the garden!"

They shouted and called out with the voice of frogs, and then the poor things transformed themselves into these animals. They live in puddles to this day.

Informant: Kasókchi ilánek

Source: Siffredi ms.

Summary

Pigeon goes far away to gather seeds. After he plants, others steal his fruits. Armadillo causes seeds to grow magically. When boys steal from his garden he makes it rain and turns them into frogs as punishment.

Motif content

A2684.	Origin of cultivated plants.
D2143.1.	Rain produced by magic.
D2157.2.	Magic quick growth of crops.
F701.	Land of plenty.
J710.	Forethought in provision for food.
Q550.+.	Rain as punishment. (Q550. Miraculous punishments.)
Q551.3.2.3.	Punishment: transformation into frog.
Q551.3.2.3.+.	Punishment: transformation into toad. (Q551.3.2.3. Punishment: transformation into frog.)

39. Kíxwet-Aséta: The Magic Pregnancy and the Introduction of Food Fish

There was a very beautiful girl, and all the armadillo "shell people" were looking at her. Kasókchi (*Dasypus* sp.) was watching her. He wanted to have sex with that girl because she was very beautiful. However, realizing that this would never be, he went away in order not to be close to her anymore.

There was another armadillo, Ithlió (*Tolypeutes matacus*), who said: "I am going to try. I am going to try it with this young girl!"

The girl was sitting there, grinding algarrobo fruit in the mortar; she was grinding and grinding. Ithlió dug a hole close to where the girl was sitting. But he could not accomplish anything either and left her alone. Then Ithlió remembered Aséta (armadillo, *Chaetophractus villosus*), who was bigger and stronger than he.

Since she was such a beautiful girl, and since the others had not
been able to do anything, Aséta agreed to give it a try. "I am going
to try!" he said.

But trying was not all that he did. He dug a hole and came out
where she was sitting. There he had sex with the girl without her
feeling a thing. When Aséta had finished, the girl saw a little hole in
the ground where she had been sitting. Aséta had used it to put his
penis through and, moving around, he had inserted it into her. The
girl could not have avoided it. Aséta was clever; he had succeeded.
He went to his friends. The following day the girl gave birth to a boy.
Nobody knew who the father was, but it was Kíxwet-Aséta.

There was a bottle tree that had something like a lagoon inside.
All the water was inside this tree and Kíxwet was taking care of it.
When he approached the people no one knew who the baby's father
was, but the baby said: "There comes my father, for Aséta had sex
with my mother, and he is my father."

Then the others knew.

In this lagoon inside the bottle tree there were many fish. Aséta's
son said to the people: "I am going to open it so you will see the fish,
and then we are going to eat them."

Aséta's son was the Father of Fish. He went to his grandmother's
house, and played with her there. Then he made some arrows, and
the grandmother asked him what they were for.

"To go over there and look for some animals."

"All right," said the grandmother. "But don't go far or you will get
lost."

"No, I am going over there, close by."

The boy went to see the lagoon in the bottle tree. Upon arriving he
looked at the tree and saw the fish swimming in the water. He took an
arrow and shot one to take home and show to his grandmother. He
returned, and said to her: "Look, grandmother! Do you know what
this is?"

"No," she said.

"This is called a fish. It is delicious, and we are going to eat it."
But the grandmother did not want to eat that. Aséta's son said: "I am
going to scale it."

He scaled it, cut it open in the middle, and roasted it. When it was
ready he took it off, put it on some leaves, and began to eat it, saying:
"Come here, grandmother! Try it, eat it. This is food for us! I am
going to get more if you like it."

The grandmother ate some, and she liked it. She asked: "Where did
you get this, son?"

"From over there. We shall go and get some more."

When they finished eating, the boy said to his grandmother: "Now we are going to get a lot! I am going to take some of the neighbors along."

Aséta's son made many long net bags, and when they arrived at the bottle tree they put the nets in the water and immediately took out a lot of fish. Some had caught twenty, others thirty, others forty. The boy made them put all the fish together and divided them up until each one had the same amount. Then he said to them: "Now we are going to scale all of them. These we eat over here, and those we take home to the camp."

This they did. They scaled them, roasted them, and divided them up to eat there together. When they had finished, they returned. The boy made them dress the fish and roast them. He cut twigs to make platforms on which to dry them. They fried the fat until it turned into oil; the people liked it. When those who did not like fish saw the others enjoy it, they liked it too.

They ate the intestines, they ate the fat, and it seemed delicious to them. When the fish were well cooked, they were placed to dry on the platforms. Some dressed the fish and dried them without roasting them first.

This is how the practice of fish eating began. Since then people have liked it a lot.

Informant: José Romero

Source: Siffredi ms.

Summary

Pretty girl admired by all men is impregnated by Aséta, who cunningly has intercourse with her without her knowledge. Her son catches fish in magic bottle tree and introduces it as food to his people.

Motif content

A445.	God of fish.
A1420.2.	Gods teach how to seek and prepare food.
A1429.+.	Acquisition of fish. (A1429. Acquisition of food supply— miscellaneous.)
A1457.	Origin of fishing.
A1457.3.	Origin of the net for fishing.
A1527.	Custom of catching fish with nets.
F575.1.	Remarkably beautiful woman.
F721.1.	Underground passages.

F811.	Extraordinary tree.
F811.+.	Tree containing water and fish. (F811. Extraordinary tree.)
F811.5.3.	Fish-producing tree.
F986.	Extraordinary occurrences concerning fishing.
H481.	Infant picks out his unknown father.
T475.	Unknown (clandestine) paramour.
T517.	Conception from extraordinary intercourse.
T573.	Short pregnancy.

40. Séta's Son Teaches Man to Eat Fish

There was a pretty woman who had never married. Séta's son had recently been born [without knowing who his father was]. The boy started to cry. The sparrow hawk came by. He wanted to pick up the boy who was lying down. Another sparrow hawk came and wanted to take him.

The bird asked: "Who is your father?" He mentioned the names of all the animals, but the boy did not answer. The bird asked: "Is the armadillo your father?" But the boy remained silent. He named all the animals, but received no reply. Then he mentioned Séta, and only then did the boy respond.

The birds took the child with them, and the boy grew bigger. Séta ordered him: "Go to that girl's house. She must be your mother." The girl was lovely, beautiful. Nobody had married her. The boy went and called: "Mother, mother, mother, give me some milk. I'm hungry."

But the girl refused. The boy cried for two nights. Finally she picked him up and made him her son. She gave him food to eat.

"Make me a little arrow," said the boy. "I am going out to hunt."

He left and came to a pond full of fish. The boy began to fish and caught one. Our ancestors did not know about fish. He brought them a fish. "Son, what are you bringing me?" asked the mother. "What is it? Could it be poisonous?" She did not know what it was.

"It is a fish," replied the boy. "Only if you eat too much of it will you get weak." He cut it up and roasted it. The fat melted, and when it had roasted he said: "Come and eat."

"No," said the mother. "I shall die. If I eat that, I shall die."

An old woman said: "I shall eat it. If I die, I die."

"It is food," said the boy. When she had finished eating it, the old woman said: "How delicious! I shall eat it. Where did you get it?"

"Over there," answered the boy, "there is a pond."

He then returned to the pond where he met his father. The girl was still unmarried. The boy returned to her with Séta, who said: "We are bringing you a lot of fish."

From afar the people saw him and said: "Could that be the boy's father? Let us welcome him," they said. "It is his father."

Séta arrived, picked up the net bag, and began to roast the fish. He married the girl because she had never been married. After the fish was gone, he went away again.

Informant: Cepillo

Source: Mashnshnek 1972, pp. 139–140.

Summary

Unmarried girl adopts young son of armadillo, who introduces fish among people.

Motif content

A1429.+.	Acquisition of fish. (A1429. Acquisition of food supply— miscellaneous.)
A1457.	Origin of fishing.
F575.1.	Remarkably beautiful woman.
H481.	Infant picks out his unknown father.
J585.	Caution in eating.
P272.	Foster mother.
R131.	Exposed or abandoned child rescued.
T670.	Adoption of children.

41. The Origin of Fish

A man who was the Father of Fish sent his son to look for a wife for him. The father still did not have a wife. There was an old woman with a daughter. She was very lovely but he could not marry her because she was only an adolescent.

The girl said: "Mother, let us go and gather chaguar to eat!" Suddenly she looked behind her and said: "Who could that be that comes behind us?"

The Father of Fish had sent his son to get the young girl, and the boy had gone to look for her. His father wanted to marry her. He was carrying a shad fish on his shoulder.

Farther on, when the two women came to a large chaguar field, they began to dig for chaguar and made a fire. Then the boy said to the old woman: "Hello, how are you, old woman?" They did not know him, and the mother said: "Where could that boy be from?"

"I do not know," said the girl.

"Old woman," said the boy, "do you want to eat fish? I am going to roast it."

"Very well, roast it."

He took a stick and stuck it through the fish to roast it. He took out the entrails and the fat and began to melt it. The old woman did not know how to do it, but the boy knew how. When it was melted, the chaguar was cooked, and the boy smeared the fish with the oil. First he called the old woman: "Come try it, old woman!"

"No, I am going to poison myself! It will kill me!"

"No, old woman, it is delicious! Come try it!"

Finally she dabbed her hand in the oil and tried it: "How delicious!"

"Yes, it is delicious," said the boy. When the fish was ready he took it out, and the old woman said: "What do we do? Where shall we put the roasted fish?"

"I know, old woman!"

The little boy was very clever and knew how to talk. "Old woman, cut some grass and spread it out on the ground. Then I shall take the fish and place it on top."

This they did and began to eat. The boy called the daughter of the old woman: "Come and eat, friend!"

And she also began to eat.

But that shad was large; it looked like a dorado. She ate a lot without being able to finish it. The boy asked the old woman: "What are you going to do with the rest? Are you going to throw it away?"

"No, I am going to take it to my husband."

"Good, do that," he said.

She wrapped it in the grass and tied it up. She also packed the chaguar, and they carried everything home.

When they arrived, the old woman said: "I have roasted meat here."

"What roast could it be?" asked her husband.

"We met a boy who gave it to me. He named it, calling it fish."

"What could it be?" said the husband, adding: "Well, I am just going to eat it; if I die, I die."

"It is good," said the old woman. "We already ate, but since I was very thirsty, I did not get full. I want to eat some more."

And so they ate together.

When the boy sent them home he had told them: "Tomorrow I shall return and bring lots of fish."

He went to inform his father. Then he made a cord, like the ones fishermen have, to string the fish together by the eyes. He strung up many fish. Around eight-thirty he appeared. "Here comes the boy, loaded with plenty of fish," said the old woman.

Loaded down like this, one cannot go slowly. One must go half-running, fast. That is how the boy was going. Then the old woman's husband said: "What a pity! How can he carry all these fish alone? Go to meet him!"

The old woman went and began walking around the boy, wondering how she might undo the string to get at the fish.[12] She did not dare to admit that she did not know how to do it. Finally she said: "Son, I cannot undo it. How is it done?"

"Well," said the boy, "I am going to rest a little. I am very tired."

When he was rested, he got up and undid the knot. The old woman thought: "I am going to watch how he takes it out."

He grabbed the end of the string and pulled it away from the fish: "This is how it's done."

The boy began to distribute fish to everybody. At first he wanted to give each person two, but when he saw that there was not enough he gave each only one so that it would go around. He gave them the fish, but did not tell them who was sending it to them.

"Well then," he said, "tomorrow I shall come back. I shall bring more fish."

He left and went to his father, saying: "I think the girl is going to want you now."

"Good. Let us get ready, son! I am going to shoot all the fish there is," said the Father of Fish.

He shot the fish, took the string, and inserted it through the eyes of the fish, making three lines, one on top of the other. He had already tied the rope to carry the fish on his shoulder but was unable to lift the weight. Then he called his son: "Come, help me carry these!"

The boy helped him by taking some of the fish himself, and they left.

The boy arrived first where the old woman was. The Father of Fish had remained some fifty meters behind. As soon as the people saw him they said: "Here comes the boy again! Hurry, go to meet him."

They took a sheepskin and spread it out to hold the fish.

Then the old woman asked: "Could that be the boy's father?"

---

[12]Once dead, the fish are strung together on a cord by the eyes, and are transported by tying the cord around the waist or slinging it over the shoulder.

And the boy began to talk with the old woman: "Do you think your daughter could marry him? That man wants to get married. He needs a wife."

The boy sat down and the Father of Fish arrived, his shoulders laden with fish. He carried a lot! They unloaded the fish and placed them next to the fish his son had brought. Now the old woman grabbed the girl by the arm and sent her inside the hut to wait there for the Father of Fish. Then she also took him by the arm and sent him to her daughter. And the two lay together.

Once married, the Father of Fish provided much fish. They roasted the fish, and when none were left he said: "I am going to catch some more."

Everybody grabbed a bag and went after him. They came to a large lagoon, and there were the fish. The Father of Fish taught his son how to count the people and then divided them into two parties: one party to go with him, and the other to follow his son to the other side of the lagoon.

This done, father and son began to shoot all the fish. Only the two of them were fishing. While shooting, the father realized that he had caught many. "Maybe we are catching too many?" he said.

"I do not know," said the boy.

He began to talk to all his friends: "Let us see! Each one gets a fish and keeps it in his bag!"

They began to gather the fish, and there were enough for everybody. Then the Father of Fish said: "Put the fish in your bags! This is too much! Let us go!"

They went home and began to roast the fish. "How are we going to do this? And where shall we put the roasted fish?" The Father of Fish thought for a while and said: "It's best that each one makes a platform. That is what we shall do!"

When they were done roasting the fish, each person placed it on top of his platform.

Suddenly, at dusk, a lean dog came, and they gave it the entrails of the fish. "Poor little dog, we shall feed you!"

The Father of Fish said to them: "Just give it to him so he may gain some weight!"

Then they asked him: "The roast we are saving, is it all right to keep it indoors?"

"No, it is better to leave it outside," said the Father of Fish.

The thin dog was walking around, spying, and saw that each house had a lot of fish. "There is no danger here. There is no Thlamó here or anything," said the people.

But around midnight the bony dog began to devour the roasted fish. He finished them all, not leaving a single one! It was Kíxwet who had transformed himself into a dog!

When the sun came up someone said: "Let us eat fish!"

But he did not find it! Then the Father of Fish became angry and said: "I am going to throw out my wife because she does not watch the fish well enough. You will not see it again. The fish will not appear again!" And the Father of Fish went to join the fish. He took on another form: with a fishtail instead of legs, and the chest and head of a man.

Then suddenly Ahóusa, the hawk hero, appeared. The people said to him: "What are we going to do with that lagoon? It is just sitting there. What shall we do? We are not going to get anything like that again! We are not going to find any fish!"

Ahóusa said to them: "I had better do something about this, but do not watch me."

He began to make a big gully and the water ran into it. Then he said: "Let us see now. Turn around!"

And they saw a big river, like this one (the Pilcomayo). That is how Ahóusa made the river. He said: "Now we shall be able to catch fish. With the water all dammed up in a lagoon, who can catch fish? However, one can fish when there is a current."

Then he said: "I thought of something. It is not a good idea to shoot with arrows in running water. I am going to make some nets: dip nets and scissor nets." Ahóusa was not distressed. At around eight-thirty in the morning he began to work, making dip nets, and by evening he finished. The nets were well made! The following day he made the others, the scissor nets.

When they went to fish, Ahóusa told them: "First we make an enclosure. Then we wait for the fish."

They began to work, making the weir. The fish piled up. After finishing the fence they stayed there to sleep, and they caught fish all night.

The next day they returned home and roasted the fish. But one fell on the fire and the Father of Fish became angry. Then another fell, and the Father of Fish got even more angry, saying:

"Now I am really not giving them more fish. There will be no fish anymore!"

Informant: Centawó

Source: Cordeu ms.

Summary

Old man (Father of Fish) who wants to marry young girl repeatedly sends his young son to girl's village where he gives people fish and teaches them how to prepare it. When old man finally appears he marries girl.

Old man and his son take people to water hole and catch large quantities of fish for them. After trickster appears in form of dog and eats all their fish, Father of Fish angrily turns into fish-man. Then hawk culture hero arrives, and he creates river and teaches them how to fish with nets.

Motif content

A445.	God of fish.
A522.2.3.	Hawk as culture hero.
A533.	Culture hero regulates rivers.
A547.	Culture hero dispenses food and hospitality.
A930.	Origin of streams.
A930.1.	Creator of rivers.
A1420.2.	Gods teach how to seek and prepare food.
A1429.+.	Acquisition of fish. (A1429. Acquisition of food supply— miscellaneous.)
A1457.	Origin of fishing.
A1457.3.	Origin of the net for fishing.
A1527.	Custom of catching fish with nets.
B80.2.	Monster half-man, half-fish.
D141.	Transformation: man to dog.
D655.	Transformation to receive food.
D657.	Transformation to steal.
D682.	Partial transformation.
F575.1.	Remarkably beautiful woman.
H1381.3.1.	Quest for bride.
J585.	Caution in eating.
J1113.	Clever boy.
T51.	Wooing by emissary.
T91.4.	Age and youth in love.
T111.	Marriage of mortal and supernatural being.
T121.	Unequal marriage.

42. Kíxwet Introduces Fish and Creates the River

In times long past Kíxwet did not have a wife. Then one day he closed his hand and fertilized it. It became pregnant, and the next day a baby boy was born. Within three days the boy was already walking.

Kíxwet had a kind of platform above a lake which he used for fishing. He left the boy there. Four girls came by and heard the boy cry. One of the girls wanted to pick him up, but he cried even harder. Another one tried but the crying got worse. When a third girl held him, he became quiet, and she took him home.

Next day Kíxwet came to inquire where they had taken his son. Everyone looked at him. "Ah! You must mean the boy we tried to hold, but who did not seem to like us. Only when that other girl held him did he calm down. She is over there!"

They showed Kíxwet the one who had accepted his child.

And he married her because she had his son. At dawn he went to fish again and brought a big catch. In those days people did not eat fish, as they did not know it was food. Kíxwet cut the fish open, removed the fat, and boiled it in a clay pan. Then he ate it like that. Nobody else did. Not one of all the people who lived there was familiar with this practice. But now they began to wonder! "What could it be? Could it be food? What custom is this?"

Kíxwet showed the people, and soon they asked him: "How is it to eat? Is it good?"

"It is delicious; it's fish," he answered.

While Kíxwet was eating, one of the old people smelled food and asked everybody: "Where does that smell come from?"

"Somebody brought fish," they said, "and we saw him eat it."

"All right, let's see if it is any good. If yes, we eat it, if not, we won't. Since I am old, I am going to try it first. Better that *I* die!"

He ate and seemed to like it. Then the people began to eat fish; one by one they began to eat fish for the first time.

Then Kíxwet went to show them where he was getting the fish. There was a bottle tree that was bigger than all other bottle trees. It had a covered hole in its middle and whenever he took off the lid, a fish like a dorado jumped out. Kíxwet would calculate how many fish he wanted to get and would then close the lid again.

Since Kíxwet is powerful and clever he tried to change his shape. On the way the people saw a lignum vitae tree, slender and with buds.

It was Kíxwet who had taken this form of a lignum vitae with buds. All the girls coming along the road, his sisters-in-law, looked and looked at him, saying: "Ah, how wonderful it would be to have him for a husband!"

Then blood began to flow from the tree. It was Kíxwet's way of doing things. His ways were different.

When night came Kíxwet went to look for that girl, his sister-in-law. He came to a hut and asked: "Which one acted like my wife? Which one will you give me, brother-in-law? Was it that one?"

"No, it was not I," denied the girl. "It was that one."

But Kíxwet, who knew, said: "No, it was you. If you let me marry you, I shall make a river." The whole family was thinking: "Will he be our master, he who is going to make an entire river?"

Kíxwet married this young girl. Then in the morning, as was his custom, he went to fish in the tree. Before reaching the bottle tree he met a friend, Wóiki, the Fox, who asked him: "Friend, where are you going?"

"I am going to fish."

"Can I come along?"

"No."

Kíxwet was reluctant because Fox was a rogue. Fox said to him: "But I really would like to, and I shall follow you anyway."

Then the two went to see where they could fish. Arriving at the bottle tree, Kíxwet removed the cover again, and ten fish jumped out. He caught them, scaled them, and put them into his bag. He said: "Fox, let's go! You are not staying here!"

"No, I am coming with you," said Fox. And the two were on their way. They arrived home where Kíxwet's wife was. After a while Fox hid himself and, taking another path, went back to see where Kíxwet fished. He went alone, thinking: "I would also like to give fish to a woman and get married."

He arrived and removed the cover, but when so many fish came out he forgot to put it back on again.

Then the water burst out from all sides and rose to a great depth. Fox climbed up a palm tree. He was at the top and spat down below to find a firm place to jump, using his saliva. Of course, water like this gathers a lot of trash. Because it looks like land Fox was deceived. He jumped from up there. Wham! His life was over.

Kíxwet had a very good stick, a powerful staff that he used. Starting from where the water had stopped he went planting it at intervals in the ground. This way he made the water return to the bottle tree. Then he had the idea of making a river instead of containing the fish inside the tree. Otherwise bothersome people would always come to take every-thing that was inside.

Absorbing all the water the bottle tree swelled up again, but Kíxwet had his thoughts on making a river. Since he had his powerful staff, he would mark a course for the river right beside his own tracks. He said to his wife: "I am going now. I am going to make a river so the people will have food. Instead of keeping the fish over there, I shall have to multiply them. I shall give them to all my descendants."

Such were his thoughts. Then he created the river, the Pilcomayo, just as we see it today. That is how it turned out for him: narrow and full of turns. He let it go far away. When we see the Pilcomayo over there, we always say: "It is like that because Kíxwet gave it many curves."

When we walk along the river, fishing, and we get tired, we say: "Why did Kíxwet turn around so much? Why did he not make it straight?" Kíxwet was walking along with his staff. He would plant it and wait for the river to come, and when it came he would pull the stick out, walk a stretch, and plant it again. The river was looking for Kíxwet's path. He would plant the staff in the ground wherever he was going to sleep, and when the river came it stopped there without bothering him. At dawn Kíxwet would start again. He was walking all over, bringing plenty of fish everywhere. When he had finished his task he returned the way he had come. But now he met many people, who, when they saw the river, had come to live alongside it.

Informant: Kasókchi ilánek

Source: Siffredi ms.

Summary

After giving birth to baby boy from his hand, Kíxwet marries girl who is taking care of baby. He introduces people to fish, which he catches in magic fish-producing tree. Trying to do same, fox causes water to gush out of tree, and he drowns. Kíxwet makes water return to tree. He creates Río Pilcomayo by making water follow his magic stick as he walks. River fills with fish, and population grows.

Motif content

A521.	Culture hero as dupe or trickster.
A527.3.1.	Culture hero can transform self.
A533.	Culture hero regulates rivers.
A547.	Culture hero dispenses food and hospitality.
A924.3.	Sea released from tree-top.
A930.	Origin of streams.
A930.1.	Creator of rivers.
A934.4.+.	River where culture hero drags his staff. (A934.4. Rivers where god drags his staff.)
A1011.	Local deluges.
A1023.	Escape from deluge on tree.
A1429.+.	Acquisition of fish. (A1429. Acquisition of food supply— miscellaneous.)
A1457.	Origin of fishing.
D215.	Transformation: man to tree.
D1254.	Magic staff.

D1549.3.8.+.	Staff stuck in river bed stops water. (D1549.3.8. Spear stuck in river bed stops water.)
D2151.2.	Magic control of rivers.
F811.	Extraordinary tree.
F811.+.	Tree containing water and fish. (F811. Extraordinary tree.)
F811.5.3.	Fish-producing tree.
F811.20.	Bleeding tree.
F986.	Extraordinary occurrences concerning fishing.
J580.	Wisdom of caution.
J620.	Forethought in prevention of others' plans.
J1117.+.	Fox as trickster. (J1117. Animal as trickster.)
J1810.	Physical phenomena misunderstood.
J2400.	Foolish imitation.
P272.	Foster mother.
Q428.	Punishment: drowning.
R311.	Tree refuge.
T111.	Marriage of mortal and supernatural being.
T425.+.	Brother-in-law marries sister-in-law. (T425. Brother-in-law seduces (seeks to seduce) sister-in-law.)
T517.	Conception from extraordinary intercourse.
T517.1.	Conception from hand or foot.
T541.+.	Birth from hand. (T541. Birth from unusual part of person's body.)
T573.	Short pregnancy.
T615.	Supernatural growth.
T670.	Adoption of children.

43. Kisbar Introduces Fishing

There was a man named Kisbar. He fertilized his own hand, and it became big, pregnant. A boy was born from the hand, the son of Kisbar. "Well, my son, go out on the road and wait. There is a twelve-year-old girl who is going to be your mother," said his father. But the girl did not want the little boy. Later she grew sleepy, and the boy suckled. She did not want him because he was not her son. Only when he grew up did she accept him.

They went out into the bush to look for fruit, gathered a lot, and put it in a heap to eat. The boy went to tell Kisbar, his father, who had his house in the middle of the river. On his way back he brought five fish with him. "Look at that! This we have never seen. Maybe it is poisonous," said the girl. "It is no good for eating." Her grandfather was there, and the girl said to him: "Well, Grandfather, we have to cut up this fish and remove the fat. Then we shall put the fruit over it, and that's how we shall eat it." They ate it. After a while Kisbar's son said: "Grandfather, we have to make nets for the fish." The old man began to make nets to place in the water, dip nets, as the boy showed him. Thereupon the water began to flow in the river; previously it did not.

Informant: Alipa

Source: Verna ms.

Motif content

A541.	Culture hero teaches arts and crafts.
A547.	Culture hero dispenses food and hospitality.
A930.	Origin of streams.
A1429.+.	Acquisition of fish. (A1429. Acquisition of food supply— miscellaneous.)
A1457.	Origin of fishing.
A1457.3.	Origin of the net for fishing.
A1527.	Custom of catching fish with nets.
P272.	Foster mother.
T517.	Conception from extraordinary intercourse.
T517.1.	Conception from hand or foot.
T541.+.	Birth from hand. (T541. Birth from unusual part of person's body.)
T670.	Adoption of children.

44. Fox Discovers a Trough Full of Fish

The primeval world was many leagues wide. Located in the north, toward Bolivia, it was pure pasture land with wild plants, beautiful grasslands.

In those times there were also very fierce enemies, and one did not know which ones were brothers (Chorote). Fish was unknown, and there was hunger. In the center of the world there was a trough[13] next to a palm, but no one knew it existed.

There was a youth who used to roam about. He found the trough, well covered with a lid. The youth looked at it but dared not go near. He was afraid and thought: "What could it be?"

---

[13]*Atés i-wét* is the name of the large receptacle containing fermented drinks (*atés*), made from a base of wild and cultivated fruits or honey. The *atés i-wét* mentioned in the tale was made from a section of the trunk of a hollowed-out bottle tree.

Finally he decided to approach it. He raised the lid a bit and saw that there was water inside. He also saw a creature in the trough, going around in the water. He thought it was alone. Then he went home, thinking: "What could that creature in the water be?" He did not ask his father or his mother. "Tomorrow I am going to take a big bag. I am going to taste it."

Next day he arrived very early at the trough, removed the lid, inserted the bag, and extracted a large number of those creatures. They were shad. He took out about twenty, killed them all, threw them on the fire, and then removed one to try it. "Let's find out if it's poisonous!" He gave a piece to a little mongrel that always accompanied him and wondered what would happen. The dog was satisfied immediately and went off contentedly. Then the youth thought: "Maybe this food is delicious." He tried it and then ate more and more.

"I am going to scale all the shad." And he scaled them, passed a line through their eyes, and carried them home attached to his belt.

When he arrived, no one in his family wanted to try the new food because they did not know what fish was. The youth roasted them. He was eating and eating and did not return to the trough until his supply was exhausted.[14]

The boy ate for a week. He grew big and fat, while the others, who were not eating fish, remained skinny. When the fish were depleted, he went back to get another twenty shad. He advised his mother to eat fish, too. While he was roasting it she wanted to know whether one could die from eating fish. But he told her: "Nothing is happening to me. This is exquisite food. Look at my body! It appears to have helped me!"

He prepared a fish soup and made his mother taste it. She liked it, and then one by one his brothers came to eat also, forming a line. They were tasting it. Fox also approached. He came to watch them. "What could they have eaten? Maybe I should eat also. I shall try it." And he tasted the fish and liked it.

Then Fox began to observe the youth to see when he would go to procure more fish. Seeing him leave to get more, Fox followed him, spying and watching everything he did. After the youth had taken the fish, Fox walked toward home, wondering how he could get some fish, too. When the boy arrived home, Fox went out. He reached the trough, and instead of uncovering it only partly, he did so completely, taking off the entire lid! The water burst forth in a stream and covered the entire

---

[14]Such conduct is based on the rules against wasting food, imposed by the Lord of the Water Species.

land. When the youth realized that the water was overflowing, he ran out. Fox had already climbed up the palm that grew near the trough. He spat and spat, believing it was dry below, but it was just water. Since there was high pasture he believed it was dry, but there was nothing but water. He said: "I am going to jump. I am going down!"

He jumped onto the pasture, fell into the water, and drowned.

The owner of the trough, who had gone to find out what had happened, saw Fox floating on the water, dead. He grabbed a stick, reached for him, and got him out. Fox returned to life, as he always did.

The youth scolded him: "Why did you go alone without asking me first? Now the water flowed out!"

From then on there was a lagoon here, and another one over there. When Fox uncovered the trough in the center of the world, the water gushed out and spilled over, so that the lagoons that we see now remained. But in those times there still were no rivers.

Informant: Kíki

Source: Siffredi ms.

Summary

In primeval world where fish is unknown, young man finds covered trough containing fish and water. He introduces fish as food among people. Fox discovers trough and removes cover, causing water to gush out. Lagoons are created. Fox drowns but is revived by man.

Motif content

A940.+.	Origin of lagoons. (A940. Origin of other bodies of water.)
A1011.	Local deluges.
A1023.	Escape from deluge on tree.
A1429.+.	Acquisition of fish. (A1429. Acquisition of food supply— miscellaneous.)
D1030.1.	Food supplied by magic.
D1171.	Magic vessel.
D1472.1.19.	Magic food-basket (vessel) supplies food.
D1652.1.10.	Inexhaustible fish.
D1652.5.	Inexhaustible vessel.
E1.	Person comes to life.
E151.	Repeated resuscitation.
F986.	Extraordinary occurrences concerning fishing.
J585.	Caution in eating.
J1117.+.	Fox as trickster. (J1117. Animal as trickster.)
J1810.	Physical phenomena misunderstood.
J2400.	Foolish imitation.

N440.+.   Secret learned. (N440. Valuable secrets learned.)
Q428.   Punishment: drowning.
R311.   Tree refuge.

45. Fox Discovers a Container of Food

When they had finished punishing Fox and had thrown him out of
Istón's house, he came to a place where he met a young man, Pasá, the
jabiru stork. The stork was living there alone with his mother, just the
two of them. Having fled from Istón's house, Fox stayed with them.
He went to bed pretending he had a toothache. But this was not true.
Instead, he had found a wild fruit, *xuethlie*, which he had stuck inside
his cheek. He said it was a swelling caused by a tooth, but that was a lie.

The mother would always ask Pasá: "Son, could you go and look
for frogs? I am hungry! You might go to your little lagoon."

And Pasá would go. Fox just lay there, saying he was ill.

Pasá had a little lagoon with a cover—like a water hole—where there
were plenty of frogs and eels. Whenever he went there, he used to lift
the lagoon's cover a little, and a frog and an eel would jump out. He
caught them and closed the lagoon again. Then he would make a fire
and put the eel and the frog on to roast. While he was turning them over
the fire, more frogs and eels came out of the lagoon. He always kept one
eel and one frog in his sack and ate those that were roasting. But when
he was about to grab his bag and leave, lots of frogs and eels would
appear, to be carried off promptly by Pasá. Upon returning, the youth's
bag would be full.

Now, as always, Pasá handed the frogs and eels to his mother who
boiled some and roasted others. When they were done, Fox went to sit
next to his hosts and received some, too. Fox was thinking: "Where could
my friend keep these frogs? I would like to know that place."

After this, as he was playing sick, he went back to bed. Then the
youth spoke very softly: "Look, mother, I want to go out again to look
for eels and frogs."

He spoke in a very low voice, but Fox heard him all the same. Of
course! He was not sleeping; he was only pretending. He asked him:
"What was it you were saying, nephew? It seemed to me you were
saying: 'I am going to look for frogs.'"

"No, I did not speak. I did not say anything to anybody," said Pasá.

"But I understood: 'I am going to see my lagoon, my frogs.' It seems
to me you said it like that."

"No, I did not say anything."

Then Fox went to bed again. Soon afterward Pasá left quietly, going out very softly. When Fox got up again he missed the youth and asked his mother: "Where did Pasá go? I think he has gone to look for frogs!" "No," said the old woman, "he just went to urinate."

"Oh no, I heard that he was going to bring frogs!" said the Fox. He went to bed again, waking up only when the sun was already high. He thought: "How would it be if I should find the place where he gets the frogs."

At about noontime Fox could not stand it in bed anymore and got up. He took his little bag and left for the place. Halfway there he saw Pasá, returning with his bag full. But Fox avoided him and hid. Then he continued on his way, and when he approached the lagoon he looked around. "What shall I do now? What is it my friend would do?"

When the youth got home he gave the frogs and the eels to his mother, and she cooked them as usual. Meanwhile Fox was over there, and the sun had risen over the lagoon. He searched around to see if he could see Pasá's footsteps; then he looked into the distance and saw a tall carnauba palm. "Maybe it is over there! I shall have a look."

He went there, walked around, and, seeing the small lagoon, said: "Ah, that is where Pasá always goes to look for frogs and eels!"

There was a lid, and it was the boy's custom to take the lid off once, let one frog and one eel jump out, cover the lagoon again quietly, and run behind these two and catch them. Fox, on the other hand, thought: "I am going to leave the lid off for a long time to let many come out quickly! Then I am going to catch all the ones that come out."

He removed the lid, but while he chased the frogs the water gushed from the opening into the lagoon, until it overflowed. Catching the frogs, Fox ate them immediately. Then the eels came out and he ate them, too. He just ate them raw.

He had filled himself up and had a big belly. His intention was to return to the lagoon. But it was impossible. More water was coming out, a lot of water was pouring out. "What am I going to do? How can I get away from here?" He looked around.

"Ah, there is the palm! I shall climb up on it, it is very tall!"

He started to climb up. Halfway up he paused, thinking the water was going to stop, but it continued to rise. So he climbed up higher, resting twice, but the water continued to rise to the top of the palm. When it reached the top, Fox did not know what else to do. From high up he looked below and saw a spot that looked dry. "I think that by jumping I can reach that dry spot to save myself."

Over and over again he tested by spitting to see if the saliva would remain where it fell. And since it seemed not to move he finally thought: "I am going to jump because if I don't, the water will kill me."

So he jumped, but rather than earth it was water where he landed, and he drowned. He died. He drowned, full of water. It entered through his mouth, and his belly swelled up a lot. He had been unable to get out because he was so full; he was heavy from all the food he had eaten.

Pasá, who was at home, looked up and saw that there stood some very dark clouds over the lagoon. "What could this be? After all there was strong sun!"

Then he realized that Fox must have done something evil. He asked his mother: "Have you seen Fox?"

"Yes, he went over there."

"Ah, it must be he! I think he is into some mischief. I am going to catch him."

"All right, go ahead," said the mother.

Before arriving at the lagoon Pasá saw a lot of water that looked like a swamp. "How sad; I think Fox is dead!" Pasá continued by swimming, and almost in the center he found him. There was Fox with a huge belly full of water!

Then Pasá began to chant, calling for Akoié, the rosy-billed pochard, and for Ixñéni, the plumbeous ibis. He was calling them so they would agitate the water with their wings. Akoié and Ixñéni began to make the water run back. It spiraled like a whirlpool toward the lagoon and inside again. When all the water had returned, Pasá closed the lagoon. Since he was the owner, he knew how to make the water run back. Then he went to see Fox. He grabbed him by the tail and held him upside down so that all the water he had swallowed could drain out. Then Fox seemed to come alive again, and Pasá said to him: "You have misbehaved! Truly, you are a rogue! If it had not been for me saving you . . . I order you not to return here again, because you do not know how to catch frogs. This will be the only time that I save you!"

Fox said: "Ah, it seems I have been sleeping!"

"No, you were not sleeping. The water killed you because you opened the lagoon. It was your own fault. But today I saved you."

Fox was alive again.

Informant: Kasókchi ilánek

Source: Siffredi ms.

Summary

Young man (Pasá) owns covered lagoon containing eels and frogs. Having learned his secret, fox removes lid of lagoon to steal animals. Water gushes out and fox takes refuge in tree, but eventually drowns. Pasá makes water return to lagoon and then revives fox.

Motif content

A1011.	Local deluges.
A1023.	Escape from deluge on tree.
B450.	Helpful birds.
D1652.1.	Inexhaustible food.
D2106.1.2.	Animals miraculously multiplied.
D2151.	Magic control of waters.
E1.	Person comes to life.
F713.	Extraordinary pond (lake).
J514.	One should not be too greedy.
J1117. + .	Fox as trickster. (J1117. Animal as trickster.)
J1810.	Physical phenomena misunderstood.
J2650.	Bungling fool.
K1868.	Deception by pretending sleep.
N440. + .	Secret learned. (N440. Valuable secrets learned.)
N455.	Overheard (human) conversation.
Q428.	Punishment: drowning.
Q432.	Punishment: ejectment.
R311.	Tree refuge.

46. Fox, Releasing the Waters, Causes the Great Flood

The owner of the water caught a lot of frogs. Fox came and asked him: "Where did you get all these frogs?" The man said: "There is a cover on the water, and when you want some you remove the cover and take them out one by one." He would get the frogs and roast and eat them. Then when he had finished, he would remove the cover again and stuff a load of frogs into his net bag. Then he would go home.

One day the owner of the water returned to get frogs, and Fox asked: "Can I go with you?" "No, you stay here," was the answer. But Fox paid no attention and followed him anyway. "So you came," the man said to him. He ordered Fox to make a fire while he himself pulled out the frogs. They cooked and ate them. On the way back to the house the

owner of the frogs said to Fox: "You must not go alone or you will die."
"No, I won't go," replied the fox.

Nevertheless, he did go to steal some frogs. As he did not quite know
how to do it he uncovered the water too much, and the frogs began to
jump up and out. He tried to catch them one by one but could not
manage. Then he removed the cover completely and all the frogs came
out. He turned around and saw a lot of water behind him. In the middle
of a small lagoon there stood a palm tree, and Fox climbed up and spat
on the water. Thinking that the water had receded he started to climb
down. But he found himself surrounded by water, and there he died.
He lay there, all swollen.

When the owner of the water came and saw this he seized him by one
of his legs and held him upside down so the water would drain out of
him. The man stood him on the ground. "What a way to sleep!" said
Fox. "You were not asleep. You were dead," replied the owner of the
water. He added: "Did I not tell you not to go and take frogs!" Fox said
to him: "I am going to try it again." "You will die," answered the owner
of the water, and left.

Informant: Petiso

Source: Verna ms.

Summary
    Ignoring warning, fox causes flood by uncovering magic lagoon.

Motif content

A420.+.	Owner of water. (A420. God of water.)
A1011.	Local deluges.
A1023.	Escape from deluge on tree.
E1.	Person comes to life.
F713.	Extraordinary pond (lake).
J652.	Inattention to warnings.
J1117.+.	Fox as trickster. (J1117. Animal as trickster.)
J1810.	Physical phenomena misunderstood.
J2650.	Bungling fool.
Q428.	Punishment: drowning.
R311.	Tree refuge.

47. Fox Causes the Great Flood

Séta, the armadillo, met Fox and said to him: "Do not come this way because the lake is very dangerous. If you catch the dorado, the water will overflow."

Fox paid no attention and continued on his way.

Séta said: "Do not come here, Fox, because the water will kill you."

"All right," said Fox. "I shall not go. I am afraid," he said.

Three days went by, and Fox went there. He went to the edge of the water and began to shoot arrows at the dorado. The water overflowed. Fox began piling up sticks to hold the water back, but it was moving fast. Séta saw clouds and realized what had happened. He said: "I think Fox has gone to the water and done something wrong. I shall go and see."

Some three hundred meters away from the house he saw the water. It was moving fast. "Did I not say that Fox was into some mischief?"

Séta put his hands into the water and found some small animal hairs.

Fox climbed up a tree and, seeing that there was foam on the water, assumed that it was solid land. He started to spit. "It is dry, I can step down," he said.

He stepped down, fell into the water, and drowned. He floated at the edge of the water with his belly swollen. Séta saw him. "Did I not say it was he who had made a mess of things?"

Séta stepped on him and Fox stood up: "I was sleeping."

"Sleeping!" said Séta. "You were being carried off by the water. You were dead! Did I not tell you not to come here alone? What did you catch?"

"I do not know," answered Fox. "I was asleep."

"Asleep!" said Séta. "You were dead!" Séta began to push the water back with his hands. It moved back to the pool, and things returned to normal.

Informant: Cepillo

Source: Mashnshnek 1972, p. 140.

Summary

Ignoring armadillo's warning, fox shoots magic fish in pond. Flood results and fox drowns. He later comes back to life, and armadillo contains flood.

Motif content

A1011.	Local deluges.
A1018.1.	Flood as punishment for breaking tabu.
A1023.	Escape from deluge on tree.
B175.	Magic fish.
C841.9.	Tabu: killing certain fish.
C923.	Death by drowning for breaking tabu.
D2151.	Magic control of waters.
E1.	Person comes to life.
F713.	Extraordinary pond (lake).
F986.	Extraordinary occurrences concerning fishing.
J652.	Inattention to warnings.
J1117.+.	Fox as trickster. (J1117. Animal as trickster.)
J1810.	Physical phenomena misunderstood.
Q428.	Punishment: drowning.
R311.	Tree refuge.

48. Fox Discovers the Container of Food

Long ago there was an old man who had a well inside the earth. It was round and had a lid. And since there is always a fox around, Fox overheard the old man saying to his son: "I am going to my lagoon, the one with the lid. Tomorrow I shall go and take the lid off, for if I don't someone else will do it, and a jet of water will gush over us."

Fox heard what he said about the covered well in the earth, and wondered how he could get there. In the morning, when the old man was about to leave, Fox said to him: "Look, my friend! Where are you going?" The old man told Fox: "Nowhere, just to see the well." Then he grabbed his bag, slung it over his shoulder, and left. He went along a narrow path through the forest. Suddenly he looked back and saw Fox following him: "Why have you come?"

"Oh . . . because you are my companion. I do not want to be apart from you. I must always go where you go."

"All right, but only so far."

When they got close to the well, the old man went to the edge alone and told Fox to make a fire. When the fire was burning he said to him: "You must lie flat on the ground! Do not look at me for I am going to uncover it!"

When Fox was face down the man uncovered the well and took out a big shad, only one. Then he covered the well again.

He cut it in half and put it on the fire to roast. Fox was watching the old man work. When they finished eating, the man said to him: "Listen, Fox, do not look because I am going to uncover the well again! You have to lie down with your forehead on the ground. Do not look at me!"

Removing the lid the man took a single shad from the well and put it down. Immediately there was a whole pile of them.

Now that he had lots, he told Fox: "Look at me!"

There were a lot of shad. Although he had taken only one from the well, soon afterward there were more. There was plenty of fish because of his power! He and Fox each took twenty, thirty. They were filling their bags to go home. The old man said to Fox: "Look, you are not coming here alone, only with me. If not, you will die."

But since Fox is wily, the next day he went alone to the well and uncovered it. A jet of water gushed out from the well in the earth. It flowed out, hitting the people and killing them all. When the old man saw this he rushed to the lagoon and commanded the water: "Water, return to the well!" The water returned. The man caught the bodies that the water was dragging along, and pulled them to the edge of the well. When all the water had retreated, he covered the well again.

Informant: José Romero

Source: Siffredi ms.

Summary

Against old man's warning, fox raises lid covering secret lagoon. Water gushes out, drowning people. Old man magically makes water return to lagoon.

Motif content

A1011.	Local deluges.
C310.	Tabu: looking at certain person or thing.
D1030.1.	Food supplied by magic.
D1652.1.10.	Inexhaustible fish.
D1711.	Magician.
D1765.	Magic results produced by command.
D2106.1.2.	Animals miraculously multiplied.
D2151.	Magic control of waters.
F713.	Extraordinary pond (lake).
J652.	Inattention to warnings.
J1117.+.	Fox as trickster. (J1117. Animal as trickster.)
J2400.	Foolish imitation.
N450.	Secrets overheard.

49. Fox Releases the Waters, Causing the Great Flood

The owner of the bottle tree has a key to the door in it, for it contains all the water and the fish. Because Fox is mischievous, he stole the key from him. He went to the door and turned the key, and the door opened. The water burst out, lots of it. Fox died right there. Not being the owner of the bottle tree he had not expected all that water to come out. Finding himself surrounded by the water he jumped, but died anyway.

The owner of the bottle tree said: "Much water ran out here." Getting closer he saw Fox floating on the water, dead. The water continued to flow, more and more. Then the dorado came out, and the *surubi*, and all the other fishes.

Informant: Esteban Mariano

Source: Verna ms.

Motif content

A1011.	Local deluges.
A1429.+.	Acquisition of fish. (A1429. Acquisition of food supply— miscellaneous.)
F811.	Extraordinary tree.
F811.+.	Tree containing water and fish. (F811. Extraordinary tree.)
F811.5.3.	Fish-producing tree.
J1117.+.	Fox as trickster. (J1117. Animal as trickster.)
Q428.	Punishment: drowning.

50. The Origin of Fire

In days of old there was no fire at Hawk's village. The only ones with fire were Aláta, the anaconda, Sieliénaj, the partridge, and Acúte, the rabbit. It was very cold, and Hawk's people had no fire. He went to visit the ones who had fire, but they did not want to part with any. He asked Aláta to allow him to sit next to the fire, as it was cold, but Aláta refused because he said that this place was reserved for him. So Hawk went to see Sieliénaj, and begged for a place near the fire. But Sieliénaj would not allow him either, because that was his own place. He finally went to see Acúte, requesting a place next to the fire. The rabbit offered him one, but told him not to poke the fire. Hawk, however, stirred it, and realized what fire was.

Looking for honeycombs, the owners took the fire with them to chase the bees away. Aláta warned them to be quiet so that Hawk would not find out about it. But while Aláta was chasing the bees, Hawk took advantage of the opportunity, quickly stole a firebrand, and carried it away on his shoulder. He brought it to the others, and that is how we got fire.

Informant: Espinosa

Source: Mashnshnek 1973, p. 62.

Motif content

A522.2.3.	Hawk as culture hero.
A1414.	Origin of fire.
A1415.0.2.+.	Original fire property of certain animals. (A1415.0.2. Original fire property of one person (animal).)
A1415.2.1.	Theft of fire by bird.
J1118.	Clever bird.

51. The Origin of Fire

In primordial times Ahóusa, the hawk hero, had no fire. Nobody did, and everybody was freezing with cold. Ahóusa traveled through the country in search of those who had fire, but they were stingy with it and did not want to share. That is how Ahóusa came to think about stealing fire.

Miyóki, the sparrow hawk, was traveling about. He had fire. Then he found *mahsás* (bees), and since they always live in the earth, he dug and made a fire to get at the honey. Ahóusa was watching, and when he saw the smoke he thought: "There are the ones who make fire."

Sparrow hawk went off to gather firewood, going far away. Ahóusa came, stole the fire from him, and carried it away. When Miyóki returned he looked for one of the kindlings he had lit, and found that it was missing: "Who took my fire? Who stole it?"

He went to find it, tracking it down. "Ah, it must be Ahóusa. I am going to catch him at his place."

Ahóusa's children were freezing to death, naturally, since they had no way of warming themselves. That is why Hawk was so distressed and was forced to find fire he could steal. When Miyóki arrived where they lived, Ahóusa was making a fire and his children were around him. He said to him: "Then it was you who stole my fire."

"Yes, but my family are like cadavers with cold. How can you be so stingy?"

"I am stingy because I am owner of the fire. But look. There is a cactus over there which is called *siñéluk*. It always has fire because it never goes out. If you do not take care of this fire it will go out and you will end up like before. You have to take good care of it!"

Since Miyóki had to return to dig for bees, he said to him: "Look, Ahóusa, I shall come back later and explain to you carefully how to take care of the fire. If you do not tend it well, people or children will burn their bodies. Everyone will burn."

Then Miyóki left.

Informant: Kíki

Source: Siffredi ms.

Summary

Hawk steals fire from sparrow hawk. Latter follows him and warns him to take good care of fire or he will lose it.

Motif content

A522.2.3.	Hawk as culture hero.
A1414.	Origin of fire.
A1414.6.	Bird as guardian of primordial fire.
A1414.7.1.	Tree as repository of fire.
A1415.0.2.	Original fire property of one person (animal).
A1415.2.1.	Theft of fire by bird.
J1118.	Clever bird.
N440.+.	Secret learned. (N440. Valuable secrets learned.)
W152.	Stinginess.

52. The Origin of Fire

There is another thing for which people are grateful to Ahóusa. In those days many were suffering for want of fire. Only some knew how to make fire, not all. Ahóusa knew a man who was an expert gatherer and who always got honey wasps out. He used fire to get them out, since those wasps are very fierce. Ahóusa heard that he was going to look for honey again, and thought: "How can I follow and catch up with him, to see how he drives these bad wasps away? The people are suffering. They have no fire."

In the morning the gatherer left, and Ahóusa went after him. When the gatherer saw wasps in a vizcacha burrow, he stopped. Ahóusa was watching him. He saw how the man used one stick that seemed rotten, and another that was firm and hard. He rubbed the latter vigorously against the other to heat it and to produce sparks. That is how he made a fire. Now he was able to get the wasps out. Ahóusa continued watching him, but the man was careful. He put the fire sticks into his bag, put the embers into the ground, covered them up, and left. After he had gone Ahóusa went to see if there were any embers. He poked around in the earth but could not find any. They had already gone out. "What now? I shall have to follow him once more. Maybe he is going to burn other honeycombs."

He followed the gatherer. Farther on the latter saw another hive and prepared to get the wasps out. He repeated what he had done before to make fire, and when he had produced it he set out to get the wasps out. Afterward he put the sticks in his bag again and covered up the fire, because he did not want the people to see it. As soon as he left Ahóusa rushed forth, poked in the earth, and found some live embers. He blew and blew and then went home, carrying the embers.

At night they saw fire in Ahóusa's home, and all the people were watching. "How come Ahóusa has fire? Nobody else does, only he."

The people came to his house and asked: "What did you do?"

"I followed a man who drove wasps out with fire."

"Ah, very good, so that's how come," they said.

"Yes, I suffered a lot to capture the fire for you all."

That is how it happened. That man had fire. But although Ahóusa obtained fire for the people living near him, those in other places still were without, and many people were in dire need of it. All those who owned fire were stingy with it, refusing to share even one ember with those who had none.

There was a woman called See. She had fire, and a man who had come from another village asked her: "See, can you give me a corner to warm myself?"

"No," she said.

"I am cold!"

"No, I won't give it to you."

The man grabbed a stick and stirred up the fire, and when wasps came out he jumped aside. Then See grabbed the fire and carried it off.

That man went to another village to look for fire and found Aláta, the boa. He asked: "Aláta, would you give me some room to sleep near the fire?"

"No, go out to the countryside. There is no room here." And he showed him something like a round lagoon: "You see? That is what I do. Around here there is no room for you. There is only enough for me." Then the man continued again and came to the village of Alená, the tapir. He saw him also by his fire and asked him: "Listen, brother! Can you allow me to sleep by your fire?"

"No," said Alená, "I can't, because I am very large and there is no room." He put first one shoulder, then the other, one leg, and then the other, his head . . . near the fire. "Do you see now that there is no room?"

Then the man went off again. He arrived at another place and met Aié, the jaguar. He asked him: "Is there any room to sleep? Can I lie down beside your fire?"

Aié said to him: "No, it is difficult because I do not have enough room for myself, but there is the countryside. If you do not want to go I may eat you. Go on!"

He went off again, and farther on he remembered the Master of the People, Ahóusa, and thought: "Why is it that that fellow always wins? I always heard that when he needed fire he would follow someone. I am going to do what he did."

And he planned to imitate him.

When another man went out to look for honey, he followed him as Ahóusa had done. He could not reach the first fire that the honey-gatherer had left, for it had gone out before he got to it. But he was able to reach the second fire, and then he was content. From this moment on the people of all the villages had fire, not only those in the area where Ahóusa lived. All the people who lacked fire got it, and they have it to this day.

Informant: Kasókchi ilánek

Source: Siffredi ms.

Summary

Hawk steals fire from honey-gatherer. Another man visits several people successively, asking for permission to warm himself by their fire, but is refused. Following Hawk's example, he steals fire from honey-gatherer.

Motif content

A522.2.3.	Hawk as culture hero.
A1414.	Origin of fire.
A1415.0.2.+.	Original fire property of certain animals. (A1415.0.2. Original fire property of one person (animal).)

A1415.2.1.	Theft of fire by bird.
A1415.4.	Vain attempts to circumvent theft of fire.
J1118.	Clever bird.
N440.+.	Secret learned. (N440. Valuable secrets learned.)
W152.	Stinginess.

53. The Origin of Fire

Before, there was no fire like this fire (hearth). Some men had fire but it did not look like this. It was guarded jealously. Only when looking for honey wasps would they make fire. The only one who did not have fire was Ahóusa, the hawk hero, so that when he removed the wasps they would sting him and his hands would swell up.

Then Ahóusa thought: "Why is it that when those people take out wasps, they do not get stung? I think they have fire. That is why the wasps do not sting them. I am going to see, to spy."

He saw a man going off to look for wasps. When he located them, he set out to make fire. He took a little stick, put it in the middle of another, and began to rotate it, rubbing it. Ahóusa heard him say to the other people: "Let us make fire!"

Ahóusa watched and said: "Let us make fire!"

He continued watching quietly and thought: "These men have fire."

The others continued rubbing the little stick which, when it was tightly inserted into the hole of the other stick, made a loud sound.

"Do not make so much noise," said the other men, "or Ahóusa will come!"

When they spoke, Ahóusa repeated after them: "Do not make so much noise, or Ahóusa will come!"

And he would say his own name. "Give it to him!"

They gave the stick to another man so that he would rub it. The stick on the bottom would begin to sound and they would say: "No, no, Ahóusa will come!"

Ahóusa was listening, and he would repeat what those people were saying. Another said: "I am going to start rubbing!"

"You make so much noise that Ahóusa will come!"

Then they called Sén, the hummingbird. He began to rub, and as he did the stick made a sound. "No, do not make so much noise because Ahóusa will come!"

Ahóusa continued to listen.

Then Pétohoi, the great kiskadee, came and he, too, began to rub. He said: "Give me that stick! I know how it is done, and I don't make that much noise."

He began to rub and rub until smoke came out of the stick on the bottom and it got warm. When it lit up, he took a dry teasel and placed it in the center so that it would ignite. After it started to smoke, they placed it near the honeycomb to chase the wasps away. There was some other kindling there that was not giving off smoke, so the men got angry and said: "This will not work! It does not smoke!"

Then Ahóusa stepped up and asked: "Do you want me to throw away this wood that won't smoke?"

The others were angry because it did not smoke, and they threw it away. The firewood fell near Ahóusa, and as it did he picked it up and ran. It was already lit. "Hurry, hurry," said the others, "let us catch him and take it away from him!"

Ahóusa ran away, and when the others got tired of following him, they cried: "The fire you carry does not have to be shown to everybody. When you get home, keep it hidden under some refuse."

Ahóusa continued and paid no attention to them, not he. He immediately lit a fire, a very big fire, and set out to distribute it to all the people. Only then did fire become available the way it is now. Ahóusa made it appear because he took it from the others.

Informant: Centawó

Source: Cordeu ms.

Summary

Hawk culture hero, who is without fire, tricks honey-gatherers into throwing burning kindling at him. He runs off with it and distributes fire among people.

Motif content

A522.2.3.	Hawk as culture hero.
A1414.	Origin of fire.
A1415.0.2. +.	Original fire property of certain animals. (A1415.0.2. Original fire property of one person (animal).)
A1415.2.1.	Theft of fire by bird.
A1415.4.	Vain attempts to circumvent theft of fire.
J1117. +.	Bird as trickster. (J1117. Animal as trickster.)
J1118.	Clever bird.
N440. +.	Secret learned. (N440. Valuable secrets learned.)
W152.	Stinginess.

54. How the Hawk Stole Fire

Traná, the woodpecker, was the owner of fire. At one time there was no fire. The people would collect honey from wasps inside a hole. But since they were without fire, the wasps would sting their entire faces. However, they did not sting those who had fire.

Jóisa tiptoed out to see who was making fire, to watch Traná. The latter was hunting wasps, and Jóisa watched from afar how he made fire. The bird took one long stick and a second, longer one. He made a small hole in one of the sticks, fashioned a point on the other, and stuck it inside the hole. Twirling the second stick around, he heated the sticks and a flame sprang out. He added some kindling, some sweepings, and then threw on some large, black sticks. The fire grew bigger. He carried it over to where the wasps were, dug a hole, and blew on the fire. Smoke rose, and the wasps flew up. Jóisa watched this, squatting down on the ground. Then he stole the fire, carrying off a firebrand. Traná ran after him, but could not catch him. He wanted to take the fire away from him. But Jóisa brought it to us, and thus we now have fire.

Informant: Esteban Mariano

Source: Mashnshnek 1972, p. 127.

Motif content

A522.2.3.	Hawk as culture hero.
A1414.	Origin of fire.
A1414.6.	Bird as guardian of primordial fire.
A1415.0.2.	Original fire property of one person (animal).
A1415.2.1.	Theft of fire by bird.
A1415.4.	Vain attempts to circumvent theft of fire.
J1118.	Clever bird.
N440.+.	Secret learned. (N440. Valuable secrets learned.)

55. Why the Indians Are Poor

It rained for three nights, stopping only during the day. A man came down amidst the Indians of the north. He told them not to be afraid, because he was peaceful. He had brought them good news. He gave them a cow, but the Indians would not accept it out of fear. He gave

them a horse to herd the cow with, but they did not know how to ride.
He asked them what they wanted, whether they wanted dogs and goats.
If only they accepted his good message, he would make a fence inside
which they could live. But they did not want to be Christians. So the
man proceeded southward. He told the people there that if they received
his message, they would have cows, horses, dogs, goats, and pigs. They
would be rich. The people of the north are called Indians. Those of
the south are called Chaqueños. This is why the latter are rich.

Informant: Olivera

Source: Mashnshnek 1973, p. 61.

Motif content

A1600.	Distribution and differentiation of peoples—general.
A1614.4.	Origin of tribes from choices made.
A1618.	Origin of inequalities among men.

56. Moon Teaches the People to Construct Houses

Moon used to be a man who lived here on earth. He gathered all the
tribes together, the Mataco, the Toba, the Chulupi, the Tapiete, and the
Chiriguano. He instructed the Toba to go build their village. He proceeded to build other houses in the Mataco village and continued in this
manner until he arrived where we live now, La Merced. Afterward he
went to La Gracia. Moon built the people's houses and then said to them:
"Now I'll return to the sky." He went back up above. We always see
a man appearing directly in the middle of the moon; it is Moon himself.
The Moon is extended like a large mirror, and this man is standing in
the middle. It looks as though he is praying, with his hands uplifted.

Informant: Esteban Mariano

Source: Mashnshnek 1972, pp. 123–124.

Motif content

A185.3.	Deity teaches mortal.
A747.	Person transformed to moon.
A751.	Man in the moon.
A753.	Moon as a person.

A1435.   Acquisition of habitations.
F30.   Inhabitant of upper world visits earth.

57. Fox Seduces the King Vulture's Daughter

When Istón, King Vulture, heard that Armadillo was the first to have a harvest, he advised his youngest daughter: "Would it not be a good idea if you looked for Armadillo to make him your husband? When I sow I have plants after six days, but not he. . . . He can do it quicker! You could marry Armadillo."

"All right, father," said the daughter. "Then I must look for him."

When King Vulture came to Armadillo's place, Fox was still lying there with indigestion. King Vulture said: "How are you, friend? Have you been sowing here?"

"Yes, here I am," said Armadillo.

"Well, I came to look for you."

"But why?"

"Well, my daughter loves you very much. You are better at sowing than I am. I could give you my youngest daughter."

When Fox heard this he jumped up in a flash: "What do you want from me?"

"Nothing. You get out of here!"

Fox went home. But soon he approached again, just as King Vulture was repeating: "Armadillo, I came to ask you to marry my daughter, because you sow more quickly than I do."

"Ah!"

Fox sat there wondering what he should do. In the evening he said: "I am going first to where King Vulture's daughter is."

He went and arrived when it was quite dark. The girl asked him: "Are you Armadillo?"

"Yes, I am Armadillo," said Fox.

Then she received him.

Her father said: "I sleep here, daughter."

She went to bed with Fox some distance away. But soon she smelled an odor and sniffed: "It smells like fox urine to me! Let us change places."

They did, but a little later he said: "What's wrong?"

"It seems a fox has urinated here. Let us move."

They moved again. But Fox, with his indigestion, could not stay awake anymore and fell asleep, snoring. Then they recognized him by his teeth, and smelled him close up. "Ah, this is Fox."

Fox heard that they wanted to flog him. He pretended to be asleep, but was not. When they were about to hit him, he dashed off.

Then the girl said to King Vulture: "Father, I had better go myself. I myself must go to Armadillo."[15] She went, and when she arrived she asked him: "Are you Armadillo?"

"Yes, what is it you come for?"

"Nothing. I am going to sleep here, at your side."

"No."

"But why not?"

"Because I am afraid of your husband," said Armadillo.

"But I do not love him! He smells very bad!"

Thus it came about that Armadillo married King Vulture's daughter.

Informant: Kasókchi ilánek

Source: Siffredi ms.

Summary

King Vulture tries to win armadillo as husband for his daughter. Hearing this, fox pretends to be armadillo, and sleeps with girl. She discovers his trickery, and starts to court armadillo herself.

Motif content

H30.+.	Recognition by smell. (H30. Recognition through personal peculiarities.)
H50.+.	Recognition by teeth. (H50. Recognition by bodily marks or physical attributes.)
J641.	Escaping before enemy can strike.
J1117.+.	Fox as trickster. (J1117. Animal as trickster.)
K1315.	Seduction by impostor.
K1915.	The false bridegroom.
T51.	Wooing by emissary.
T55.	Girl as wooer.

58. The Origin of Chicha and of Shamanism

Long ago there were no shamans, nor chicha, and no chants. The people were perfect and did not have such customs. Then, in the recent

---

[15]In the beginning the story inverts the guidelines of courtship, which among the Chorote is initiated by the young girl, the parents intervening only when dealing with the selection of a permanent companion. At the end of the story, the decision by King Vulture's daughter to take over the courtship of Armadillo forms the basis of the customary pattern, brought about in the myth by the deceit of which they were victims.

past, all of a sudden a man got the idea of performing chants, witch-craft, and dances. He sent his wife to look for fruit and made her grind it. They put the fruit in a gourd as if preparing chicha. Two days later, the man thought: "This is probably delicious to eat!"

He thought it was going to be something to eat, like food, and not like drink that would make him dizzy. Since the people liked *añapa* he thought: "With two days of preparation maybe we'll have a more deli-cious drink. But I do not know yet how it will taste!"

He tried it, and immediately thought: "How I like this drink. Now I shall attempt to sing!"

He did not know how to sing, but suddenly he felt like he did. He could not restrain himself and say: "No, I won't!"

It was as if suddenly something had entered his mouth that forced him to sing, and he sang. The people of the village said: "Why is he sing-ing? What is he doing? Where do these chants come from?"

After he had chanted, the man tasted the drink and said it was good. Although he did not realize it, it was chicha, and very delicious. He thought it was going to fill him up like food, nothing else, and he had no idea that it would intoxicate him. He thought: "I want to show this to the people so they will acquire the custom of eating like this. By taking out these seeds and letting it sit for one or two days, they will have this rather than the usual thick *añapa*." That's what he intended to do, but instead he ended up drunk without knowing it. Everyone, his wife and children, said: "He is about to die!"

But it was not that he was dying, he was just drunk. Of course they did not realize it because such things were unknown to them. Everybody became frightened upon seeing this first inebriated man. They had never seen or heard one before. When he controlled himself a little they asked him: "So you are all right?"

"Very much so."

"What was it like?"

"Very good! I thought I was going to die, but no. When it comes on, you just get dizzy. One no longer feels inhibited and sings away."

Later, when the young men heard that the man had made chicha again, they went to his house to find out about it. They tried it to see how it tasted. Unaccustomed as they were, they soon felt dizzy. But the man told them: "It's nothing! It is good! It is so that we may have songs. Let us sing!"

Then the people played, saying: "Yes, it is good; let us make a habit of drinking chicha."

A year later the man had another idea: "What could I do in order to cure? What could I use?"

He cut off the top of a gourd and put hard seeds inside so it would sound. This rattle was to help the man with his song, like a drum which also helps. That is what the man thought. He liked it, and he tried it: "Ah! It would be nice if I sang accompanied by this little gourd. It would give more pleasure, and the people might say: 'What a beautiful voice! How nice it sounds!' "

That is how the people began to use the rattle. The first man to do so did not know why he was using it; nobody knew. Finally, however, they heard the spirits as the man was becoming the first shaman. The spirits said: "This rattle will belong to us, too. Our people will use it frequently, and a shaman shaking it will make a spirit live inside."

Previously the man did not realize that all of this happened because of the gifts of Thlamó,[16] because of the power that he had bestowed on him. Thlamó causes people to contemplate how to receive his words (shamanic practices).

And that is how shamans came to live with rattles. That is why when someone comes through the air—any animal (shaman helper) sent by another shaman—one rotates the rattle or shakes it, so that it hits this animal and brings it down. The rattle is powerful. Not that it has power of itself; rather, it has the power of the spirit that resides inside. That is why to this day we use rattles to catch the spirit helpers of other shamans.

Once the people had seen this the custom was adopted. It started downriver, to the east, but then it came little by little toward this area. The man who made the songs said to the others: "All those who sing, all those who are shamans, will be my namesakes. My name will be Taxés-po, 'the scaly one.' "

When a woman fell ill in the camp, Taxés-po, seeing her, thought: "What if I could cure her? What would happen? Maybe I will succeed in curing her."

But the others said: "No, how are you going to heal!"

"I think I can cure her. She has to get well!" He thought: "I am going to see how it works. What song could I sing? What song did the good birds have?"

He continued to think and to think, until he said to himself: "I could try the song of Atá, the vulture, or the song of Sén, the hummingbird. . . . Better that I try Sén! Yes, I shall try Sén!"

He began to chant at the sick woman's side; he sang and sang. Then all the young people said: "What is going on? Let's go and see what he is doing!"

---

[16]Underground deity which is responsible for the visionary experience of a class of shamans.

They teased and made fun of him because they doubted that he could cure a sick person. Upon finishing his chant, Taxés-po rested briefly and told them: "Look, I think I am going to cure this sick woman!"

But the others continued in their disbelief: "Who knows, maybe you will," they said.

"Of course! I am going to cure her because I am not acting on my own. Rather, I practice what I have heard."

"Very well, we shall see tomorrow."

"So be it! He who is first at my side will become the first shaman!" He said this because while many men were watching him chant again, none came closer. Then one man began to accompany him. "I believe this man will become a shaman if she gets well! We shall see."

They continued singing and singing. They paused a while and sang again. But at dawn, the woman was well.

The young people said: "How wonderful! I should also like to be able to heal, my sister perhaps, or my mother when afflicted with illness. How nice that would be! We are going to imitate Taxés-po and continue his work."

Thus the people began to cure at the side of a shaman. Even when still at a tender age the apprentice begins to chant and to learn the songs he will use.

And Taxés-po promised, saying: "What I did here will spread everywhere. All the peoples around us, even those of different languages, will have their healers. Everyone! A shaman who works well will enjoy many things, but he who does not work well will be killed. He who does not do his duty will be killed by his chief (an allusion to Thlamó), or by the people. But someone who imitates my practice, someone who cures, will do good deeds and receive many gifts."

That is what he said, as everybody was listening to him.

And that is how this practice reached us, and why it retains its form. It has taken a while but we followed Taxés-po. Thanks to that one man this practice began. But Thlamó worked in him to increase the number of shamans, and he continues to do so to this day. From that time on, we have learned everything from him.

Informant: Domingo

Source: Siffredi ms.

Summary

Man discovers how to make fermented drink by mixing ground fruit and water. After initial reaction of fear, custom spreads among people. Same man then makes rattle to accompany his songs, and spirit helpers teach him how to use it and how to cure. (Origin of shamanic practices.)

Motif content

A300.	God of the underworld.
A1101.1.	Golden age.
A1426.2.1.	Introduction of brewing.
A1427.	Acquisition of spiritous liquors.
A1438.	Origin of medicine (healing).
A1461.4.	Origin of the use of the rattle.
A1654.	Origin of priesthood (shamanism, etc.).
D1212.	Magic rattle.
D1500.1.24.	Magic healing song.
D1711.	Magician.
D1711.0.1.	Magician's apprentice.
D1711.0.3.	Means of becoming magician.
D1726.	Magic power from deity.
D2060.	Death or bodily injury by magic.
D2161.	Magic healing power.
F403.2.	Spirits help mortal.

59. The Origin of Honey-Chicha

There was a man who was a gatherer. Every day he would go in search of honey and would invariably bring some for his family. Once he said: "No matter how many times I bring honey it never lasts. None of it ever remains! Would it not be better to mix it with water to make it last longer? What would happen if I let it stand with water for two or three days? Raw it doesn't fill us up. We should add water so as to have more. It might possibly become stronger this way so that I would not have to go out all the time after honey. 'You have to go, you have to go!' This way we can eat our fill easily, because it will be stronger."

After thinking about it, the man mixed the honey with water in a bottle tree trough and tasted it. Two days later he tried it again. The other men he had called asked him: "Look! Why is it like this? Could it be bad?"

"No, this way it settles more and is stronger," answered the man.

Then they tasted it and began to like it. They continued drinking and drinking without anticipating what would happen to them. One of them said: "Hey! What is happening to me? It seems that when I look at you I see two people."

And the other one said: "So do I, I see the same. I don't know what is going on. Could this be like drinking? Could it be due to the kind of honey we are making?"

Since in those days there were already evil spirits, one spirit who was with that man said to him: "What you are making is chicha, but it is not harmful; it just gets you drunk. It is a drink. That was a good idea you had!"

"Ah! Then it is good! We shall have the custom of making chicha."

It was not the man who gave it its name. Rather it was the evil spirit who said to its owner: "What you are making is chicha!"

Yet, when they were drunk, the owner told the people: "What I made is called chicha. It was I who gave it this name."

But it was not true that he named it; it was the spirit.

At first they enjoyed the chicha, but when they felt dizzy they began to get angry. The people who saw how it was prepared continued drinking it. When there was no chicha they would not get angry so often. But when they began to drink their tempers rose, they fought, and then the bad habits remained. When someone wants to get angry he says: "I am going to drink chicha. That way I am not going to be ashamed, and if I die, I just die. If I am lucky I shall kill someone else."

For this reason people drink chicha to this day. They drink it made of honey, *mistol*, watermelon, and many other fruits, in order to become strong and dizzy. However, afterward it causes bad blood, and then families divide.

Informant: Aió

Source: Siffredi ms.

Summary

In order to make honey last longer man adds water to it, thereby accidentally inventing chicha (fermented drink).

Motif content

A1427.	Acquisition of spiritous liquors.
F402.	Evil spirits.

60. The Origin of Honey

In the time of our ancestors the people who used to hunt tuco-tucos said: "Look! Why should we have to eat meat all our lives? We are bored with this already! Might there not be another kind of food so we could eat different things?"

Then one of them said: "Would it not be better to ask our old man (shaman)?"

Their old man lived with them, and one afternoon they got together and asked him: "Look! We often say: 'Why do we always have to eat meat?'"

"Well, because it is very difficult to find other food!" said the old man.

That is what he said. Then he went on to answer the people who were asking him. He continued talking and spoke many words: that perhaps he would not be able to, that it was going to be difficult to make other foods appear. The young hunters continued begging him to show them how to find other food. They asked him all these questions, and finally he said to them: "I can't, but I believe there is a kind of food called honey."

The people said to him: "All right, maybe you could point it out to us."

"Very well! Tomorrow evening all of you who have axes can sharpen and prepare them well. There is a food called honey, but you will have to use axes to get it."

The young men looked at each other, and when they were alone they said: "What could it be? We were asking for something else!"

One said: "Why did we not tell him what we needed? Now that the old man has named it (honey), we cannot but accept it."

Later, while they were preparing their axes, each one thought: "What can it be that we are going to do tomorrow? What can it be that the old man will show us?"

Very early in the morning the old man got up and called the one who had asked him first to show them another kind of food. "You can go to the woods, and take one other man along. You will find some bees that come out from inside the trunks of large trees. That is the food you asked me for!"

"Old man, had you not better accompany us?"

"All right, but since I cannot walk well it will go very slowly."

Then the others said: "We can carry the old man; we shall each carry him a distance. That way we shall get to the forest quicker."

They did so, and when they arrived the old man walked very slowly. Suddenly he said: "Look! That is what is called honey! Now you must chop at the trunk that it is in."

When they prepared to take the honey out they asked the old man: "How are we supposed to get it out?"

"You have to fill that rabbit skin bag you have. The food you asked me for you will put inside it."

"All right, old man. Would it not be best if we tasted a little first?"

"It is all right. Do not be afraid because it is not bad. You can eat it without worry."

Each one went to look for honey in a different place, and instantly the noise of many axes was heard. Someone shouted with happiness, and then all did the same. Finally they returned to the village. The women did not recognize what the men had brought either. Each one would arrive with his little rabbit skin bag, and would open it and say to his wife: "Look, this is called honey! We already tried it. Put your finger in it and try a little. You will see how good it is! Our old man says it will be our food. When we search for it we first have to get an ax, then a rabbit skin bag. But the old man says that one cannot play with these tools, and he also said: 'If you do not take care of these things and the dogs come to eat honey, you will never have luck in finding it again!'"

Before the men went back, the old man had said to each one of them: "Tell your wives to take good care of everything in your home that is used to gather honey, because if you or they do not look after everything well, it will not work anymore. If you do not store the honey and tools well, the bees will go away. They will give little honey, and there will only be bees."

Such was his advice, and the people said: "All right, that is good."

Thus the people got honey in those days. Before that they did not have anything. They live only on meat.

Then the little old man said to them: "There is the Owner of Honey, the bee called *thliténte*, little old lady. When you hear her buzz loudly and clearly, it indicates that there is a lot of honey. But there is another *thliténte* that buzzes very oddly, very softly and hard to hear. That means there won't be honey. Then one cannot chop or get honey. But you do not have to worry, knowing that there will be some in the future."

This is the sign that we have to this day. When we hear the *thliténte* buzzing weakly, although we see many bees come out, we do not get honey. We must find another one with a louder voice. Then, although few bees come out, we know that this honeycomb will have enough honey.

Informant: Aió

Source: Siffredi ms.

Summary

Primeval people, tired of living on meat alone, ask shaman for alternative food. He gives them honey, showing them how to extract it.

Motif content

A1420.+.	Acquisition of honey. (A1420. Acquisition of food supply for human race.)
N825.2.	Old man helper.

61. Tséxmataki, the Cannibal, and the Origin of Tobacco

Tséxmataki[17] had devoured all the people of a village. She felt full because she had eaten a lot, and decided to leave a boy, the only one remaining, for the following day when she would have regained her appetite. Holding him firmly between her legs she began to snore.

The boy summoned Ihñé esekié, who is very slippery, and said: "Enter me!"

He asked Eel to come into him, and having adopted his form he was able to slide down little by little until he was free of Tséxmataki's legs. Then he changed back into human form and ran away. It was not long before Tséxmataki woke up. Realizing the direction in which the boy had escaped, she went in pursuit of him. Now the young man summoned Ele, the parrot. He entered Parrot and flew off inside him.[18] But Ele, who cannot fly too well, grew tired from carrying so heavy a burden, and the boy had to escape on his own. Since they were close to where there were people, Ele warned them: "Tséxmataki is coming, Tséxmataki is coming!"

There were two (parallel) paths that led to that village, and two shamans placed themselves in the middle, waiting for Tséxmataki. They put wax on the tips of their arrows and heated them. They listened to ascertain by which path she was coming and took up their positions. When the giant came into sight they seized their arrows and shot her in the eyes, for they knew that those were her vulnerable spots.

The hot wax scorched her eyes, and she died. Afterward the shamans burned her, and from her ashes grew a tobacco plant.

The two shamans said: "Would it be all right to try this? Maybe it's good for smoking."

And one said to the other: "All right, tomorrow we shall see whether it is good."

They began by smelling the tobacco, and then they tried to smoke it. "This is good," they said. "It is very tasty and makes you feel good.

---

[17]The expression *tséxmatax*, fem. *tséxmataki*, designates both the mythical personage (a shamanic helper) and the state of being possessed which brings out the traits and behavior of the personage. It contains the root *tsé*, stomach, the particle *ma* which indicates movement, and the augmentative suffix *ta, tax*. The Chorote translate it as "big-belly, big eater," with the express intention of emphasizing the insatiable, cannibalistic character of the creature.

[18]The story describes two typical shamanistic recourses. The *iwít tátam* is based on the concept of transformation through penetration by a helper. The *iúxiam* refers to the entry of the shaman into one of his helpers, without implying a change of form.

This plant must have seeds. Let us leave it so it will grow and have flowers and fruit; then we shall have the seeds."

And that is what they did. Had it not been for Tséxmataki there would be no tobacco.

Informant: Máki

Source: Siffredi ms.

Summary

Boy escapes from ogre's clutches by turning into eel, after which he flees inside parrot helper. Pursuing ogre is killed by two shamans and then burned. From her ashes grows tobacco plant.

Motif content

A2611.	Plants from body of slain person or animal.
A2611.2.+.	Tobacco from ashes of bad woman. (A2611.2. Tobacco from grave of bad woman.)
A2691.2.	Origin of tobacco.
B469.9.	Helpful parrot.
B476.	Helpful eel.
B542.1.	Bird flies with man to safety.
B552.	Man carried by bird.
D173.	Transformation: man to eel.
D631.1.1.	Person changes appearance at will.
D642.	Transformation to escape difficult situation.
D2165.	Escapes by magic.
F1034.	Person concealed in another's body.
G11.6.	Man-eating woman.
G312.	Cannibal ogre.
G346.	Devastating monster.
G512.	Ogre killed.
Z310.+.	Eyes only vulnerable spot. (Z310. Unique vulnerability.)
Z356.	Unique survivor.

62. Tséxmataki, the Cannibal, Goes to the Sky: The Origin of Tobacco

There was a man who used to harm and kill a lot of people. Once they tried to beat him to death, but since he would not die they burned him with thick rounds of quebracho wood. He was still alive, however, and thought: "What am I going to do with these people? I am still suffering! They do not kill me all at once! I shall take revenge."

When they finished cremating him an unfamiliar personage emerged from the ashes of that man. The shaman who had burned him asked: "Who are you?"

"I shall become Tséxmataki right away. You people will call me Tséxmataki."

"Very well," said the shaman.

Tséxmataki's body was that of a big-bellied woman. What was different, though, were her nails, her eyes, and her teeth. What red eyes! And what long teeth and nails! She also had a tail, long, thick, and very red, with stiff, coarse bristles, like those of a horse.

She began to jump around, slowly at first, because she was still weak. Then she grew strong and jumped long distances, shouting: *"Eám, eám!"*[19]

She wanted to eat the people. She was dangerous to everyone, for she turned into a cannibal, a devourer of men, and they had to kill her once more.

So they burned her, and from her ashes rose the tobacco plant. It was a single plant, but a very large one! When they burned her she spoke these last words: "Although you burn me I shall go on living. This plant which I leave you means that I am still present. Though I won't be on earth any more, my customs will prevail. I shall be Tséxmataki forever, the one who perpetrated and will continue to perpetrate evil on earth and in the land up there (sky).[20] You throw me out but you will use my smoke; the smoke vanishes but this plant persists. I should no longer like to remain on this earth, for you want to kill me, but you will never succeed in killing me completely. Now I am moving to a place far from here (the sky). I leave you this plant so that you will go on using it, so that you will realize that I live even though you take me for dead."

That is why Tséxmataki will always be.

While the plant grew the old shaman watched it, saying: "What kind of plant could it be?"

Some asked: "What can we do with it?"

"Tonight I am going to see. I am going to think about the purpose of this plant, whether it might be food, perhaps."

The following morning he said to them: "I think I am going to try it now, but leave me alone. I am afraid it might be something that kills people. We don't know yet!"

---

[19]Onomatopoeia for "eat."

[20]Besides her customs of primordial times Tséxmataki persists in the tobacco plant. She persists as a very powerful and indeterminate shamanic helper; as a state in which she personifies a kind of possession; and as a celestial creature who devours the moon god, being associated with lunar eclipses.

"All right," said the men. "We shall wait until you have figured it out."

The old man made a pipe. He dried some leaves, put them inside the pipe, and tried them. The others asked: "Grandfather, how do you feel?"

"I am fine."

"Do you feel something in your body?"

"No, nothing. Would you like to try?"

He gave them some, and they tried it: "How good it tastes! What is it called?"

"I don't know its name, but tonight I shall see."

Early in the morning the old man said: "Ah, I kill myself, I smoke. I am going to smoke tobacco!"

The others heard him say this and immediately repeated those words, which they do to this day. The old man who was the first to try tobacco said: "I was afraid that if I smoked suddenly, something might happen to me. I was afraid that it might kill me, that it might be poison, but it was not. It is very good for smoking!"

Informant: Aió

Source: Siffredi ms.

Summary

People try in vain to kill murderous man, who then turns into ogre to avenge himself. After they burn him in ogre form, tobacco plant emerges from his ashes. Shaman learns how to utilize tobacco leaves and teaches everybody to smoke.

Motif content

A2611.	Plants from body of slain person or animal.
A2611.2.+.	Tobacco from ashes of bad woman. (A2611.2. Tobacco from grave of bad woman.)
A2691.2.	Origin of tobacco.
D91.	Transformation: normal man to cannibal.
D94.	Transformation: man to ogre.
D1840.	Magic invulnerability.
D1841.3.	Burning magically evaded.
E631.5.1.	Reincarnation as tobacco plant.
F515.2.2.	Person with very long fingernails.
F518.	Persons with tails.
F541.6.2.	Person has red eye.
F544.3.5.	Remarkably long teeth.
G11.6.	Man-eating woman.

G30.	Person becomes cannibal.
G312.	Cannibal ogre.
G346.	Devastating monster.
G360.	Ogres with monstrous features.
G512.3.	Ogre burned to death.
J580.	Wisdom of caution.

63. The Origin of Green Tobacco

There was an old woman who wanted to eat her children and everybody else. She was mad. There were a lot of mad women. Once the woman accompanied her husband on a honey search. When they found honey in a *moro-moro* nest, the wife said to her husband: "Come on down, I shall hold you."

As the husband climbed down, the wife took him by the testicles and squeezed them. She killed him and cut off his testes. "Now I have teasel fruit," she said.

She married another man and the same thing happened. They went to gather honey, and when her husband came down from the tree, she grabbed his testicles and killed him. In all, she had four husbands. When the last one came down, she grabbed him by his testicles and penis and cut them off. The woman had two sons. Back home, she said: "I bring something to roast." She got out a stirring stick and a frying pan in which she put the genitals. When the penis was frying, her daughter stepped back a good distance and sang: "There's my mother, eating my father's penis!"

"Come now, how could this be your father's penis?" the old mother asked.

"But it is, I recognize it," the girl replied.

"Enough of that. How wicked you are!" From then on the woman went mad. She wanted to eat everybody. She even thought of killing people everywhere. She walked away, and when she came across other villages she ended up devouring everyone in them.

Her two sons stayed with their grandmother. The elder one said to his younger brother: "Brother, let's go hunting. Let's look for peccaries!"

When they saw the peccaries they picked up a handful of earth and threw it over them. The animals fell on the spot.

"We could go and get the old woman, if you want to," the older boy said. Day and night they traveled.

"Maybe we should kill our mother," one of them said.

"Let's," said the younger boy.

"Let us catch up with her."

Four days later they departed. When one of them got tired, the other one would carry him. When he in turn got tired, the other would carry him. They poked around in an old fireplace and slept there. The next day they continued onward, traveling night and day. Poor fellows! Each time they came across an old fireplace they stirred it up. They stirred up three fires that the old woman had made, and arrived at one that was still warm. "We shall soon catch up with her," they said. And they traveled night and day. They came to another fireplace and said: "Now she is nearby. There is a beach, and I have seen a lot of people."

They were holding hands, going single file.

"Now we shall catch up with her," one of them said. He picked up a handful of earth and threw it ahead of them. The people whom the woman was leading away fell to the ground. "She must still have another fifty of them," the younger boy said. They picked up another handful of earth and threw it at her. The old woman nearly fell. She stood among the people she was taking away. They recognized the boy, and someone said: "That one is our brother." The boy threw more dirt, and the old woman nearly fell. Then he threw a final handful, and only then did the woman fall. She sat right down on the ground. When the boys reached her, the old woman said: "Do not kill me! My sons, how are you? Why would you want to kill me?"

"Well," said the boys, "we believed you were already dead. Now we shall kill you because you ate our father."

They picked up a handful of earth and threw it in the old woman's eyes. She was blinded. They picked up a stick and flogged her hard. "My heart is not in my chest," the old woman said. "It is in my ankle. That is where my heart is."

"Right you are," said the boys. So they hit her there, and she died.

"Let's find a beach," the boys said.

"But I am so tired," said one of them. "Then I shall carry you," said the other. He picked up his brother and they left. They arrived at a beach. "Let us sit down here. I am happy; we have killed our mother," said one boy.

"Let's see if we cannot find our father," said another.

"You know what we ought to do? We should pile up some sand."

"Turn around," said the older boy. The other turned around. "Don't look." And there appeared a big mound covered with maize plants. Then they burned the old woman. When they returned the next day to inspect the place where she had burned they found a green tobacco plant.

Informant: Cepillo

Source: Mashnshnek 1972, pp. 141–142.

Summary

While out gathering honey, woman kills her successive husbands one after another. One day her children recognize their father's genitals being roasted. When challenged, woman leaves, attacking people everywhere. Her sons pursue her, and after many attempts finally manage to kill her by throwing earth over her. They burn her. Tobacco plant grows from her grave.

Motif content

A2611.	Plants from body of slain person or animal.
A2611.2.	Tobacco from grave of bad woman.
A2691.2.	Origin of tobacco.
D2061.	Magic murder.
D2061.2.+.	Murder by throwing earth over victim. (D2061.2. Means employed in magic murder.)
D2178.+.	Maize plants produced by magic. (D2178. Objects produced by magic.)
E714.4.	Soul (life) in the heart.
F559.7.+.	Heart in ankle. (F559.7. Remarkable heart.)
G11.6.	Man-eating woman.
G61.1.	Child recognizes relative's flesh when it is served to be eaten.
G72.1.	Woman plans to eat her children.
G81.	Unwitting marriage to cannibal.
G310.+.	Ogre kills by squeezing testicles. (G310. Ogres with characteristic methods.)
G312.	Cannibal ogre.
G346.	Devastating monster.
G512.8.	Ogre killed by striking.
H1397.	Quest for enemies.
Q411.6.	Death as punishment for murder.
Q422.0.1.	Punishment: beating to death.
S139.2.2.	Other indignities to corpse.
S176.	Mutilation: sex organs cut off.
Z310.	Unique vulnerability.

64. Tséxmataki, the Great Cannibal, and the Origin of Shamanic Helpers

Whenever the ancients heard that Tséxmataki was coming, there was panic in the villages. She used to come from the north, so everybody would rush off in the opposite direction. To save themselves

from this evil they had no choice but to flee, for they knew that
Tséxmataki is bad and ferocious. She always traveled at night, and
when she reached a village she would soften the ground so that the
people had to remain there, unable to run away. She had large teeth
and devoured everything that came before her: old and young people,
dogs. . . .

Once, knowing that Tséxmataki was on her way and that everyone
was doomed to die, the people deserted their homes. But one of them,
a shaman, said: "Never mind, my children, I shall stay. You go.
I'll do what I can. If I cannot do anything Tséxmataki will come and
find you in your hiding places, but if I kill her you will be all right."

Earlier the old man (*kihíl*)[21] had cut some thick quebracho, and
planted logs in the ground until he had made a small house. He left
only a tiny window to be able to see. It was ready just as Tséxmataki
approached, and as she came closer and closer the old man heard
the earth moving (earthquake). She was the one who made it move
through the magic of her power.

As she walked along she was saying: "Where am I going to find
people? Where am I going to find my nieces and nephews and my
grandchildren?"

When she reached the village of the escaped people she asked:
"Where can they have gone? What could they possibly be afraid of?
What messenger (shamanic helper) could have warned them?"

Arriving at the old man's hiding place, she saw that it was a log
house of quebracho, and she smelled fire. When she went closer the
logs shook, but she was unable to pull them up. So she said: "Hey,
you in there! Can you give me some fire, even if it is a small firebrand?
I must warm myself; I am cold!"

The old man said: "All right, but my fire is still weak."

Meanwhile he had been heating some wax on the tip of his arrow
until it was very hot. Facing her squarely he aimed at Tséxmataki's
eye and let fly. No sooner did it hit her than she fell over backward
and died. As she expired there was a terrible noise. All the people
who had retreated to other places heard it, for the earth was shaking
and moving. They realized that perhaps the old man had killed her:
"Let us listen and see what happens next. Maybe the old man has
killed her."

After a while the shaman summoned Wisiénik, the woodcreeper
bird, and said: "Wisiénik, go and take a look! I do not know whether
she is really dead!"

[21]The term *kihíl*, old man, is used in the story, referring to the *aiéu*, shaman. In fact,
the cultural norms prohibit the use of the latter term, people resorting instead to various
indirect references.

The bird went, jumped about on top of Tséxmataki, singing, and came back: "She seems to be dead!"

The old man called yet another bird, Sólolok, and sent him to look. Just as Sólolok always steps on the ground, so he stepped all over her. "She is dead!" he said.

Then the shaman left his house to cut off her tail. Tséxmataki had a long, intensely red tail. He tied it around his dog's neck and sent him to notify the people who had fled: "Go and find the people, and take Tséxmataki's tail with you!"

Previously he had told the people: "I'll cut off her tail if I kill her, and this little dog will bring it to you, tied around his neck. Then you will know that peace has returned to this earth."

All the people who lived on the earth were afraid and had moved to other places. The shaman's people had gathered dry husks and placed them along the path so as to hear if anyone approached. By their steps they would be able to tell whether the old man, the dog, or Tséxmataki was coming. When the small dog came the people heard the dry husks and were afraid. But then they realized that it was not the heavy steps of a person, and when the dog suddenly appeared, they were very happy. They saw that he had something red around his neck.

The dog went to yet another group of people who had escaped earlier. When he reached them those people had to send him to look for people who had gone before them and who were even farther away. Thus, the following day, the little dog continued on his way, going to distant places which he did not know, for he was from another land. He kept going to where the people had halted to rest and where they had left ashes. He would touch the ashes to see whether he was close: "They are cold, so the people are still far away, but I shall go on anyway."

He traveled all day until noon, when he came to a hearth and touched it to see if it was warm. "No, it is very cool; I am going on."

He spent one day, two days on the road, and after four days he saw ashes again and touched them with his paw. "Ah! They are a bit warm! It will not be soon that I catch up with them, but I shall not give up."

The next day he found another hearth which was a little warmer. "Aha, this is it! It is not long since they left."

He was pleased and went on his way. When he got to another hearth he touched it with his paw and found embers: "Aha, now I am close!"

Once more he set off, and after one night, two nights, a fire was visible ahead. "Could it be this one?"

The people heard the little dog calling from the roadside, and thought: "Is that not the dog we left with the old man a long time ago?"

Everyone knew that the old man had remained where Tséxmataki was. When they saw the dog they recognized him: "Ah, yes, that's the one!"

They asked him: "Did the old man kill Tséxmataki?"

"Yes, he did, and he wants you to come back to our country."

The people were overjoyed and said to the dog: "You lead the way!"

"No, I cannot walk. I have a lot of blisters."

So they put him in a bag to carry him, and all the people returned to the old man who had saved them.

Some time before they arrived the old man who had killed Tséxmataki burned her. From her ashes came many things: vampires, and different kinds of birds, such as the rufous ovenbird, the *sólolok*, the chalk-browed mockingbird, the burrowing owl, the striped cuckoo, the dark-billed cuckoo, the large *wokó*, and others. That is why we say that in the beginning Tséxmataki was the Mother of Birds. From her ashes originated other things as well, which, like the birds, became shamanic helpers, such as the howler monkey and a pair of Guardians of the Forest. Finally from the ashes of Tséxmataki there came the tobacco plant.[22]

At first it only had some buds, and our remote ancestors realized that they were from a plant that no one was familiar with. They did not know what kind of plant it was until the next season, several moons later. Then they saw that the stem of the tobacco plant was very thick. The plant had grown as tall as a person and had large, broad leaves.

Everybody wanted to pull off the leaves, but the old man said: "No, don't do that now, for then the plant will not reproduce. It must have something that makes it sprout."

Then the old man dried a leaf by the fire and tried it to see how it was: "This is good," he said. "Henceforth we shall cultivate tobacco. But we must not remove the seeds until it has flowers and fruit. That way we shall be able to cultivate it."

Thus they waited until the fruit was ripe and had seeds. Then everybody took some and planted them in various places. But the plants no longer attained the height of the first one; they were small. The tobacco that came from the ashes of Tséxmataki is the one we see on

---

[22]The beings that emerged from the ashes of Tséxmataki are defined as both human and nonhuman at the same time, a lack of distinction inherent in Chorote representation of primordial creatures. Their differentiation is ascribed to the actions of Ahóusa, Hawk, the hero.

this earth. The one that man plants is different from the tobacco that comes from the underworld, from the earth deities.

Informant: Kasókchi ilánek

Source: Siffredi ms.

Summary

People flee in terror from ogre. Shaman who stays behind succeeds in killing her, after which he sends out his dog to notify fugitives. Before they return, shaman burns ogre's body, and from its ashes come birds (later shamanic helpers) and tobacco plant.

Motif content

A181.2.	God as cultivator.
A300.	God of the underworld.
A1724.1.+.	Birds from body of slain monster. (A1724.1. Animals from body of slain person.)
A1861.+.	Creation of howler monkey. (A1861. Creation of monkey.)
A1895.	Creation of bat.
A1900.	Creation of birds.
A2611.	Plants from body of slain person or animal.
A2611.2.+.	Tobacco from ashes of bad woman. (A2611.2. Tobacco from grave of bad woman.)
A2691.2.	Origin of tobacco.
B291.2.2.	Dog as messenger.
B421.	Helpful dog.
B450.	Helpful birds.
B563.6.	Birds as scouts.
D2148.	Earth magically caused to quake.
D2157.	Magic control of soil and crops.
F441.	Wood-spirit.
F518.	Persons with tails.
F544.3.+.	Large teeth. (F544.3. Remarkable teeth.)
F942.	Man sinks into earth.
G11.6.	Man-eating woman.
G310.	Ogres with characteristic methods.
G312.	Cannibal ogre.
G346.	Devastating monster.
G360.	Ogres with monstrous features.
G512.	Ogre killed.
H84.	Tokens of exploits.

H105.4.+.	Tail of monster as token (proof) of slaying. (H105.4.
	Head of monster as token (proof) of slaying.)
J613.	Wise fear of the weak for the strong.
J641.	Escaping before enemy can strike.
J670.	Forethought in defenses against others.
J1100.+.	Clever dog. (J1100. Cleverness.)
K730.	Victim trapped.
K839.2.	Victim lured into approach by false token.
K910.	Murder by strategy.
N845.	Magician as helper.

65. The Death of Tséxmataki, and the Origin of Green Tobacco

Tséxmataki was big and fat-bellied; she went about knocking down the houses with her chest. The people began to run away; they had already stopped planting. Everyone was afraid of Tséxmataki and escaped into the bush.

The only one left was an old man who was sitting in his house together with a young girl. The old man placed quebracho logs around his house so that the big-bellied one could not knock it down. Tséxmataki came and tried to push the house over with her chest, but it was solidly built and could not be destroyed. Then she asked permission to enter through the door, saying: "I am cold!" But the old man paid no attention. He put little balls of grease or wax on his arrows and took aim at Tséxmataki. He shot her in the eyes, and, because the wax is powerful and burns the eyes, the creature died.

This old man had a little dog, which he sent outside to see whether the big ogre had died. "She is dead," said the little dog. Then the old man cut off the creature's red tail, and with a string he fashioned a collar which he put around the dog's neck. Thus carrying the creature's tail the dog went to look for the other people who had fled into the bush. He reached a campfire and touched it, but since the embers were quite cold he continued searching. Finding another fireplace he touched it again, and its embers were a bit warmer; he was getting closer to the people. He reached another fireplace, still smoking, and with warm embers. The people had placed pieces of dry tree bark on the road, and as the little dog came along he stepped on the bark chips and broke them. A man who was listening said: "Tséxmataki is coming. It is she!"

He wanted to run. But the dog said: "No, it is I!" Everybody stopped, and the dog told them: "The old man has killed the creature." All the people returned to their houses, and the old man was pleased that his family was back again.

The little girl who had remained with the old man prepared an oven and put firewood in it. When the kindling was all consumed she placed squash and all kinds of fruit on the oven to cook them well. She covered them so the smoke would not escape. When the food was cooked she took it out. It was ready for the newly arrived people to eat.

The old man looked for a dry bottle tree, took the dead Tséxmataki, placed the firewood on top of her, and set fire to it. A few hours passed but the creature did not burn. Eventually, however, it did catch fire. In the very same place where the burned ogre had lain, a tobacco plant appeared.

Informant: Petiso

Source: Verna ms.

Summary

Villagers flee from devastating ogre. Old man single-handedly kills ogre, then sends his dog out to bring back fugitives. Upon their return they burn ogre's body. Tobacco plant appears on same spot.

Motif content

A2611.	Plants from body of slain person or animal.
A2611.2.+.	Tobacco from ashes of bad woman. (A2611.2. Tobacco from grave of bad woman.)
A2691.2.	Origin of tobacco.
B291.2.2.	Dog as messenger.
B421.	Helpful dog.
F518.	Persons with tails.
G310.	Ogres with characteristic methods.
G346.	Devastating monster.
G512.	Ogre killed.
H84.	Tokens of exploits.
H105.4.+.	Tail of monster as token (proof) of slaying. (H105.4. Head of monster as token (proof) of slaying.)
J613.	Wise fear of the weak for the strong.
J641.	Escaping before enemy can strike.
J670.	Forethought in defenses against others.
J1100.+.	Clever dog. (J1100. Cleverness.)
K910.	Murder by strategy.
N825.2.	Old man helper.

66. The Death of Tséxmataki, and the Origin of Green Tobacco

There was a mad woman named Tséxmataki who was cannibalizing the people. She came from underground.

One day an old man took an ax and went to cut heavy logs to place around his hut. He was a shaman. The mad woman came to the old man's house and wanted to knock it down. He took some wax, put it on his arrow, and let fly at the forehead of the woman, who fell to the ground as if dead. But when the pain subsided she rose again and climbed on top of the shaman's house. He continued shooting at her, and since the wax was hot it kept scorching her entire body. Eventually she died of the burns.

There was a little dog which was tied up. It said: "I'll go to check whether the mad woman is dead." "No, no," said a big fly, "I'm going." "No, she is not dead," said the dog. The fly circled around the body, saying: "I'll enter through her mouth and emerge at her anus. That way I can tell whether she is dead." He did so, and found her dead. "I want to see for myself," said the shaman. He went there and saw that she was dead. "I am going to cut off her tail and send the dog to look for the people who fled into the bush."

When the others saw the dog with the ogre's tail attached to it, they immediately returned to the village. The old man had already started to burn Tséxmataki. The toads were circling around the fire. Early the next day the old man and his people went to inspect what they had burned. They saw a tobacco plant. From the ashes of Tséxmataki's body grew the tobacco plants.

Informant: Centawó

Source: Verna ms.

Motif content

A2611.	Plants from body of slain person or animal.
A2611.2.+.	Tobacco from ashes of bad woman. (A2611.2. Tobacco from grave of bad woman.)
A2691.2.	Origin of tobacco.
B291.2.2.	Dog as messenger.
B421.	Helpful dog.
B483.1.	Helpful fly.
F518.	Persons with tails.
F900.+.	Crawling through the body of another. (F900. Extraordinary occurrences.)

G11.6.   Man-eating woman.
G312.   Cannibal ogre.
G346.   Devastating monster.
G512.3.   Ogre burned to death.
G630.+.   Ogre lives underground. (G630. Characteristics of ogres.)
H84.   Tokens of exploits.
H105.4.+.   Tail of monster as token (proof) of slaying. (H105.4.
                     Head of monster as token (proof) of slaying.)
J613.   Wise fear of the weak for the strong.
J641.   Escaping before enemy can strike.
J670.   Forethought in defenses against others.
K910.   Murder by strategy.
N845.   Magician as helper.

67. The Man Who Turned into Tséxmataki: The Origin of Birds and Wild Animals

There was a man who was ill for many months. He was in bed with no one to look after him. His family left, and sometimes he lay there by himself for up to two weeks without anyone giving him anything to eat. Then he would cry, and when a neighboring family heard him they would bring him some food. His own family went out into the bush (hunting and gathering) as they pleased, without bothering about the father. Thus the poor man began to wonder what he could do to kill them in order to take revenge.

He felt that he had magic power although he was thin. He felt that he had as much power as a healthy man. Seizing his penis he pulled and pulled at it until it looked like a tail, changing color. His power increased as he was pulling his penis, making it into a tail; now it stuck out behind him, very long, thick, and red. He also pulled at his fingernails which began to look like knives, long, sharp, and pointed.

He was shut up inside his house, and thus no one saw and was upset by the fact that he no longer had a human body, that he was something else: he was very close to turning into Tséxmataki. When he realized that he was on the verge of being transformed he felt like eating all the people in the village, and he pushed the house over and went out. The people were screaming in fear! But they could do nothing, and running away was impossible. If someone ran he would make a sweeping gesture with his hand, only a gesture, but the person would fall, unable to run anymore, and would remain there paralyzed, immobilized, even without Tséxmataki's touching him. That way he was able to get close to those people, and he killed and ate them all. As he had been transformed he ate all the people, everything, including the bones, and he ate them raw to boot.

The ancestors were very frightened. They could not make fire with just any kind of firewood the way we do. The only thing they would throw on their fires was quebracho, for it does not create smoke. Any other kind of wood would immediately make smoke, and then the transformed man, who used to walk about at night, would smell the smoke and go there at once, saying: "The people are over there!"

But those who made fire using quebracho he could not find.

The transformed man always sounded as though he were a bomb: *Buum, buum, buum! Tsium! Tsium, tsium! Eam, eam, eam!* (onomatopoeia for "eat"). Then the other people realized who he was. Because of the noise and his shouting they said that he was Tséxmataki, which is like saying "eater of people." Knowing that he was drawing near they were forced to run, fleeing far away.

The transformed man had already wiped out two villages, killing everyone. When he was on his way to two more, an old man, a shaman, said to all his neighbors: "You go. I am going to stay here."

He made only a little girl and a dog stay behind to live with him. Then he planted tall quebracho poles in the ground in a circle, like a fence, joining the upper ends (a conical house). He made sure that the hut was well closed, with only a small opening in order to be able to see the transformed man.

When the latter was approaching the village they heard the noise. The earth was moving; there was an earthquake! Since he had been transformed, whenever he lifted his foot the earth shook. The little girl who had stayed with the old man was frightened but he said to her: "Be patient; I know what to do. I am going to kill him."

He had magic power and knew how he was going to do it. He kept touching the quebracho sticks so they would not move.

The transformed man quickly reached a hut. As he stood up he touched it slightly, without pushing it, and it fell. What power he had! When he came close to the old man, who always kept a small firebrand burning, he smelled the fire, and he searched and searched until he found the man's place. He pushed against the quebracho poles, but they did not move. Then he said: "I am cold! Open the door so I can come in! Have pity on me!"

As he spoke his eyes were keeping a sharp lookout.

The old man was heating wax on a firebrand for the tips of his arrows, and while the ogre was looking around he shot off an arrow into his eye, which was glued completely shut by the hot wax. The transformed man began to run to and from outside the fence, and the old man shot him again, this time in the other eye. With both eyes full of hot wax he looked like a shivering animal. His body was trembling, he was wandering back and forth aimlessly, and when he fell, what noise echoed from all around! When he fell, when he died, there were earthquakes that lasted four hours.

When the shaman and his daughter saw him fall they were pleased, and the old man went out to look at him from a distance. He was still distrustful, believing that Tséxmataki never died, and he went on looking and looking, for his daughter was afraid that the ogre might arise again. Then he ordered Kataaki, the fly: "Go and make sure that he is really dead!"

Kataaki went, crawled into the mouth of the transformed man, and emerged through his anus. "He is dead!" he told the old man. The latter slowly moved closer, inch by inch, and when he was right next to the body he touched the tail, moving it in all directions. "It is true, he is really dead!"

He was very pleased. Cutting off the monster's tail he called his dog and said: "Go and find those who went away and tell them to come back! Take Tséxmataki's tail with you, tied around your neck, so they will see that he is dead."

The dog traveled for about two months to find them. When the people saw a dog walking around wearing a tie they were frightened and nearly shot him. Later one of them realized that he was the dog that they had left with the old man. He had said to them: "When I have killed the transformed man I shall send my dog after you."

Then they took the tail from him: "He killed him already!"

They returned home very happy. When they got to where the old man was they began to burn Tséxmataki. As they burned the body a whirl-wind came up from the ashes, and after the whirlwind all the animals of the bush appeared, the ostrich and all the birds. All those animals came from the ashes of Tséxmataki, and the people saw them. Afterward each animal named itself, for the people did not know what they were.

Informant: Kíki

Source: Siffredi ms.

Summary

Sick man abandoned by family turns himself into ogre pulling his penis into long red tail. He attacks own village, killing and eating everyone in it, and causing people from nearby villages to flee. Old shaman alone stays, hiding in specially built hut, and he kills ogre with wax-tipped arrows. He sends dog to tell people to return. They burn ogre's body, from which birds emerge.

Motif content

A1700.	Creation of animals.
A1724.1.	Animals from body of slain person.
A1900.	Creation of birds.
A2571.	How animals received their names.
B291.2.2.	Dog as messenger.
B421.	Helpful dog.
B483.1.	Helpful fly.
D91.	Transformation: normal man to cannibal.
D1720.	Acquisition of magic powers.
D2072.	Magic paralysis.
D2089.6.	House destroyed by magic.
D2142.1.	Wind produced by magic.
F515.2.2.	Person with very long fingernails.
F547.3.1.	Long penis.
F771.	Extraordinary castle (house, palace).
F900.+.	Crawling through the body of another. (F900. Extraordinary occurrences.)
F960.2.5.2.+.	Earthquake at ogre's death. (F960.2.5.2. Earthquake at witch's death.)
F969.4.	Extraordinary earthquake.
G30.	Person becomes cannibal.
G310.	Ogres with characteristic methods.
G312.	Cannibal ogre.
G346.	Devastating monster.
G360.	Ogres with monstrous features.
G512.	Ogre killed.
H30.+.	Recognition by sounds. (H30. Recognition through personal peculiarities.)
H84.	Tokens of exploits.
H105.4.+.	Penis of monster as token (proof) of slaying. (H105.4. Head of monster as token (proof) of slaying.)
J613.	Wise fear of the weak for the strong.
J641.	Escaping before enemy can strike.
J670.	Forethought in defenses against others.
K730.	Victim trapped.

K910.	Murder by strategy.
N845.	Magician as helper.
Q291.	Hard-heartedness punished.
S0.	Cruel relative.

68. The Hunters in the Sky: The Origin of Certain Animals

Two hunters could not find a single animal here on earth. There were no animals here. Then the star came to fetch the men and took them up to the sky. All kinds of animals were up there: armadillo, rhea, deer, iguana, *pichi, chachalaca,* six-banded armadillo. They caught them and roasted them. When all the game had been prepared the hunters descended, carrying the meat.

The other people came and asked them: "What did you bring?" "Come here and you will see. This is rhea meat, this is chachalaca, this is armadillo, this is iguana . . . ," the hunters were saying. "We are going to have a real feast now!" said the people.

When the meat was finished they returned to the sky, and the star encouraged them to hunt more game for the rest of the people on the earth who were without. Thus they continued going up and coming down until finally the star decided to send the animals down here. Today there are birds and all kinds of animals on earth so that the people can hunt them here. All originated above.

Informant: Esteban Mariano

Source: Verna ms.

Motif content

A1700.	Creation of animals.
A1795.+.	Animals drop from sky. (A1795. Animals drop from clouds.)
F10.	Journey to upper world.
F10.1.	Return from upper world.
F11.3.	Man goes to heaven for limited time.
F15.	Visit to star-world.
F166.11.	Abundant food in otherworld.
F167.1.	Animals in otherworld.

69. The Origin of Wild Animals

A long time ago, all the wild animals were people. From the north Miyóki, the sparrow hawk, came to this region and began to chop trees to make a plaza. When the place was completely cleared he dug a big hole in the center and made a fire with the trees he had chopped. He filled the hole with coals and covered it. Then he called the people who lived in the area: "Come, come, we are going to dance!"

The people came to join Miyóki and began to dance. They immediately fell into the hole with coals. Miyóki covered it with the people inside. Next morning he returned, uncovered the pit, and called the people. But when they came out they did not look like people anymore. They had changed into animals.

Two men who had been gathering honey met a pecccary (*Dicotyles tajacu tajacu*), but they did not know what it was. They said: "Let's catch it to see if it is good to eat."

They killed it and carried it to the wife of one of them so she might cook it. When they tasted it they did not like it. It did not taste very good, and they threw it away. A little later Miyóki came and said to them: "Why did you throw it out? It must be good to eat."

"No, we threw it away because it was not good to eat. It tasted like a human being."

Miyóki returned to the plaza, where he made a fire again and filled the hole with coals. He called all those people who had turned into animals, put them in the hole again, and left them there all night so that they would become well burned. Very early the next day he went to call them. He separated each one (grouping them according to species), put them to one side, and gave them names. "You will be called Kíxnie (peccary), and you will be fierce toward the people who hunt you. To defend yourselves I give you sharp knives (hooves)." Miyóki also gave them a place in the dense forest where they could live: the brushwood and the closed forest. Afterward he gave them advice: "You will eat wild potatoes and cactus fruit." They went off to the place Miyóki had indicated.

Then Miyóki called Ausa, the wild boar (*Tayassu pecari albirostris*): "You will be called Ausa," he said. "That will be your name. There is a place here called *kísí* (open woodlands); you will have to live there. You will have to eat *espinillo* and those tiny yellow fruits. You will also be fierce toward hunters; you will bite them."

Then Aié, the jaguar, arrived, and Miyóki said to him: "You will be called Aié. You have to look for old paths to travel on, and where you find roots you have to scratch them so that people will say: 'A bad jaguar passed by there. It is a sign.'"

For this reason, if we see an old path and his tracks along it, immediately some distance away we see roots that he was scratching. We know that Aié is very bad; he eats people, too, not just animals.

That was the advice that Miyóki gave Aié when he came out of the oven. And when he sent him to the forest, Aié thought: "What am I going to eat? Maybe I should look for a deer?"

Thus when he saw a deer he had to kill and eat it. He also said: "What am I going to drink? Now I have to look for water."

For that reason, when Aié finds water he is just like a person. He must walk cautiously, very slowly, and look at the water to make sure that there is nobody around. Now he tried to drink the water: "It is good. So then I shall eat meat, and afterward drink water. This is going to be my lagoon."

That is what he said. Therefore when he is around we know where he is going, along this old path directly to the lagoon. It is his custom to come and go on the same path to drink water, because Miyóki ordered him to do it that way. After a few days he returns to the lagoon by that same path. He is always walking around.

When Iwáxla, the puma, arrived, Miyóki instructed him this way: "You are to be called Iwáxla. You will have to go all over the woodlands, and when you find something you will have to eat it. Just go! I do not give you a fixed place to rest; you will rest wherever you can."

For this reason Iwáxla goes everywhere in the forest. If he is in a forest he traverses it completely. We see his tracks all over. Miyóki gave him animals to eat—fox, rabbit, armadillo—so that we always see in the forest a lot of shells of all types of armadillo that became his meals. When Iwáxla wants to rest, he rests beneath a tree where there is shade. Afterward he goes wherever he wants because it was ordained for him that way. Aié may have a cave somewhere, but not Iwáxla; he goes where he wants. That is also why he goes where the peccaries are, to eat their young. He was given these habits, for which reason he never stops. One day we see his tracks, and the next day we don't. But people who go hunting in another place find him, because if Iwáxla is in a large forest he travels through it from one end to the other. He goes where there is a path and where there is not. He rests where he wants to rest, and he is hardly seen. He is very wild!

Then Miyóki said to Siláxkai, the wildcat: "You will be Siláxkai. Before it gets very late you will have to go hunting, but you will have to go at night. If you find a rabbit you must eat it, and if you see an agouti, a *charata*, a pigeon, or a guinea pig you will eat them. All night you will have to walk about, and when it is nearly dawn you will have to drink. Then, before daybreak you must look for a place to hide and sleep."

This is why Siláxkai is difficult to find, because he goes looking for beautiful, high places in which to make himself comfortable. At times he crawls into an old nest up in a tree, or inside an old tree, like a cave. In the evening, around six o'clock, he climbs down, as Miyóki had told him. Then he begins to wander all night again. Close to dawn he has to rest, and he sleeps all day. These are the habits given to Siláxkai. That is why today if we see a nest, we think that the wildcat is there, and we always throw a stick. He comes out immediately, walking lazily. Then we have to kill him. He is weak because he just woke up, and the morning is not his time to be strong; the afternoon is.

Miyóki also instructed Alená, the tapir: "You will be called Alená and you will also have to wander at night. You will eat the fruit of cactus and prickly pear. When you find a place where they are, you must remove the thorns, and then pound and eat the pulp. That shall be your food."

That is why, when Alená encounters these fruits, it takes him a long time to knock them down, for they have many thorns. He begins to rub them, but since he cannot do it with his hands or hooves, he rubs them with his snout; that is why his snout is rough. When he finishes getting rid of the thorns, he can pound the fruit. Seeing one of these places, it appears as if there had been many tapirs, but there was only one. What happens is that it is difficult for him to eat quickly because of the thorns. That is what they gave him. Miyóki ordered him to go and eat like that. He also said: "All night you must wander and then look for water. You must not look for water close by; you have to search far away. To calculate the time well, you will leave and arrive at the water close to dawn. You will drink and then go back to eat some more until sunrise. When the sun is a bit higher, you search for a place to lie down and sleep. So look for a quiet place, beneath a white or red quebracho with lots of shade."

Tapir searches for a white quebracho and goes to sleep. At that time it is early in the day because he wandered all night long and needs sleep. Now Miyóki said to him: "When you are tired and lie down, turn from one side to the other, because you have to be calculating time."

That is why when Tapir sleeps he always wakes up at the slightest sound and then goes back to sleep. He turns his head from side to side, so that when we see a place where he has slept it looks as if a sick person

had slept there. It is his custom to move around. They also said to him:
"When you see that the sun is in the zenith, you will know that the
hour is near in which you have to leave."

That's why at noon Tapir says: "I am going to sleep again."

He goes to sleep again, and just when evening falls he wakes up to
eat again.

Tapir is an animal that wanders all night without resting, all over,
because they have not given him a fixed abode. If there is a lagoon, in
order to drink he must immerse his entire body. When he comes out
his tracks are wet and hunters know he is close by, because from sunrise
on Tapir has to sleep. When we see those wet tracks, we follow them
because he is not far away. He looks for a place close by because he
cannot wander by day. This is the task they gave the tapir. It is nice,
but it is dangerous for him because he always has to greet dawn in the
water and, since it is light, hunters can come close. It also takes him a
long time to eat, so that before he can travel very far it is day again,
and he has to settle down to sleep. Then all we have to do is follow
him, knowing that we will catch him.

Long ago, when the wild animals were humans, Tapir was a shaman,
and that is why after his transformation he did not sleep at night. He
was also very bad, and when he was transformed he continued that
way. Since Miyóki told him that if he was being chased he should turn
on the hunters and their dogs to bite them, he does just that.

When Miyóki distributed the tasks among the animals he did not
know what to assign to Soóla, the anteater, because she was a little old
woman. He thought it better not to give her any, since she was not going
to be able to do anything. He said to her: "You are already old, unlike
the others who are young and strong and who can find their own food
and take care of themselves in the forest. I worry a lot about what to
give you so that you can go on living. I believe it is best that you walk
around all night, very carefully and slowly. Also, since you do not have
teeth, it is difficult for you to eat a lot of things. I was thinking of giving
you ants to eat."

Immediately she answered: "Yes, yes, I am happy!"

But Miyóki said to her: "I think there are ants that are bad and that
can bite your tongue or stomach."

She said: "Yes, but there are other ants that are not bad, and those
are the ones that I am going to eat in order to continue living. I am also
going to catch spiders with my tongue, and eat them."

"All right, that is good. I give you this, but you have to go by night
to eat these ants, because it is at night that they gather together. I will

also tell you that it would be better if you had a knife in your hands (claws) so that you could dig in places where there are lots of ants. When you have dug you will put your tongue in there, and maybe you will catch many and have a meal. That is how you are going to live."

"All right, but I still do not have a place to sleep. Where shall I hide when I want to rest?"

"You must look for old trees, those that look soft and crumbly. Open the trunk a little and sleep inside there. Since you are a little old lady who cannot stand the cold, I shall give you this coat (which was her tail) so that you can cover yourself when you lie still. But wander a lot at night so that you will find something to eat. It is a good idea for you to wander in different areas and not return to the same place to sleep."

That is why Soóla behaves that way; she wanders at night. During the day she goes into her hiding place where not even dogs can find her, only the dog that knows her. Those who do not know her do not see her, although they may pass right by her. She is difficult to see because she looks like a branch. We cannot track her, either. Her feet make it very difficult because they do not leave clear tracks. We can catch Soóla only if we have good dogs.

When Kiliéni, the deer, came out, the man called Miyóki asked him: "Are you going to be Kiliéni?"

"Yes, I am going to be Kiliéni. But what are you going to give me?"

"I advise you to wander all over, because you have better meat and the hunters are going to like you. So you do not have to stay in a fixed place; you must stop a little and rest, continue going, and stop a little bit more. For food I am going to give you shoots of young grass and some cactus fruits. These will be your plants; you will have no others to eat. You must be very careful. Walk around very early and rest a little when the sun is high. When it is hotter, you will also have to rest. But it is not good for you to stay in the same place. You must wander everywhere and stop where you think it is best for you. You had also best wander at night. If you remain in one place during the day, hunters or animals will definitely come looking for you because your meat is the best, and they will want to eat you. I shall give you hearing better than anyone else's, even in your sleep. At least you will be able to hear from a distance and that will be your salvation."

That is why, although he is sleeping, the deer wakes up immediately, because they have given him keen hearing in order that he may live in this form. At times we see a deer standing there, asleep; he rests just a little bit, and in any way he can. If we pass quietly alongside he looks at us peacefully, and when we are far away he is already watching. He never fails to do this, because Miyóki had told him: "You have to watch intently, very closely!"

That is why, when Kiliéni watches us, he is certain that we are watching him. He is not going to yield an inch. When he realizes that we are enemies he has to run, and he goes far. He runs and runs, always looking behind; he does not look where he is going. That is why the hunters know how to kill a deer. When he runs like that they have to circle around ahead of him and catch him from the front. Kiliéni is very wild, but he always watches everything, and especially if he sees something red he never stops looking at it. He does not get tired. So all the hunters use red ponchos. Kiliéni watches red things a lot; even if one comes close he continues to watch. So it is easy to catch a deer. Since they ordered him to watch intently, Kiliéni has to comply to this day.

Then the man who was giving these orders (Miyóki) said: "You will be called Athlu, iguana (*tupinambis teguixin*)."

He answered: "Really?"

"Yes, that is it, you will be called Athlu."

"All right, that is fine. I shall be called that."

"Since you are going to have a hole in the earth to live in, you will live not in the woodlands like the others, but in open places, on grasslands with a few trees and on the savanna. You have to go there. I will give you food, like *sachasandia*, *bola verde*, *mistol*, and cactus. The fruits that fall will be your food."

"All right, that is good."

"But you must not eat anything else, only these fruits."

"All right. Then I am called Athlu?"

"Yes, your name is Athlu."

"Good, then I am going.

He began to walk, and when he came to his assigned place he saw the fruits that Miyóki had told him about, and he tasted them: "This is what he gave me to eat. How delicious!"

He continued walking, and close to noon he stopped: "I am going to rest. I have a lot of food now, many fruits that I can eat."

He saw that there were some holes and said: "I am going to see whose hole this could be."

When he looked at it, he thought: "This is good. I am going to enter and rest a little, since I have already eaten."

A little later he looked out: "It is late now. I am going to go out. I shall just take a little walk and it will be night."

He hurried to get some *sachasandia*: "This is for tonight. I shall not suffer; there is fruit for me."

When night came he had to lie down. Near midnight he ate and was very happy. That is why in the morning he continued looking around for fruit. The iguana already knew how to stay alive.

Almost in the middle of the fruit season he thought: "I am going to gather all there is and place it in a hole that I shall prepare, because I know that within a short time there will be no more fruit. I am not like the other animals that can eat anything. They only gave me fruit, so I am going to gather them in my burrow."

So when there are a lot of iguanas in one place, one sees many criss-crossing tracks. Iguanas hurry about, heading for their deep burrows where water does not reach, to hibernate.

The one who had given these orders (Miyóki) had said: "You, Athlu, have to go into a hole because it will be difficult for you to remain outside during the winter months. You are not going to have anything to eat."

"Yes," said Athlu, "that is why I am gathering food."

"That is good. See if the constellation of the Seven Little Goats (the Pleiades) is far away; then it will be time to come out. That means that the tree blossoming season is drawing near, and that another growing season of many fruits will come." Then Athlu went inside without being distressed, for he had food to eat.

When he hides he does not come out until almost a year later. But one night when his food supply begins to run out he sticks his head out to look at the stars: "Soon it will be my time to come out, but I am going to hide a bit longer. I still have food."

When it is thundering, he turns around: "It is thundering. . . . The earth must be wet and the trees are going to have new leaves. Then they will have flowers and fruit."

When the growing season arrives and it thunders again, Athlu turns around again. Then he stretches out well to be able to walk, because he has been rolled up, weak, and motionless. The third time he says: "I am going to try. I know it is all right now." Then he goes out.

When he first comes out he is very weak; he walks slowly and imme-diately returns to his burrow. Then we can catch him easily. At first Athlu is very fat, but when he has been out a long time he is rather skinny, because he wanders and wanders, and also because of the heat. These were the instructions that Miyóki had given to Athlu. That is why the iguana fulfills them to this day.

When Amla, the rhea, came out, Miyóki said to him: "You are going to be Amla.[23] You will be called Amla."

[23]In Chorote taxonomy the ostrich does not belong to the generic category of *mithlúi* (four-footed animals, generally forest-dwelling) nor to that of *axuénas* (birds), because

"All right. I am very tall. What will I do?"

"Well, I ordered the others to go to the dense forest, but since you are tall you are not in any danger. You will have to look for open spaces like the savanna or sparsely forested grasslands, so that you can escape when you are frightened. Wander as you wish, wherever you want. When you are bored with a place you can leave. But you will always be in open places so that if danger arises you can see it because of your long neck. If you lived under the trees, you would not be able to watch. That is how you are going to live, and your descendants will have this same life."

"All right. But what will I eat?"

"You will eat green grass, fruit if you see some, and pieces of old trees. That is what your nourishment will be; it will not be very delicate. When the time comes for you to lay eggs you will have to look for a quiet place, dig a little hole, and put them there because you are going to have a lot of eggs. Then you will have to sit on them, and when your chicks come out, they will walk the following day. The next day you will have to take them to the plain so that they get used to running." That is why when we see ostriches, although they are small, they run quickly because at that time they were given strength to walk and run. And they are very wild also, because Miyóki had said to the first one that it was better to be in the open country than in the forest where it would be difficult to see a man or any danger approaching them.

This is the plan that they gave to Amla, and he has fulfilled it up to this day. That is why sometimes we find rheas and at other times we do not. They change the places where they eat and where they live.

Informant: Aió

Source: Siffredi ms.

Summary

Sparrow hawk pushes people into hole full of burning coals. They emerge, all burned, in animal form. Sparrow hawk divides them into species and gives each its characteristic habits, food, and dwelling place.

Motif content

A522.2.3.	Hawk as culture hero.
A630.+.	Animals created after initial unsuccessful experiment.
	(A630. Series of creations.)

---

although it has wings it does not fly. The remaining species to which the narrative alludes are classified as *mithlúi*.

A1101.2.+.	Primeval animals human. (A1101.2. Reversal of nature in former age.)
A1710.	Creation of animals through transformation.
A2218.	Animal characteristics from burning or singeing.
A2376.+.	How anteater got its claws. (A2376. Animal characteristics: claws and hoofs.)
A2376.+.	How peccary got its hoofs. (A2376. Animal characteristics: claws and hoofs.)
A2378.1.+.	Why anteater has tail. (A2378.1. Why animals have tail.)
A2428.+.	Origin of deer's sharp hearing. (A2428. Animal's hearing.)
A2432.+.	Anteater's dwelling. (A2432. Dwelling of other animal than bird.)
A2432.+.	Why iguana lives in burrow. (A2432. Dwelling of other animal than bird.)
A2432.+.	Why puma has no permanent dwelling. (A2432. Dwelling of other animal than bird.)
A2432.+.	Wildcat's dwelling. (A2432. Dwelling of other animal than bird.)
A2433.+.	Deer's haunt. (A2433. Animal's characteristic haunt.)
A2433.1.	Establishment of animal haunt.
A2433.2.1.+.	Why peccary lives in woods. (A2433.2.1. Animals that live in woods.)
A2433.2.1.+.	Why wild boar lives in woods. (A2433.2.1. Animals that live in woods.)
A2433.4.+.	Why rhea lives on the plains. (A2433.4. Haunts of birds.)
A2435.+.	Food of anteater. (A2435. Food of animal.)
A2435.+.	Food of deer. (A2435. Food of animal.)
A2435.+.	Food of peccary. (A2435. Food of animal.)
A2435.+.	Food of puma. (A2435. Food of animal.)
A2435.+.	Food of tapir. (A2435. Food of animal.)
A2435.3.2.+.	Food of wildcat. (A2435.3.2. Food of cat.)
A2435.3.14.	Food of pig.
A2435.3.16.	Food of jaguar.
A2435.4.+.	Food of rhea. (A2435.4. Food of birds.)
A2435.6.+.	Food of iguana. (A2435.6. Food of fish, reptiles, etc.)
A2461.+.	Deer's means of defense: sharp hearing. (A2461. Animal's means of defense.)
A2461.+.	Peccary's means of defense: hoofs. (A2461. Animal's means of defense.)
A2461.4.	Why deer run, stop, and run on again.
A2470.+.	Tapir's habitual bodily movements. (A2470. Animal's habitual bodily movements.)
A2481.+.	Why iguana hibernates. (A2481. Why animals hibernate.)
A2491.+.	Why anteater is nocturnal. (A2491. Why certain animals avoid light.)

A2491.+.	Why tapir is nocturnal. (A2491. Why certain animals avoid light.)
A2491.+.	Why wildcat is nocturnal. (A2491. Why certain animals avoid light.)
A2524.+.	Why peccary is pugnacious. (A2524. Why animal is pugnacious (brave, bold).)
A2524.+.	Why tapir is pugnacious. (A2524. Why animal is pugnacious (brave, bold).)
A2524.+.	Why wild boar is fierce. (A2524. Why animal is pugnacious (brave, bold).)
A2540.+.	Why jaguar scratches trees. (A2540. Other animal characteristics.)
A2571.	How animals received their names.
D100.	Transformation: man to animal.
D576.	Transformation by being burned.
J710.	Forethought in provision for food.
J711.	In time of plenty provide for want.
K700.	Capture by deception.
K735.	Capture in pitfall.

70. The Origin of Peccaries and Other Wild Animals

There was a man who went to hunt and got lost. Suddenly he saw a white quebracho and said: "I think I ought to go that way. That is it, so it seems."

Many days had passed since he had gotten lost. So he made a fire, gathered the ashes, and smeared them on his cheeks. Then he calmed down a bit and recognized where he was. "Now I know!"

And he went off. When he approached his home, the other men said: "Here comes the lost one."

But he still had ashes on his cheeks, and upon arriving he became a peccary.[24] He had three hairs on each side, but when he became a peccary he got many; he became like a pig. He began to settle himself next to the men of his house, rubbing them with his cheek, and then they, too, became peccaries. There was a small boy who also turned into a peccary, but a smaller one. Then they began to grunt as peccaries do.

The first one to become a peccary saw all the people and said: "It is not good for us to be so few. Let us look for another house."

[24]See glossary under peccary.

They left. Arriving at another house they surrounded it and settled near the people, and all turned into peccaries. The house was surrounded by peccaries. They were people who had turned into pigs. The first one said: "No, this is not good. Let us look for some more. We are too few." They went off, got to other houses, and did the same thing. All the people there turned into pigs. Then they said: "Now it is all right."

When all the people had turned into peccaries they lived in the forest; they were not people anymore. They said: "When we want to lose our tempers we will drag along a prickly pear. That way, when the hunters come and find our tracks, they will say: 'We are not going to track them because they are bad and they are many. It is better to leave them and look for other boars, those that walk about in smaller groups (*chancho rosillo*).'"

A man who had remained in those houses said: "I am going to visit my brothers at the other houses."

He went, and before arriving he sat down: "Why are the people not making any noise? Could they be sleeping? What could it be?"

As soon as he arrived at the houses he said: "Nobody has been here."

A little farther on he saw the tracks the boars made when they had gone to the forest. He got there, and hardly had he stepped on the tracks when he crouched down. He became a peccary and followed the rest.

Since this man did not return, another went to look for him. As soon as he arrived at the houses he saw the peccary tracks. He looked at them and was about to crouch down, too, but then he did not do so. He did not become a peccary. Instead he immediately went back to give warning: "I have seen the tracks of peccaries."

Then all the old men got up: "Now we are going to hunt them because we have dogs."

They called the dogs and left. They found the tracks, but the peccaries had left about two days earlier when they had gone to the forest. The old men began to track them. The peccaries had turned around to run in their old tracks. The men turned and followed the fresh tracks. They animated the dogs and sent them off. Farther on they heard them bark. They had reached the peccaries. The men hurried to catch up, and about a hundred meters off they heard the boars making a terrible noise, roaring angrily. To the men it seemed like the noise a quebracho tree makes when it burns in the pit: "What could they be burning?"

"No, it is a boar," said another man.

The dogs ran toward the men followed by the peccaries, which were beginning to bite them. The dogs were able to catch and kill only one small peccary, but the boars killed all the dogs. Since there were many peccaries the men were afraid and climbed a tree. The boars surrounded the tree and would not leave. Then a young man who was also a shaman spoke to the old men: "Why don't you chant so the peccaries will go away?"

Then the old men sang, and the peccaries understood them. A boar that was far away called them and they left.

The men came down, put the small dead peccary in a bag, and returned home. The old men said: "How are we going to prepare it? Roasted or boiled?"

"Let us boil it," they said.

When it was cooked they started to eat it, but they did not like it. It tasted like human flesh. They threw it out and went again to look for peccaries. They caught a large one and boiled it, but they did not want to eat that one either. It did not taste good.

Suddenly there came from the north a bird who was a person (Miyóki) and asked them: "How are the peccaries?"

"They taste bad."

"What happened to the other people? Could the peccaries be those people?"

"They must be because they are not here," said the men.

Miyóki began to cut down trees to make a plaza. He piled up firewood and dug a large, deep pit, put the wood inside, and set it on fire. It heated up until it was very red. When only the coals remained, he summoned all the animals that exist and said: "Let us put in that big one called Tapir. We are going to put him in first."

They pushed him into the pit, and he burned. You see, none of the animals that existed were good to eat.

Then he called the jaguar and said: "This one goes together with Tapir." He pushed him in and burned him. "Who else?" said Miyóki.

That is how he burned all the animals: the peccaries—*quimilero* and *rosillo*—the rabbit, the wildcat, the puma, and the vizcacha.

When Miyóki had put all the animals into the pit, he covered it with weeds and earth and left. Next day he uncovered the pit, and the animals came out. They were burned but came to life again. The men went to hunt and caught a *quimilero* peccary. They boiled it and tasted it, and it was good to eat, for now it was a wild boar.

Since the tapir, the jaguar, the wildcat, the puma, and all those animals had not roasted well, the creature from the north (Miyóki) put them back into the oven. He began to stoke it with old quebracho and *mistol*, lit it, and cooked all the animals again. It had become night. Next day, around eight o'clock, he went to see them, saying: "Let us dance!"

He called the animals, and when they came out of the oven he lined them up on the plaza he had cleared. Then he began to chant so that it would become night. He thought: "I am going to do something. Let's see you form a line, all of you!" (He wanted them grouped by species.)

They formed a line. Since Miyóki had cooked them they paid attention to him. They surrounded him, and he was asking them: "What will you be called?"

"I shall be called Tapir."

"What will you do?"

"What am I going to do? Hunters who find me will turn their dogs on me. When I get tired of running from the dogs I shall stop to bite them, or smash and eat them. That's what I shall do."

The bird from the north said: "That is not a good idea; the others will be afraid of you."

He continued asking: "What will you be called?"

"I shall be called Wildcat."

"Then if you are going to live in the forest, what are you going to eat?"

"Only rabbit."

"All right. Let's see. Rabbit, come here! Run! Let's see how the wildcat goes about catching you."

The rabbit streaked off and the wildcat followed him. Up ahead he caught him and the rabbit screamed, but it was just a test. They returned from there and the wildcat said: "I think I shall be able to catch rabbits when I am in the forest."

Miyóki called another animal: "And you, what are you going to be called?"

"I shall be called Jaguar."

"What will you eat when you are in the forest?"

"I am going to eat wild boar, I am going to eat dogs, I am going to eat people. I am going to have a lot to eat and shall not lack food when I am in the forest. I shall also catch lamb. That is what I am going to do!"

"Let's see, try! Come here, boar! Run, let's see if it is true!"

The boar dashed off and the jaguar followed him. Farther on he caught him, and they came back. The ground was already trampled from so much running. The jaguar said: "It seems I am going to catch a little something."

Others came out when Miyóki called them, and he asked them: "What will you be called?"

"I shall be called Anteater."

"What are you going to eat?"

"Just ants, nothing else."

"Come here, ant, pass by there!"

Anteater stuck out her tongue, caught the ant, and ate it: "That's how I shall eat ants." Then he called another animal and asked him: "What will you be called?"

"I shall be called Puma."

"What are you going to catch when you are in the forest?"

"I shall eat only deer or goats."

"Come on, deer, since you are fast! Let's see, run!"

The deer ran and the puma pursued him. Up ahead the deer screamed; he had been caught. Puma ran after a goat and afterward they returned.

Miyóki asked other animals that had come out of the oven: "What are you going to be called?"

"I shall be called Quimilero (peccary)."

"And what are you going to eat when you are in the forest?"

"Nothing. If the dogs chase me I am going to hurt them or kill them, and the people, too."

"Good."

He called one more, the *rosillo* peccary, who said the same: "I am going to bother the dogs and the people also."

He called the rabbit and asked him: "What are you going to eat?"

"Only grass. That is what I am going to eat."

"All right."

Then the bird who came from the north (Miyóki) said: "Let's hurry because it is getting light."

It must have been close to two in the morning when they had begun to assign names. Now the bird from the north began to sweep the air with his hand, waving it from one side to the other, and the animals rushed off. In the distance the jaguar was heard. He was going to eat the boar, but now it was for real. Far away the rabbit was heard eating. All of them had gone.

Informant: Centawó

Source: Cordeu ms.

Summary

Man transforms himself into peccary by rubbing his cheeks with ashes. He then turns other people into peccaries as well. Hunters catch and cook small peccary boy but are unable to eat him because his flesh tastes like human flesh.

Then sparrow hawk tricks all animals into gathering, and pushes them into earth oven where he twice bakes them. They emerge, burned, but tasting truly like animals. Hawk assigns to them their dwelling places and individual characteristics.

Motif content

A522.2.3.	Hawk as culture hero.
A630.+.	Animals created after initial unsuccessful experiment. (A630. Series of creations.)
A1710.	Creation of animals through transformation.
A2210.	Animal characteristics: change in ancient animal.
A2218.	Animal characteristics from burning or singeing.
A2435.+.	Food of anteater. (A2435. Food of animal.)
A2435.+.	Food of puma. (A2435. Food of animal.)
A2435.3.2.+.	Food of wildcat. (A2435.3.2. Food of cat.)
A2435.3.12.+.	Food of rabbit. (A2435.3.12. Food of hare.)
A2435.3.16.	Food of jaguar.
A2524.+.	Why peccary is pugnacious. (A2524. Why animal is pugnacious (brave, bold).)
A2524.+.	Why tapir is pugnacious. (A2524. Why animal is pugnacious (brave, bold).)
A2571.	How animals received their names.
D114.3.1.	Transformation: man to peccary.
D576.	Transformation by being burned.
D2146.2.1.	Night produced by magic.
D2197.	Magic dominance over animals.
E3.	Dead animal comes to life.
J670.	Forethought in defenses against others.
K1800.	Deception by disguise or illusion.
R311.	Tree refuge.

71. The Sparrow Hawk Gives Names and Habits to the Animals

A man who was a bird cleared away all the dry trunks from the plain and piled them up. Then he dug a nice, long pit which was eight meters deep. This bird who had come down from the north was Okináwo. He summoned all the animals, lit the fire, and placed all the wood in the pit. When the wood was burned, the pit became hot and appeared very red. The earth burned. When the fire went out, the pit was hot. Okináwo summoned all the animals that existed: "Who is going to get in first?" he asked. The bird from the north said once again: "Let us put this big animal called Tapir in. We shall put him in first." He pushed him inside and the animal burned. All the edible animals that existed had no flavor. Okináwo said: "Who will be the next one?" He summoned Jaguar. "He will go in with Tapir." He pushed in the jaguar, who was also burned. "Who else?" he asked. "The wild boars, *quimilero* and *rosillo*." All the animals were burned—the rabbit, the cat, the puma, the vizcacha—all of them.

When all the animals were dead, the bird from the north covered the hole with weeds, filled it with dirt, and left the bodies there. The next day he took them out. All the animals who had been burned came out.

When the hunters went out on the plain they caught peccaries. They boiled and ate them. They tasted them, and now they had flavor. Since the cat, the tapir, the jaguar, and the puma were not roasted enough, the bird from the north put them back in to bake once again. He began to cut old quebracho colorado and *mistol*, and then he lit another fire and burned them. He roasted the animals once more. Night fell. The next day, around eight in the morning, the bird came to see the oven. He moved the cover to one side, and the animals who had baked came out. "Let us dance," said the bird from the north. He summoned all the animals. They formed a line. The bird from the north began to sing. "I shall do something," he thought. "Let us see. Get in line according to your kind."

They lined up. Okináwo asked: "What will your name be?"

"My name will be Tapir," was the reply.

"What will you do?" asked the bird from the north.

"You know what I shall do?" he answered. "If the hunters find me, they will set the dogs on me. But if I get tired from their chase, I shall stop. The dogs will bite me. I shall bite the runner, or wound him. That is what I shall do."

The bird from the north said: "That is not good; you will frighten the others."

The bird set the tapir aside, and there he remained. Tapir did not leave yet. Now Okináwo asked someone else who was coming out: "What will your name be?"

"My name will be Wildcat."

"If you live in the forest, what will you eat?" asked the bird.

"The only thing I shall eat will be rabbit," he replied.

"All right," said the bird from the north. "Let us see. Come here, Rabbit. Run so that we can see how Wildcat will catch you."

Rabbit ran off with Wildcat in pursuit. "I think I shall be able to catch him when I am in the forest," said Wildcat.

The bird from the north called another animal over. "What will you be called?" he asked.

"I shall be called Jaguar."

"What will you eat in the forest?"

"I shall eat pigs, dogs, and people. I shall eat a lot of things. I shall lack for nothing in the forest."

"Let's see. Let's find out. Come here, Peccary."

"Let's see. Run."

The peccary ran off with Jaguar after him. Farther along Jaguar caught him. They came back. Paths were already crisscrossing the plain from all the running. "Ah, if I could only catch something else," said Jaguar.

Another one came out. The bird from the north asked him: "What will you be called?"

The animal replied: "I shall be called Anteater."

"What will you eat?"

"I shall eat ants, nothing else."

"Come, Ant, come over here," said the bird from the north.

Anteater stuck out his tongue to get the ant and ate it.

"Now I shall really eat ants," he said. The bird from the north summoned someone else. "What will your name be?" he asked.

"I shall be called Puma," he replied. "What will you catch in the forest?" Okináwo asked.

"The only thing I shall catch is Deer."

"Come, Deer, because you are nimble." He sent the deer forth. "Let us see. Run!" Deer ran off.

Puma went after him. Farther down the path Deer screamed. The puma had caught him. The bird from the north summoned another. "What will your name be?"

"My name will be Quimilero," was the reply.

"And what will you eat in the forest?"

"Anything. If the dogs chase me, I shall wound them and kill them. People, too."

"All right," said Okináwo. He called another, the *rosillo* peccary, who said the same thing, that he would hurt dogs and people. Okináwo summoned Rabbit: "What will you eat?"

"The only thing I shall eat is grass. That is my food."

"All right," said the bird from the north.

"Let us hurry," he said. "It is almost daybreak."

Okináwo started to wave his arms, and all the animals dispersed. Shortly thereafter he heard Jaguar eating a peccary. This time he was eating him in earnest. A little later he heard Rabbit eat (grass).

Informant: Sentawó

Source: Mashnshnek 1972, pp. 137–138.

Summary

Bird burns primeval animals in earth oven in order to give their flesh better flavor. Afterward he gathers them together, and all acquire their present names and characteristic food.

Motif content

A522.2.3.	Hawk as culture hero.
A630.+.	Animals created after initial unsuccessful experiment. (A630. Series of creations.)
A1710.	Creation of animals through transformation.
A2210.	Animal characteristics: change in ancient animal.
A2218.	Animal characteristics from burning or singeing.
A2435.+.	Food of anteater. (A2435. Food of animal.)
A2435.+.	Food of puma. (A2435. Food of animal.)
A2435.3.2.+.	Food of wildcat. (A2435.3.2. Food of cat.)
A2435.3.12.+.	Food of rabbit. (A2435.3.12. Food of hare.)
A2435.3.16.	Food of jaguar.
A2524.+.	Why peccary is pugnacious. (A2524. Why animal is pugnacious (brave, bold).)
A2524.+.	Why tapir is pugnacious. (A2524. Why animal is pugnacious (brave, bold).)
A2571.	How animals received their names.
D576.	Transformation by being burned.
E3.	Dead animal comes to life.

72. The Sun and the Origin of Some Domesticated Animals

Sun was a man with a body and legs like ours. One day he came down to the earth and began to round up all the domesticated animals like cows, horses, goats. He created them and left them here for us. Afterward he happily returned to the sky, for his work was done. Now there were many of those animals.

Informant: Esteban Mariano

Source: Verna ms.

Motif content

A1.1.	Sun-god as creator.
A21.	Creator from above.
A84.	Creator of animals.

A736.	Sun as human being.
A1703.+.	Sun creates useful animals. (A1703. Culture hero creates useful animals.)
F30.	Inhabitant of upper world visits earth.

73. The Origin of Chickens

A newly married man built his house at the edge of the water. Ahead he saw some eggs which were already turning white. His mother-in-law said to him: "I feel like eating hens' eggs." So the boy finished his house, and then he waited for the birds to descend, the chachalacas, all the birds.

The chachalacas were the first to descend. The man thought: "I shall not kill these because my mother-in-law wants hens' eggs." The chachalacas drank some water and left. Soon the hens came, and the man went into his house. Many wild roosters and hens came flying, raising a cloud of dust behind them. Previously there were none. It was this man who was going to get some chickens from these hens. As soon as they were near he began to shoot arrows at all of them. As the young man was trying to catch them the roosters crowed, the way we always hear them crowing.

He ran out of arrows, and the hens went off into the bush again with the man in pursuit. About five hundred meters away there was a big hill, and there in front he saw the eggs which were turning white under the trees. One by one he took them and put them in his net bag. When the bag was full he picked up the roosters and hens that he had killed and carried them home.

When his mother-in-law saw him coming with everything she was happy. She separated the eggs that had chickens inside. After a few days the chicks emerged. (If it had not been for this man there would not be any roosters or chickens; he was the one who brought them.) They gave the chickens food so that they would grow. Thus the people were pleased. The rooster began crowing at four in the morning, and then the people were even more pleased, for now they could tell the time. Whenever they heard the cock crow they would get up. Since that day the cock has been waking up all the people.

Informant: Esteban Mariano

Source: Verna ms.

Summary

Man brings home eggs, from which first chickens are hatched.

Motif content

A1988.   Creation of chicken.

74. The Origin of Felines

Jaguar descended from the sky to this earth. At first she was alone, but later she gave birth to many jaguars and also to wildcats, pumas. . . . All came from the belly of this jaguar.

Informant: Esteban Mariano

Source: Verna ms.

Motif content

A1795.+.   Jaguar drops from sky. (A1795. Animals drop from
                     clouds.)
A1810.   Creation of felidae.
F980.+.   Jaguar gives birth to other felines. (F980. Extraordinary
                     occurrences concerning animals.)

75. The Chief of the Anteaters

When Miyóki named the first anteater that came out, he gave her this name and then sent her to the forest. There were several anteaters that followed the first one. In the middle of their journeys they began to bear young that were a bit different, and so the anteaters said: "Children, you will be called honey bear because you do not reach our size and are a different color. You are of a generation that is a bit changed."

In the beginning the first anteater was the chief of all the anteaters, but when the honey bears were born and they saw their skills, they made one of them the chief. They did this because the honey bear is more clever than the others. The anteaters are very lazy. The honey bear, despite being smaller, knows how to take care of the anteaters. It is difficult for the latter to drink water in the lagoons because they cannot go in, and so they just put their tongues in. But since the honey bear can climb trees, he looks for hollow ones that store rainwater. He makes a hole in them, and the anteaters can put their tongues in there and drink. The chief did this for the anteaters and taught them how to drink like that.

Also, when there is honey, the honey bear can break the hive and leave it open so that the anteaters can get honey. Since the honey bear has longer and stronger claws, he can break termitaries for the anteaters.

The honey bear does all these things to sustain the anteaters; he is very intelligent. Unlike the anteaters, when something happens the honey bear survives because he does not sleep on the ground, but hidden above in the treetops. If it were not for the honey bear, the anteaters would suffer a lot because they are very slow and lazy. All this is why the anteaters made Honey Bear their chief.

Informant: Aió

Source: Siffredi ms.

Summary

Honey bear is made chief of anteaters because of his cleverness.

Motif content

A1700. + .	Origin of anteater. (A1700. Creation of animals.)
A1700. + .	Origin of honey bear. (A1700. Creation of animals.)
A2433.2.1. + .	Why anteater lives in woods. (A2433.2.1. Animals that live in woods.)
A2571. + .	How anteater received its name. (A2571. How animals received their names.)
A2571. + .	How honey bear received its name. (A2571. How animals received their names.)
B241.2. + .	Chief of anteaters. (B241.2. King of the various kinds of beasts.)
J1100. + .	Clever honey bear. (J1100. Cleverness.)

76. The Chiefs of the Iguanas

When the men turned into iguanas[25] (*Tupinambis teguixin*) and were sent by Miyóki to the open country, they first had as their leader the *aléxkina* iguana (*Tupinambis rufescens*), who was producing more iguanas. Then her husband, who was another *aléxkina* iguana, was also named chief.

[25]*Tupinambis teguixin*, very abundant in the Chorote habitat and an important source of food to the Indians, is a large lizard with no crest.

He said to his wife: "I know you are my wife, but I do not want to follow in your path. You are a woman, and you will have to go with the rest of the women (female iguanas). I shall go with the men (male iguanas). Only when we want to have sex will we look for each other somewhere."

And they left, the men in one direction, one by one, and the women in their own direction.

The chief would always say: "Where could my wife be? Well, she knows where to find a good place. I am eating, so she must be eating also."

When the time comes for them to join, the female bites the male's tail. He has to drag her along, so they proceed very slowly and go into shallow holes together. At this time, when they go in pairs, men can kill them easily. "We poor things! Why are they allowed to kill us?"

But later the male iguana said: "Well . . . what can we do? We are food for men, so it has to be like this. But we shall never disappear, we shall live on! We do not end!"

His wife was very distressed and he continued saying to her: "Do not worry, because we shall not die. We shall live always because that is what Miyóki told us: 'People will eat you, but you shall live again.'"

This is true, because although we kill many iguanas, many still come out and live again. It is the only wild animal that always lives again.

Informant: Aió

Source: Siffredi ms.

Motif content

A2140.+.	Origin of iguana. (A2140. Creation of reptiles.)
A2210.	Animal characteristics: change in ancient animal.
A2433.2.1.+.	Why iguana lives in woods. (A2433.2.1. Animals that live in woods.)
B244.+.	Chief of iguanas. (B244. King of reptiles.)
D197.1.	Transformation: man to iguana.

77. The Chief of the Peccaries

When Miyóki gave orders to the white-lipped peccaries (*ausá*) and sent them to the forest, they gathered together because they had some doubts: "What shall we do now that we are alone? Would it not be best to elect someone as our chief?"

They did not know what to do, and they argued, a custom that had stayed with them since they were men. Then one of them said: "Who is going to lead us?"

At that moment another answered him: "Look, that one is going to be our chief!"

The chief is a very small peccary, but he is not young; he is an old fellow. They immediately said: "All right, now we are strong! We can do what Miyóki orders us to do in the forest. Now we can go!"

They prepared to leave in a group and set off.

At noon the chief said to them: "Look, children, we are going to go over there, and since it is pretty far away we shall prepare a place to sleep tonight. We shall camp out here to rest."

The peccaries said: "All right. That seems best to us: to have elected someone to lead us, because alone we can do nothing."

The *kawós* (peons, referring to the peccaries) went walking in front and the chief, who was last, followed them. Then he heard a noise; it seemed that they were pushing one another. Upon arriving he asked them: "What are you doing? Are you fighting?"

"No, we are digging."

They were all putting their snouts in the earth to make a hole. The chief said to them: "That is good. We shall use it to rest inside."

They continued working all night until a large hole was formed in which they could stretch out safely. The chief said to them: "Children, this is our home. Another night we shall be able to return. Then we shall make another in another place, so that when we tire of walking we shall be able to stay there. We shall work like that!"

"Good idea!"

That is the custom that the peccaries have: in the place where they are going to sleep, before lying down, they make such a hole. The chief of the white-lipped peccaries and his group are worse than the collared peccaries (*kíxnie*). When there is a north wind and if someone passes by, they smell and perceive his presence. The chief says to them: "Look, here comes a man! Charge him in a group!"

Then they run toward him, but later they leave because their chief says to them: "Stop, children, because the man has left. But now he knows where our home is, so we shall move to another place. He will come back to bother us here. He will not stop doing it, so we shall have to leave now."

They followed their chief's order, and in the afternoon they made another house farther away. Then he said to them: "When you go hunting again and if you do not have time, remember the home we left, so you can rest there even if it is only for one night. That way we shall have one house here and another there. They will not find us easily."

Informant: Aió

Source: Siffredi ms.

Summary

Primeval peccaries elect leader who tells them to dig holes as shelter from men.

Motif content

A1871.2.	Origin of peccary.
A2432. +.	Peccary's burrow. (A2432. Dwelling of other animal than bird.)
A2433.2.1. +.	Why peccary lives in woods. (A2433.2.1. Animals that live in woods.)
B241.2. +.	Chief of peccaries. (B241.2. King of the various kinds of beasts.)
D114.3.1.	Transformation: man to peccary.
J641.	Escaping before enemy can strike.
J670.	Forethought in defenses against others.

78. The Chief of the Peccaries

The collared peccaries met to name their chief, and they elected a very small, yellow peccary. He appeared young, but was very old, which is why he has big teeth. He is the chief of the male peccaries, and his wife is the chief of the females. They never gave up the customs they had when they were human. That is why at night, before going out to hunt, he always talks to his wife and advises her: "You will have to take good care of the females. You have to be careful because we are still not safe, and many enemies (hunters and their dogs) may come. When we go out we shall encounter many *tséxmataki!*" Actually these are dogs, but they call them *tséxmataki.*

When the two of them dream of anything bad, they immediately tell the rest. Then all the peccaries travel together. They are not careless, and wherever they go they always listen.

One night the chief had bad dreams and warned the peccaries: "I had bad dreams because I dreamed that Tséxmataki came and ate one of us. So we must be careful! Sons, you should sharpen your knives well and have them ready because I know there will be danger. One of them will kill one of my children today or tomorrow."

The chief knew that the hunters were bound to come to the forest where the peccaries were. That is why they go running out in the morning. We hunters see by their tracks that they are running, and that is because their chief makes them hurry because of that dream which he always remembers.

Informant: Aió

Source: Siffredi ms.

Motif content

A2275.	Animal habit a reminiscence of former experience.
B241.2.+.	Chief of peccaries. (B241.2. King of the various kinds of beasts.)
D114.3.1.	Transformation: man to peccary.
D1810.8.3.	Warning in dreams.
D1810.8.3.1.1.	Dream warns of illness or injury.
D1810.8.3.2.	Dream warns of danger which will happen in near future.
J580.	Wisdom of caution.
J670.	Forethought in defenses against others.
J1050.	Attention to warnings.

79. How the Tapir Got a Prominent Nose

Long ago when animals were men, they had a party and drank chicha. Already pretty drunk, the Chief of Tapirs began to get angry and wanted to fight with Kasókchi, the nine-banded armadillo. Tapir believed he could kill Armadillo, because the latter was a very short man. He wanted to fight at any cost, but Armadillo told him: "We cannot fight because we are friends!"

Tapir did not want to give in and insisted on fighting.

Then Aséta (white-bristled hairy armadillo) said to Kasókchi: "Look, you have to try out with Tapir which one of you is more manly, which one is stronger! Now we shall see."

Then they began to fight. Kasókchi hit him hard in the face and won. That is why Tapir has a big nose. It stayed that way since Kasókchi hit him.

Informant: Aió

Source: Siffredi ms.

Motif content

A1101.2.+.	Primeval animals human. (A1101.2. Reversal of nature in former age.)

A2213.5.   Animal characteristics from being struck.
A2335.3.2.   Why tapir has long nose.
B241.2.+.   Chief of tapirs. (B241.2. King of the various kinds of
                              beasts.)
H1562.   Test of strength.

80. How Armadillos Got Their Distinctive Features

Okosa, the giant armadillo, was in charge of all those of the same race (armadillo-men). Because his daughter had died, he lit a bonfire at dusk and said to them: "You have to be by the fire!"

So the *ókosa* armadillos surrounded the fire. Okosa wanted to show them the tradition that we present-day people still have: when a family member dies we light a fire, and the family sits beside the fire in order to continue living. If they do not do that, they will also die. The *ókosa* said: "We shall do what you say! We do not want to die soon! We shall continue this example."

Then the Chief of Armadillos took some charcoal and painted all the giant armadillos that surrounded the fire. This went on all night. In the morning he took a jaguar skin, spread it out some distance away, and told his people: "Try to fight against the jaguar!"

They tried, as if it were a training exercise. They practiced being quick; each one would throw his club and hit the jaguar skin: *wham!*

Since they were next to the fire they were stronger. And this black paint that their chief had put on them stayed on because they had been warming themselves all night, and their skin remained a little black because of the heat.

Then Okosa, the giant armadillo, asked Kasókchi, the nine-banded armadillo, and Aséta, the white-bristled hairy armadillo, to do the same, but the latter said to him: "No, we are not going to do what the giant armadillos did!"

That is why you see that Kasókchi and Aséta are not that same black color; they did not do what Okosa had told them. If they had, they would also be the same color.

When we see a giant armadillo on the plain he is very swift, very quick to get into his cave, quicker than Kasókchi. This is because they had instruction. When they encounter danger they can escape easily, because their chief had taught them to stay beside the bonfire all night, and to fight. That is why they have this power.

All the other armadillos—*ithlió, isténik lampé, kasókchi, aséta*—were men who refused Okosa's instructions. They followed Guasét (armadillo, *Dasypus hybridus*) who from then on was their chief. Guasét had told them: "If you want to paint yourselves black, do it, but it is better that you do not. It is all right if the giant armadillos who lost a daughter want to paint themselves. They can do whatever they want! But you, my children, should not pay any attention; just go as you are. Why should you take off the painting you have? It is bad to remove it. You are all right the way you are! We are ugly, but as long as we are not the ugliest, it is best to keep this color. Let the giant armadillos do what they want!"

Since then, the *isténik lampé, ithlió, aséta, kasókchi* and all the other armadillos, except the *ókosa*, go together with Guasét, because he did not let them go with Okosa.

Informant: Aió

Source: Siffredi ms.

Summary

Okosa armadillos acquire their black color, strength, and speed by obeying their chief's instructions.

Motif content

A1547.+.	Origin of custom of lighting fire after death of family member. (A1547. Origin of funeral customs.)
A2210.	Animal characteristics: change in ancient animal.
A2217.	Appearance of animal from marking or painting.
A2411.+.	Color of armadillo. (A2411. Origin of color of animal.)
A2528.+.	Why certain armadillo is strong. (A2528. Why animal is strong.)
A2555.+.	Why certain armadillo is swift. (A2555. Why certain animals are swift.)
B241.2.+.	Chief of armadillos. (B241.2. King of the various kinds of beasts.)
P681.	Mourning customs.

81. The Origin of the Capybara

The Chief of Vizcachas lives alone in a burrow. He would order the vizcachas that were living in other burrows to go out at night to look for food, saying to them: "You must return when it gets close to sunrise.

Then you have to go to sleep and be quiet. You must hunt at night and return for the day."

One day our recent ancestors found the burrows of the vizcachas and poured water into them, killing several animals. One vizcacha floated along this current of water, thinking: "I cannot return because now the burrow is destroyed. The house is useless now."

He continued living in the water and, later, did not want to come out. His hair began to grow longer, and he became accustomed to eating herbage, not much, at the edge of the water. But afterward he could no longer eat what he ate as a vizcacha[26] and would eat anything from the water, like *mojarras* and small fish.

Some days he would come out of the water to rest, but would always return, thinking: "If I do not return to the water, I shall not eat anything. I had better return!"

He continued living like this until he was completely used to it and stayed in the water forever.

It seems that the water in which he was living was changing the color of his hair until he took on another form. He grew more because he ate more, and he became bigger. The vizcacha turned into a capybara. The capybara did not live in the water before. He lived on land like the vizcacha, but when the people flooded the burrows he floated with the current and got used to living in the water. That is why the capybara does not forget the time when he was living on land. From time to time he goes far away from the river, but returns when it gets hot, because he is now used to its coolness.

Later the capybara met a female vizcacha, and when their children were born they were like the father. They shed his previous characteristics and grew up like their father, living in the water.

The vizcacha that had escaped from the burrows, the one that transformed into the first capybara, became the chief of the rest of the capybaras because he had made them. When the Chief of Vizcachas saw the change in this vizcacha who had turned into a capybara, he told him: "You will let us live like we always did, before you changed a little."

So they agreed to care for his children: "You will live in the water and will have to take good care of your newborn children. You should not let them leave the water when they are small. Only when they get bigger will you let the young capybaras leave."

Since that moment the transformed vizcacha ruled everything he had produced in the water; he was the Chief of Capybaras. From then on he hides in the deep of the lagoon, in a hole inside, and he hardly ever comes out. Only his children come out. The water does not reach his

---

[26]The vizcacha prefers to eat herbage and seeds, but also eats roots.

house, because after going in he covers his burrow with mud, and lives in peaceful coolness. The rest of the capybaras live on the banks of the river and the lagoons, and in the water.

The Chief of Vizcachas, though, got tired of seeing the Indians kill and bother the vizcachas whenever it rained. It hurt him: "These are my children, and Indians are eating them all year! I am going to try to arrange it so that they cannot catch them so easily."

So whenever the people were going to flood the burrows he would begin to cover the place where the water would enter and would divert the direction of the water by perforating the floor of the burrow. The place where the vizcachas lived no longer filled up. This is the work of the Chief. It is not known whether he hurts or injures men; it is only known that he diverts the water.

Informant: Aió

Source: Siffredi ms.

Summary

Vizcacha stranded in water after attack by humans learns to live in water, where he is gradually transformed into capybara. His children likewise take on his new features. (Origin of capybaras.)

Motif content

A1700.+.	Creation of capybara. (A1700. Creation of animals.)
A2275.	Animal habit a reminiscence of former experience.
A2433.2.2.+.	Why capybara lives in the water. (A2433.2.2. Animals that inhabit water.)
B241.2.+.	Chief of capybaras. (B241.2. King of the various kinds of beasts.)
B241.2.+.	Chief of vizcachas. (B241.2. King of the various kinds of beasts.)
D410.+.	Transformation: vizcacha to capybara. (D410. Transformation: one animal to another.)
D681.	Gradual transformation.

82. The Chief of Tapirs

The Chief of Tapirs is like a tapir, but very short, very strong, and very bad. He has a good build, and although he is tiny, he is very strong.

He always takes care of his animals. That is why when a tapir is lying down resting, he suddenly moves and leaves. It is because his chief has warned him: "Look, I think somebody is coming behind you!"

The tapir decides instantly: "I must get up and run!" And he goes far away. Even if they search and search for him until noon, they will not be able to reach him.

The chief always warns his *kawós* (peons, referring to the tapirs) because he does not want to give them to the hunter. But a shaman with a tapir among his spirit helpers is able to tame and catch them easily, because the chief is very good and gentle with him. With those Indians who do not have such a spirit, he is very bad and wild.

Once a youth who encountered a tapir shot him. The wounded animal got rougher and began to chase him so that he had to flee. Later, one night the Chief of Tapirs met a shaman who had a tapir spirit, and said to him: "I do not like it when the young people treat my animals like that. I do not want them to hurt them, and if they do, I am going to get angry."

"Just relax and be patient," said the shaman. "Surely your animal will be healthy again within a few days."

"All right, that is good," said the Chief of the Tapirs. "But they had better not bother them again."

Informant: Aió

Source: Siffredi ms.

Motif content

B241.2. + .	Chief of tapirs. (B241.2. King of the various kinds of beasts.)
D2197.	Magic dominance over animals.
F403.2.2.1. + .	Tapir as shaman's spirit helper. (F403.2.2.1. Familiar spirit in animal form.)

83. The Mistresses of Doves

The Mistresses of Doves take care of the doves (*Columba picazuro*) so that they are not killed for no reason. They allow them to be killed only in reasonable numbers. These mistresses do not live here on the plain, but on the hills (the Andean foothills). We call them strange women, because we do not see them as we do human women, and they have powers like underworld spirits. We only hear them always laugh like humans. It is very dangerous to see them because they kill those who do. They keep their victim's soul and take it to the caves in the hills where they live.

When they see a young man they like pass by the hills, they make a rock fall from above and kill him, and then they carry the soul away for themselves. That way they have a common husband. Since they are single women, they are always on the lookout for men.

There was a boy who had very good aim with a sling. Whenever he went out he brought back about forty doves, while we kill hardly ten or fifteen. Each time he had more and more luck, until one day when he went out during a storm. Sitting under a tree he saw a cariama and wanted to shoot it with his sling, but missed. Leaving the place he accidentally left his spare sling behind. All night he was lost in the forest and heard those spirits laughing. Upon returning home in the morning he became ill.

A shaman who knew about such things went to see him and asked: "What did you hear out there?"

"I heard laughter, as if there were women."

"Yes, those are the Mistresses of the Doves."

The shaman said that when the boy returned home they followed him, as they always do. The shaman approached them and asked: "What do you come to find here?"

"We came to look for the boy because we like him. When he goes about the countryside, we always give him many things. Now he has to pay us back. He has killed many of our doves and he must admit it. We do not want clothes or money; he has to give us his body so we shall have his soul."

"No, please!" said the shaman. "He is my grandson, the only one who feeds me! Perhaps you can pardon him."

"Very well, we shall pardon him, but he had better not go and kill doves ever again. If we see him around he will lose his life, and we shall take him down below to the underworld."

The next day the boy was well, and he went back to look for the sling he had forgotten. It was new, but he found it in pieces. The Mistresses of Doves had broken it.

The shamans say that they look like women, but they are different: big, very white, and ugly. They are like white women.

Informant: Kasókchi ilánek

Source: Siffredi ms.

Summary
Spirit-women cause magic sickness in boy as punishment for excessive hunting.

Motif content

B242.2.2.+.	Mistress of doves. (B242.2.2. King of doves.)
F402.1.5.	Demon causes disease.
F402.1.5.1.+.	Demons carry off man's soul. (F402.1.5.1. Demons seek to carry off king's soul.)
F402.1.10.	Spirit pursues person.
F402.1.11.	Spirit causes death.
F402.1.15.+.	Demon suitors of boy. (F402.1.15. Demon suitors of girl.)
F402.6.4.1.	Spirits live in caves.
F403.2.3.2.	Spirit gives warning.
F412.1.+.	Invisible spirit laughs. (F412.1. Invisible spirit speaks.)
F661.	Skillful marksman.
F679.5.	Skillful hunter.
G302.3.3.+.	Demon in form of white woman. (G302.3.3. Demon in form of old woman.)
G302.7.1.	Sexual relations between man and demons.

84. The Chief of Batrachians

Tásena, the big toad, is the Chief of Frogs and Toads, and of the *pái, potié,* and *sóxuatana* (other batrachians), because when he was sent from heaven with the rain, he laid many eggs, which hatched in different ways: like frogs, toads, and so on. Since that time they produced other children, different from Tásena, but he continued taking care of them.

When Tásena finished laying eggs on the water, he finally made a *siwólo* (fish that turned into a *nátisat* [*armado*]), thus giving us food at the end of his life. Tásena is very poisonous because he secretes that white juice (poison) all over his body. But we always remember that he was good to us, because instead of coming to the earth without doing anything, he gave us frogs and *armados* as food.

Informant: Aió

Source: Siffredi ms.

Motif content

A1420.3.	Creator of food items.
A1795.+.	Toad drops from clouds. (A1795. Animals drop from clouds.)
A2110.	Creation of particular fishes.
A2160.	Origin of amphibia.
B245.+.	Chief of amphibians. (B245. King of amphibians.)

85. The Origin of Wild Pigs

A child had some pigs in the pigsty. The child's mother was not around, so he was all by himself. The pigs had to be fed, and the child was angry with his mother for not coming. So he took one of her dresses and put it on a pig. When the woman returned she saw her dress and said: "Who gave my dress to the pigs? Could it be that stupid bastard?" The boy was sitting there. She ordered him to take off the dress, but he refused. Finally he went, but could not get it off. Instead he ran to the pigs and beat them. The pigs headed for the brush forest, and the dress tore. When they finally arrived in the brush, the dress was torn. The woman picked up a stick and beat her son, telling him not to take her dresses. She then killed him (he was a dunce), and she strangled him with a rope. Now she had no more son. The old woman was alone in the house. The pigs had gone. As she had killed their keeper there were no more pigs. The pigs did not return home but ran off to the woods. The old woman went in search of them, but not a single pig showed up, so she returned home.

Informant: Esteban Mariano

Source: Mashnshnek 1972, p. 124.

Motif content

A1871.1.	Origin of wild boar.
Q424.	Punishment: strangling.
Q470.	Humiliating punishments.
S12.2.	Cruel mother kills child.

86. The Chief of Pumas

The Chief of Pumas looks a little different from a puma. He has a bigger head, black stripes on his feet, and his coat is more reddish.

Before looking after his animals he said that he had to go and find out where the deer were going to drink. When he found the place, he said to himself: "Now I know where my animals will have to come!"

Then he taught them how to hunt deer: "When you sight deer and a north wind blows, you must be to the south of them so they do not sense that you are near. To be able to hunt, you should always go against the wind. When the deer approaches, you must be well prepared, pressed against the ground and hidden behind a tree."

The pumas follow this custom to this day.

Informant: Aió

Source: Siffredi ms.

Motif content

A2452.+.	Puma's occupation: hunting. (A2452. Animal's occupation: hunting.)
B241.2.+.	Chief of pumas. (B241.2. King of the various kinds of beasts.)

87. How an Old Husband Turned into a Bird

Long ago there was a very old man who lived with a beautiful girl about fifteen years of age. Pretty young for that old man!

The two went to the forest, and when they arrived the old man said to her: "We have to make a fire!"

She gathered wood, piled it up, lit it, and made a fire. Then the old man lay down by the fire to warm himself. He was cold!

The girl had a big dagger and planned to kill her husband, that old man who had married her. When the old man realized that she wanted to murder him, he got up and jumped to the top of a tree. From there he began to call: *Ché pé, ché pé, ché pé!*

The girl stood there looking at her husband, who had become a bird.

There is a lovely colorful bird which we can never catch and whose nest we never see. In its human form it used to be that old man (*kihíil*), and that is why we call the bird Kihíil.

When the girl saw her husband flying around she returned to the fire and thought: "What do I do now? I am all alone here!"

She did not know what to do and finally returned to where her mother was. When she got there, her mother asked her: "And your husband?"

"I don't know. . . . My husband is like a bird now; he has wings. I don't know what could have happened!"

"Why should it be? What could he have done to change into a bird?"

"I do not know, Mother. I was going to ask him, but the old man, my husband, flew away. I wanted to know what was going to happen with us."

Since the girl did not realize that her husband had become a bird, she did not know what was going to happen to him, either. So then the girl remained all alone.

Informant: Kíki

Source: Siffredi ms.

Summary

Realizing that his young wife wants to kill him, old man turns into bird.

Motif content

A1715.+.	Bird from transformed man. (A1715. Animals from transformed man.)
A1900.+.	Origin of *kihil* bird. (A1900. Creation of birds.)
D150.	Transformation: man to bird.
D642.2.	Transformation to escape death.
J445.2.	Foolish marriage of old man and young girl.
J641.	Escaping before enemy can strike.
R311.	Tree refuge.
S60.+.	Cruel wife. (S60. Cruel spouse.)

88. The Constellations and the Origin of Birds

There once was a rhea up in the sky who came down to earth. Then he began to bring down many of his companions: rheas, *charatas*, doves, all the birds that used to be with him up there. He also brought down the tuco-tuco.

In the sky they had been stars. The ones you see spread out apart from each other are the rheas. A small star which appears together with an even smaller star and which shines only faintly is a *charata*. A star that appears to have two little feet is the dove. Others are hens. These are the homes of the animals which are all located close together. Where you see that patch which appears all white, that is where the road of the animals is. The tuco-tuco lives farther away, where you see a white star, a black star, and then another white one. Those birds never separate; they live together. It is just like our homes, all living together. When it was time for them to go they descended to earth, and here they bathed and spent several days. Some birds never again returned here; they remained up there. But here below it was a lovely place, since nothing was wanting, and there was no lack of fruit. So the dove, who flew better than the others, went to call those who were still in the sky. The birds came down and have remained here where they have their houses.

Informant: Esteban Mariano

Source: Mashnshnek 1972, p. 125.

Motif content

A760.+.	Stars as birds. (A760. Creation and condition of the stars.)
A761.6.	Stars thought of as living beings.
A762.+.	Stars descend as birds. (A762. Star descends as human being.)
A1795.	Animals drop from clouds.
A1900.	Creation of birds.

89. Killing the Sharpened-Leg Cannibal: The Origin of Kiésta

Long ago Kiésta, the chalk-browed mockingbird, was a very handsome boy, just as today he is a very beautiful bird. Even his singing then was as beautiful as it is today. But he was an unpleasant young man with bad manners. For the smallest thing he would take offense and become angry with the other men, cursing, shouting, hitting, and fighting. The people did not like that, for it made them anxious. Whenever he sang the girls loved to listen to him, and that is exactly why he always liked to sing. It was common in those days for the young man who sang the best to be the most popular with the girls. Kiésta sang better than anybody, and for that, too, the men did not like him. Nearly all the girls were fond of him. Thus he got into the habit of singing every night, as he does now, but he always got the better of anyone who sang with him, and this caused bad blood.

One night he wanted to sing with another man who today is Káhopo, the cuckoo. Káhopo does not get sleepy and always sings at dawn. Kiésta wanted to be like him and said: "Let us sing together to see who will win."

They began to sing and sing next to the fire. Because Káhopo is not easily overcome by sleep he went on singing, but Kiésta grew drowsy and fell asleep. His right leg fell into the fire and was burned.

Meanwhile the rest of the people were saying in hushed voices: "When we move we shall leave Kiésta behind, for he is a bad man."

Toward morning they began to leave, fleeing from Kiésta. He woke up a bit later and looked around, but did not see anyone. Then as was his wont he became angry: "What shall I do with them? They have left me. I know why they do not like me."

Seeing that his leg was burned and foul-smelling, and realizing that there was nobody to look after him, he started to pick out and eat pieces of his skin. When finished with the skin he was still hungry. So he ate the flesh up to where he had burned himself, to the knee. Eventually nothing remained but the bone. He thought: "Maybe I should sharpen it and use it as a spear? I think that would be a good idea for my revenge, to look for those people wherever they may have gone."

From then on the people became afraid of him. He had turned into a cannibal and grew more and more savage. By tasting his own skin and flesh he acquired bad habits. He wanted to eat his food raw, and to eat people.

Kiésta sharpened the bone of his leg like a knife and tried to thrust it. When a rat passed by, he almost stabbed it. He sharpened the bone again, and as there are always a lot of ovenbirds in abandoned places, he lay down and stabbed one. He said to himself: "Very well, this will be my weapon. I shall have this sharpened leg and shall continue using it."

Going into the forest in search of honey, the men would hardly begin to cut with their axes when Kiésta heard them. His hearing reached everywhere around him. He would approach unseen from behind. But the honey collectors, noticing something, would ask: "Who's there?"

And Kiésta, without showing himself, would say: "It is I, whom you abandoned."

Then he would drive his leg into the man's back and would kill and eat him. Like that this cannibal went from one village to the next, destroying people.

Since in the afternoons there would always be some honey gatherer missing, the people became distressed. They summoned Ahóusa, the crested caracara [Hawk, the culture hero], who was very clever and powerful, and who knew. In the night, while he was playing the drum, he thought: "Surely it is Kiésta who is doing such bad things. What could I do to bring back happiness and peace to the people? I am going to look for a very soft tree, a bottle tree. Then, if I dodge him, he will stab the tree and his leg will get stuck in it. Thus I will be able to kill him."

And that is what Ahóusa did. In the morning he took his ax and left for the forest. When he saw a bottle tree, he climbed up and tried to open it with his ax. But there was no honey. Yet, looking back from beneath his wing, he continued chopping diligently so that Kiésta, who always listened into all parts of the forest, would approach. You see, whenever he heard the noise of an ax he knew that someone had climbed a tree to gather honey. From this position it was easy to grab a man.

Ahóusa pretended to be chopping, hoping that Kiésta would come. Suddenly he heard someone stepping on dry branches. He settled himself comfortably up there, all prepared.

Then Kiésta called out: "Hello there, how are you?"

"Well. I am up here," said Ahóusa.

"Can you invite me to a little of what you are gathering?"

"Yes, but later. Wait for me down below."

Kiésta knew very well that Ahóusa was clever and very powerful. He wanted him to move a little to the left, all the better to stab him with his right leg. But Ahóusa anticipated this already and said: "No, it is better that I move over to the right."

That way he could see Kiésta better beneath his wing and could move aside and dodge his blow if he jumped. They argued a great deal, but in the end Ahóusa won. Had Kiésta not given in, Ahóusa might eventually have moved to the left and been gored.

Later Kiésta said to him: "All right, try to get that honey out."

So then Ahóusa began to chop again . . . but not for real. . . . He was looking behind him from under his wing. Kiésta had already gotten ready to jump by aiming his foot of pure bone. But Ahóusa was quicker and more clever. He suddenly turned around, and the pointed foot drove into the bottle tree, where it broke. Kiésta resharpened it and tried once more to stab Ahóusa. Again the latter dodged the thrust and the leg broke against the tree. Resharpening it he finally reached the knee, and there was nothing left for him to do.

Then Ahóusa descended to pile up firewood to burn him, because he was their enemy. He clubbed him hard, and Kiésta died. He set the branches on fire and burned him. Ahóusa was waiting for that moment to see what would emerge afterward. When only the dust of the ashes remained he saw a tiny thing moving about above the ashes. From it emerged a tiny bird that we call Kasólala. Kiésta continued his evil ways by means of Kasólala. He transformed himself into Kasólala so that the people would not realize that it was he. In that way he continued with his wickedness, killing the rest of the people.

Since the people who went to collect honey began to disappear again, they went to tell Ahóusa what was happening: "What could be happening now? We believed it had ended already."

Ahóusa thought: "It must be that bird that came out of the ashes of Kiésta. It must still be he. It appears that he has not stopped what he was doing."

Then he asked the people: "What does he say when he arrives where a man is gathering honey?"

They answered him: "The one who is gathering honey always has to ask: 'Who is there?' And his answer is: 'I am the one whom you abandoned in the camp.'"

At this Ahóusa said: "So then Kiésta lives on, because those were his words. I am going to do the same thing, and I am going to burn him again."

He went to look for a bottle tree and began to cut again, pretending to gather honey. When he heard Kiésta coming, he tentatively spoke those words that they always would say: "Who goes there?"

Kiésta answered like this: "I am the one you abandoned in the camp."

Ahóusa said to himself: "That is it; those were the words of the man I burned before. He still lives."

He began to look under his wing, and Kiésta believed that because he was busy chopping, Ahóusa was not watching. Then Kiésta jumped to gore him, but he only stabbed the bottle tree. Ahóusa had to kill and burn him again. He waited to see what form would emerge. When Kiésta had turned into ashes, another bird emerged which was a bit unfamiliar. It was of a different color than Kasólala and was a bit larger. When it emerged from the ashes it said to Ahóusa: "What do you want me to do?"

"It would be better if you were the true Kiésta. Try it; try to fly."

Kiésta tried and tried. "All right, that is good," said Ahóusa.

"Do not kill me," said Kiésta. "I am going to be the true Kiésta. I am going to be good. When you hear me sing it will be close to daybreak. Thus you will be able to say: 'Now it is going to be day because we hear Kiésta.' And you will know that it is the hour to go hunt tuco-tucos, because I will sing when they begin to come out of their holes. Then you will think of me. That is how I am going to be, this will be my custom now."

Informant: Aió

Source: Siffredi ms.

Summary

Handsome but quarrelsome man is envied by others for his success with women. After his leg is accidentally burned in fire they abandon him. He sharpens burned leg and turns into ogre, stabbing and eating all passersby. People enlist help of hawk, who twice kills and burns ogre. On both occasions latter turns into bird.

Motif content

A1724.1.+.	Bird from body of slain person. (A1724.1. Animals from body of slain person.)
A1900.+.	Origin of mockingbird. (A1900. Creation of birds.)

B34.	Bird of dawn.
B455.4.	Helpful hawk.
D441.6.1.+.	Transformation: ashes into birds. (D441.6.1. Transformation: ashes into animals.)
D642.2.	Transformation to escape death.
D642.5.	Transformation to escape notice.
D1810.	Magic knowledge.
F548.0.1.	Pointed leg.
F575.2.	Handsome man.
F688.	Man with marvelous voice.
G30.	Person becomes cannibal.
G36.	Taste of human flesh leads to habitual cannibalism.
G51.	Person eats own flesh.
G312.	Cannibal ogre.
G341.1.	Ogre with sharpened leg.
G346.	Devastating monster.
G512.	Ogre killed.
H38.+.	Person's identity betrayed by habitual conversation. (H38. Person's rank betrayed by habitual conversation.)
H503.1.	Song duel. Contest in singing.
J1118.	Clever bird.
J2424.	The sharpened leg.
K800.	Killing or maiming by deception.
K810.	Fatal deception into trickster's power.
K839.2.	Victim lured into approach by false token.
K910.	Murder by strategy.
K959.4.	Murder from behind.
K1626.	Would-be killers killed.
N397.	Accidental self-injury.
S115.	Murder by stabbing.
S160.1.	Self-mutilation.
W188.	Contentiousness.
W195.	Envy.

90. The Origin of the Mockingbird

There was once a little creature whose name was Likiku. He spoke to Kiastáj, the mockingbird, and told him: "I shall make you a bet."

"Go ahead," replied Kiastáj.

"Which one of us can stay awake the longest?" said Likiku.

"Let us see," replied Kiastáj.

They got out the gourd and began to shake it around. They stirred up the fire. It was very cold. Around midnight Kiastáj said: "I am going to lie down a while; my waist hurts from sitting up so long."

He leaned back on his elbow. Shortly thereafter he fell asleep, with his feet near the fire. The heat from the fire burned his shin. He went to sleep. Likiku said: "I hope he sleeps well. I shall beat him."

Kiastáj's foot fell into the middle of the fire and was burned. Two days went by, and his shin was rotting. So the other animals cast Kiastáj out and left. Likiku said to Kiastáj: "How come they say that you can stay awake a long time?"

"That is what they said," Kiastáj answered.

"But that's not true," said Likiku.

Kiastáj smelled a piece of flesh. "I am hungry," he said.

He tore off a piece and ate. The shin was totally bare since he had eaten so much flesh. He started to sharpen the tip of the bone. Along came a little bird named Ovenbird. "I think I shall jump and catch him," said Kiastáj.

From a distance of fifty meters he jumped and pierced the ovenbird with his bone. The bird died. He roasted and ate it.

Kiastáj thought of something else. He wanted to catch up with the people who had gone away. He found campfires, but no people. He proceeded onward, traveling day and night. Whenever he arrived at a spot where they had built a fire he put his hands in, but there was nothing. Farther along he found another spot where they had built a fire. He touched it, and the embers were still warm. "Now I shall find them," Kiastáj said.

Suddenly he ran into someone who was looking for honey. "This is where I shall find them."

He heard them cutting wood. Kiastáj entered the brush forest. "Who is coming?" the man asked.

"No one, just me," Kiastáj said. "The other day you left me back there at home."

The man asked: "Where will you sit? Sit over there in front of me."

"No," said Kiastáj. "I prefer to remain behind."

The man was cutting wood. Suddenly Kiastáj jumped on him and with his sharpened leg pierced the man's back all the way through. The man fell down, and Kiastáj began to club him. He then baked him. In the afternoon he took him out of the oven and ate him. Within two days he had finished him off. He went to look for another one. When he heard another man felling wood, Kiastáj went directly toward him. He broke a little stick and the man said: "Who made that noise?"

"Just me. You left me alone at home," Kiastáj replied.

"Come over here," the man said. "Sit down in front of me."

"No," said Kiastáj. "I prefer to be behind you."

The man was busy chopping wood, and once again Kiastáj jumped on him. He pierced him with his bone, wounded him, killed him, roasted him, and then ate him.

He met another man with his son. The child was nearby as his father was felling trees. Then Kiastáj broke a stick. "Who is it?" asked the man.

"Just the one whom you left behind," answered Kiastáj.

"Come over," said the man. "Where are you going to sit? Sit down here in front of me."

"No, behind you is better," replied Kiastáj.

The man was chopping wood. Once again he jumped on him. However, this time the boy got up and went to inform the others: "This is what is happening to the people we have lost."

"Who is the man killing them? Go call the chief."

Joisá was the chief. The little boy went to tell him. "Keep quiet for a while, son," said Joisá. The boy was jumping around, and Joisá could not hear. "My family is dead," said the boy who had gone to inform him.

Joisá thought that there was a battle in progress, and thought of the Mataco, the Chulupi, the Coya, the Paraguayans, the measles, the jaguar. "All right, I shall go and investigate," he said. He combed his hair, took out a rope, and put it in his net bag. Then he departed and ran into the boy who had come to inform him. "What is happening?" asked Joisá.

"I have simply come to tell you what is happening. This is what is happening to the people who have disappeared. There is a man killing them."

"What are you saying?" asked Joisá.

"Someone asks him who he is, and he answers: 'I am the one you left behind alone at home.' Who might the man be?" the boy asked.

"Soon I shall find out," answered Joisá.

The boy went with Joisá to get honey. They found a tall bottle tree and threw the rope up to sit on it. There was no honey, but Joisá started to chop down the tree nonetheless. He was pretending to be looking for honey. In a little while Kiastáj came by. They heard a stick break. "Now you will see what he says," the boy said to Joisá.

Another stick broke.

"Who is there?" asked Joisá.

"Just the one you abandoned back at home," Kiastáj replied.

"You see! That is what he says," the boy said.

Kiastáj began to chop wood and put his head under his wings. "Where are you going to stand?" asked Joisá.

"Behind you will suit me fine," answered Kiastáj.

Joisá began to chop while he watched from under his wing. Suddenly Kiastáj jumped and Joisá quickly moved to the side, hanging from the rope. Kiastáj broke his bone, and Joisá climbed down quickly. "Damn it! I fell!" said Kiastáj.

He started to sharpen his pointed leg again. By now it was quite short. Once more he jumped, and it broke again. Quickly Joisá picked up the ax and struck and killed Kiastáj. He built a fire and burned him. He then stirred the ashes. When they began to scatter they asked one another: "What is going to be my name?"

"I'll be called Kiastáj (mockingbird)," they answered themselves. "When you go out hunting, I shall sit and sing to the dawn. You will say: 'Let us go quickly, the mockingbird has sung. It is the time when the animals come out.'"

Informant: Sentawó

Source: Mashnshnek 1972, pp. 128–130.

Summary

Man accidentally burns leg in fire. After rest of people abandon him he eats burned flesh and sharpens bone and starts out in pursuit of them. Finding them one by one in forest he pierces them with his pointed leg and kills and eats them. Small boy finally asks for help after ogre kills his father. Hawk defeats ogre and burns his body. Ashes turn into birds.

Motif content

A1724.1.+.	Bird from body of slain person. (A1724.1. Animals from body of slain person.)
A1900.+.	Origin of mockingbird. (A1900. Creation of birds.)
D441.6.1.+.	Transformation: ashes into birds. (D441.6.1. Transformation: ashes into animals.)
F548.0.1.	Pointed leg.
G30.	Person becomes cannibal.
G51.	Person eats own flesh.
G312.	Cannibal ogre.
G341.1.	Ogre with sharpened leg.
G346.	Devastating monster.
G512.	Ogre killed.
H38.+.	Person's identity betrayed by habitual conversation. (H38. Person's rank betrayed by habitual conversation.)
H1540.+.	Contest: staying awake. (H1540. Contests in endurance.)

J1118.	Clever bird.
J2424.	The sharpened leg.
K800.	Killing or maiming by deception.
K810.	Fatal deception into trickster's power.
K839.2.	Victim lured into approach by false token.
K910.	Murder by strategy.
K959.4.	Murder from behind.
K1626.	Would-be killers killed.
N397.	Accidental self-injury.
S115.	Murder by stabbing.
S160.1.	Self-mutilation.

91. The Origin of the Black Vulture

There once was a man named Atá who always ate boys. He would play with them and make them put their hands on his chest where he had cavities. Then he would lift them up and beat them against the bottle trees. When the boys died, he would eat them.

One day Joisá [Hawk] said to his son: "Son, go and see what the one who is eating all the boys is doing. I shall instruct you carefully."

"All right, father," answered the son, and he left.

He met Atá. "Hello, son," the man said. "Go and stand over there on the plain."

The boy went there. Atá asked him: "Son, are you standing on the plain?"

"No, grandfather," he answered. "I am standing in the brush forest."

The boy proceeded onward.

Atá asked once more: "Have you reached the plain?"

"Not yet," replied the boy.

"Tell me when you get there," said Atá. "That is where you have to stop."

"All right," replied the boy. Hawk had already instructed him: "Stop behind the tallest trees. If he asks whether you have reached the plain, answer him."

When the boy saw a big tree, he hid behind it.

"Have you reached the plain yet?" asked Atá.

"Yes," answered the boy.

"Are you sure?" asked Atá.

"Yes," replied the boy.

Atá picked up a rock and aimed it where the boy's voice was coming from. "But are you sure you are standing on the plain?" he asked.

"Yes," replied the boy.

"All right," said Atá, and he threw the stone. It struck the tree where the boy was hiding. Quickly the boy looked for it and picked it up. The rock was broken in half. He took it to where his father, the hawk, was. He ran.

A long time after the boy had left, Atá asked: "Son, where are you?"

There was no reply since the boy was not there. He had gone to get the stone. The man repeated his question: "Son, are you dead?"

There was no response.

Atá laughed. "I have killed the boy," he said. He rose and went to where the boy had been. He could not find him but saw the tracks. Atá went to catch him to take back the stone with which he had killed the other boys. He saw him far off in the distance. Upon arriving in a large clearing he saw the boy. "Son," Atá said, "give me the stone. It is mine."

The boy paid no attention and went on. Then he started to shout: "Come and get me, father. I am tired."

There was no response. The boy called again, because the man was catching up with him. "Father, come and get me," he cried.

Then Joisá got up to meet his son. The boy ran and gave his father the stone. Joisá knew he would bring it. He had built a big fire. When the boy gave him the stone he turned around and went to the fire. It was blazing. He threw the stone into it. The boy fell down exhausted. The stone burned up.

Much later, Joisá saw Atá coming after his son. Atá was coming right at them with great speed. He saw the fire and landed right in the middle of it. He burned. When Atá was completely burned up, the hawk began to stir the ashes that were left. "What will your name be?" he asked them.

The ashes replied: "Now I shall be called Atá, Black Vulture." They added: "When you see me in bad weather, when I fly over you, you will say: 'Now the sun will come out. Now we shall have nice weather.'"

Informant: Sentawó

Source: Mashnshnek 1972, pp. 130–131.

Summary

In order to catch child-eating ogre, hawk sends his son to act as bait. Following father's instructions boy hides behind tree, thus deflecting stone with which ogre tries to kill him. He runs off with stone, pursued by ogre. Hawk burns first stone and then ogre in large fire. Ogre's ashes turn into birds.

Motif content

A1724.1.+.	Bird from body of slain person. (A1724.1. Animals from body of slain person.)
A1931.	Creation of vulture.
D441.6.1.+.	Transformation: ashes into birds. (D441.6.1. Transformation: ashes into animals.)
F800.	Extraordinary rocks and stones.
G310.	Ogres with characteristic methods.
G312.	Cannibal ogre.
G366.+.	Ogre with cavities in his body. (G366. Ogre monstrous as to trunk.)
G512.3.	Ogre burned to death.
J1118.	Clever bird.
K800.	Killing or maiming by deception.
K810.	Fatal deception into trickster's power.
K910.	Murder by strategy.
K1626.	Would-be killers killed.

92. Killing the Blind Man Who Ate Children: The Origin of Atá

Long ago there was a blind man who was very evil. He approached the children and, acting as if he wanted to play ball, would tell them to come with him to the clearing to play catch with him. Once there, and when the boy was ready, he would warn him, but then would not throw a ball but a deadly stone at him. This way he killed many boys and ate them afterward.

The people were distressed, and since they did not know what was happening they sent word to Ahóusa who was our great chief and savior. "What could it be that is making the children disappear?"

"Let us see," said Ahóusa.

He knew how the children were disappearing. He said to his son: "We are going to finish off this blind man who eats all the children. When he tells you to go to the clearing behind the village, get behind the trees that surround it, and when he asks you if you are in the clearing, tell him yes."

Ahóusa's son went, and when he found the blind man the latter immediately asked him to play ball, saying: "Go to the clearing, and when you are there let me know."

The boy hid behind the trees, and when the other asked him if he had arrived in the clearing he told him that he had.

Then the blind man threw the stone in the direction of the boy's voice, but it hit a tree and broke in two. The boy took it and ran away. Finally he called Ahóusa to help him. The blind man, who was very angry, wanted him to return the stone. He was getting closer all the time. He could clearly hear the sound of the boy's footsteps and was following him quickly. Ahóusa had already made a great fire. He met his son, seized the stone, and threw it into the fire where it burned. The blind man, who was running rapidly, went straight into the fire and also burned.

When only ashes remained, Ahóusa stirred them with a stick, searching. Suddenly the ashes moved like a whirlwind. A bird emerged and said: "Now I am going to be Atá, the black vulture, because now my human form has died. Ahóusa has changed me into a bird and I am going to be good; I shall not eat children anymore. When there is a storm and the people see me flying over the village, it will be a sign that it is going to clear. That is what I am going to do now, and that is how you will remember me."

"All right, that is good," said Ahóusa.

He was a great chief at that time.

Informant: Aió

Source: Siffredi ms.

Summary

Ogre who kills and eats children is defeated and burned by hawk. Ashes turn into bird.

Motif content

A1724.1.+.	Bird from body of slain person. (A1724.1. Animals from body of slain person.)
A1931.	Creation of vulture.
B455.4.	Helpful hawk.
D441.6.1.+.	Transformation: ashes into birds. (D441.6.1. Transformation: ashes into animals.)
D1810.	Magic knowledge.
F800.	Extraordinary rocks and stones.
G121.+.	Blind ogre. (G121. Blind giant ogre.)
G310.	Ogres with characteristic methods.
G312.	Cannibal ogre.
G512.3.	Ogre burned to death.
J1118.	Clever bird.
K800.	Killing or maiming by deception.
K810.	Fatal deception into trickster's power.

K910.   Murder by strategy.
K1626.   Would-be killers killed.

93. Killing Atá, the Old Man Who Ate Children

Atá was an old man who always went where the children were playing and sat down there. He had a very deep hollow in his back. The children liked this hollow; they would put their hands inside and play. "How pretty it is, old man! It is pretty, this hollow!"

And Atá would say to them: "All right, come on, we are going to play."

When the other children saw that he was good to them, they came to play with him. But when they put their hands in the hollow, Atá grabbed them and carried them up to his place in order to eat them.

The people did not like what Atá was doing and wondered how they could kill him, but they did not succeed: "We cannot do it. Let's ask our chief, Ahóusa. Perhaps he can kill Atá." Then they called him. All the people gathered and told him that Atá was doing great harm to the children. "When they play over there he's already there, and he takes more and more children."

Ahóusa said: "If I am not brave, I shall not kill him, but if I am brave, I shall. We'll see."

He sent a message with Katáki, the fly: "Katáki, go to Atá and tell him to come. I want to speak with him."

Katáki went there, and Atá asked him what he wanted. "I am here because Ahóusa sent me to ask you to come and talk with him."

"But what is wrong?"

"I do not know, he wants to see you."

"All right, I shall come."

Then Atá came down to earth and went to Ahóusa's place: "Hello, how have you been?"

"I am all right, more or less. But why have you done this?"

"What have I done?"

"You ate many children! All the parents have come to tell me about it. This is very bad!"

Atá went a little farther away: "Very well, Ahóusa, if you are brave like I am, I shall not kill you. But if you are not, then you will die."

"All right. We shall just fight here!"

They fought here, on this earth. Atá was not in his territory when he fought with Ahóusa. Ahóusa, on the other hand, fought in the place where he lived. Therefore, when he got tired he called to the people:

"Help me! Let us kill this one!"

And everyone helped him kill Atá.

Then Ahóusa sent another message to notify the chiefs of the birds. First he sent notice to the chief of the king vultures: "Let him know that Ahóusa has killed Atá."

The messenger went. It was Katáki. "Why have you come?" asked the king vulture.

"I am here to tell you that Ahóusa has killed Atá. The two chiefs fought, and he killed him."

"But why?"

"I do not know. They argued, then they fought, and in the end Ahóusa killed Atá."

"All right, go and tell the other chiefs!"

He went again to notify everybody.

Afterward the chiefs of the carrion-eating birds thought of how they could kill Ahóusa: "We are going to get even!"

They united to kill him, but in the end one chief said: "No, we are not going to do this, because if we do, we will put an end to ourselves. Ahóusa killed Atá because he harmed the children: he was right in killing him. But now if we kill Ahóusa we would end up badly, because revenge would follow. Better to forget all this. Our sons must be able to look for our food without having to worry. Let us leave our sons in peace!"

That was how they thought. It was better to discontinue the battle, so that the earth remained in peace.

Informant: Kasókchi ilánek

Source: Siffredi ms.

Summary

Old man carries children up to sky where he eats them. Hawk kills him in fight. Chiefs of other birds refrain from killing hawk, fearing consequences.

Motif content

B242.2.+.	Chiefs of the various kinds of birds. (B242.2. King of the various kinds of birds.)
B291.+.	Fly as messenger. (B291. Animal as messenger.)
B455.4.	Helpful hawk.
F30.	Inhabitant of upper world visits earth.
G310.	Ogres with characteristic methods.
G312.	Cannibal ogre.
G366.+.	Ogre with cavities in his body. (G366. Ogre monstrous as to trunk.)

G512.	Ogre killed.
G630.+.	Ogre lives in sky. (G630. Characteristics of ogres.)
J580.	Wisdom of caution.
J647.	Avoiding enemy's revenge.
K800.	Killing or maiming by deception.
K810.	Fatal deception into trickster's power.
K815.	Victim lured by kind words approaches trickster and is killed.
K827.	Dupe persuaded to relax vigilance: seized.

94. The Origin of Pottery and of the Ovenbird

In primordial times, when Sáti, the ovenbird, was human, her work was dedicated to making pottery containers for water. Sáti would work on this and the other women did not know what she was doing, nor did they think of imitating her.

She would always search for clay elsewhere and would bring it from afar little by little. She would moisten it and would first make it in the shape of a plate, very thin and small. Then she would fire it and break it to mix with new clay. This would protect the container that she was going to fashion, making it stronger.

When she was human, Sáti would spend all her time working. A lot of people used to make fun of her. They did not like her work because they did not know what it was going to be. When the day came that the containers were ready, she had to haul firewood in order to put them on the fire and bake them. After this, the people saw that Sáti was making genuine jars, and they tried to put water inside. They could use them. They saw that her work was going better.

That is the example Sáti gave, and afterward the other women adopted the custom which continues to this day. She was the first to make water jars and she taught the others, showing them that this work is only for women.

She always worked a lot, baking clay to make water jars and other things. The other women did not like this. They would always come up to her and say: "Sáti, what are you doing all day? We have never seen you rest. Always making clay, clay, clay!"

Every time she answered them like this: "It is my own business what I make. If I did not do this, where would you put water? And how would you cook? For I also make pots. I am not like you! I work as I like!"

She never tired of making things, and the people saw that she continued to do so. They acquired more and more large earthen jars and pots! They kept advising her to stop, but she did not want to. She continued gathering wood and bringing it to bake clay and make containers.

The third time the women went to counsel her, she answered them: "I know what you are doing with me! From now on I am going to withdraw and go wherever I want. I am leaving! But remember that I am Sáti, who helped you a lot. If someone did not have a water jar, I gave it to her so she could get water. But when I am not with you, you will suffer a lot. I shall not be here anymore because you do not like me. Now I am going to hang up my pot (nest) where I want to, since I do not have a family anymore."

The other women did not want her to be there always working. They were ashamed of not doing anything while she continued working. Then she thought: "It is best that I leave this place. I shall go where I want!"

Since she was in an angry mood, she began to walk. Further on, worried that the people did not like her, her thinking turned bad. She stopped looking for food and began to eat any old worm. She would walk and walk aimlessly, almost without resting. Then she thought: "It is best not to live with people anymore. Maybe I should transform myself into an animal? That way the people would not see me anymore, and I would have no more problems. How would it be if I were a *sáti*?"

She did not know what the job of this bird was going to be, but she knew what her own was. She continued wandering about and did not return to where the others were. Then she ran out of food. She was suffering, and she began to cry out from hunger and want. That cry was what was transforming her into Sáti. She began to walk quickly back and forth without stopping, as we now see the ovenbird do. She learned to be like the ovenbird, and then suddenly she was Sáti.

Informant: Aió

Source: Siffredi ms.

Summary

Woman works hard making pottery for people, to whom this craft is still unknown. Tired of their mockery she eventually leaves and turns into bird.

Motif content

A1451.	Origin of pottery.
A1900. + .	Origin of ovenbird. (A1900. Creation of birds.)
A2441.2.	Cause of bird's walk.

D150.+.   Transformation: woman to bird. (D150. Transformation:
                 man to bird.)
D520.+.   Transformation by calling out. (D520. Transformation
                 through power of the word.)

95. Killing the Hidden Murderer: The Origin of Sáti

There was a woman who had an oven[27] as big as the tire of a car.
It was up in a tree in the middle of the road. She used to hide inside
it. She was also dangerous and destructive. When people passed by
she dropped the heavy oven on their heads, killing them. She had killed
many people, for up there she was well covered by leaves, and the
people had to pass by that way.

Only one man had been able to escape. He had halted below the
oven, but when it came down he moved aside, and the oven fell to the
ground. Realizing what had happened he went to inform Ahóusa so
that he could look into the matter. "There is a large thing that is stuck
to a tree, but I do not know what it is. I stopped there and—*wham!*—
it came down on me. Had I not moved aside it would surely have killed
me. This is what must have happened to all the people who have died."

Ahóusa listened carefully to what the man was telling him and said:
"In the morning we shall go. Right now I myself am going to see."

Since Ahóusa is clever he went quietly looking all around: he looked
to the back, to the front, and above. When he was near the tree he
piled up firewood and made a large fire. Then, when he stopped below
the oven and saw it coming down on top of him, he moved to one side.
The oven broke into pieces, and the owner who had fallen on the ground
said: "It is over for me, now that I have seen Ahóusa."

As always when there is danger, Ahóusa simply burns what is dangerous until only ashes remain. He picked up the woman and the oven,
threw them on the fire, and waited to see them burn to ashes. He wanted
to see what would come out of them.

When they were completely burned, Ahóusa took a stick and separated the ashes. He saw a little thing moving inside the ashes that
became like a whirlwind. Then the little thing in the middle of the ashes
spoke, saying to Ahóusa: "Now I shall become what is called Sáti, the

---

[27]This term refers to the elevated, domed oven, made of earth, which is used by the
indigenous population of the area. It also refers to the ceramic vessels made by the Chorote
and to the kiln.

ovenbird. Now I shall go around only as a bird, not as someone who kills people. No longer will I cause trouble, now that I turned into an ovenbird. I am going to be gentle. I shall hang my oven from the trees, well secured; not as before when it was loose and when I let it fall down."

"All right, then that is good," said Ahóusa.

Since Ahóusa is powerful he made her emerge as a bird, but as a real bird.

Informant: Kíki

Source: Siffredi ms.

Summary

Ogress kills passersby by dropping heavy oven on them. Hawk kills and burns her, and her ashes turn into bird.

Motif content

A1724.1.+.	Bird from body of slain person. (A1724.1. Animals from body of slain person.)
A1900.+.	Origin of ovenbird. (A1900. Creation of birds.)
B455.4.	Helpful hawk.
D441.6.1.+.	Transformation: ashes into birds. (D441.6.1. Transformation: ashes into animals.)
G310.	Ogres with characteristic methods.
G321.2.	Ogress at a spot along the road takes toll of lives.
G512.3.	Ogre burned to death.
G512.3.2.	Ogre burned in his own oven.
G637.	Ogres live in trees.
J1118.	Clever bird.

96. Origin of the Ovenbird

Saatí, the ovenbird, had a little mud house. Whenever someone passed by underneath, the house would descend. Someone went to inform Joisá, the hawk. Saatí would watch the person walking underneath and would lower his house.

Joisá went to where the mud house was and watched from the side. When he saw the little house come down he moved sideways, and the little house disappeared. Quickly Joisá went back, picked up a stick, and began to strike the house. He then built a fire. When the fire grew strong, Joisá burned the clay house. When he had burned it thoroughly, he started stirring the ashes with a stick. The ashes moved around. They said: "Who is moving us? It must be Joisá."

"No," they added. "I am not going to be angry."
Joisá asked: "What will you be called?"
The ashes replied: "My name will be Saatí."
"Very well," answered Joisá.

Informant: Sentawó

Source: Mashnshnek 1972, p. 132.

Motif content

A1900.+.	Origin of ovenbird. (A1900. Creation of birds.)
B455.4.	Helpful hawk.
D441.6.1.+.	Transformation: ashes into birds. (D441.6.1. Transformation: ashes into animals.)
G310.	Ogres with characteristic methods.
G512.3.	Ogre burned to death.
J1118.	Clever bird.
K812.	Victim burned in his own house (or hiding place).

97. The Origin of the Burrowing Owl

There once was a man named Kioít (Burrowing Owl). He began to sing softly. Whenever he sang more loudly it would arouse the people, and they would come to see him. Kioít lived inside a big hole. The people came over and went inside, and everyone died. Some five houses fell into the hole; it was a large village. One man said: "Go and call the chief."

Joisá, the hawk, was the chief. The man who went to inform Joisá was shouting. "Calm down, my son," said Joisá. "Who is shouting?"

"My family is dead," the man replied. "Now I am alone."

"What are you trying to say?" asked Joisá.

"There is a creature who sings. It seems to be Kioít. It starts off singing softly, but then it becomes louder, and the people go to look at it. There is a large hole, and when the people go in they die." Joisá was upset and said: "I shall go and straighten things out."

He got all his tools and an *ucle* with which to build a fire. He arrived at dusk. "By day Kioít does not sing," they told him. "Only at night."

Around eight o'clock, Kioít began to sing his first small song. When he began to sing more loudly, the people came to see him.

"So this is what is happening," Joisá said.

For a short while he sang softly.

"This is how he sings at first," they told him.

Joisá wanted to go out to see him.

"Wait a while," they suggested. "He is not singing loudly yet. That is when the people go out to see him."

"All right," agreed Joisá. When they heard loud singing the people said: "That is it." All the Indians got up to see him. Joisá remained behind. He lit the *ucle* and proceeded. "Step aside. Here comes the chief," the people said.

"Yes, companions, step aside because I have fire," was Joisá's response.

When he arrived at the hole, he set it aflame. He burned it, killing Kioít. He began to stir up the ashes. The ashes moved and said: "Now I shall be called Kioít, Burrowing Owl, King of the Birds."

Informant: Sentawó

Source: Mashnshnek 1972, p. 128.

Summary

Loud song of ogre sitting inside big hole attracts people. When they enter hole, everybody dies. Hawk comes to people's rescue by setting fire to hole, killing ogre. Its ashes turn into bird.

Motif content

A1724.1.+.	Bird from body of slain person. (A1724.1. Animals from body of slain person.)
A1958.	Creation of owl.
B242.+.	Chief of birds. (B242. King of birds.)
B455.4.	Helpful hawk.
D441.6.1.+.	Transformation: ashes into birds. (D441.6.1. Transformation: ashes into animals.)
G310.	Ogres with characteristic methods.
G421.	Ogre traps victim.
G512.3.	Ogre burned to death.
J1118.	Clever bird.
K700.	Capture by deception.
K810.	Fatal deception into trickster's power.
K812.	Victim burned in his own house (or hiding place).

98. Killing the Hidden Murderer: The Origin of Kioí

Long ago Kioí, the burrowing owl, was a human enemy, not a bird like now. Since Ahóusa killed him he has been heard singing at any hour of the night, but now it is the true Kioí, not like before. At that time he would kill people. He had a large hole inside the earth with a cover on it, and there he would hide himself. At any hour of the night he would begin to whistle and whistle. At night he would just whistle until he woke up the people, and he would call to them: "Come, come, we are going to have a dance!"

Then everyone would want to go to see him where he was living, which was away from the village. And when they arrived Kioí would take away the cover and they would disappear, all falling into the hole. He would cover it again and they would suffocate. In this manner he killed those who saw him.

Then Kioí ceased to sing and began to think and think: "Where am I going to go now? Because now all the people of this village are finished."

He went to another village and sang again as always so that those people would come to see him. Kioí took off the cover and made them fall into the hole, killing all of them. Only a little girl had remained above and was very distressed. "What am I going to do now all alone like this? They have taken my entire family. Who is going to feed me?" She went to ask advice from Ahóusa, and she said to him: "My entire family is gone. The other night there was someone outside the village who first was singing very softly, then loudly, and who was calling: 'Come, we are going to have a dance here!' Then the people got up and went. They did not appear again. What could have happened to the people?"

Ahóusa said to her: "I know."

When night fell Ahóusa began to sing, playing the drum until dawn. The next night he did not sing anymore; he was waiting for Kioí. Kioí came and sang again. Then Ahóusa said to those people: "Be careful with the one who is singing! He is dangerous! Do not go near when he calls you, although you want to see him, because he is going to kill all of you."

Ahóusa made a bundle of dry grass and went close to the hole to wait for Kioí to sing loudly. When the latter sang loudly to the people, he set fire to the weeds and put them in the hole and, as he is strong, seized the cover and placed it over the opening. Kioí wanted to take it off but his hands bent and he could not do anything: he remained inside the hole.

Then Ahóusa gathered a lot of firewood and threw it on top of the hole. When Kioí was dead and completely burned, and no more than the ashes remained, Ahóusa jabbed the ashes with a stick and they formed a whirlwind, rising up like smoke. When the tip of the cloud of smoke was up in the sky a bird appeared, flew down, and said to him: "Now

I will never again be the way I was in those days when I would call all the people, and would kill them and eat them. Now I am going to call myself Kioí and I am going to eat any type of bird. When the people hear me whistle from afar, it will be a signal that they have to go away from that place because enemies are coming."

When Ahóusa killed and burned that man, he turned into the burrowing owl. If it were not for him, all people would long since have died.

Informant: Kasókchi ilánek

Source: Siffredi ms.

Summary

With beautiful song ogre lures people to approach, then traps and kills them. Finally hawk traps and burns him in his own hole. Smoke from burned ogre turns into bird.

Motif content

A1724.1.+.	Bird from body of slain person. (A1724.1. Animals from body of slain person.)
A1958.	Creation of owl.
B143.1.	Bird gives warning.
B455.4.	Helpful hawk.
B521.3.	Animals warn against attack.
D441.6.1.+.	Transformation: ashes into birds. (D441.6.1. Transformation: ashes into animals.)
D1810.	Magic knowledge.
G310.	Ogres with characteristic methods.
G421.	Ogre traps victim.
G512.3.	Ogre burned to death.
J1118.	Clever bird.
K735.	Capture in pitfall.
K812.	Victim burned in his own house (or hiding place).
K815.	Victim lured by kind words approaches trickster and is killed.
S113.2.	Murder by suffocation.
Z356.	Unique survivor.

99. The Origin of Parrots and Herons

There were many boys out bathing. They bathed for a long time. One of them got cold. He was shivering in the water. The other boys had already gotten out.

"Come out, brother," they said to him.

"But I am not cold yet," he answered.

"Why are you shivering so?" they asked.

"You are really cold."

"I am not cold yet," the boy replied. After a while he climbed up on dry land. Right there he turned into a white heron. He tapped the ground with his beak as if he were a peccary.

"What is happening to our brother?" the other boys asked.

"Did we not tell you to get out?"

"But I was not cold yet," answered the heron. He had done this to himself in order to get out. "Let us play one more time," he said.

"All right," the others replied. There were a lot of boys. They began playing, screaming, and yelling. They built little houses. The boys treated each other badly and then turned into parrots. They started to play and scream as parrots do. One of them said: "I shall make my house up in that tree. My house will be a nest. This is what I am going to do." And the parrots screamed.

"Climb up there," one of them said. "This is my place."

"No," the other parrots said. "We like this place."

"How shall we build our houses?" they asked.

"We shall cut thorns and build a little house, a nest."

They began to gather thorns. "How do we cut them? With our hands?"

"No, with our beaks. We shall cut them with our beaks because they are sharp."

They cut the thorns and built a little house. But the house was actually a nest.

Informant: Cepillo

Source: Mashnshnek 1972, p. 142.

Summary

Bathing boys turn themselves into birds and build nest.

Motif content

A1710.+.	Creation of birds through transformation. (A1710. Creation of animals through transformation.)
A1964.	Creation of heron.
A1994.	Creation of parrot.
A2431.3.	Origin of birds' nests.
D150.	Transformation: man to bird.

100. Killing Sákiti, the Man-Eating Celestial Eagle: The Origin of the Color of Birds

Sákiti, the harpy eagle, lives in the heavens close to the places of other big birds, like the black-and-chestnut eagle, the black vulture, and the king vulture. In the beginning Sákiti would come from above whenever he wanted to eat and would look for tuco-tucos. He had four children, and when he returned home they would hear a noise from afar like a wind and would become content: "Our father is coming!"

When Sákiti arrived he fed them tuco-tucos. Then he would say: "Children, I am going to look for more, you have already eaten it all."

He would begin at dawn, by hunting tuco-tucos. In the afternoon he would return to look for something else. Sometimes he found snakes and had to fight because they were difficult to kill. He tried to seize them by the head and struggled fiercely for about one hour. That was why he sometimes returned tired to his home. With snakes it took him a long time, but tuco-tucos he dispatched quickly. This was the food he fed to his children when he began his work.

Eventually he exhausted this small game and realized that all the food he used to hunt—snakes, tuco-tucos, red brocket deer—was not enough for him. He thought of humans and wanted to try to eat a man: "It is better that I eat a human being, for they have much more meat, even enough for me. I am not going to bother going to the open country every day; one person will be more than enough for me."

He became very dangerous when he began this! Whenever Sákiti descended and saw someone killing tuco-tucos in the country or gathering honey in the forest, he had stones on hand to throw and kill the man.

When the men disappeared nobody knew who was killing them; no one realized. And for Sákiti it was easy to carry his victim home to his children. In time there were a lot of bones in the place where he cut up the people for food. His children used to play with the bones, throwing them as though they were sticks, making noise. Every day they played with these bones, and when they saw their father coming they would leave their game, return to where their mother was, and wait for Sákiti to arrive. Eventually, however, he began to have difficulty with his work.

There was a very fine young man by the name of Wiskilióte, the laughing falcon. Like Sákiti, he was a good hunter. He had a grandmother who took care of him. He lived with her close to Sákiti's place and did not like the noise of the bones that the children were throwing around. He always said to himself: "What could I do to Sákiti's children to stop them from making such a racket? How could I catch and kill them?"

One afternoon his grandmother called Wiskilióte. He threw himself down next to her the way he always did and said to her very clearly: "Look, grandmother, would it not be better if I went to visit Sákiti?"

As soon as the woman heard this she began to cry: "No, my grandson, he will eat you!"

"All right, grandmother, then I shall attempt to kill him first!"

"What do you mean, you are going to kill him? You are not going to kill him!"

"I am going to kill him. You will see. Do not be afraid. I shall kill him."

"No, grandson, you are the one who feeds me. Don't concern yourself!"

"All the same, I am going to kill Sákiti. He is dangerous. He has already killed a great many people."

"Don't go! Why will you go?"

But the young man said: "Well, I am going. I want to pay him a visit."

He considered how to handle it. Later, at night, he walked across some dry lagoons and found a rattlesnake. He seized it and, while holding it live in his hand, cut off its head and took it home. His grandmother asked him: "Where have you been?"

"I went to look for frogs, but there weren't any. You must sleep, grandmother!"

That night he thought and thought of how he was going to kill Sákiti. Very early in the morning he packed his bag and put the head of the rattlesnake inside. He painted himself with color derived from a certain root: yellow, but very bright, very beautiful. Then he went off prepared. Sákiti had already left to look for someone to eat, and the young man remained there, waiting to hear the children. Around nine o'clock they went to play where the bones were, and Wiskilióte heard them. He thought: "Now the children are coming. I am going to kill them! No matter how. I am going to kill them!"

While they were playing, he quietly began to move in closer, softly. Sákiti's children saw him, and one said: "Look at that young man. How pretty!"

"How handsomely he is painted!"

The other said: "Brother, it was I who saw him!"

"No, I am the one who saw him first! I am going to call him."

They called him, and Wiskilióte was pleased because this gave him the opportunity to move in. When he arrived, the children were looking at him: "Look how handsome he is! What does my uncle do to have such good paint?"

"I do it with a certain thing I own, something good."

"What is it?"

"Here," he said as he poked about for the head of the rattlesnake in the bag. "This is it."

"And what do you do with it?"

"I hold it, make it pull gently on my tongue, and then bite it. Then I lie face down, and in a moment, when I stand up, a lot of paint comes out. Beautiful! That is how I do it."

"Ah, then you can do this to us?"

"Yes, if you like."

"Well now, which one of us will you take first?"

Wiskilióte thought: "The biggest, for there are four of them."

And he began. "Let us see. Open your mouth, son, wide open, and tongue out!"

Then he grasped the head of the rattlesnake, and alive and poisonous as it was, it bit him in the tongue.

"Ow, ow!" said the boy.

"Don't scream; it will be all right. Lie face down!"

He obeyed, but the other children thought he was too still, and asked: "Is he dead?"

"No." Wiskilióte had a way of making the lying child move. "Look, he is moving. Do you want it also?"

"Yes, why not."

He did it to the others. But the last child sat there thinking, and asked: "Why does he not get up?"

"Well, he is going to get up soon," said Wiskilióte. "You should do the same. If not, you won't get any paint."

"All right, I shall do it, too." So Wiskilióte grabbed him, and thus killed the last child. Then he thought: "What am I going to do now? If Sákiti finds out that I killed his children he will kill me for sure. I shall go see his wife."

Wiskilióte went to Sákiti's wife. She looked like an old woman unable to walk. But she could walk, only Sákiti did not want her to go out. Since he was evil, he did not want his wife to go around and kept her locked up. When the young man arrived he looked at the old woman, and she looked at him: "Well, young man, what is the matter? Why have you come? My husband is very dangerous, and it is almost time for him to come home."

"It does not matter. Let him kill me!"

Then he thought: "I am going to figure out where he keeps his spears."

Sákiti kept them in a place like an oven in the form of a large earthen jar. He owned four different spears for different purposes: one for people, one for large animals, and another for small animals. He had taken one with him, and three remained inside.

Wiskilióte asked the woman: "Grandmother, where does Sákiti keep his spears?"

"Over there."

"Then, old woman, I am going inside. Do not tell Sákiti."

Said the woman: "Upon arriving he always throws the spear into the oven. It will hit you!"

"It does not matter, let it . . . old woman, I am going to try."

The young man entered the oven, but soon came out again to ask: "Old woman, what time does Sákiti usually get home?"

"Look, young man, he always arrives a little before noon."

"All right, old woman, if he asks for his children, I killed them a little while ago," he told her.

"Oh! Why did you kill them?"

"Well, I killed them . . . if he wants to kill you for that, old woman, let me know."

Then Wiskilióte entered the oven and prepared different colors like butterflies; he made many butterflies. He divided himself up so as to be able to escape Sákiti. The old woman warned him: "Look, young man, did you hear? Sákiti is coming! Whenever he is about to arrive, some drops of blood fall to the ground from above. Be careful; he will be here any minute!"

"It's all right, old woman."

Although Wiskilióte was inside the oven, he could hear him come. When Sákiti was still some distance away, he got angry because he could not hear his sons play from a distance as he always did. "What happened to the children that I do not hear them? Could they have been killed?"

He came quickly, descended, and asked his wife: "Where are the boys?"

"I don't know. They went out to play," she said.

"But why didn't I hear them from afar?"

"Well, I don't know. Go see for yourself!"

"But where are they?"

"I don't know."

"No one came?"

"No, no one."

The young man was inside listening.

Then Sákiti said: "We are going to find out what is happening to the children."

They went to where they had been playing on the cleared land and then saw them dead.

The father asked his wife: "Who killed my children? Tell me or I'll kill you, too!"

"But I don't know who killed them. I have no way of knowing! You ordered me not to go anywhere. What can I say if I did not see anyone?"

But Sákiti insisted: "Tell me who killed them! If you do not tell me right now, I'll kill and eat you."

"But how can I tell you if I do not know anything?"

"You did not hear any noise around here, like a man going by?"

"Nothing, nothing!" said the wife.

"But there has to be something because all the children have lost their lives. There has to be something!"

They continued talking and in the end the old woman became frightened, because Sákiti held his spear at the ready to kill her. Pointing to the oven she said: "Well, someone went in there."

"You saw him? Why did you not tell me?"

When he poked the spear inside the oven a butterfly flew out, and Sákiti ran to catch it. He asked his wife: "Is this it?"

"No, it is not."

"But what color was it?"

Again he put the spear in, and another butterfly came out: "Is this it?"

"No, it is not. It was not that color."

"Well, tell me then what color it was!"

Many more butterflies came out, more and more and more. Finally he could not catch them any more. As soon as he tried to catch one, another one came out; and catching them all was impossible.

"Is that the one? Is that the one?" he asked.

"No, not this one," his wife kept saying.

Then five butterflies came out followed by five more, and yet another five. The one in the middle was Wiskilióte. He was like a red butterfly! He fled far away. Sákiti asked: "Where is it?"

"It came out a little while ago," said the wife.

"There it goes," he said. "I am not letting it get away. I am going to kill it." He dashed off immediately to catch the butterfly. It flew without direction. Then Wiskilióte thought: "Oh, here comes Sákiti! What am I going to do? How can I save myself?"

Sákiti had seen him. He had already passed by many butterflies and was catching up with him. He would grab one butterfly and let it go, grab another one and let it go; it was not Wiskilióte. Letting them all go he said to himself: "Ah, that red one must be the one that killed my children!"

He went in pursuit. But the moment he was about to catch the butterfly, the young man changed into flowers. Sákiti flew right over the flowers, which were beautiful. He could not see the butterfly anymore. He saw nothing and returned to where he had been before, far away from the young man. He continued looking for him and found him, and when he was about to grab him, Wiskilióte transformed himself into Sén, the hummingbird. He flew around there pecking at flowers, and Sákiti did not realize who it was. He passed far beyond Wiskilióte until he saw that there were no butterflies. Then he returned, but Wiskilióte was far away again. This is why Sákiti had to travel from one end of the sky to the other. Catching this young man really took some doing.

Wiskilióte had become very tired, naturally—he had changed into so many forms. He thought: "May Sákiti find a way to catch me, what do I care."

Sákiti was stronger than Wiskilióte. But then he remembered: "To the north where my grandmother lives there is a tree."

There was a big bottle tree and two other big trees. He said: "I am going to my grandmother. Maybe she can save me. I am going to her place."

Finally he was getting there; he was very close. Wiskilióte could not transform himself anymore. He had used up all the forms he could assume. So from afar he cried: "Grandmother, let me in, for I am tired!"

And this other old woman who was a tree said to him: "No, grandson, I cannot because I have only one deep root. Go to that other old woman who has something like five roots. She will be able to help you."

So he just continued on, and upon arriving said to her: "Grandmother, take me in!"

"Certainly, grandson, hurry, hurry up. Hurry before Sákiti gets you!"

Then she took him inside. She opened her trunk and the young man entered it. Sákiti was about to catch him. He was right behind him, when, *whoosh*, the old woman closed the trunk and seized Sákiti by the neck. Wiskilióte fell inside the old woman and sat down. He had arrived on all fours, so exhausted was he.

Then Sákiti, caught by the neck, began to move. He called several powerful winds to shake this bottle tree. The winds severed one root, then another, and another. The old woman had five roots, but the winds continued cutting them, at the same time that Sákiti was fighting to free himself. When only one root remained, the one that went deepest, she touched the young man and said: "Grandson, get up! I have only one root left!"

Wiskilióte rose on all fours, grabbed an ax, and cut off Sákiti's head. He killed him. The old woman said: "Well done, grandson! You knew

I had only one root left and that I was about to die. Now you must return to your home!"

Wiskilióte took some of Sákiti's reddish feathers and returned to the south where he lived with his own grandmother. But first he went to see Sákiti's wife. He got there and said: "Old woman, I have killed Sákiti."

"Really?"

"Yes, I killed him!"

"Good. I always wanted to do that, because my husband was very bad to all the people. I did not like him. He even wanted to kill me!"

Then Wiskilióte continued on to where his grandmother lived. From afar he heard the old people lamenting! They had been thinking a lot, knowing how dangerous Sákiti was. Since the young man had been missing for several days, they believed that Sákiti had eaten him. But then he arrived, and while he looked down on them from above, his grandmother said: "Oh! Why do you make us cry, grandson?"

"All is well. Stop crying; I am back."

"Where have you come from?"

"From afar!"

He did not tell her that he had killed Sákiti. Later on, as is the custom, Wiskilióte asked her: "Grandmother, can you examine me for lice?"

He drew near her and she began looking for them. When she was about to come to the place where he had hidden the feathers, he said to her, indicating the other side: "There is a louse!"

But examining his entire body, she eventually found the feathers of Sákiti, which were well known. She said: "Grandson, what is going on here?"

"Grandmother," said Wiskilióte, "I killed Sákiti."

"Really?"

"Really."

"How?"

And he told her.

All the people rejoiced upon learning that Wiskilióte had killed Sákiti. The following day an order was issued: everybody was to go to the place where Sákiti had died, where he had gotten caught.

"Very well, we'll go," everyone said. "Let's go see."

They needed the strongest people to chop firewood, or those with the sharpest axes. Everybody proclaimed the woodpecker to be the best with the ax, the next best being another woodpecker who had the sharpest ax. Then came various other woodpeckers and other, different, birds that were men then. All went to see the spectacle. When they arrived, Sákiti was there with his belly all putrid and swollen. So the people tried to puncture Sákiti with their axes but could not do it. Not even the great woodpecker was able to. While they were trying they lit fires, one next to the other, in order to sleep there, just waiting. They had come to carry Sákiti to their village. But since several days had passed they could not draw Sákiti's blood which initially was red. After the large woodpeckers had all tried, Eskiníni—who is now a piculet with a tiny beak—said: "Maybe I can puncture Sákiti."

The other larger ones said: "What are you, the smallest one, going to do? Your ax does not work. We have fine axes, and we cannot do it."

"I believe I can do something," said Eskiníni.

Another man who now is a bird said: "Let him try!"

Since he was very small they brought him a branch to stand on. Everybody drew close when he began to chop. They realized that if he punctured Sákiti, they were going to be able to enter. Eskiníni did puncture Sákiti with several blows, and the blood came gushing out. Eskiníni wanted to yell like when a tree comes falling down. But the people grabbed him and tossed him far away.

A heavy stream of blood came out of Sákiti! His blood was of different colors. The strongest people went into the stream, stayed there, and were colored. Each one selected the colors he now has; they all came from Sákiti's blood. That was how all the people who are now birds got their colors, for earlier they had none; they were white. Wosiét, the cardinal, immersed himself in the blood and painted himself red; Péto-hoi, the great kiskadee, painted himself yellow; Ele, the parrot, painted himself green; Sóm, the blue magpie, painted himself yellow and blue.

But they had pulled Eskiníni away from the blood, and that is why he does not have enough color. Only at the end did everyone say: "What about the one who opened Sákiti, where is he?"

Well, he was a small man and could not get there. They called him and smeared the sparse red color on him that he has now. Then all the colors had been used up, and only Sákiti's meat remained. They did not invite Eskiníni to partake of the meat, either. Everybody was eating, except he. He had punctured Sákiti for little gain.

Eskiníni used to sing close to these people at dawn. After they had eaten and slept, they waited for it to become day, but no, day did not come. So they said: "What is happening to us? Could it be because we did not share with Eskiníni? Could that be why we are still in the dark?"

At that hour it was always day, but Eskiníni let it be night for about two days. The people became tired of waiting, but day would not come because Eskiníni was angry. So they finally invited him, and then he sang again. "Oh, now it is day!"

Someone said: "You saw that nobody listened to me when I said 'We have to share with him'?"

When the people returned to their homes, they were happy to have done away with that menace (Sákiti). One morning Eskiníni thought about moving. Since he was tiny, he took his small bag and packed it. Everyone said: "Where are you going?"

"I want to move, to look for a new place."

"That is not a good idea. What are you going to do?"

They had seen how he had made Sákiti burst, but just to make fun of him they said to him: "How will you get food?"

"I have an ax."

"Well, try to use it."

Everyone looked at Eskiníni and someone said: "Why make fun of our friend? He is brave!"

Then Eskiníni left. Night came and he had not returned. Wiskilióte said: "He went away because you did not share with him. You should have shared. After all it is because of him that each of us has his own colors. They were not ours; it was he who gave them to us! So we can't say a thing against Eskiníni."

Later they sent a messenger to look for him. He asked him: "How are you, Eskiníni? The people want you to return."

"No, I can't. I am busy. I can't."

The messenger returned to notify the people: "He does not want to come because he is angry."

Eskiníni remained in the open country, never to come back to the others. He went far away and never returned.

Informant: Kasókchi ilánek

Source: Siffredi ms.

Summary

Man-eating eagle brings human victims for his children to eat. Latter play noisily with bones. Irritated by noise, young man goes to kill children. In eagle's absence he deceives them into allowing themselves to be bitten by poisonous snake head, and all die. To help him escape eagle's revenge, latter's wife hides him in oven in form of butterfly. Eventually he flies off, pursued by eagle. Helpful tree (woman) opens trunk to hide him. When eagle tries to cut roots of tree, man kills him with ax. Birds gather by dead eagle's swollen body. Woodpecker punctures his belly and multicolored blood spurts out, giving birds their present colors. Offended by not being included in subsequent celebration, woodpecker leaves, after first delaying return of dawn after night.

Motif content

A2210.	Animal characteristics: change in ancient animal.
A2217.1.	Birds painted their present colors.
A2411.2.	Origin of color of bird.
B16.3.	Devastating birds.
B33.	Man-eating birds.
B34.	Bird of dawn.
B191.6.	Bird as magician.
B200.+.	Birds in human form. (B200. Animals with human traits.)
B720.+.	Eagle with multicolored blood. (B720. Fanciful bodily members of animals.)
B755.	Animal calls the dawn.
D150.	Transformation: man to bird.
D186.1.	Transformation: man to butterfly.
D212.	Transformation: man (woman) to flower.
D631.1.1.	Person changes appearance at will.
D642.2.	Transformation to escape death.
D671.	Transformation flight.
D950.	Magic tree.
D1380.2.	Tree (plant) protects.
D1393.1.	Tree opens and conceals fugitive.
D1556.	Self-opening tree-trunk.
D1610.2.	Speaking tree.
D2142.1.	Wind produced by magic.
D2146.	Magic control of night and day.
D2146.2.2.	Night magically lengthened.
D2178.4.	Animals created by magic.
F679.5.	Skillful hunter.
G353.1.	Cannibal bird as ogre.
G510.4.	Hero overcomes devastating animal.
G512.1.2.	Ogre decapitated.
G530.1.	Help from ogre's wife (mistress).
G630.+.	Bird ogre lives in sky. (G630. Characteristics of ogres.)
G691.+.	Bones of victims in front of ogre's house. (G691. Bodies of victims in front of ogre's house.)
H84.	Tokens of exploits.
H105.	Parts of slain animals as token of slaying.
H1362.	Quest for devastating animals.
J652.	Inattention to warnings.
K649.1.	Confederate hides fugitive.
K800.	Killing or maiming by deception.
K825.+.	Victim persuaded to hold out his tongue: bit by snake. (K825. Victim persuaded to hold out his tongue: cut off.)
K910.	Murder by strategy.
K930.	Treacherous murder of enemy's children or charges.

K1013.	False beauty-doctor.
K1892.	Deception by hiding.
Q280.	Unkindness punished.
Q552.20.1.	Miraculous darkness as punishment.
R13.3.	Person carried off by bird.
R311.	Tree refuge.

101. Killing Sákiti, the Man-Eating Celestial Eagle: The Origin of the Color of Birds

Long ago Sákiti, the harpy eagle, came down to earth. But he was not like eagles from here. This one came from heaven. What a bird—as large as an ostrich! He does not live on this earth; he always stays in the heavens.

Around noon there was a woman sitting outside her hut and . . . *bang!* He came shooting down like an arrow! He was accompanied by something like clouds, obscuring the sun. Seizing the woman with those huge fingernails of his, he carried her up above. In this manner he ate all the women; he would take them by night and by day. Even if they were sleeping inside their huts, he would still pull them outside. He is an animal (enormous and strong).[28] That was how every day a woman disappeared, and no one knew who did it or what was happening. The people said: "Who could be finishing off all the women? Who could it be that does not leave tracks?"

Since they did not know, they called Ahóusa who is wise and told him what was going on. He said to them: "I know what is happening. The one who is carrying off the women comes from above; that is why you did not see him or his tracks. I am going to take care of it."

Sákiti was living above, but on this earth he had four small children whom he provided with food. Ahóusa painted stripes on his cheeks by using his four fingers which he had rubbed in charcoal and went to where Sákiti's children were playing. When they saw him they wanted him to paint them like him, but Ahóusa told them that to do this they had to stick out their tongues. When they obeyed he simply cut off their tongues and killed them.

---

[28]Of the six versions presented, this is the only one which comes from a woman, and which claims that Sákiti confined his victims to women. Conversely, those narrated by male informants describe the victims as men who were seized without warning while they were watching the burrow of a tuco-tuco, motionless and with bows drawn, ready to shoot as the animal emerged.

When Sákiti learned about this he went to ask the people: "Who killed all my children?"

"I do not know."

He asked Ahóusa, the most clever of all: "Are you Ahóusa?"

"No," said Ahóusa, who was painted, but he ran away just the same. He put himself in the middle of beautiful butterflies of all colors that looked like flowers. Sákiti was catching butterflies, asking them: "Is this it? No, it is not."

Then the butterflies flew away and Ahóusa escaped too. But in the end Sákiti could see him and went like a bullet toward Ahóusa, who had climbed a tree. Since he is quick he was able to dodge the attack. Sákiti got his head caught in the tree and died.

Now Ahóusa called all the birds who in those days were men. All the woodpeckers came to try to open Sákiti's belly with their beaks, but none could do it except Eskiníni, the piculet, who perforated it with his tiny beak. The blood of Sákiti gushed forth like a stream. All the birds that were white approached, and received the colors we see today. But they grabbed Eskiníni by the foot and tossed him aside. They wanted to enter the stream. It was already night, and it continued being night. Since the dawn did not come, they were afraid. Then they invited Eskiníni to take some of Sákiti's blood for himself. He felt sorry for them and sang until finally everything lit up; it dawned again.

Informant: Kíki

Source: Siffredi ms.

Summary

Cannibal bird (Sákiti) abducts and eats women. Hawk in turn kills Sákiti's children. Trying to take revenge, Sákiti dies. Small bird punctures his stomach, splattering blood all over nearby birds who thereby receive their present-day colors.

Motif content

A2210.	Animal characteristics: change in ancient animal.
A2217.1.	Birds painted their present colors.
A2411.2.	Origin of color of bird.
B16.3.	Devastating birds.
B33.	Man-eating birds.
B34.	Bird of dawn.
B191.6.	Bird as magician.
B200. +.	Birds in human form. (B200. Animals with human traits.)
B455.4.	Helpful hawk.
B755.	Animal calls the dawn.

B872.   Giant birds.
D1810.   Magic knowledge.
D2146.   Magic control of night and day.
D2146.2.2.   Night magically lengthened.
G353.1.   Cannibal bird as ogre.
G510.4.   Hero overcomes devastating animal.
G512.   Ogre killed.
G630.+.   Bird ogre lives in sky. (G630. Characteristics of ogres.)
H1362.   Quest for devastating animals.
J1118.   Clever bird.
K800.   Killing or maiming by deception.
K825.   Victim persuaded to hold out his tongue: cut off.
K910.   Murder by strategy.
K930.   Treacherous murder of enemy's children or charges.
K1013.   False beauty-doctor.
Q280.   Unkindness punished.
Q552.20.1.   Miraculous darkness as punishment.
R13.3.   Person carried off by bird.
R311.   Tree refuge.

102. Confrontation with Sákiti

There was a man hunting tuco-tucos with his arrows. Since these creatures are in their burrows, the man had to be like a soldier on guard. He had to watch the cave without moving, with his arrows ready, and once they came out, since they were wild, shoot them quickly. He had to wait about an hour, and during this time Sákiti, the harpy eagle, came, the largest eagle there is. The man could not look behind him, so Sákiti grabbed him without warning and flew away with him.

That was why every day a tuco-tuco hunter was lost. Those who were skillful were disappearing, but no one knew who did it or what was happening. Finally a man saw him: "I do not know what animal it could be that is descending over there. It came down and flew away with someone. Could that be why we are losing people? Who could it be? Maybe he eats those he takes away." They lost more men every day, and it was Sákiti who was killing them.

There was a shaman who knew how to become an eagle. When Sákiti grabbed another hunter, the shaman called his own Sákiti so he might enter him. He became the same as the eagle.

When Sákiti caught another man, the shaman who had become an eagle flew after him. He was spying on Sákiti to see where he was taking the man to eat him. Upon arriving, the shaman became a man

again. There was Sákiti, nibbling at the one he had seized. He was
eating him! He did not know the shaman had come, and he continued
nibbling. The shaman took from his side a large club and with all his
might hit him in the back of the neck, killing Sákiti.

Informant: Axués pa

Source: Siffredi ms.

Motif content

B16.3.	Devastating birds.
B33.	Man-eating birds.
D152.2.	Transformation: man to eagle.
D651.1.	Transformation to kill enemy.
G353.1.	Cannibal bird as ogre.
G510.4.	Hero overcomes devastating animal.
G512.8.1.	Ogre killed by striking with club.
H1362.	Quest for devastating animals.
R13.3.	Person carried off by bird.

103. Confrontation with Sákiti

Sákiti, the harpy eagle, would come from the sky and kill people.
When he came for people, he approached like a vulture, very quickly.
He would dive like a bullet! Then he would seize the men by the nape
of their necks and carry them up there. He was strong!

The people who remained said: "Someone is missing! Where could
he be? Who could it be who is killing the people? Could it be an animal?
And if so, which one?"

Then they ordered an old man, who was a shaman, to go watch. The
old shaman began to chant, looking for who it was, and he began to
fly in the air.

The people thought the killer was a person on earth, but after having
sung, the shaman told them: "I believe an animal has come from above
and has killed all the people. That is why you did not know, that is
why you did not see anything—no trace of him—because he comes from
above! When he sees a man, he hurls himself downward, grabs him by
the neck and carries him up as food. Now I know who it is! He is like a
sparrow hawk, only very large. He has huge claws! It is Sákiti! I fought
with him up there and think that he will not return again. The danger
is over!"

The people were more at ease. Many had died, and had it not been for the shaman, Sákiti would have finished them off.

Informant: José Romero

Source: Siffredi ms.

Motif content

B16.3.	Devastating birds.
B33.	Man-eating birds.
D1781.+.	Knowledge from singing. (D1781. Magic results from singing.)
D1810.	Magic knowledge.
D2135.0.3.	Magic ability to fly.
G353.1.	Cannibal bird as ogre.
G510.4.	Hero overcomes devastating animal.
H1362.	Quest for devastating animals.
N845.	Magician as helper.
R13.3.	Person carried off by bird.

104. Confrontation with Kiliéni Thlásini

Long ago the black-and-chestnut eagle, Kiliéni Thlásini ("cry of the deer"), was bigger than the ostrich and had large claws. He would come down at night, around twelve o'clock, but since the people were asleep they would not hear anything. He seized someone with his talons and flew off with him to his place where he ate him. He let the bones of those he had eaten pile up there. Once he had finished the people of one village, he would look for another. In this fashion he was gradually eating all the people on the earth.

Later, the people of a certain village said: "There is a huge kind of bird! What could it be? It always eats at night, and each time it carries a person away."

They gave warning of this in another place where there were many old shamans, in order to find out what was happening in the settlement where the people were dying. A shaman said: "Do not get careless tonight! We are going to see what's going on."

All the neighbors were anxious to know what the shaman was saying in order to know what was happening. They still did not know whether it was a wild animal, a bird, or a man. They were soon going to find out.

Around midnight, the old shaman lay down on his back waiting. Suddenly there came a strong wind, like when an airplane lands with spread wings. The old man said: "It must be this!"

It seems that the animal (Kiliéni Thlásini) knew how to speak. He said: "The shamans do not know me! I eat everyone! I do not spare a single man. I eat every one of them when I come down."

The old man was listening to him. The bird had to know that he was a shaman! It did not carry him off. He was watching it! Then he warned the other shamans and also called the neighbors, to wake them up: "Get up, get up, the one who eats us has arrived already."

Everyone got up to fight. The old man said: "If I were not a shaman and as clever a man as Ahóusa, I would kill him myself."

Then the old man fought the eagle, and since many were helping him, and since the bird was all alone, they finally knocked him down. Fifteen men took hold of him and pinned him to the ground: five held him by one foot, five by the other, and five by the neck. Fifteen men on their hands and knees could barely hold the eagle to the ground! They began to hit him and killed him.

When they finished killing the eagle, they carried him away to be burned, and then they burned him again, because that is the rule in such cases, ever since Ahóusa long ago ordained it so. Even today, if there is danger, if there is a bad animal, we won't bury it because it would be dangerous for us. It might come out again! We must burn it so it will not return.

Informant: Axués pa

Source: Siffredi ms.

Summary

People enlist help of shaman to catch man-eating eagle. After killing bird they burn it.

Motif content

A522.2.3.	Hawk as culture hero.
B16.3.	Devastating birds.
B33.	Man-eating birds.
B211.3.	Speaking bird.
B872.	Giant birds.
E431.13.	Corpse burned to prevent return.
F1084.	Furious battle.
G346.	Devastating monster.
G353.1.	Cannibal bird as ogre.
G512.8.	Ogre killed by striking.
G691.+.	Bones of victims in front of ogre's house. (G691. Bodies of victims in front of ogre's house.)

J580.	Wisdom of caution.
J670.	Forethought in defenses against others.
N845.	Magician as helper.
R13.3.	Person carried off by bird.

105. The Origin of Snakes

There once was a woman who was menstruating. She saw a snakeskin and placed it in her vagina. Soon she conceived. Her stomach grew very large! A young man who slept with her died because the snakes bit him. Then she had sex with another boy, and he died as well. Almost all of them died. Then a man went to fetch Joisá (the hawk). Some three hundred meters from the house the man called: "We are being killed off."

The hawk could not hear him clearly and replied: "What is happening? Who is killing the boys? Is it the Mataco? The Chulupi, the measles, or jaguars?" So he got ready, combed his hair, and went to see the woman. He carried a gourd with him. He came to a spot where there was a lambskin. "I shall go to the one who is killing off the young men," he said. Departing, he suggested: "Let us sing." The boys began to congregate and Joisá started to chant. Inside the gourd was a man's tooth, and with it he made the gourd rattle. Joisá said: "Wait, leave me alone for a while. I am going to sleep."

He went to bed with the killer woman. He had cut a piece from a palo verde tree, made a hole in it, and stuck a finger inside. He tied the small piece of wood to his hand. When he touched the woman's legs, the snakes bit the wood. She tried to embrace him, but failed because her stomach was so big. Joisá went outside with this woman who had killed the others. He said to the boys: "Make me a fire." The boys started to sweep under a tree. But Joisá stopped there, saying: "No, I had better go far away. There was a beautiful forest. I shall take her there to kill her." The other animals asked: "When are you going to take her there? We shall set fire to the brush." Joisá answered: "I'll choose the one who cries the most beautifully." He named all the animals, the sparrow hawk, everyone.

Joisá departed, saying: "I think I shall go look for honey."

"Let us go," said the woman.

Joisá was taking her to the forest. He took her to the middle of the brush. As there was a lot of dry grass, it began to burn.

"What do I have on my head?" asked Joisá. "Delouse me."

He sat down on the ground with his elbows on his knees and began to look at the woman from below. Between the woman's legs there appeared several big snakes. The woman looked up. "Why is there smoke here?" she asked.

"That is just my friends hunting for food," replied Joisá.

But the fire was coming closer. It was very near. Joisá did not budge. Only when the fire was right there did he begin to worry, saying: "The fire is definitely here. I am fleeing right away."

"Wait for me," the woman said." I am taking out my babies."

She pulled out a big rattlesnake and hurled it at Joisá, but the latter threw himself to the ground. The fire was approaching. Joisá spoke to it: "Fire, fire, go out, go out, go out."

The fire abated slightly. He then jumped to the other side and was now beside the *nuca*. All the animals approached the pampas and surrounded him. Joisá was waiting. Soon he heard the woman. One of her eyes had burst from the fire. "Ah! Now she will go back and kill the rest of the men," said Joisá. When the fire subsided they could see the snakes coming out of the woman and being burned. Some snakes escaped into the water and others stayed on land. These are the ones that survived. When the woman burst, the snakes came out.

Informant: Sentawó

Source: Mashnshnek 1972, pp. 130–131.

Summary

After woman inserts snakeskin into her vagina, snakes start to grow inside her. They bite and kill every man trying to have intercourse with her. People ask Hawk for help. He lures her into forest where she is burned to death in fire started by people. Snakes emerge from her stomach. (Origin of snakes.)

Motif content

A2145.	Creation of snake (serpent).
B455.4.	Helpful hawk.
B524.2.	Animals overcome man's adversary by strategy.
D2158.	Magic control of fires.
J580.	Wisdom of caution.
J670.	Forethought in defenses against others.
J1118.	Clever bird.
K910.	Murder by strategy.
K955.	Murder by burning.
T173.	Murderous bride.
T182.	Death from intercourse.
T510.	Miraculous conception.
T532.1.+.	Conception from snakeskin in vagina. (T532.1. Conception from contact with magic object.)
T554.7.	Woman gives birth to a snake.

106. Killing the Woman Impregnated by a Snakeskin: The Origin of the Vampire and of Snakes

Long ago Ehéie, the vampire, was a pretty girl. Once she went out in the rain although then, as now, it was customary for menstruating women to stay indoors. But Ehéie went out anyway, not realizing that right there a snake had shed its skin. The skin entered her vagina and impregnated her. Then many snakes grew in her womb, not just harmless ones but some with poison. The mixture of menstrual blood with that skin produced poison.

Ehéie was very fat, nice, and beautiful. All the men liked her and wanted to have intercourse with her, but because she had snakes inside, whenever someone slept with her the snakes promptly bit his penis. Getting up she would ask the man: "What is the matter with you?"

But he remained lying there, and she covered him. In the morning her brothers-in-law would ask her: "Where is your husband?"

"In the house, still asleep."

But when they went to wake him up, they saw that he was dead.

"What is wrong, Ehéie? What have you done? It seems you have killed him."

"No, I wanted to wake him up, too, but I don't know what is the matter with him."

Every man who went to have intercourse with her lasted only for one night. In the morning the people found him dead. The following day the man's brother had to have relations with her, for she was the wife of his dead brother. As was customary an old man would say: "It is better if the widow does not go to another village; we had better give her to another man."

Of course all the young men liked Ehéie, for she was very nice, nicer than the other women. So they kept going to her. But it was always the same. Every single man who had intercourse with her died, until there were many dead, and nobody knew what was the matter with her. At dawn when they asked her: "What have you done to your husband?" she would answer: "Nothing; he was sleeping, that is all. I have not done anything."

Then the people of the village remembered Ahóusa, and they said to someone: "Why don't you inform him so that he will investigate what is wrong with this woman?"

The man told Ahóusa who said to him: "Let us see if I can. I shall go at once. What is the matter?"

"I do not know, but whenever a man wants to possess her something stings his penis."

"Aha, I do not know what it is, but I shall kill it," said Ahóusa.

Then, as is customary when a man wishes to have sex with a woman, Ahóusa went to see her, and he said: "I came because I would like you to be my wife."

"All right."

She was pleased! Ahóusa had heard what her problem was, but he still had not discovered what caused it. In the evening he prepared a piece of hollow reed and put it over his penis. As he lay down next to Ehéie he felt some things moving in her stomach and thought: "What can it be?"

He began to have intercourse with her, but no sooner had he touched her than he felt a hard blow, something biting the reed. Only then did he realize that it was snakes: "Aha, no wonder all those young men died having relations with her! So that was the danger!"

Ehéie stayed indoors. She never went out, for she was a widow, and those who have recently become widows must not go out. Every night that a husband died she grew more ashamed.

Ahóusa gave a lot of thought to getting rid of that danger. He went from house to house to tell the young men: "I am going to take Ehéie to that little lagoon that is surrounded by grass. When the sun is high you must set fire to the grass, for at that time there blows a strong north wind."

"I shall burn the grass," said one.

"No, I prefer the one who can whistle the best. You, Miyóki (hawk), who can whistle very loudly, must whistle when you have burned the grass all around the lagoon."

"All right, I shall whistle."

Ahóusa went back to his wife: "Why do we not go over to that lagoon and bathe?"

But the widow told him that she did not feel like it. "It does not look good if a married man is not accompanied by his wife," he insisted.

Finally Ahóusa persuaded her, and they left. When they got to the lagoon he asked her to delouse him. He put his head on her lap, and she unsuspectingly began to hunt for lice.

Meanwhile the men were already around the lagoon, and Miyóki had started to burn the grass. Suddenly Ehéie saw smoke and was frightened: "Look, Ahóusa, maybe they are burning the area we are in right now?"

"Don't worry, it is probably the children; they always come here to look for frogs."

She continued to delouse him, but when she looked up again she saw a large blazing fire: "Look, Ahóusa, it is burning all around us."

"Don't worry, I know where they are burning. It is somewhere else." Ehéie fell silent.

Suddenly Miyóki whistled loudly, and Ahóusa looked around to see where he could escape. He had very long hair which he wore tied back with a string. He said to Fire (Eti): "Slow down a little and let me through."

He ran quickly and immediately afterward it blazed up again, but it had already allowed him to pass through. The flames caught part of his hair, and to this day Ahóusa has this mark: the feathers on the back of his neck are a bit short.

The fire kept growing in intensity. When it reached Ehéie she began to scream and shout, and the snakes she had inside were anxious as they heard her shouting: "*Aum, áum!*"

When she was all burned her stomach exploded, and the snakes that emerged went into the lagoon to hide, saving themselves there, while others burned. The woman was burned to death. When the fire had died down and there was only smoke and ashes Ahóusa came back and stirred the ashes with a stick. He saw a small worm moving about. "Now I am going to be Ehéie, a real vampire bat. I am going to be evil. At night I shall bite people and suck their blood."

Ahóusa looked into the lagoon and saw a large number of snakes of different colors and types. He said: "This one I am going to call *ápa* (*yarará, Bothrops gen.*);[29] this one I shall call *ahláta* (*Boa constrictor*); and this one I shall call *topéna* (rattlesnake, *Crotalus durissus*)."

He named all the snakes that came from Ehéie's stomach, and they are the ones we see today: water snakes, land snakes, tree snakes.

First of all Ahóusa called Apa and said to him: "Let us see, show me your mouth."

"Why?"

"You have to show me so I can see if you have teeth."

"No, I do not."

And he hid them, for he knows how to do that. When Ahóusa touched him he did not have any. Then he went straight to Topéna, asking him whether he had teeth. "But I do not have any," said the latter. He, too, had hidden them. That is why these snakes are poisonous, because Ahóusa did not discover their teeth. Then he went to the other snakes, the ones that are not poisonous, like Ahláta, and asked them: "Let me see, show me your mouth."

---

[29] A very poisonous Argentine viper [translator's note].

They did so, and he pulled out all their teeth. They grew out again, but because of what Ahóusa had done they did not have poison.

Informant: Kasókchi ilánek

Source: Siffredi ms.

Summary

Ignoring tabu, menstruating girl goes out during rain and is impregnated by snakeskin. Snakes grow in her stomach, killing every man she has intercourse with by biting his penis. Finally people ask help of Ahóusa, who marries her. After discovering snakes he lures her into firetrap, and she burns to death. Escaping snakes take refuge in lagoon. Some have their teeth extracted by Ahóusa, but those who do not become today's poisonous snakes.

Motif content

A1710.	Creation of animals through transformation.
A1895.	Creation of bat.
A2145.	Creation of snake (serpent).
A2210.	Animal characteristics: change in ancient animal.
A2218.	Animal characteristics from burning or singeing.
A2313.+.	Why hawk's neck feathers are short. (A2313. Origin of bird's feathers.)
A2531.+.	Why some snakes are harmless. (A2531. Why animal is harmless.)
A2532.1.	Why snakes are venomous.
A2571.+.	How snakes received their names. (A2571. How animals received their names.)
B455.4.	Helpful hawk.
B524.2.	Animals overcome man's adversary by strategy.
C141.	Tabu: going forth during menses.
C898.+.	Tabu: widow not to go outside. (C898. Tabus concerned with mourning.)
D100.+.	Transformation: woman to bat. (D100. Transformation: man to animal.)
D2158.	Magic control of fires.
F575.1.	Remarkably beautiful woman.
J580.	Wisdom of caution.
J670.	Forethought in defenses against others.
J1118.	Clever bird.
K910.	Murder by strategy.
K955.	Murder by burning.
P681.	Mourning customs.
T173.	Murderous bride.
T182.	Death from intercourse.

T510.	Miraculous conception.
T532.1.+.	Conception from snakeskin in vagina. (T532.1. Conception from contact with magic object.)
T554.7.	Woman gives birth to a snake.

107. Killing the Man-Eating Water Snake: The Discovery of Aquatic Animals, and the Origin of the Drying Up of Lakes

Long ago there was a young man who lived by a lagoon. The water in the lagoon was never exhausted, like a great watercourse.[30] Since it was very hot, the young man said: "Mother, I want to take a swim."

"All right, go ahead."

He went to swim. Hardly had he gotten into the water when a giant snake (*Eunectes notaeus?*) swallowed him whole. What an animal!

After a long time while his mother and other relatives were waiting for him, they wondered: "What time will he get back from swimming?"

"I do not know. You could go to find out. Maybe something has happened to him, for that lagoon is very dangerous. A lot of snakes live there!"

The women went to look and did not find anything . . . nothing.

At night, a shaman in the village began to watch the lagoon, going there in spirit with his soul image. He had a vision which revealed to him that a large snake living in the lagoon had swallowed the young man. In the morning he told the mother and the relatives of the boy. They began to cry, as is the custom when we lose someone.

One of them, who was the older brother of the one who had disappeared, was not crying. He was planning: "What am I going to do? How will I get even?"

At noon he began to sharpen his knife until very late. Afterward he said: "All right, I am going to take a swim." He went away very quietly. A woman saw that he had gone off with a knife. Later they also missed him. He did not return. This young man, arriving at the lagoon, had done the same as his younger brother, and the same thing happened to him. He went swimming, and immediately they swallowed him.

---

[30]These particular lagoons (*madrejones*) are zones of water constantly supplied with an abundance of sediment produced by the meandering of the Río Pilcomayo.

Inside the snake the young man was making himself at home. First he went to stand with his head next to the tail, and then he turned around toward where he had entered. He searched for the heart, and when he found it he cut it and said: "It seems that I have killed this one!"

When they missed the young man because he had not returned, the shaman sent another young man to find out if someone had seen him. He went around asking, and a woman who had seen him said: "He went over there with his knife!"

"Oh, he has to take revenge! We must go and see!"

Everyone went to the lagoon, and the moment the huge snake died all the water dried up. The lagoon dried up! He remained there. What an animal!

When the young man who had cut the heart felt that the snake had stopped moving in all directions and was lying very still, he slit the belly and went out with his brother. Then they cut off a piece of meat, built a fire, roasted it, and tasted it. They liked it, and so everyone ate. It was delicious, pure fat!

When the lagoon was dry they found different water inhabitants. At that time it was discovered that there are different snakes like *ithlá* and *itiúlai tos* (black snake) that live in the waters, of different sizes, some with colors and others without, and also that alligators and caimans exist.

Informant: Aió

Source: Siffredi ms.

Summary

Man-eating snake living in lagoon devours two brothers. One of them kills snake from within, and both emerge. Lagoon dries up, revealing water animals.

Motif content

B16.5.1.2.	Devastating (man-eating) sea-monster (serpent).
B875.1.	Giant serpent.
D1810.8.1.	Truth given in vision.
D2151.0.2.	Waters made to dry up.
E721.	Soul journeys from the body.
F911.	Person (animal) swallowed without killing.
F911.7.	Serpent swallows man.
F912.2.	Victim kills swallower from within by cutting.
G354.1.	Snake as ogre.
H1385.8.	Quest for lost brother(s).

K952.	Animal (monster) killed from within.
R155.2.	Elder brother rescues younger.
V514.	Non-religious visions.

108. Killing the Mother of the Man-Eating Water Snakes and the Mother of the Alligators: Origin of the Drying Up of Lakes and of Dangerous Storms

There was a shaman who one day said to his younger brother: "Let us go look for parrot chicks!"

They went and found a large palo santo tree. There were the parrot nests.

The older brother said to the boy: "Go up there. Climb up! Go take the nests!"

"No, it is better that you go up since you are bigger."

So he climbed up and began to take the nests, and the young birds were falling out. When he had taken all the nests in the palo santo, a little parrot came out and flew into a swamplike lagoon that was nearby. The boy went to catch it while it was flying over the water, going into the lagoon up to his waist without being able to reach it. He started sinking deeper and deeper, slipping under the water which was swallowing him more each minute, until he vanished completely; the mud was running over him.

The older brother said to him: "Do not go there!"

Esiníni (little woodpecker, *Picummus* sp.) began to cry. He sang: "Do not go there, son!"

But he went into the water anyway and just disappeared there. When the other brother got down from the tree he gathered up all the parrot chicks and put them in the sack. He had a bunch! When he got home he said to his mother: "Boil the little parrots quickly! We are going to eat!"

They plucked them and put them on to boil. The mother waited a long time, then asked: "What has become of my son?"

"I do not know. He was looking for an arrow; it seems he got lost."

He did not tell her anything about the mud. Hurriedly he said: "That is it; now they are cooked!"

And he poked the fire so the little parrots would boil faster. She continued asking about the son: "What has happened to him?"

"Maybe he has not found the arrow."

He did not want to tell her. He grabbed a knife that was well sharpened: "Well, I am going to try out my knife to see if it is good and sharp."

He grabbed a thick branch and cut it in half: "Now I am satisfied; it is sharp!"

"It is done now. I am going to take it off," said the mother.

"All right, take it off. I am anxious to find my brother!"

When she finished taking out the parrots she divided them up among all the people who were there. Right after they finished eating the soup he wanted to tell them, but he did not have the courage.

Later he said: "I am going to tell what happened. My brother is dead. He is under the mud, so I am going to look for him. That is why I am sharpening my knife!"

His mother did not want him to go: "I also want to die next to my son!" She cried and cried, insisting that he must not go. But he went anyway to look for his brother. When he arrived at the spot where his brother had disappeared, he sat down at the side of the lagoon and began to think. It sounded as if there were frogs there. All the insects around there were singing, and Pétexuai, the great kiskadee, had begun to sing.

He said: "Go ahead and sing! I also want to make a home here!"

Meanwhile he had begun to slip into the mud. He went a ways and stopped. Pétexuai continued singing. Suddenly the boy began to sink more and more, just like the one who had gone in before. He was going to where his brother had disappeared, inside the lagoon, to look for him. Suddenly a big snake swallowed him, and he asked it: "Where did my brother go?"

"He went over there."

He escaped from inside the snake, and another came and swallowed him.

He asked it: "Where did my brother go?"

"He went over there."

In this way he went along asking the snakes that were in the water, the water inhabitants. He went along tracking down his brother to where they had taken him. He would enter one, would ask where his brother had gone, and would leave it and enter another one.

There were about five snakes still ahead of him. He went in, asked, and came out again. Now there were four snakes, and when the next swallowed him, he asked it: "Where has my brother gone?"

But this snake did not want to answer him: "I do not know. I did not see him."

"Tell me! If you do not, I shall kill you!"

He took out his knife, and then it told him: "He went over there. He passed that way."

He came out, went, and found another that swallowed him. He asked it: "Where did my brother go?"

"I do not know, I did not see him."

"How could you not help seeing him when his tracks pass right by here!"

"I do not know."

"Tell me! If you do not, I shall kill you!"

He took out the knife and showed it. Then it became afraid, and to avoid being killed it told him. Up ahead another snake swallowed him. He searched for his brother inside and did not find him: "Tell me where my brother went!"

"I do not know."

"How is it that you do not know? What do I have here? It is a knife, is it not?"

Then it only said to him: "Your brother is up ahead."

He was where the Mother of Snakes was living. They said it was a huge snake, as big as a house! It swallowed the man, who remained standing inside it. That is how big it was. It was there that he found the boy, but he was already dead: "Here is where my brother has been!"

He began to walk about inside the Mother of Snakes, looking for its heart. When he felt something beating, he grabbed it, took out his knife, and cut next to the heart. Immediately the water moved; it was like a whirlpool. The Mother of Snakes died, and the lagoon began to dry up.

"How do I get out of here?" he said. "I had better not go out through the mouth."

He began to cut through its middle, where its ribs were, until he could get out. When he halted on top of the snake, he saw that the water had disappeared; the lagoon was dry. He lifted his brother and pulled him out, put him on the steep shore, and touched his head with his hand. Although he barely touched him, already his hair started to come out. He touched him firmly, gripping his head well so that his hair would settle. Then he squeezed his whole body which had become very soft, and finally he stepped on him. The boy got up: "Oh! I was sleeping!"

"No, you were not sleeping. The big snakes swallowed you!"

The snakes appeared, all dried up. "I fixed you up a little. I squeezed your whole body and your head. Are you all right, brother?"

"Yes, now I am all right."

The older brother had begun to look for the Mother of Snakes and said: "Will it not be nice to eat it? I am going to cut off a little piece."

He went to cut off a piece, put it in his sack, and said: "What could my old mother be doing? I think she must be hoarse from crying so much. Let us go quickly!"

They set off for home, and when the people saw them from afar, they said to the mother: "Be quiet, old woman, stop crying! Is that not your son?"

When they arrived she became very happy. No sooner had they sat down than her older son asked her: "Do you want me to show you the meat I brought?"

He took it out and it was pure fat. He began to roast it, and when it was done he tasted it: "Great! Let us call everybody!"

Everybody came, and when they finished eating they asked him: "Where did you get this wonderful meat?"

"If you want, we shall bring more."

Immediately every woman grabbed her sack. Everyone went, and they began to cut until each one had filled her sack with the meat of the Mother of Snakes. There were many women, and still there was more than enough meat.

There were two girls who had said they were not going to eat that meat, but they had eaten it. In the afternoon they passed gas, gas that burned as if it was lightning. "Why did you say you were not eating? Why are you eating on the sly?" said their parents.

When the meat was all gone, the people went out to look for more since they still liked it, but they did not find any. They continued on until they came to a large tree next to a swamplike lagoon. Someone said: "There is a large snake!"

They made a fire and began to dig where it was dry, next to the tree. When they reached the water they took some burning pieces of wood and put them inside the hole to heat up the water and kill the creature. But it was not a snake; it was the Mother of Caimans, a large caiman. They continued to put in more and more burning pieces of wood until there was no more fire. Then the water began to surge forward. The men did not move back. They did not think the water was going to do anything to them, but they began to sink and sink.

Then Ixñéni, the plumbeous ibis, came and perched inside the lagoon. Suddenly a strong wind came up and the men put out their hands to intercept it. It stopped a little, but then it came from the other side and pushed them toward the hole out of which water was coming, and they all fell inside. Everyone died, remaining in the swamplike lagoon.[31]

Informant: Centawó

Source: Cordeu ms.

Summary

Ignoring shaman brother's warning, man enters lagoon where he disappears. When shaman goes to lagoon to look for him he meets several snakes which all swallow him. Escaping from each he follows their directions in search of brother. Finally he finds dead brother in stomach of giant Mother of Snakes. He kills snake and emerges with brother, whom he revives. Lagoon magically dries up. People eat dead snake's meat with relish. Looking for more they try to catch Mother of Caimans, but instead all drown in lagoon.

Motif content

B16.5.1.2.	Devastating (man-eating) sea-monster (serpent).
B143.1.	Bird gives warning.
B244.+.	Mother of caimans. (B244. King of reptiles.)
B244.1.1.	Queen of watersnakes.
B461.1.	Helpful woodpecker.
B491.1.	Helpful serpent.
B563.	Animals direct man on journey.
B875.1.	Giant serpent.
D906.	Magic wind.
D921.	Magic lake (pond).
D2151.0.2.	Waters made to dry up.
F911.	Person (animal) swallowed without killing.
F911.7.	Serpent swallows man.
F912.2.	Victim kills swallower from within by cutting.
F921.	Swallowed person becomes bald.
F921.1.+.	Swallowed person becomes soft. (F921.1. Swallowed person becomes boneless.)
F1041.+.	Burning intestinal wind. (F1041. Extraordinary physical reactions of persons.)
G354.1.	Snake as ogre.
H1385.8.	Quest for lost brother(s).
J613.	Wise fear of the weak for the strong.
J652.	Inattention to warnings.
K952.	Animal (monster) killed from within.

[31]The Chorote attribute to caimans and alligators the ability to unleash dangerous storms, and to cause the lagoon in which they have been captured to dry up. For this reason they go after these animals with great caution.

| Q552.19. | Miraculous drowning as punishment. |
| R155.2. | Elder brother rescues younger. |

109. The Man Who Was Swallowed by the Big Snake

There was an old woman who had choked on a bone in a fish which her son-in-law had brought her. Then she said to him: "I would like to eat something that does not have bones." Her son-in-law thought: "I wonder what she wants." He went to a large water hole where there was a giant snake, and climbed up in a tree that stood in the middle of the water. The water began to move, waves formed, and the big snake appeared and swallowed him whole.

The boy had a knife with him, and when he was inside the animal he began to search for its heart to cut it in two. Seeing something move he said: "That is it!" He cut it, and the snake died. At once all the water dried up. Taking the opportunity he crawled out. Outside he saw a lot of snakes and started to kill them. Afterward he went to his mother-in-law and said to her: "Could this be what you wanted to eat? It is nice!" After cutting the meat into many pieces he melted it, and everyone started to eat.

There were many girls there. One of them broke wind, and it burned. "Who among you did not eat of the snake?" asked the young man. "I did not," replied the girls. In the evening one girl again broke wind, and it burned. "Did you see that they did not eat the snake?" repeated the boy.

The old woman was talking. She said: "I want something else. I want a red head." "I wonder what that could be?" said the boy to himself. He took out a fish for her to eat, but the old woman said: "No, I want the red head." "I think she wants to have sex," he thought, and he had intercourse with her. Then his mother-in-law said: "Now I ate the red head; that is what I wanted. Let us go home."

Informant: Cepillo

Source: Verna ms.

Motif content

B16.5.1.2.	Devastating (man-eating) sea-monster (serpent).
B875.1.	Giant serpent.
F911.	Person (animal) swallowed without killing.

F911.7.	Serpent swallows man.
F912.2.	Victim kills swallower from within by cutting.
F1041.+.	Burning intestinal wind. (F1041. Extraordinary physical reactions of persons.)
G354.1.	Snake as ogre.
H580.	Enigmatic statements.
K952.	Animal (monster) killed from within.
T417.1.	Mother-in-law seduces son-in-law.

110. The Indian Swallowed by a Snake

In a lake dwelled a snake that was as thick as the distance between the fingertips of two outstretched arms. It devoured a Chorote, but the latter killed the snake by stabbing it in the heart and then found his way out of the snake's body. From the heat in the snake's stomach the Chorote turned completely red and lost all the hair on his head. When he got home his wife did not recognize him. He told her the story of how he had been devoured by the snake.

Source: Nordenskiöld 1926, p. 88.

Motif content

B16.5.1.2.	Devastating (man-eating) sea-monster (serpent).
B875.1.	Giant serpent.
D57.	Change in person's color.
D682.4.	Partial transformation— color changed.
F527.1.	Red person.
F911.	Person (animal) swallowed without killing.
F911.7.	Serpent swallows man.
F912.2.	Victim kills swallower from within by cutting.
F921.	Swallowed person becomes bald.
F1082.	Person changes color.
G354.1.	Snake as ogre.
K952.	Animal (monster) killed from within.

111. The Man-Eating Wasps

Two wasps were walking through the village. Suddenly they saw a little boy, and they seized him, cut him in half, and roasted him. When they ate him and realized how tasty he was they wanted to kill all the people.

Two men came across these man-eaters. They shot them but the wasps did not die until one man shot one of them in the foot. The animals fled into the bush. Quickly the men set off in pursuit. The wasps entered a hole, and after a while a mass of wasps emerged. One of the men grabbed one and burned it. Immediately all the other wasps came to look at the one that was burned, surrounding it. Then they surrounded the man. More and more wasps came, crowding together, and from those wasps a man was made.

Informant: Esteban Mariano

Source: Verna ms.

Motif content

B16.6.+.	Devastating wasp. (B16.6. Devastating insects.)
D380.+.	Transformation: wasp to person. (D380. Transformation: insect to person.)
G350.+.	Wasp as ogre. (G350. Animal ogres.)

112. The Headhunter

There was a Chorote man who began looking for people from different tribes. Finding some Mataco he killed them all, cut off their heads, and put them in his net bag. He carried the bag with all the heads of the Mataco inside. When he arrived home he removed the skin from the heads and placed them on the embers. From inside each head a liquid trickled out which he drank. After drinking it he grew very strong, increasingly so every time he drank. Nobody could do anything against him. That is why he was able to kill all those people from different tribes.

This man had a woman living with him. Whenever he got a new scalp she would be pleased, and would take off her dress and dance. Seizing the scalps she would sing and jump happily.

The man who drank the liquid from the heads became the chief because of all the strength he possessed.

Informant: Esteban Mariano

Source: Verna ms.

Motif content

D1335.2.	Magic strength-giving drink.
D1830.	Magic strength.

F610.	Remarkably strong man.
G10.	Cannibalism.
G310.+.	Headhunter. (G310. Ogres with characteristic methods.)
P11.4.+.	Chief chosen on basis of strength. (P11.4. King chosen on basis of strength and exploits.)
S139.2.1.1.	Head of murdered man taken along as trophy.

113. Killing the Bird Catcher's Wife Who Was Possessed by Tséxmataki

There was a woman who was seriously ill with shamanic possession; she was turning into Tséxmataki once more. When they summoned the shaman of her village to cure her[32] she would not permit him to come close to her: "Why are you coming here? Maybe you want to kill me?"

"No, not at all. Do you not want to help me to cure you?"

But she refused and would not let anyone approach, not even her husband and children. She wanted so badly to eat them, however, that first she ate one child, then another, and then another, without her husband finding out.

Later they went to look for young parrots to eat. The husband climbed up into a tree to take them and threw them down to his wife who caught them from below and ate them raw. When the husband looked down he saw her eating them, and grew very frightened. "Now, what am I going to do to get down? If I climb down I am sure she will eat me, too."

Then the woman said to him: "Jump down, and I shall catch you with my hands!"

But the man did not want to, for he realized that she was going to eat him: "I had better stay; there are still many young parrots left."

"Come down, or I shall push over the tree!"

Finally the man had to jump. What was he going to do? He was afraid. When he jumped Tséxmataki seized him with those long fingernails that she had grown and sank her big, sharp teeth into his neck until he died, and then she ate him.

When her mother-in-law saw the daughter-in-law returning home in the distance, she went to receive her happily, as is the custom. She believed that the other had really been hunting young parrots. But

---

[32]Usually the Chorote assign the practices of inflicting harm to shamans of another village and of curing to a person of one's own village.

they were not parrots! When she showed her, there was the head of her son in the bag.

Everybody grew frightened, and they called together many people to kill her. They hit her everywhere, raining blows over her, but were unable to kill her. They looked for a way to kill her, striking her with heavy sticks and with clubs, but to no avail. So much did they beat her that her body was all battered, but not even that made her fall: she could not die. Then one of them who was a shaman and who knew many things thought that they should hit her not in the chest but lower down: "If you hit her below, on her ankle, maybe she will die."

And when they hit her there she died at once. Only on the ankle was she vulnerable; that was where her heart was.

Informant: Kasókchi ilánek

Source: Siffredi ms.

Summary

Woman possessed by Tséxmataki eats her husband while out bird hunting with him. Upon her return villagers try to kill her, at first in vain, until shaman discovers her one vulnerable spot and she dies.

Motif content

D2070.	Bewitching.
E714.+.	Ogre's heart (life) in foot. (E714. Soul (or life) kept in special part of body.)
F515.2.2.	Person with very long fingernails.
G11.6.	Man-eating woman.
G11.6.4.	Woman devours her husband.
G30.	Person becomes cannibal.
G72.+.	Unnatural mother eats children. (G72. Unnatural parents eat children.)
G512.8.	Ogre killed by striking.
J613.	Wise fear of the weak for the strong.
J640.	Avoidance of others' power.
S12.2.	Cruel mother kills child.
S139.2.1.1.	Head of murdered man taken along as trophy.
S183.	Frightful meal.
Z311.	Achilles heel. Invulnerability except in one spot.

114. Killing the Bird Catcher's Wife Who Was Possessed by Tséxmataki

There was a pregnant woman who said to her husband: "Let us go and get some young parrots to eat. I know where the parrot's nest is."

They went off, bringing the rope, the ax made of palo santo wood, and the bag. Soon the woman saw the nest: "That is the one I was talking about."

The husband climbed up into the tree to take out the young birds, supporting himself with the rope in order to be able to cut into the trunk where the hole was.

Taking out a young bird he said to his wife: "Here is one!"

She caught it, opened the bag, hid her head inside, and ate it, leaving only the little wings in the bag. "Here is another one!"

That one, too, she ate. She had eaten about four young birds when her husband looked down and began to realize: "What have you done with the little parrots? I think you eat them."

"No," she said and began to beat the little wings that she had kept in the bag, all the while calling like a parrot.

The husband went on pulling out the birds: "Here comes another!"

But this time he watched her, and saw her eat the bird as soon as she had caught it. He said: "I want some, too. I want us to eat them together!"

"But I am not eating!"

"Of course you are. I saw you."

But now the husband was afraid of climbing down: "How am I going to get down? She will do some mischief. Now it is my turn to be eaten."

The woman began to urge him: "Come on down! It is late already!"

When it was late the husband threw the ax at his wife, but it merely grazed her head and fell to one side. Blood came out of her head, and as it trickled down she caught it and began to lick it. The husband thought: "I am sure she is going to do some mischief. She is going to eat me."

For a long time the woman urged her husband: "Come down quickly, it is late! Hurry up, let us go home!"

"If I climb down she will eat me," he was thinking. Then he looked at the sun: "It is late already; I shall climb down anyway. If she wants to eat me, let her."

And he began to descend. When he was nearly down the woman got ready to seize him. Throwing her arms around him she bit him on the back of the neck, killed him, and ate him. She left only his testicles, which she put in the bag, and went away. Farther on she found some edible leaves and cut them off.

When she reached the village she ground the testicles, put them on a plate, and said: "I have some teasel fruit. It is very good when it is mixed with leaves."

She began to cut it up without anyone realizing what it was. When it was ready, with salt, chili pepper, and everything, the people helped her eat, but when they tasted it they said: "This is not fruit. What is it that is mixed in with the leaves?"

Suddenly they saw the skin of the testicles and realized that this was not the fruit that she claimed. Then the other families were frightened and went away.

That woman had four children, two boys and two younger girls. She said: "I am hungry. I am going over there to look for something to eat."

She went, and around two o'clock in the afternoon she came home again: "I am thirsty, son."

She went to take a look in the clay jug and shook it. There was no water, and she was thirsty. She called her daughters: "My daughter, come here a minute. Why do you not fetch water? Did you not see that I went out to look for food?"

The mother seized her daughter, gouged out one of her eyes, and ate it. She was angry.

The next day she went out in search of food, and when she came back it was late. She came straight home, saying: "I am thirsty, son."

She shook the jug to see whether it had any water, which it did not. Once more she began to grow angry, grabbed the younger daughter, removed one of her eyes, and ate it.

When the mother had eaten the eyes of the girls, their two brothers thought: "What can we do? Let us try something. We shall set a snare for her in the door opening for when she comes back from the brush."

They asked: "Who knows how to make a snare?"

Then the fox came: "I know how."

And he began to sing:

> "Now indeed, now indeed
> am I going to have myself a feast . . .
> to kill an old woman."

"Brothers, if you want to sing along with me we shall talk."

"All right," said the boys.

Then they made a snare. They planted a pole deep in the ground, and Wóiki climbed up to the top of it, took a very strong rope, and tied it to the end of the pole. Then he climbed down, grabbed the rope, and began to run in order to bend the pole. He placed some sticks in the form of a square for her to put her feet on, and coiled the rope so that when she stepped into it, it would detach itself and be pulled upward. They left the snare there, and the boys went to the river.

It was late. "I am thirsty," said the old woman when she got home, but she did not find her sons there. "Where have they gone?"

Her daughters were there, for since she had gouged out their eyes they did not leave the house.

"Why do you not bring water?"

"How can I do that if I do not have eyes?"

Then the old woman seized the girl and ate her. When she had eaten her two daughters she took the jug and went to the river to fetch water.

There she found the boys, her two sons: "So this is where you were."

"Yes, we are here. We were looking at the animals that walk by here. We are going to snare them."

"What is that thing over there by the door, my son?"

"That is a snare that we placed there to get food."

Then Wóiki emerged, happily jumping around and saying: "Now our feast is very near! But seriously, brother, are you not going to help me sing?"

"Come on, let us catch the old woman!" said the boys to him.

The woman was approaching the house, and when she saw the snare she asked: "What is that?"

"Do not be afraid. Go ahead and step on it. The sticks are very soft; they will not harm you. That is for the animals," said her sons. The old woman put her foot on one of them, and immediately the snare was released, pulling her up into the air while she was furiously shouting at them.

The boys grabbed an ax and began to administer blows all over her body. Then they gave her a blow on the head so that her brains oozed out, but still she kept on talking; she did not die. When all her bones were broken she said: "Listen, my sons, how come you do not feel sorry for me? Do not hit me so! Do not cut me up like that! Here is my heart, in my foot. Hit me there!"

They began to do so, and the old woman started to scream. She screamed so loudly that it seemed like thunder, and the earth was shaking. While she was dying she said to her sons: "Why did you kill me? Why?"

"If we had not done it we would not survive. You killed several of us, and you were going to finish off all the others as well."

Afterward they burned her, and Wóiki was saying contentedly while circling the fire: "Now I am going to eat a fat woman. Let us see, do you know my song? Try it!"

> "Now I am really going to eat a fat old woman.
> The day of the feast is here, now we have done it."

They went on burning her, and the fox in turn continued to sing happily.

Informant: Centawó

Source: Cordeu ms.

Summary

From top of tree man throws down young birds to his wife, who eats them raw. Seeing this he fears for his life but is finally persuaded by wife to climb down. She kills and eats him and takes his testicles back to villagers, claiming them to be fruit. Frightened people abandon village, leaving only cannibal woman and her four children.

After she has gouged out and eaten her daughters' eyes, her sons decide to kill her, and with help of Fox they set snare in which she is caught. They try in vain to beat her to death until she reveals her one vulnerable spot, that is, her foot. She dies and they burn her, singing happily.

Motif content

B435.1.	Helpful fox.
B524.2.	Animals overcome man's adversary by strategy.
B560.	Animals advise men.
E714.+.	Ogre's heart (life) in foot. (E714. Soul (or life) kept in special part of body.)
G11.6.	Man-eating woman.
G11.6.4.	Woman devours her husband.
G72.+.	Unnatural mother eats children. (G72. Unnatural parents eat children.)
G512.8.	Ogre killed by striking.
G514.3.	Ogre caught in noose and killed.
J613.	Wise fear of the weak for the strong.
J640.	Avoidance of others' power.
K730.	Victim trapped.
S12.2.	Cruel mother kills child.
S12.4.+.	Cruel mother blinds daughter. (S12.4. Cruel mother blinds son.)
S165.	Mutilation: putting out eyes.
S183.	Frightful meal.
Z311.	Achilles heel. Invulnerability except in one spot.

115. The Bird-Men Ascend to Heaven on a Chain of Arrows

Once, when all the birds were men, they were very distressed. While they were making arrows, Sén, the hummingbird, said to them: "Make a lot! Here comes the crazy woman (Tséxmataki)! She is going to destroy us!"

A bird shot an arrow up to the sky, but the arrow did not get there. When other birds shot, they could not reach it either. One after the other tried, and the arrows returned to the earth. Sén wanted to shoot, but the others did not believe his arrow would arrive because he was tiny. He said: "I am capable of reaching the sky!"

"How can you, you are too small!"

And the other birds continued shooting their arrows, which all returned to earth. Sén was the last, and when all the birds finished shooting they said: "Now, let us try Sén, to see if it is true."

He crouched down and shot. The arrow reached the sky and remained there: "They shall see, I think it reached the sky."

Then Sén stopped, while the others were waiting for the arrow to return to earth. They got tired of waiting and said: "Could it be true that it got there? Let us see, shoot another one!" He began to shoot again.

Where the arrow had stuck in the sky Sén shot another, and its tip stuck in the tail of the first. He shot one arrow after another, and they were locking together. When Sén had finished his arrows, he took some from the other birds and continued shooting. When these were finished he grabbed another bunch and continued shooting. Since the sky is high up, he had used thousands of arrows. The other people (birds) had few arrows left when they began to see them, just barely, turning white in the rear of the line. Then Sén was distressed. He continued shooting and shooting and shooting and the arrows were coming closer and closer, but they had only very few left. Sén continued shooting and the arrows were coming low. When the line was very low, he grabbed it and put the arrows on with his hand until they reached the earth.

Then they sent Siwálak, the spider, up on it. They said to him: "All right, Siwálak, go up there, along this line."

Siwálak began to spin a web and reached the sky. Then a rope appeared that Siwálak made up above. When the rope was finished, the birds began to jump, grabbing the rope to go up to heaven. The last one to climb up was Sén, but since Ele (parrot) was understood, the other men (birds) gave him an order: "You are Ele, you are understood! When

Crazy Woman comes close, climb up to the sky on the rope and pull
it up, but do not rush off quickly."

When Crazy Woman arrived, she grabbed the rope to get to Ele. He
was going very slowly upward, and since Crazy Woman wanted to
reach him, she began to yell. Then someone spoke to him from above,
from the sky: "Ele, when you are close to the sky, cut the rope before
Crazy Woman gets here."

When he reached the sky, Ele began to bite the rope and he cut it.
Then Crazy Woman let go and fell to the earth.

Ele had gone up there, and the other men (birds) also stayed there.
They did not come back down again.

Informant: Centawó

Source: Cordeu ms.

Summary

Spider climbs up to sky on arrow chain made by hummingbird. From there
he throws down rope to bird-men on earth, who climb up to escape from dangerous woman. When latter follows them on rope, Parrot cuts rope and woman
falls to earth.

Motif content

A1101.2.+.	Birds were men in former age. (A1101.2. Reversal of nature in former age.)
B50.	Bird-men.
F53.	Ascent to upper world on arrow chain.
F661.7.3.	One arrow shot into end of last one to make rope of arrows.
G512.	Ogre killed.
J613.	Wise fear of the weak for the strong.
J640.	Avoidance of others' power.
J641.	Escaping before enemy can strike.
J1118.	Clever bird.
K678.	Cutting rope to kill ogre who is climbing the rope to kill his victim.
K963.	Rope cut and victim dropped.
L112.2.	Very small hero.
R323.	Refuge in upper world.
U110.	Appearances deceive.

116. The Sexual Excesses of Kíxwet

"Prick" is what we call Kíxwet. He had a long penis which he wound around his waist as if it was a belt; it was ten meters long. For that reason, whenever he wanted to have a woman, he would uncoil it and, although he was far away, he would still have sex with her and he would kill her. That Kíxwet was always having sex with women, and he would kill them in doing it. Since he had such a huge penis, when he had intercourse with them it was immediately fatal.

Kíxwet would always go around looking for adolescent girls. When he could not get a young girl he would make himself into a woman and would go out in a woman's form, with breasts and all. The women did not recognize him and would then not be afraid anymore. They believed he was not Kíxwet, but a man, a transvestite, one might say. They believed he was a woman and would go with him, calling him "companion." In that way Kíxwet joined the women. They did not know it was he.

When the women went out together, Kíxwet would say: "Let us go with the companions!"

When the women entered the forest, they saw those wasps that have their nests in the earth (máhsa).[33] A younger girl began to dig there by herself to get honey. Some went off in one direction and some in another. Kíxwet returned to where the lone girl remained digging at the nest, and he grabbed her and had intercourse with her. Ugh! When he did it, a lot of blood came out and ran down to the girl's feet!

Then the girl called to her companions, but when they realized what had happened, Kíxwet had already gone down into the earth, where he was digging in the form of an armadillo (Chaetophractus villosus). He squeezed himself in, and when they arrived they said: "He entered over there!"

They were not able to get him out. They could not dig because he was well inside.

Afterward when Kíxwet came out again from below ground, he returned to where the others were. He arrived there, and the mother of the girl he had had intercourse with received him. He said to her: "You are not going to kill me; you are never going to kill me. You

---

[33]Máhsa refers to a honey-making wasp of the extremely aggressive subgenus Trigona, and to the nest and the honey it produces. It nests in tree trunks and more frequently underground. To extract the honey, it is necessary to make a fire in order to drive them out.

believe you kill me, but you cannot. I am always going to live. Nobody kills me!"

Informant: Kíki

Source: Siffredi ms.

Summary

Man with extraordinarily long penis rapes all young girls he can find, killing them.

Motif content

D12.	Transformation: man to woman.
D100.+.	Transformation: man to armadillo. (D100. Transformation: man to animal.)
D631.1.1.	Person changes appearance at will.
D658.3.	Transformation of sex to seduce.
F547.3.1.	Long penis.
K515.6.	Escape by hiding in the earth.
K1321.	Seduction by man disguising as woman.
K1391.	Long distance sexual intercourse.
T182.	Death from intercourse.
T471.	Rape.

117. The Sexual Excesses of Kíxwet

Whenever Kíxwet heard the sound of dancing he would go toward the village, and before arriving would take on the shape of a woman, with breasts and all. He would grab his penis, and because it was so long he would fold it, wrapping it around him like a belt. He was a man, but would always act like an adolescent girl when he wanted to do bad things.

Kíxwet was a rogue. He did not like older women, only young ones. Upon arriving at a dance, even in the dark of night, since he is powerful he would know which ones were the youngest. He would always look for two girls and would deceive them, saying: "Hello! Are you going to accompany some man?"

"No, we are afraid. We are still young girls!"

"I do not know if you have a bed around here, but I am sure you are going to catch a man."[34]

---

[34]During the evening dances, each young girl would choose a boy, having sex with him, until a steady relationship was formed with one boy. Thereafter the decision for the most part would rest with the parents of the young girl.

"We never do because we are not used to it."

"Well, I am not, either," said Kíxwet. "You could take me to your house."

It was customary for the young girls to sleep together in order to talk, and since Kíxwet looked like one of them, they said: "All right, we have to call our companions before the dance ends!"

The three girls went off together, but one of them was Kíxwet. They began to chat and then, when they were going to sleep, he was there watching them. No sooner had they gone to sleep than he began to uncoil his penis and aim it to have sex with the girls. What a huge penis! Kíxwet would always say: "Grow, grow!"

As big as it was, he would make it grow more! Then he left the girls full of blood. He deflowered all of them.

When dawn came they said: "Oh, it looks like Kíxwet has been here! We did not realize!"

They did not know where he had gone. He would take off to wherever he wanted. No sooner would he finish than he would leave for another camp. Kíxwet molested all the girls! He was always looking for them just to copulate, and then he would leave.

When he fled, he would first turn himself into a *quirquincho* armadillo, then he would become a *pichi* armadillo, and finally he would become a six-banded armadillo.

Informant: Máki

Source: Siffredi ms.

Summary

Man with long penis transforms himself into woman in order to get close to young girls and rape them.

Motif content

D12.	Transformation: man to woman.
D100.+.	Transformation: man to armadillo. (D100. Transformation: man to animal.)
D489.+.	Penis made larger. (D489. Objects made larger—miscellaneous.)
D631.1.1.	Person changes appearance at will.
D658.3.	Transformation of sex to seduce.
F547.3.1.	Long penis.
K1321.	Seduction by man disguising as woman.
K1340.	Entrance into girl's (man's) room (bed) by trick.
T471.	Rape.

118. Kíswet Deflowers Girls

There was once a man named Kíswet who resembled a giant. "I am going to the dance," he said. When he went out he heard the sound of the drum. Near the house he found a bottle tree. He pulled out the long thorns and put them under his shirt, making himself look like a woman. He made himself smaller, like a twelve-year-old, but actually he was a giant. He imitated little breasts with the thorns of the bottle tree. He laughed: "I think I shall pass myself off just fine."

When he arrived at where the drum was playing, he looked like a twelve-year-old girl, very plump and fair-skinned, with hair down to her waist. Just like a young woman. There was a crowd at the dance. One girl told him that her brother would receive him. The brother motioned to him with his hands, calling him over. The giant said, no, he would not go. He joined the girls instead. A young boy came by, looked at him, and greeted him: "Where are you from?" he asked.

"From over there," replied the giant. The other asked: "Who is your father?"

"My father is the fox," replied the giant.

"Why did you come alone?" he asked.

"I hid myself, ran off, and came to see the dance," answered Kíswet. He then asked: "Who is the biggest woman?"

They pointed out to him several girls. "And who are the smallest? Because I am not big yet, I am still little."

So they pointed out several who were the youngest. They asked him: "How old are you?"

"Twelve," he answered.

"All right," he added. "I am going to join the young girls. They are going to be my companions, for I am afraid of their brothers." The boys began to clap their hands. "Yes, now we shall go try them," they said.

When night fell, the giant said: "Companions, let us sleep together because I am afraid of your uncles. I want to lie in the middle."

He went to bed. "Are not your brothers naughty?" he asked.

"No, the other men are," the girls replied.

"All right, let's sleep together." They went to sleep. Around midnight the giant began to move because he wanted to wake up the girls who were sleeping with him. He moved, but the girls did not hear anything. "What shall I do?" he asked himself. He began to have intercourse with the youngest. "I want my penis to grow big, just like a watermelon," he said. And his penis grew. He started to have sex with the youngest. He broke her hymen, but she did not feel anything because he was a giant. The bed filled with blood when he deflowered her. The giant then got back up to have sex with the girl on the other side. He broke her hymen, too, and there was blood. Since he had teasel thorns, he said: "Now what shall I do? I have to bleed, too, so their mothers will think that I bled along with them." He picked up a thorn and stabbed himself on the end of his penis. Blood squirted out.

At daybreak he looked at the girls. "What's wrong?" they were saying. "Why am I bleeding? What could be wrong?"

"I am bleeding, too!" said the giant. "I am going home because your uncle is such a rogue. Look what he did to me!"

The giant's dress was full of blood. The father believed that they had broken his hymen, too. But he was the one who had done it.

"All right, I am going because your uncle is a rogue. What time did he come to our bed?" asked the giant. He left.

Outside the other boys sneered at him. They began to dislike him. "We shall let her go on for a while," they said. "Then we shall follow her tracks and have sex with her." The giant ran fast. Shortly thereafter the girls' uncles came out to catch him and rape him. They ran fast to catch up with him. "Let us catch her! How beautiful this girl is!" The giant stopped to rest. The boys kept running. They made signs with their hands for him to stop. One older boy ran faster than the others and caught the giant's clothes. "What are you going to do?" asked the giant. "Why are you running after me? If this is what you want . . ." and he pulled out his penis. "Get lost!" said the boys. "We thought you were a girl. That's terrible! He was a giant all along!" they said. "It was he who deflowered our sisters!" They cursed the giant and returned home.

Informant: Sentawó

Source: Mashnshnek 1972, pp. 132–133.

Summary

Giant goes to village dance disguised as young girl. At night, while sharing house with other girls, he deflowers them all in their sleep. He flees next morning pursued by boys who want to rape him. When they catch him they find out who he is and realize what happened.

Motif content

D12.	Transformation: man to woman.
D489.+.	Penis made larger. (D489. Objects made larger—miscellaneous.)
D658.3.	Transformation of sex to seduce.
F531.	Giant.

F531.6.5.2.	Giants large or small at will.
F547.3.1.	Long penis.
J1820.+.	Attempted rape of man disguised as woman. (J1820. Inappropriate action from misunderstanding.)
K1321.	Seduction by man disguising as woman.
K1340.	Entrance into girl's (man's) room (bed) by trick.
T471.	Rape.
T475.2.1.	Intercourse with sleeping girl.

119. Kiswét Turns into a Gaucho

There was a fellow named Kiswét who threw away all his old clothes and started to change. He put on wide, loose-fitting trousers, a shirt, boots, a neckerchief, a hat, and spurs. Then he went to a feast. But he did not quite have the courage to approach. Then the host said to him: "Come here, gaucho, come over to the table!" "I am afraid," said Kiswét. "Of what? There is nothing to fear here," the host said to him. So the gaucho went over to the table and sat down.

The music began. The women came and seized him to go and dance, saying: "Come on, let us dance!" He answered: "No, I do not know how." Again they took hold of him until finally he got up and went to dance with one of them. *Cri, cri, cri,* sounded his spurs. When he started to dance all the women were looking at him, saying: "Look at that man, how well he dances!" The other women were saying: "How come we have not noticed him before?"

When the music was over they went to rest, and the woman sat down next to him and started a conversation. She asked him: "Who are you?" "I'm a gaucho." "How about the two of us going to your house?" asked the woman. "If you like . . . it is in the forest," answered the gaucho.

The party ended, and they went off together. When they reached the house there was a heap of clothes there. He asked the woman: "What kind of clothes do you like?" "Everything, all this," she replied. "All right, then choose; pick out what you want. I shall not say anything." She took the clothes, and immediately she became pregnant. Kiswét gave her a child. Later he gave her many children, and she never returned home again.

Informant: Petiso

Source: Verna ms.

Motif content

F699.1.	Marvelous dancer.
K1810.	Deception by disguise.
T55.	Girl as wooer.
T532.5.1.	Conception from touching another's garment.

120. Confrontation with Kíxwet

When the shaman threw out Siéhnam, the people could continue sleeping peacefully, but later another came: Kíxwet, the man who had a long penis. When he copulated he would stand far away, but he reached anyway because his penis was very large. His penis would actually come out of the woman's mouth and would kill her. There were five women with whom Kíxwet had intercourse and whom he killed at night.

So they had to order the shaman again to go at night and watch to see who this killer of women was. No one knew who it was.

That night the old man began to dream. He dreamed that a man was standing far away and displaying his penis in the direction where the people were living. It was a real man whom he was seeing in his dreams. He had not only dreamed it; since he was a shaman he had seen him. Kíxwet was not standing nearby there; he was quite far away, but since the old man was a shaman he could see him all the same. Then the shaman told him not to return anymore: "If you continue killing women, no families will remain."

The next day they asked the shaman: "How did it go, old man? Did you find out anything?"

"I think we shall be all right. I had a dream about a man with a large penis, and later he pointed it in the direction of the women. He prods and prods, and since it is big, he kills them with it. But tonight I do not think there will be any danger. I am sure that man went far away. Now we shall be able to sleep peacefully. Nothing will bother us."

Informant: José Romero

Source: Siffredi ms.

Motif content

D1810.8.2.	Information received through dream.
D1810.8.3.	Warning in dreams.

F547.3.1.	Long penis.
F1068.	Realistic dream.
J157.	Wisdom (knowledge) from dream.
K1391.	Long distance sexual intercourse.
N845.	Magician as helper.
T182.	Death from intercourse.
T471.	Rape.

121. Misdeeds, Deaths, Resurrections, and Transformations of Kíxwet

Kíxwet had found a nest of black wasps underground, and since he had found it, it was his. He had a sister-in-law who, while he remained sleeping at home, went out to look for honey. Her mother and her husband had also gone to look for honey. The sister-in-law knew where Kíxwet's nest was, and when she arrived there she found it and broke off some pieces of a dry cactus. Then she began to dig for the nest, which was large.

The giant (referring to Kíxwet) got up and said: "I am going to take out what I hid the other day."

He passed by his sister-in-law's house and saw that she was not in: "How awful! I am the stupid one because I went and showed her the things I found! It does not matter, I am going to look for her!"

He went off, and when he was near the spot where the nest was he smelled the smoke from the fire that she had made to get the wasps out. He found her digging with her backside in the air, and since the nest was very deep, she had to bend over lower and lower to get the dirt out. "Oh," said the giant, "what am I going to do? I shall just go there, that is all! Why has she taken from me what I found? She is going to pay for what she has done!"

He did not know what to do with her and sat down to look at her. "When she bends down to dig out the dirt, I shall walk over there very slowly."

When he got up the girl stopped digging, and so he hid. She squatted down again to continue removing the dirt. The giant, who had a sharp digging stick, left it and went closer. As he did so he was singing, calling to the *cipoy* plant (a wild cucurbitaceous plant, as large as a watermelon): "*Cipoy, cipoy*, come, come and put yourself here on the head of my penis!"

And that is what happened. It came and attached itself to his penis.

She continued to dig and dig, but suddenly he arrived, lifted up her dress, and began to have intercourse with her. While he was doing this he was gradually pushing her inside the nest. She realized and said to him: "Giant, let me alone! Take your penis out and have sex with me outside the nest!"

The wasps had begun to sting her face. He continued pushing: "I do not want to pull it out. I also want to know my brother's path (*i-kai*, road, uterus)!"

When he finished with her he took out his penis and gave a sound as if he were a donkey mounting a mare. He yelled and began to laugh: "Oh, I am happy! I am going home." Quickly he grabbed the digging stick and went off contentedly. Farther on, before arriving home, he started to shout: "Come here, someone is shooting at me with an arrow!"

Seizing an arrow he stuck it in his chest and went running to his house. He went inside to where his bed was and threw himself down on his belly. When he did the arrow went in deeper and broke, and the tip remained in his chest. He died. He pretended to be dead, but it was a lie.

After a while the woman came out of the nest screaming, with her face very swollen from the wasp stings. She could not see and did not know where she was going. How she was screaming!

"What could be going on? What could that giant have done?" said the people.

"I am going to see what happened!" Her daughter went to look for her: "What is wrong with you, mother?"

"Nothing, daughter. Your uncle held me inside the hole, next to the nest. That is why I am blind."

Her daughter gave her a stick and began to lead her home. She could not see; she was blind. Upon arriving home she sat down, and all the people asked her: "What has happened to you?"

"Nothing. Your uncle grabbed me and pushed me inside the hole, and so all the wasps stung me."

Soon the giant's brother arrived, bringing a peccary, and he set down his sack. The woman always used to see what her husband had brought as soon as he arrived. When he noticed that she was taking a long time, the giant's brother said to her: "Why do you not get up to see what I brought to eat?"

"What can I see if I am blind?"

"What happened to you?"

"Your brother grabbed me, and then I became blind. The wasps stung me." Her husband said angrily to his brother: "That is why you played dumb when I called you to go hunting! You are always going around looking for women!"

The giant answered his brother: "Yes, brother, come on and kill me!"
He was speaking but he was already dead. "Of course I am going to kill you!"

The man grabbed a club and jumped to the other side until he was standing next to the giant, who was lying down. He began to club him until he killed him. Then the brother said: "Let us burn him!"

They burned him. Around noon they planned to move to another spot. "We are going to move because we have killed my uncle," said the brother, "and he has been completely burned.[35] Daughter, bring me my arrows! Since the wind is blowing, the armadillo (*Chaetophractus villosus*) is going to come out. When you find one, kill it."

"All right, father."

The giant's brother stayed behind, and his daughter went on ahead looking for the armadillo, searching along the edge of the road. In one place she found one that ran past her and into a hole. She began to shoot at it, but the arrow passed below the armadillo which went farther inside. The girl ran to grab the arrow but could not get it out. It was the giant who had gone below the ground to catch the people who were moving. He had grabbed the arrow and was pulling at it to make the girl sink into the ground. She began to shout: "Father, come! I have caught the armadillo. Here he is, underground."

Quickly the father went.

The giant let go of the arrow, and the girl who was pulling with so much force to get the armadillo out fell backward with her legs open. Then the giant appeared. His brother said to him: "You came already, giant!"

"Yes, I came but I was burned. I have returned to life." They went off together again. He did not leave the niece.

Informant: Centawó

Source: Cordeu ms.

Summary

Giant rapes sister-in-law who is trying to steal his honey. Afterward he pushes her into wasps' nest where stings of wasps blind her. Her husband kills giant in revenge. Giant revives and takes form of armadillo. He tries to abduct blind woman's daughter while she is hunting.

Motif content

D100.+.	Transformation: man to armadillo. (D100. Transformation: man to animal.)

[35]Previously, when somebody died, the Chorote would abandon the site.

D631.1.1.	Person changes appearance at will.
D1643.	Object travels by itself.
D1765.	Magic results produced by command.
D2074.	Attracting by magic.
D2136.	Objects magically moved.
E1.	Person comes to life.
E42.	Resuscitation from ashes of dead man.
F531.	Giant.
K515.6.	Escape by hiding in the earth.
K1860.	Deception by feigned death (sleep).
Q212.	Theft punished.
Q411.7.	Death as punishment for ravisher.
Q422.0.1.	Punishment: beating to death.
Q451.7.	Blinding as punishment.
Q453.+.	Punishment: being stung by wasps. (Q453. Punishment: being bitten by animal.)
T410.	Incest.
T425.	Brother-in-law seduces (seeks to seduce) sister-in-law.
T471.	Rape.

122. Kíxwet Kills the Club Murderer

Far away, from the north, a huge man used to come who had the arms of a giant. Iñó tók (giant man, strong, brave) had a club. At night he would come, enter the houses, and kill the ancient Chorote while they were asleep, clubbing them in the back of the neck. He was also bad because he would not kill just one or two but would kill many. Afterward he would pile them up and burn them. He had a lot of firewood, and all night long he would play, building fires.

Then the people who remained sent a messenger to ask Kíxwet to keep guard at night. Kíxwet would always stay on the hill because he lived there.[36] He was like a person but more powerful, as powerful as a shaman. He came and waited during the night for Iñó tók to arrive. When he arrived he grabbed him. They began to fight, and Kíxwet killed him. In this way the danger was ended.

Informant: Obispo (Axués pa)

Source: Siffredi ms.

[36]The meaning of "Kíxwet," according to the informant, is "he who inhabits the mountain." *Wet* or *et* indicates surroundings, place, position of any person, animal, vegetable, or thing.

Motif content

F531.	Giant.
F531.4.5.1.+.	Giant with club as weapon. (F531.4.5.1. Giant with iron club as weapon.)
G310.	Ogres with characteristic methods.
G346.	Devastating monster.
G512.	Ogre killed.
K959.2.	Murder in one's sleep.
N810.	Supernatural helpers.

123. The Giant Kíswet Searches for His Family

A man named Kíswet once asked an old sandal: "Where has my family gone?" The sandal answered by raising itself up and lowering itself back down. "Why do you not answer me?" asked the giant. He picked up the sandal and threw it against a tree. The sandal came back at him and struck him in the forehead. How it hurt! He sat down and began to cry. "Why am I crying?" he asked himself. "I am not a woman."

He then met a cariama. "Where has my family gone?" he asked it. The cariama replied: "That way," and pointed with its beak. So the giant said: "Ah! I shall go that way." "If you find your wife," warned the bird, "you shall see that your brother is now married to her. He has already made love to her. She loves him deeply." The giant replied: "Yes, I told her to marry him."

He met his cousin. They started to fight. The cousin chopped off a piece of the giant and threw it away. From this piece another identical man was formed, another Kíswet. Always, whenever part of him was cut off and discarded, another man would form. When they tore the giant's guts out and threw them on a tree, the lianas were created. Whenever we see the lianas, we say: "Those are the giant's guts."

Informant: Cepillo

Source: Mashnshnek 1972, p. 134.

Motif content

A1263.	Man created from part of body.
A1296.	Multiplication of man by fragmentation.
A2611.0.5.	Parts of human or animal body transformed into plants.
A2682.	Origin of creepers.
B143.1.	Bird gives warning.

B450.	Helpful birds.
B563.2.	Birds point out road to hero.
D437.	Transformation: part of animal or person to person.
D1602.+.	Self-returning sandal. (D1602. Self-returning magic object.)
F531.	Giant.
F1009.	Inanimate object acts as if living.
H1385.9.	Quest for lost (stolen) family.
T410.	Incest.
T425.	Brother-in-law seduces (seeks to seduce) sister-in-law.

124. Killing the Thlimnál I-Wós Cannibals

Thlimnál i-wó and Thlimnál i-wóki (male and female Guardian of the Forest) live in the bush where no people ever go. They are man and woman and always go around together as husband and wife. But they are strange. They are giants and look like people, but very strange. They are like devils. Previously they used to eat people.[37]

There was a young hunter of Chaco chachalacas who always used to go to a place in the bush, near a lagoon, where these birds could easily be caught. The hunters would make a tightly enclosed shelter where they would lie in wait, and thus they would be able to see the chachalacas coming down to drink water, and they would kill them. The young man wanted to go there before dawn, and his brother said to him: "All right, brother, if you want to go over there I shall accompany you."

"No, do not, because that place is always visited by two strange creatures. I don't quite know what they are. If you came and you saw them I am sure you would laugh, for when they are about to drink they pull out the hairs around the penis and the vulva, put them in the water, and drink it like that. Even I can hardly refrain from laughing. They are hairy all over. The hair on their heads grows down to their waists, and their pubic hair hangs all the way down to their feet."

"I shall keep from laughing. I want to see them."

"Do not go. You will be the culprit," said the family.

[37]The defeat and death of the Thlimnál i-wós at the hands of Ahóusa leads to the suppression of their malevolence as expressed in cannibalism. Although the latter custom is confined to primordial times, the activities of the couple extend into the present in the shamanic complex, which is also the case with the other "harmful" protagonists in the Ahóusa cycle. In this case they occur as helpers who facilitate the gathering of honey and other products of the brushwood.

But when the elder brother went off, the younger went with him. The former had told him what they were like but he did not care, thinking that either it was not true, or if it was, that he would control his laughter. When they arrived the elder brother heard a sound: "They are coming. Do not look at them; it is dangerous. You must look in the other direction."

But the younger paid no attention to him. When they approached the water he looked at them, and seeing them pulling out their pubic hair he began to laugh, but inwardly. He could not help himself. His brother put his hand over his mouth, but he could not stand it and he laughed out loud.

Then Thlimnál i-wó said slowly: "There seems to be someone here saying 'hee, hee, hee.' Let us have a look!"

They had some beautiful palo santo sticks for killing rabbits, and they poked about with these and found the brothers. The younger brother, the guilty one, they cut in half. Thlimnál i-wó said to his wife: "I'll eat the upper part (head, trunk, and arms), and you eat the lower (abdomen and legs). But the elder one we shall keep and eat when the south wind blows again. We shall stay and sleep here next to the water. Now we have food."

Then each swallowed half of the younger brother, for those creatures do not chew.

When they lay down they put the young man between them, holding him firmly for fear that he would escape. But he knew many things and could summon any kind of slippery animal. First he called a snake, as though transforming himself into that slippery creature. Thus he was able to slide down a little, but the Thlimnál i-wós felt him moving and grasped him more firmly. The young man kept calling another animal and then yet another, all the while transforming himself. He called the lizard and turned himself into that animal, which enabled him to slide a bit farther down. Meanwhile his captors slept, snoring. Then he called the eel, and in that form, which is very slippery, he was able to extricate himself and get away. He was summoning the animals and transforming himself into them to see whether he could escape from the embrace of his captors, turning into successively smaller and smaller animals. But when he had freed himself he became human once more and escaped.

When he already was far away the Thlimnál i-wós woke up and began to argue: "Why did you eat him?"

"No, you are the one who ate him."

"No, I did not."

"Let us see; vomit! We shall see if there is not something in your stomach!"

He vomited, but all he had was the boy they had eaten. Then they began to look around for the other, and soon they saw his tracks and followed them. They were very winding. Thlimnál i-wó was shouting as he went, and how he shouted! They continued their pursuit until they reached a distant place where there were many hunters' tracks. There they halted, unwilling to go on, for they live in a place where there are no people.

When the young man reached the village all the families saw that he was coming back alone and crying unhappily: "My brother is dead. He has been eaten by that man and woman who go about naked in the thick brushwood. I do not know who they might be."

Since the parents of the boys also did not know, they summoned Ahóusa again. He came, and because he is the only wise man among our ancestors he said at once: "It was the Thlimnál i-wós who ate him. I am going to look for them and kill them."

He went off, and when he found them he brought them back to the parents of the boys so they would see them and know that he was not lying. He killed them and disemboweled them, finding the upper part of the boy in the belly of Thlimnál i-wó and the lower part inside Thlimnál i-wóki. Putting together the two pieces he said: "Come on, arise, stand up again!"

And the boy stood up. "Ah, I was asleep!"

"No," said Ahóusa, "these two ate you!"

Informant: Kasókchi ilánek

Source: Siffredi ms.

Summary

Strange forest-dwelling cannibals capture two brothers. Cutting one in half they eat him, saving other for later. Although held in firm grip by his sleeping captors, boy manages to extricate himself by turning himself into succession of slippery animals. He flees to village. Parents summon Ahóusa who captures and kills cannibals, removes slain boy from their stomachs, and revives him.

Motif content

B455.4.	Helpful hawk.
B515.+.	Resuscitation by hawk. (B515. Resuscitation by animals.)
B540.	Animal rescuer or retriever.
B546.	Animal searches for dead man.
C43.	Tabu: offending wood-spirit.
C311.1.	Tabu: seeing supernatural creatures.
C460.	Laughing tabu.

D100.	Transformation: man to animal.
D610.	Repeated transformation.
D631.1.1.	Person changes appearance at will.
D642.1.	Transformation to escape from captivity.
D642.2.	Transformation to escape death.
D1810.	Magic knowledge.
D2074.1.	Animals magically called.
E1.	Person comes to life.
E30.	Resuscitation by arrangement of members.
E32.0.1.	Eaten person resuscitated.
F441.	Wood-spirit.
F441.5.2.	Wood-spirit gigantic.
F531.1.6.3.	Giants with shaggy hair on their bodies.
F531.1.6.3.1.	Giant (giantess) with particularly long hair.
G11.10.	Cannibalistic spirits.
J581.	Foolishness of noise-making when enemies overhear.
J652.	Inattention to warnings.
J1113.	Clever boy.
Q411.	Death as punishment.

125. Pasá, the *Yulo* Bird, Destroys the Bird Snatchers

Long ago, an adolescent wanted to go and take Pasá's young birds to raise them. Up in a bottle tree he saw the nests, and as soon as he saw them the young *yulo* birds came out. Then the boy began to climb up the bottle tree. Since Pasá was very bad (he used to kill people in those days), he climbed up quietly so that the bird would not notice. The boy thought that the young birds, which are tame, were alone.

Pasá hid himself in the top of the bottle tree. When he saw that a youth had climbed up, he waited until the boy turned around, and when he could not see him he gave him an arrow-shot with his long beak: *wham!* He put it in the middle of his back and killed him. That Pasá was also very dangerous. He would always kill those who climbed up to look for young birds to raise.

Informant: Kíki

Source: Siffredi ms.

Motif content

B16.3.	Devastating birds.
J613.	Wise fear of the weak for the strong.

126. Confrontation with Siéhnam, the Deer

Siéhnam was dangerous. He was destroying all the people. He would walk at night, killing people. Night after night he would go and look for villages, and since the male deer has large antlers, he would kill people by stabbing them. He continued killing and killing in this way and, since we sleep on our backs, he also used to bite people's throats. In this way he went on, and if he encountered someone, he bit him in the neck and continued. Every night he killed four people!

Finally they had to order the old man (shaman) to go at night to see who it was who was killing off the people: "What is this that always comes at night?"

Of course, the shamans do not sleep at night. Since this killer (Siéhnam) would always go around at midnight, the old man woke up a little before. Suddenly he heard a sound. He stopped, saw what was approaching him, lay down again, and said to him: "Now I have caught you! It was you who was killing all the people! I thought it was another, but it was you. You and I are going to fight!"

They fought. The old shaman knocked him down and Siéhnam did not come back again. The next day the others asked him: "What will happen now?"

The old man told them: "Now we are going to be able to sleep peacefully! I believe that the one that was bothering us will not return again."

Informant: José Romero

Source: Siffredi ms.

Motif content

B16.2.7.	Destructive deer.
G310.	Ogres with characteristic methods.
G346.	Devastating monster.
G350.+.	Deer as ogre. (G350. Animal ogres.)
G500.	Ogre defeated.
N845.	Magician as helper.

127. Confrontation with the Deer-Man

There was a man who was a deer (*Blastocerus dichotomus*). At first he would just go around as a deer, and later, when he entered the forest, would turn himself into a man. Then he would take out his arrows and would shoot a man. After killing him he would go around as a deer again, with large antlers. The people would be looking for that man who was shooting them, but he had already become a deer again, and they would be unable to find him.

There was a shaman who wanted to know how the hunters were dying. Each time someone was lost he said: "How can it be? I am going to look well! Perhaps I shall also die."

He went to the forest and saw that after having shot a person, the man turned himself into a deer and was going to run off. But since the shaman knew, he subdued him. He had a shamanic helper who was a deer, and that way he could prevent the killer from escaping. Then he grabbed a big stick that he had, threw it at the back of his neck, and killed the deer.

Informant: Axués pa

Source: Siffredi ms.

Motif content

B16.2.7.	Destructive deer.
B20.+.	Deer-man. (B20. Beast-men.)
D114.1.1.	Transformation: man to deer.
D631.1.1.	Person changes appearance at will.
D642.7.	Transformation to elude pursuers.
F403.2.2.1.	Familiar spirit in animal form.
G310.	Ogres with characteristic methods.
G350.+.	Deer-man as ogre. (G350. Animal ogres.)
G512.	Ogre killed.
N845.	Magician as helper.

128. Confrontation with the Jaguar-Man

There was a jaguar. He was bad and dangerous. At night, around midnight, he would go to the village, and since they were sleeping, they would not hear a thing. He would come up next to someone and would sink his fangs into him and kill him. He would pass on to another, again sink his fangs into the throat, and would kill the man. And in this way he would finish off all of them without anybody yelling. No one knew what was happening.

There was an old man called Kithlié, who was about seventy or eighty years old, a little old man. He knew more than anyone! The old ones knew a lot, and so they asked him: "What is going on at night?"

"I do not know! Tonight I am going to know from my dream. Tonight we shall see!"

In the morning the others asked him again: "What have you done, old man?"

"I had a dream about someone who looks like a man, but a minute later he looks like a jaguar. How can it be? Could it be that another shaman is playing tricks?"

And then immediately the old man knew what was happening.

Because the dream had let him know all this, he lay down, waiting, until midnight. He had a short spear next to his head, and this is how the old man was, with his head upright. He already knew, and he would watch a little, faking sleep. The jaguar-shaman went directly to where he was sleeping and wanted to jump on top of him, but the old man already had the spear ready, and as soon as the other approached he stuck it into his side: "Go ahead and scream!"

The jaguar-shaman was screaming: "Grrr . . ." and he woke up the others. "What was that?"

"Wake up, old people! Wake up, children! Here is the one who comes to eat us!"

They brought clubs and showered him with blows until he died.

Informant: Axués pa

Source: Siffredi ms.

Summary

Shaman in jaguar form who kills people during nightly visits is in turn killed by other shaman.

Motif content

B16.2.2. +.	Devastating jaguar. (B16.2.2. Devastating tiger.)
D631.1.1.	Person changes appearance at will.
D1810.0.2.	Magic knowledge of magician.
D1810.8.2.	Information received through dream.
G310.	Ogres with characteristic methods.
G346.	Devastating monster.
G350. +.	Jaguar-man as ogre. (G350. Animal ogres.)
G512.8.	Ogre killed by striking.
J157.	Wisdom (knowledge) from dream.
K911.3.	Sleep feigned to kill enemy.
K1868.	Deception by pretending sleep.
N845.	Magician as helper.

129. The Woman Married to the Jaguar

There once was a girl who had a mother and several brothers and sisters. They only offered her crumbs to eat. Her sisters would say to her: "How nice! Go and get corn from where Aiés, the jaguar, lives." The girl went to the brush forest carrying her net bag. On a tree trunk she strung a hammock. Aiés came by. When he spotted the girl up above in the hammock she said: "Aiés, you must not eat me."

Aiés said: "No, I am going to be your husband."

So the girl went to the brush and had relations with Aiés. The latter went in search of something to eat and brought back a wild boar. But there was no fire there. He thought about how he could make one. So he made a fire. He ate roast together with his wife, who said: "Aiés, go look for a tuco-tuco." Aiés went hunting where the girl's brother was looking for tuco-tucos and brought back the brother's foot to eat. The girl burst into tears.

"What is wrong?" asked Aiés.

"Nothing," answered the girl. "I am just plucking my eyelashes."

"It looks like you are crying," Aiés said.

"No," she answered. "I am plucking an eyelash." But the girl was actually crying because she had recognized her brother's foot.

In the morning the girl went out to get thorns to blind Aiés. She said to him: "Come here, Aiés. I want to pluck your eyelashes."

He believed her, and she put his eyes out with the thorns.

Aiés was now blind. The girl returned to the others, who told her: "Someone is missing. Your brother is missing."

"All right," the girl said. "Go to Aiés, who is now blind, and bring him back." The other brothers went to Aiés, killed him, and ate him.

Informant: Alipa

Source: Mashnshnek 1972, pp. 126–127.

Summary

Mistreated girl leaves home, goes into forest, and marries jaguar. When jaguar kills her brother during hunt she blinds him, then returns home. Her other brothers in turn kill jaguar.

Motif content

B200.+.	Jaguar uses fire. (B200. Animals with human traits.)
B531.	Animals provide food for men.
B601.15.	Marriage to jaguar.
G61.1.	Child recognizes relative's flesh when it is served to be eaten.

K1013.	False beauty-doctor.
Q411.	Death as punishment.
R227.1.	Wife flees from animal husband.
R228.	Children leave home because their parents refuse them food.
S0.	Cruel relative.
S12.6.	Cruel mother refuses children food.
S165.	Mutilation: putting out eyes.

130. The Woman Who Was Married to Aiés (the Jaguar)

There was a little girl who was always angry because she was given too little food. She began to cry. One night when the moon was shining brightly she went out, climbed up into a tree, and started moving her foot around, making shadows. Her mother said to her: "Go and marry the jaguar. He will give you plenty to eat." But the girl replied: "He is too old, mother."

The jaguar who was nearby saw the girl making shadows with her foot, and he grew annoyed and tried to catch the shadow. Whenever the girl moved her foot, the jaguar would grab its shadow. Finally he looked up and saw her. He said to her: "Come down!" She obeyed, saying: "Do not eat me!" "No, I am going to marry you," he replied, and he took her to his house. Looking at the girl he said: "She does not seem very suitable." But he married her anyway. Then he brought her many deer to eat. The girl was happy, saying: "Now I can really eat a lot because this is not my home. At home they gave me very little."

Informant: Cepillo

Source: Verna ms.

Motif content

B531.	Animals provide food for men.
B601.15.	Marriage to jaguar.
J613.	Wise fear of the weak for the strong.
J1790.	Shadow mistaken for substance.
R228.	Children leave home because their parents refuse them food.
S12.	Cruel mother.
S12.6.	Cruel mother refuses children food.

131. The Woman Who Married Aiés (the Jaguar)

A woman left her husband and went to the forest where the jaguar was. She met him and said: "Don't eat me, jaguar." "No, I am going to marry you," he said. During the night the jaguar had intercourse with the woman, and she became pregnant. The son of the jaguar was born and grew very quickly. He began to accompany his father to the forest in search of food. When the boy was as big as his father he began to think of eating his mother. He ate her.

The jaguar wanted to marry again. But the women were afraid of him and did not want to marry him. They escaped, but one of them was left behind up in a tree. The jaguar saw her, knocked down the tree, and married her.

Informant: Simplicios

Source: Verna ms.

Motif content

B601.15.	Marriage to jaguar.
B630.	Offspring of marriage to animal.
G71.+.	Animal son eats human mother. (G71. Unnatural children eat parent.)
J613.	Wise fear of the weak for the strong.
J640.	Avoidance of others' power.
R311.	Tree refuge.
S21.	Cruel son.
T192.	Marriage by force.
T615.	Supernatural growth.

132. War Between the Chorote and the Sirakua

An old man said to the other Indians: "Let us go and gather honey." Then he thought of something else to do: "Let us go and fight the Sira-kua[38] instead." "All right," answered everybody.

As soon as the rooster crowed at dawn they set off toward the houses of the Sirakua. "Watch out, for they are very bad," said the old man to them. They followed some tracks that looked like cow tracks. Then the ground began to grow very sandy. Finally they reached the houses.

---

[38]The Sirakua were people whose bodies were covered with downy hair. They lived in the desert and had very sharp eyes which permitted them to travel and hunt during the night, while they rested during the day.

"Those Sirakua are very cowardly; as soon as they see a stranger they abandon their homes," said the old man. The Sirakua had left. Looking inside they found nothing. They cut some quebracho colorado and planted it around the houses, making a wall. On top they placed some chaguar so that it would not leak when it rained. They looked inside but it was dark; all they saw was a cemetery. "Well, I shall catch up with them," said the old man.

They followed the tracks left by the fleeing Sirakua, traveling all day to overtake them. Soon they saw the oldest Sirakua, who was skinning a vizcacha. They blew on him, but he did not turn around. The Indians grew tired of waiting and started to beat their arrows. Then the old Sirakua looked behind him, and seeing the Indians he began to shout.

The Indians moved in, seized everybody by the arms, and began to fight. A Sirakua grabbed an Indian, jammed his knee into the other's back to break it, and seized his head to kill him. The Indian was able to get up, however, and did the same to the Sirakua. Again the Sirakua threw the Indian to the ground. Then he grew worried, picked up the Indian, put him over his shoulder, and ran off. The other Indians ran after him but were unable to catch up with him.

The old man thought: "What can we do now?" He called to the hummingbird to find the Sirakua, who was disappearing into the distance. The hummingbird had prepared a pitfall a bit farther away. Now he pulled back a little, and immediately the Sirakua put his foot into the hole. He was caught there, unable to get out. The Indians came and hit him with their clubs. The Sirakua was breaking wind; it looked like smoke coming out. "Stay away from that. It brings sickness," warned the old man. An Indian with a knife cut the Sirakua's throat and he died.

At once they went off to look for the rest of them. They found an old Sirakua woman who was cutting a weed. Sensing the smell of watermelon she moved her hand toward the stem, dug, and found the watermelon. As she inserted her hand to pull out the fruit, her rump was pointing upward. Slowly an Indian came up behind her, took a stick, and rammed it into her anus. He pinned her down, and then he left her in the hole.

They went to where the Sirakua were resting to look for the boys. They killed all the boys and burned them. There were two girls there, and they did not kill them, for they wanted to marry them. They took them along. As they were walking one man said: "Shall we have sex with them?" "No, let us kill them instead," said another.

After a while they heard the sound of a flute. The Sirakua were approaching, singing. Then they heard something like the noise of cows. "Look, they have already caught up with us," said the old man. "Quick, everybody, go and hide, by the path or in the trees." When the Sirakua were near the Indians began to shoot at them. The Sirakua chief was there, easily recognizable by his jaguar skin shirt and the parrot feathers on his head. They aimed at him and killed him. The rest of the Sirakua went home.

Informant: Centawó

Source: Verna ms.

Summary

Indians go on war expedition against supernatural creatures (Sirakua). After killing many, including Sirakua chief, they return home.

Motif content

B450.	Helpful birds.
B524.2.	Animals overcome man's adversary by strategy.
D1500.4.+.	Magic intestinal wind causes disease. (D1500.4. Magic object causes disease.)
F521.1.	Man covered with hair.
F541.	Remarkable eyes.
F560.+.	Asleep by day, awake by night. (F560. Unusual manner of life.)
F642.4.	Person sees equally well by night or day.
F1084.	Furious battle.
H1397.	Quest for enemies.
J640.	Avoidance of others' power.
J641.	Escaping before enemy can strike.
K735.	Capture in pitfall.
K810.	Fatal deception into trickster's power.
K959.4.	Murder from behind.
S100.	Revolting murders or mutilations.

133. The Land of Plenty

Pák, the creamy-billed thrush, was a young man, short and squat, and a shaman. In his area, far away in the north, the algarrobo harvest never ends. For he sowed all the plants that are eaten—*mistol, tusca, algarrobo*—and those that are not eaten, like the quebracho. That is why now, when it is the season of flowers, the flowers are blooming, so that the people can eat the fruit in the season of wild fruit. He who first sowed (Pák) said: "I do this so that the people will have food and will be able to live."

Pák had a wife, Woshiét, the cardinal. During the fruit season she had a lot to do. In the mornings she would make two trips to gather algarrobo. In the evening she would begin to grind it, storing the flour in the granary, and she would also dampen the flour to make cookies to store. Then she would grind *tusca* or algarrobo and put them in a gourd to make chicha (fermented drink) so that Pák would drink and sing. When he was singing, he would get drunk. He would drink and drink.

An old shaman went to look for Pák to drink with him. When he heard him sing, he said: "He is around here. I shall soon find him."

He was approaching Pák's house, and from time to time he would stop; he could barely get there. Pák's sons saw a man coming and told him: "Father, someone is coming." Pák called the man. They put a skin on the ground for him to sit on, and Pák said to him: "I do not have anything to drink anymore."

But he was lying, for that gourd with chicha was inexhaustible; it filled up by itself again. Finally he took out the gourd to invite him. When the man drank chicha he realized it was very strong, and he could not finish it. The man was sitting down, and as he looked behind, the gourd filled itself up with chicha again. Pák said: "Friend, it seems to me that you are going to get drunk!"

The man drank four times and got drunk. Then Pák said to him: "Friend, you are drunk! Before you get more intoxicated you should go home."

"All right, I am going."

Then Woshiét said to Pák: "Give him something to take home."

He took out a bag and filled it with ground algorrobo, whole algarrobo, and cookies.

When he gave him all this it was not November or December, it was January or February. So the others said to him: "Where did you get this? It is not the season."

"I went to my nephew's house. They invited me there."

The others continued saying that it was not the season for algarrobo and *tusca*, that it had already passed. The man repeated: "I got this from Pák's house."

When he arrived home and his wife saw it, she took the algarrobo that was inside the bag and began to grind it, but she asked him: "Where did you get this? Another man might go to that place."

Then another man took a bag and said he was going into the bush, but it was not true. He also wanted to go to Pák's place. He went, stopping occasionally when he heard Pák sing, listening to where the song was coming from.

Pák had climbed up in a quebracho colorado and was singing. The man wanted to approach, but when he was close he did not see him anymore. Pák had disappeared. When he heard the song again, Pák was behind him. So the man went to where Pák was singing, and when he was about to approach him again, Pák was behind him again. Many times the man tried to approach him without succeeding, until finally he was tired. He stopped looking for him and returned home.

Later, the man who had gone first told Pák he wanted to return again. Pák let him know he was going to move: "There is a lagoon. I am going next to that lagoon!"

Pák's old house reverted to being a forest (scrubs). It disappeared. Then the man went to the new house, close to the lagoon. He found it, and there, too, found a lot of algarrobo. He continued to have what was in the old place. When he arrived, he drank again with Pák. He was only a little drunk, and when Pák saw that he was about to leave, he said to him: "You have to come back!"

"All right, I shall come back later."

The man arrived home, but this time he was carrying ground algarrobo and cookies; he did not have any whole algarrobo. He gave it to his wife and she ate *añapa* (a mixture of algarrobo and water, unfermented). It was already the middle of the afternoon, so he said to his wife: "My friend (Pák) said that we should go to his house for a while."

"As soon as I finish eating."

Soon the wife finished and they went. Pák's sons saw them coming down the road, and they went to tell him: "Who could they be?"

"It must be our friend, because a while ago I told him to return."

Pák recognized him, called to him, and offered him a seat. Woshiét offered his wife some algarrobo.

Pák said to the man: "I do not have any more chicha."

He invited him to have only *añapa*, and they ate with the women. Since the visitors had several children, as soon as they finished eating the *añapa* they took out many bags of algarrobo and gave one bag each to the children. Afterward Pák and his wife took out the cookies and gave them some. Before returning home, the man said to Pák: "Friend, I am not going to return again."

When they got home they began to grind all the algarrobo they had been given until there was none left. There was no algarrobo there because the season had already passed. They continued to have it in Pák's house, but the man did not want to go again because he had told him that he was not going to return. In the far north where Pák is, the harvest of algarrobo never ends.

Informant: Aió

Source: Siffredi ms.

Summary

Pák (bird) lives in land of unlimited food supply. Three times man goes to visit him, each time returning home laden with gifts of food.

Motif content

D1652.5.	Inexhaustible vessel.
F111.	Journey to earthly paradise.
F701.	Land of plenty.
W11.	Generosity.

134. The Man Who Turned Himself into a Rhea

A man wanted to turn into a rhea. He thought: "What can I do to become like a rhea? I think I shall get some ashes from the hearth." He started swallowing ashes, and soon he had turned into a rhea. But he was not really a rhea. He had only transformed himself temporarily in order to kill the other rheas.

He went to the bush to look for the traps placed by hunters, and when he had found them he called all the rheas together and said to them: "Form a line, and then we shall see who first gets to the place that I have indicated to you." All the birds started running; then they stepped in the traps and fell. The young man came, saw them, and said: "Now we are really going to kill them all."

Informant: Sekiome

Source: Verna ms.

Motif content

D150.	Transformation: man to bird.
D551.+.	Transformation by eating ashes. (D551. Transformation by eating.)
D631.1.1.	Person changes appearance at will.
K700.	Capture by deception.
K730.	Victim trapped.
K755.	Capture by masking as another.
K810.	Fatal deception into trickster's power.

135. A Celestial Puma Hunt

The hunters' dogs were running after a puma. The latter came to a big tree and climbed up. Below, the dogs were jumping up at him. The puma descended, and the dogs continued their pursuit. The puma climbed up another tree, and the dogs followed in order to catch him. He was in the very top of the tree, holding on as hard as he could. Then he started to climb again, higher and higher toward the sky. The hunters were saying to the dogs: "Do not let him escape!" They put wings on the dogs, which dashed off in pursuit of the puma. The latter climbed up to the first sky and then he descended again. As he reached the earth, the owners of the dogs shot him with their arrows. When he was dead they skinned him and roasted him, and then they cut him into several pieces to eat him.

Informant: Esteban Mariano

Source: Verna ms.

Motif content

F10.	Journey to upper world.
F989.15.	Hunt for extraordinary (magic) animal.
F1021.	Extraordinary flights through air.
F1021.1.	Flight on artificial wings.
R311.	Tree refuge.
R323.	Refuge in upper world.

136. The Star-Woman

There once was a twelve-year-old boy. He took some blood from his shin and threw it up to the sky where Star lived. The blood drew near to her. The boy went out hunting and found a little bird, Pestiokít. He said: "I shall shoot off my arrow." He shot four arrows and had no more left. So he sat down. He looked for the arrows but could not find them. It was late. He cried. Suddenly the woman, Star, approached him from behind.

"You are crying," she said to the boy. "No, I am not crying." Star placed an arrow on his shoulder.

"Take it," she said. "This is what you are thinking about." She added: "Now you must go; it is nighttime. You do not have to sleep with your parents. Sleep far away. Around midnight I shall come to you."

The boy climbed up on his platform bed and retired. He fell asleep. When Star came to him, he wanted to scream from fear. "Do not call out," said Star.

When day broke Star arose and hid inside a gourd. She appeared only during the daytime. She saw her mother-in-law making a net bag. "I feel like working, too," said Star. "Ask your mother if I can. I want to make a bag like she does." The boy asked his mother, and she gave it to him. He kept it, because Star did not know how to work. "Ask for a plate," said Star. "I feel like urinating."

"No," said the mother-in-law, "she has dirty habits. How can you urinate in a plate?" Another old woman came by and gave Star a plate. She began to urinate, and fine crystals came out. She filled the plate. The mother-in-law said: "How beautiful your wife's urine is! I want some, too!"

"Why did you not give me what I asked for?" asked the boy.

Star then asked the boy: "Where were you planting before?"

"Right there." She began to gather all the old plants, piled them up, picked up a handful of dirt, and blew on it. New watermelons, beans, maize, and melons appeared. When they went out she once again hid inside a gourd.

The people went to another place. The boy's sister was carrying Star inside the gourd, in a net bag. When she started getting tired, the girl said: "What am I carrying? It is very heavy. Could it be Star?"

She threw it away. The gourd broke open. The people who had departed died. The boy nearly fell. "I think you have made a mess," said Star. She started throwing handfuls of dirt behind him, and then the people returned to life. When they arrived at a spot, Star left. It was nighttime. Star was angry. "If you miss me," she said to her husband, "do not digress onto another road. There are three roads, but the one that goes to my house is straight."

Some four days passed. The youth felt sad and thought about his wife.

"My house lies along the straight road," she had taught him. "One path goes to the house of the hawks, one to the (king?) vultures, and one to the *palas*, the black vultures." The boy passed by two roads and entered onto the next one, farther along. The son of the hawk upon seeing the boy said: "I saw him first."

The vulture had a cavity in his shoulders. He said: "How handsome I am! It was I who saw him first." He then said to the boy: "Do you want to play with me? If you want to, hold out your hand."

The boy held it out and the vulture lifted him up and carried him off. But around them there were a lot of *ucle* and bottle tree thorns. The vulture began to beat the boy against them, trying to kill him. "Are you dead yet?" he asked.

"No," replied the boy. The bird dropped him once more.

"Are you dead yet?" The boy did not reply.

"He is dead now; I shall eat him," said the vulture.

When he had descended, he started to eat him. The boy's eye was already gone. A fly went to tell his wife. "Is it not your husband whom the vultures are eating?"

The woman went to him. The vulture's son had already eaten an eye. She found the young vulture suffering from indigestion while the others slept. She began to beat him and to search for her husband's flesh to make a new body. The eye was missing. Star wanted to kill the vulture's son.

"No, I did not eat anything," he said. "I did not go near him." Star went to fetch a *suncho* fruit and placed it on the boy's face; then he got both eyes back. She took him with her to the sky, and he never returned.

Informant: Sentawó

Source: Mashnshnek 1972, pp. 138–139.

Summary

Star descends from sky and marries boy. During day she hides inside gourd until finally she is discovered. On several occasions she performs marvels: urinating crystals, creating fruits and vegetables. After she returns to sky, boy goes in search of her. On the way he is killed and partly eaten by vulture, but Star finds him, resuscitates him, and takes him up to sky.

Motif content

A762.	Star descends as human being.
A762.2.	Mortal marries star-girl.
B16.3.	Devastating birds.
B33.	Man-eating birds.
B291.+.	Fly as messenger. (B291. Animal as messenger.)
C15.1.1.	Wish for star wife realized.
C30.	Tabu: offending supernatural relative.
C921.	Immediate death for breaking tabu.
C932.	Loss of wife (husband) for breaking tabu.
D439.5.2.	Transformation: star to person.
D1002.1.	Magic urine.
D1454.+.	Crystals from urine. (D1454. Parts of human body furnish treasure.)
D1819.1.	Magic knowledge of another's thoughts.
D2157.2.	Magic quick growth of crops.
D2161.3.1.1.	Eyes torn out magically replaced.
D2178.+.	Vegetables produced by magic. (D2178. Objects produced by magic.)

E1.	Person comes to life.
E32.0.1.	Eaten person resuscitated.
E35.	Resuscitation from fragments of body.
E50.+.	Resuscitation by sprinkling earth. (E50. Resuscitation by magic.)
E121.	Resuscitation by supernatural person.
E781.	Eyes successfully replaced.
F10.	Journey to upper world.
H1385.3.	Quest for vanished wife (mistress).
K2295.+.	Treacherous bird. (K2295. Treacherous animals.)
Q411.	Death as punishment.
R13.3.	Person carried off by bird.
T111.2.	Woman from sky-world marries mortal man.

137. Katés, the Morning Star

In primordial times a young man was outside every night, looking at the beautiful stars, for the stars were women. He especially looked at Katés (Morning Star), thinking: "I should like her to be my wife."

In the morning he went to hunt birds. He shot off an arrow and lost it. He began to cry over the lost arrow. When he was tired of looking for it a woman appeared behind him, saying: "Here is your arrow. Why are you crying?"

"Because I had lost it."

"But why are you shooting at me? It was me you were shooting at, not the bird."[39]

"Well, I did not know. I shot at a bird."

"Here is your arrow. Go home. Tonight you must sleep some distance away from your father and mother. I shall be there at midnight."

The boy could not sleep. He was waiting. Exactly at midnight the woman came. Now he had a wife. In the morning everyone looked at the young man whom nobody had wanted previously. No girl from his village liked him. How he had suffered because of that! But that day he got a wife.

When the sun was high his wife (Katés) asked him: "Does your mother have a pan?"

"Why?"

"I want to urinate."

[39]*Pétohoi* = great kiskadee (*Pitangus sulphuratus*). The identification of heavenly beings with birds is a frequent occurrence; besides, the cosmological habitat of the latter is the sky.

He asked: "Mother, can you give me the pan for my wife to urinate in?"

Not surprisingly the old woman said: "No, why should she urinate in my pan? I do not like it."

Then another old woman who lived farther away said: "I have a pan."

And she gave it to him. But when Katés urinated it was colored beads; she urinated many-colored beads. When she was finished she saw that they were beautiful. After a while she said to the boy: "Does your mother have a net bag that she has just started to make?"

The young man asked the old woman who said: "Yes, I do."

She gave it to him. Instead of making the net bag with string alone, Katés mixed the string with the beads and ended up with a very pretty design. But the mother said: "She takes very long. If it were me I would have finished long ago."

She did not know that Katés is a night creature and never works during the day. Then Katés became angry. She gave up working before she was halfway finished and said: "Here, give it to your mother!"

When the old woman saw it she said: "Oh no, do not take it away from her, my son!"

But Katés wanted nothing to do with it.

Later they thought of moving to another place in search of food. When Katés heard that her mother-in-law wanted to leave, she asked her husband: "Do you have a *patéhna* [a large gourd used for storing necklaces, charms, and ornaments]? I want to enter a gourd. Does your mother have one?"

"Yes, we have one."

"I want to enter it so they can carry me."

Katés did not show herself in the daytime, and neither her mother-in-law nor anyone else knew her.

They went off, with a girl of about nineteen carrying the *patéhna*. "Can my younger sister carry this?" asked the boy.

When they were far away, he said: "I am going this way. I shall look for something to eat while we are traveling."

They went off in another direction. When the others arrived the girl was tired, for the gourd was very heavy: "What is it I am carrying? It seems to be Katés."

Unceremoniously she threw it to the ground, and as she did everybody died, falling to the ground.

The young man had gone out to gather honey. He had brought ropes, for the trees had few branches and he needed the ropes to hoist himself up and extract the honey. When his sister threw Katés on the ground he was hanging by the rope and so he did not fall, but he received a blow and died a little. Soon he became well again, and then he realized: "Ah, that must have been Katés! It seems they threw her to the ground."

He crossed the road to look for them and found them all dead, and there was Katés, looking at them. Her husband asked her: "What happened?"

"Your sister threw me to the ground. She was saying: 'Why should I be carrying this heavy thing? Maybe it is Katés. I had better throw it away.'"

Katés gathered earth to revive the dead people. Taking some earth she sprinkled it over them, and they all arose and said: "Ah, I was asleep!"

"No, you were not asleep. You threw me on the ground and then you died."

When they reached the place of the new camp Katés was already thinking of something else: "What is there around here?"

"There are plants, fields."

"Let us have a look."

When they arrived the cultivated plants were all dry, and the wild plants and trees had dried up as well. Then Katés gathered all the dry plants, took some earth, and blew it over them. All the plants revived— melons, maize, squash, watermelons, *ancos* (a kind of squash), *watóne*, *kehát* (cacti)—and immediately fruit started to grow.

Afterward Katés wanted to go to the sky, leaving all the plants on the earth, and she told her husband: "I am leaving now, because your mother and all your relatives do not like me. I am leaving! If you miss me a lot you can follow me later. But be careful not to take the wrong path! There are three paths. One is in the middle and goes straight; that is my path (Katés *ikái*) which leads to Wéla, my father. The other two go off to the side; the first one is *atás ikái* (the path of the vultures), and the second is *ahóusas ikái* (the path of the hawks). Along one the vultures live, and along the other the hawks."

When the young man went after his wife he followed the Katés *ikái*. Some distance along the road, where it crossed the *atás ikái*, the children of the hawk were playing with those of the vulture. Seeing somebody approaching they said: "There is a man coming."

Two of the children, one of Vulture's and one of Hawk's, went up to their respective houses to inform their fathers. Later, when the two fathers came, one was saying: "My son came to tell me first."

The other said: "No, my son came first."

Ahóusa was the more insistent one, saying that it was his son who had seen the man first and that therefore he had the right to seize the young man, take him home, and eat him. Finally they ate him.

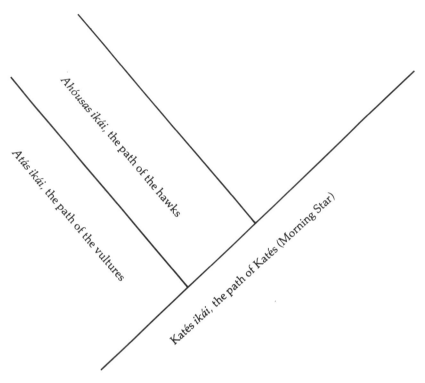

Atás ikái, the path of the vultures

Ahóusas ikái, the path of the hawks

Katés ikái, the path of Katés (Morning Star)

Kataaki (Fly), who was the niece of Katés, was there, and they did not give her anything to eat; there was not enough of the young man to go around. Then she became angry and said: "I think that the one they just ate was the husband of my aunt. I am going to go and tell her."

And she went.

The messenger came and said: "Look, my aunt, they have just eaten your husband."

"Who did?"

"Well, vultures and hawks."

"Then I am going."

Katés went to where the birds lived, and when she arrived she asked: "Who was it who ate him? Maybe you ate my husband, Atá."

"No, perhaps it was Ahóusa."

She asked Ahóusa, who said: "No, I do not know who it could have been."

Angrily Katés said: "If you do not tell me who it was I shall kill all of you."

They summoned all the hawks and the vultures before her, and the son of Atá said: "Ahóusa ate him first."

Then Katés threw him to the ground and crouched down by him: "I am going to take everything out of this fellow. Let us see if I can find all the pieces."

Ahóusa lay there quietly, for he was afraid. If they had not told Katés the truth it would have been worse. She would have killed everyone. It was better that she searched inside him. Katés extracted first one piece from him that he had eaten, then another, and then yet another, in order to make her husband a new body. Only one eye was missing, the right one. She went to look for a pigeon and gave the young man a pigeon eye, and that was why he acquired a very red right eye.

Then Katés made him over again. Joining together all the parts of his body she picked up some earth and sprinkled it over her husband, and the man was remade. Afterward she took him with her to the sky where she lives. That earth where vultures and hawks live is like this one. When the young man arrived he began to hunt deer for his father-in-law, who was Wéla (moon), and for his family.

After spending a long time with his father-in-law, the young man wanted to return to this earth to see his mother again. Katés said to him: "This time I shall not let you go alone. I can accompany you to where the hawks and vultures live, and from there you will be able to continue by yourself."

They set off quietly and reached the place where the vultures are. There Katés stopped in order to return home again, and the young man went back to the earth.

Afterward his mother asked him: "How did you get away from there? How did you get here? How come you are alive? I thought you were dead."

She knew it is dangerous there, with the vultures and the hawks. He told her what had happened to him: "First the vultures and the hawks ate me, but my wife's niece sent a message to her and then my wife came for me. She gathered all the pieces of my body which they had eaten, and remade me."

Thus the young man told his mother.

Informant: Kasókchi ilánek

Source: Siffredi ms.

Summary

Star (Katés) descends in response to young man's wish and marries him. She demonstrates her magic power by urinating multicolored beads. Starting to work on net bag begun by mother-in-law, she is offended by latter's criticism of her slowness and stops. During daytime she hides in gourd. When sister-in-law gets tired of carrying gourd on journey she throws it away, and Katés angrily kills everyone, subsequently reviving them.

Feeling unwanted she returns to sky. Husband follows her, but despite her warnings he is eaten by vultures and hawks. Katés extracts pieces of his body from bird and remakes and revives body. Later young man returns to earth to see his mother.

Motif content

A761.6.+.	Stars are women. (A761.6. Stars thought of as living beings.)
A762.	Star descends as human being.
A762.2.	Mortal marries star-girl.
A764.1.	Stars as children of the moon.
B16.3.	Devastating birds.
B33.	Man-eating birds.
B291.+.	Fly as messenger. (B291. Animal as messenger.)
C15.1.1.	Wish for star wife realized.
C30.	Tabu: offending supernatural relative.
C921.	Immediate death for breaking tabu.
D439.5.2.	Transformation: star to person.
D440.+.	Transformation: star to bird. (D440. Transformation: object to animal.)
D961.1.	Garden produced by magic.
D1002.1.	Magic urine.
D1071.0.1.	Jewels produced by magic.
D1454.+.	Jewels from urine. (D1454. Parts of human body furnish treasure.)
D2157.2.	Magic quick growth of crops.
D2161.3.1.1.	Eyes torn out magically replaced.
E1.	Person comes to life.
E30.	Resuscitation by arrangement of members.
E32.0.1.	Eaten person resuscitated.
E35.	Resuscitation from fragments of body.
E50.+.	Resuscitation by sprinkling earth. (E50. Resuscitation by magic.)
E121.	Resuscitation by supernatural person.
E781.	Eyes successfully replaced.
E781.1.	Substituted eyes. Lost eyes are replaced by those of another person or animal.
F10.	Journey to upper world.
F10.1.	Return from upper world.
F11.3.	Man goes to heaven for limited time.
F15.	Visit to star-world.

F167.1.	Animals in otherworld.
H1385.3.	Quest for vanished wife (mistress).
N699.6.	Overheard wish is realized.
Q411.	Death as punishment.
T111.2.	Woman from sky-world marries mortal man.

138. Star-Woman Marries a Man

There was a boy who used to lie at night looking up at the sky and saying to himself: "How I would like to marry that beautiful star up there!" He got blood from his leg and flung it upward, since the star was not down here on the earth. He kept saying: "How beautiful that star is!"

On the following day the boy went out to hunt for a bird, and shot three arrows at it. The fourth arrow he could not find. He wondered: "Where could that arrow have fallen?" In fact, the star had hidden it. The boy looked everywhere for his arrow. "This is where I shot it," he was saying. At that moment he stepped on a thorn which went through his foot. He tried to pull it out but was unable to, and he cried and cried, for he could not even walk.

After a while he heard behind him the sound of someone laughing: "Who could be laughing at me?" he wondered, and again he cried. Suddenly somebody softly touched his head and asked him: "Why are you crying?" "No particular reason; only I stepped on a thorn and now I cannot get it out," said the boy. "So you are the one who is always looking at me when I am going to bed. Think hard and try to remember." "Who can that be?" the boy thought. The star said: "I am going to remove that thorn from your foot right now. But tonight you must sleep by yourself; tell your mother to sleep apart from you."

In the evening the boy lay down to sleep, with his bed well made. The star came to lie down, and said: "Do not tell anyone that I am here." In the morning when the boy's mother woke up she asked him: "My son, where did that girl come from?" "I do not know; she came last night." "Well, get up; we are going to eat," said his mother. While everyone was talking the star asked the boy where she could go to urinate. When she urinated all kinds of necklaces came out—green, white, azure, all colors. Then she said to the boy: "Ask your grandmother for chaguar, for I want to make a net bag."

That evening when they went to bed the star said to the boy: "When we leave tomorrow, tell your sister to put the bag down on the ground softly. If she throws it down abruptly everybody will die." The next morning all the people lay dead, bellies in the air. "My sister must have thrown the net bag down suddenly," thought the boy. The star came and said to him: "I am going to make everybody well again. You people really make a lot of trouble for me!" Picking up some earth she threw it over the people, and everyone stood up.

The boy was sad because the star was leaving. But she had told him exactly how to get to her house. He said to himself: "I think I shall follow my little wife." He went, but mistakenly took the wrong road, the road of the hawks, and they killed him.

That night the star had a nightmare. She dreamed that the hawks had killed her husband. When she woke up she went to kill those hawks. She went to their house and asked: "Which one of you killed my husband?" Nobody knew, but she did, and when they went to sleep she clubbed them all to death, leaving no one alive. Afterward she disemboweled them, and from the pieces of the boy's flesh she reassembled his body—hair, ears, everything. The girl gathered together the flesh, and then she pressed down on it. The boy got up. "I was really sound asleep!" he said. "You were not asleep; the hawks had killed you." The star took her husband up to the sky with her.

But when it was daylight the boy had to return to the earth again. The pigeon said to him: "I shall take you home, I know the way. I always go in that direction." Then came the hawk and the vulture, and they said the same. But they were all lying. The boy climbed up on the vulture. When they were already near the bird said to him: "Get down, get down." But the boy did not want to get down, saying that he was thirsty. "All right, I shall take you to a place where you can drink." When they reached the lagoon the boy climbed onto the branch of a tree. The vulture said to him: "I am going to throw you in and then I shall lift you up, but when I throw you, you must shout." When the boy fell into the water he shouted, but he drowned there and disappeared.

Informant: Sekiome

Source: Verna ms.

Summary

Star descends to young man who has admired her beauty in the sky. She demonstrates her magic power by urinating jewelry and resuscitating dead people. After she leaves, her husband follows her but is eaten by hawks. She kills hawks and revives him from pieces of his flesh, then takes him to sky. After returning to earth on back of bird he drowns.

Motif content

A762.	Star descends as human being.
A762.2.	Mortal marries star-girl.
B16.3.	Devastating birds.
B33.	Man-eating birds.
B552.	Man carried by bird.
C15.1.1.	Wish for star wife realized.
C30.	Tabu: offending supernatural relative.
C921.	Immediate death for breaking tabu.
D439.5.2.	Transformation: star to person.
D1002.1.	Magic urine.
D1071.0.1.	Jewels produced by magic.
D1454.+.	Jewels from urine. (D1454. Parts of human body furnish treasure.)
D1810.8.2.3.	Murder made known in a dream.
D1812.3.3.11.	Death of another revealed in dream.
E1.	Person comes to life.
E30.	Resuscitation by arrangement of members.
E32.0.1.	Eaten person resuscitated.
E50.+.	Resuscitation by sprinkling earth. (E50. Resuscitation by magic.)
E121.	Resuscitation by supernatural person.
F10.	Journey to upper world.
F10.1.	Return from upper world.
F11.3.	Man goes to heaven for limited time.
F15.	Visit to star-world.
F62.2.	Birds carry person from upper world.
F827.	Extraordinary ornaments.
H1385.3.	Quest for vanished wife (mistress).
J652.	Inattention to warnings.
K959.2.	Murder in one's sleep.
K2295.+.	Treacherous bird. (K2295. Treacherous animals.)
N699.6.	Overheard wish is realized.
Q411.	Death as punishment.
Q411.6.	Death as punishment for murder.
Q422.0.1.	Punishment: beating to death.
T111.2.	Woman from sky-world marries mortal man.

139. Katés, the Morning Star Woman

There was a man who was so ugly that no woman wanted him. All the women in his village persecuted him, throwing sticks at him. At night he lay down to sleep outside and started to look up at Katés: "What a pretty girl! How I should like to marry her!"

He drew some blood from his tongue and spat up toward the sky, staining Katés's dress. He was already in love with her.

The following night Katés descended to the earth and had intercourse with the young man. When dawn was near she said to him: "I come from the sky, and at night I shall be your wife. Do not tell anybody that I have come. I do not go about during the daytime, and so that no one will see me I am going to hide inside that gourd."

After a few days the people of that village decided to move to another spot. The previous night Katés had told her husband: "Tell your younger sister to carry the gourd carefully, and when she wants to rest, to put it very gently on the ground. If she drops it all the villagers will die."

When they left the young man's sister carried the gourd with Katés inside, but it was very heavy, and when she grew tired she threw it on the ground. Everybody died, lying stretched out, face up. Only the young man was left alive, sitting there. When he saw that all had died he asked Katés to revive them. "All right, I will, but afterward I shall go back up there (to the sky), for you people mistreated me."

Picking up a fistful of earth she sprinkled it over the dead bodies, and everyone stood up once more.

The women went to gather wild beans, but when they got there they found only leaves. Then Katés spat into the hands of her sister-in-law, the one who had thrown her on the ground, and at once many beans appeared. But afterward she went back up to the sky as she had said she would.

Informant: Kíki

Source: Siffredi ms.

Summary

Star descends from sky to marry unpopular man. When his sister drops gourd in which she is hiding she kills all villagers, then revives them and returns to sky.

Motif content

A762.	Star descends as human being.
A762.2.	Mortal marries star-girl.
C15.1.1.	Wish for star wife realized.
C30.	Tabu: offending supernatural relative.
C921.	Immediate death for breaking tabu.
C932.	Loss of wife (husband) for breaking tabu.

D439.5.2.	Transformation: star to person.
D451.8.+.	Transformation: leaf to beans. (D451.8. Transformation: leaf to another object.)
D560.+.	Transformation by spitting. (D560. Transformation by various means.)
D2178.+.	Vegetables produced by magic. (D2178. Objects produced by magic.)
E1.	Person comes to life.
E50.+.	Resuscitation by sprinkling earth. (E50. Resuscitation by magic.)
E121.	Resuscitation by supernatural person.
F576.	Extraordinary ugliness.
N699.6.	Overheard wish is realized.
Q411.	Death as punishment.
T75.0.1.	Suitors ill-treated.
T111.2.	Woman from sky-world marries mortal man.
T475.	Unknown (clandestine) paramour.

140. Star-Woman Marries a Man

There was a very ugly man who was always running after the women, but they did not like him and would hit him. Once this man took blood from his tongue and flung it up to the sky. Then a star descended, and she stayed here on earth. She married the ugly man.

The star took the man to another place along with all his people. In order to be able to carry her he put her inside a gourd and covered it, and then his sister placed the gourd in a net bag which she carried as she went. After a while the girl grew tired from carrying such a heavy load, and she let it fall to the ground. All those who were out in the brushwood with their axes, gathering honey, died. The star said: "We have to pick up some earth and throw it up toward the sky." She did it, and immediately all those who had died reappeared, alive and working.

Later they looked for something to eat, but found nothing but leaves. There was not a single fruit in that place. Then the star said to her sister-in-law: "Take a leaf from any tree." When the sister-in-law obeyed, the star spat in her hand, and the wild beans appeared.

Informant: Alipa

Source: Verna ms.

Motif content

A762.	Star descends as human being.
A762.2.	Mortal marries star-girl.
C30.	Tabu: offending supernatural relative.
C921.	Immediate death for breaking tabu.
D439.5.2.	Transformation: star to person.
D451.8. + .	Transformation: leaf to beans. (D451.8. Transformation: leaf to another object.)
D560. + .	Transformation by spitting. (D560. Transformation by various means.)
D2178. + .	Vegetables produced by magic. (D2178. Objects produced by magic.)
E1.	Person comes to life.
E50. + .	Resuscitation by sprinkling earth. (E50. Resuscitation by magic.)
E121.	Resuscitation by supernatural person.
F576.	Extraordinary ugliness.
Q411.	Death as punishment.
T75.0.1.	Suitors ill-treated.
T111.2.	Woman from sky-world marries mortal man.

141. Moon Remakes an Ugly Man

There was a young man who was very ugly, and the women whom he went after did not want him. They were always mistreating him, picking up firebrands and putting them on his body, until they really frightened him.

Thus the young man said to his mother: "Do not be afraid. I am going away, for the women intimidate me. They do not leave me alone; they burn me all over. I cannot stand it any more! I am going to Moon's house to see what he can do."

He went off, and when he got there (to the sky) Moon's children saw him coming and said to their father: "Look, someone is coming. Who could it be?"

When the young man arrived he said to Moon: "I came to visit you to see if you would like to change my face and my whole body, for nobody likes me. Those women go after me and throw burning sticks at my face and body. I want you to remake my entire body—improve it, change it to look beautiful."

Moon did as he asked, and said: "The women who did not treat you badly you must love, but the worst ones you must mistreat in turn."

After Moon had made him handsome the young man returned to the earth again, and then all the women who previously did not like him suddenly wanted him. All the women wanted him.

Informant: Kíki

Source: Siffredi ms.

Motif content

A745.	Family of the moon.
D52.2.	Ugly man becomes handsome.
F10.	Journey to upper world.
F10.1.	Return from upper world.
F16.	Visit to land of moon.
F576.	Extraordinary ugliness.
N818.1.+.	Moon as helper. (N818.1. Sun as helper.)
T75.0.1.	Suitors ill-treated.

142. Moon Remakes an Ugly Man

There was a boy whom nobody wanted. His face was pockmarked from smallpox, and he was very ugly. No woman wanted him, and all the villagers were always hitting him. One day he got tired of the situation and said: "I am going to Moon."

Moon asked him: "What do you want?"

"I am suffering a lot down there, for the people are very mean and they all hit me. I have come to ask you for magic power."

Moon changed his face, making him handsome, and said to him: "You have to hit the bad ones with your right hand, and then they will die. The others you must hit with your left hand, and they will live."

The boy returned to the village, and when he struck some people with his right hand they died. Those that he struck with the left hand did not die. He was able to get rid of all those who used to hit him, for he alone possessed the magic power that Moon had given him.

Informant: Alenta

Source: Siffredi ms.

Motif content

D52.2.	Ugly man becomes handsome.
D1720.	Acquisition of magic powers.

D2060.	Death or bodily injury by magic.
F16.	Visit to land of moon.
F576.	Extraordinary ugliness.
N818.1.+.	Moon as helper. (N818.1. Sun as helper.)
Q280.	Unkindness punished.
Q411.	Death as punishment.
T75.0.1.	Suitors ill-treated.

143. Moon Grants Strength to a Man

There once was a man whom the people did not like. They beat him everywhere—his eyes, his body, blackening one of his eyes. "I shall go to the place where Moon lives," he said, "to see if he will give me strength." So he went to Moon's house. The man's face was deep purple. "What happened?" Moon asked.

"Have you not seen my face?" answered the man.

"Come, my son," said Moon, calling the man over. The latter approached. Moon was seated on a chair. "I have suffered a great deal here among the others," the man said. "They do not like me. None of my people like me." Moon changed his face so that his eyes were no longer swollen; he changed his face, removing all the wrinkles. Moon said: "All those who like you a lot you need only touch with your left hand and they will live; those who do not like you, you must touch with your right hand and they will die. Thus the men of your country will leave you alone. They will stop beating you." The man returned home. His enemies, those who liked to beat him, approached and once again began to beat him. The man struck them with his right hand, and they died. The ones he struck with his left hand were knocked over, but remained alive.

He then called the remaining men who used to beat him and said: "May those who beat me come back."

The ones who were still alive returned.

He struck them and killed them all. That was the end of them, since this man now had the strength Moon had given him. Since he alone had Moon's strength, he killed everyone else.

Informant: Esteban Mariano

Source: Mashnshnek 1972, p. 123.

Motif content

D52.	Magic change to different appearance.
D1720.	Acquisition of magic powers.
D2060.	Death or bodily injury by magic.
F16.	Visit to land of moon.
N818.1.+.	Moon as helper. (N818.1. Sun as helper.)
Q280.	Unkindness punished.
Q411.	Death as punishment.

144. Fox Deceives Bee and Has His Bodily Orifices Stopped Up

Naákiwoki, the *moro-moro* bee, had a daughter. As she was about to go out to the country she left the girl in the house, saying to Fox: "Take care of my daughter! Do not do bad things!"

"No," said Fox.

Then Naákiwoki left her there and went out.

Since Fox is roguish he grabbed a little rabbit-skin bag, one of those they use to put honey in, and said to the daughter: "Come on, let us eat!"

They ate and ate until they finished the honey. Then, as Fox is a rogue, he planned to kill Naákiwoki's daughter. After he had killed her he put her in the bag where the honey was. He threw her in, tied the bag again, and hung it in the same place. Then he went to hide among the weeds.

Around noon the mother returned. When she was nearly there she said: "Daughter, come outside!"

Nothing happened.

"What is wrong, daughter?"

She kept talking and talking, but no one answered. Then she realized: "Maybe Fox killed my daughter. It is just possible."

She looked into all the bags she had, poking about everywhere, but her daughter did not appear. She began to insult him: "The miserable Fox! Now he has killed my daughter. I am sure he has!"

Finally Naákiwoki found the bag, which was inside the house. She touched it: "Could this be my daughter?"

When she untied it she realized that it was, and took her outside. "She is dead!"

She ordered her cousin to call the rest of the Naákiwos family, and they gathered where she was. She told them what had happened when she had gone to the country, leaving her daughter behind. On their way there the Naákiwos had seen Fox playing with the other child of Naákiwoki, and so they all went over there. They were many.

When they got to where Fox was they grabbed beeswax and they all began to rough him up. One put wax in his eyes, another in his nose, another put it in his mouth. Finally Fox could not breathe anymore. How he was yelling! They hobbled him and continued putting wax in his eyes, in his anus, everywhere. When they had stopped up all his orifices, Fox had to die. And he died. Then the eldest of the Naákiwos stepped on his head, saying: "Don't be such a miserable creature! What a rascal!"

After having murdered Fox they went to have a party at Naákiwoki's house. Each person had brought a bag of honey, and each contributed it for the party, so that the daughter would be resuscitated. Since they were many, and each one had brought a bag, there was a lot of honey. When they all began to eat this honey together, Naákiwoki's daughter was already moving. They said: "Now she is going to come alive again! Now she will eat with us!"

When they had all eaten well, they went to lift up the girl. They lifted her up and she greeted the whole family, all her brothers and her grandmother. When she finished greeting all the relatives, they gave her a bag of honey. She ate and then said: "I am tired of sleeping; I am tired of it." But Naákiwoki told her: "You were not sleeping! The one who made you die was Fox. He is the one who killed you!"

Informant: Kíki

Source: Siffredi ms.

Summary

Pretending to guard bee-woman's daughter, fox kills her instead. Bee family gather and kill fox by stopping up his bodily orifices, then resuscitate dead girl.

Motif content

E1.	Person comes to life.
J1117.+.	Fox as trickster. (J1117. Animal as trickster.)
K1461.	Caring for the child: child killed.
K2295.+.	Treacherous fox. (K2295. Treacherous animals.)
Q211.4.	Murder of children punished.
Q411.6.	Death as punishment for murder.
Q450.+.	Punishment: bodily orifices stopped up. (Q450. Cruel punishments.)
S302.	Children murdered.

145. Fox Makes Fun of the Women Who Grind Algarrobo

There were some naked women who used to live alone in the north. They did not have any clothing, not even a rag, but they had a lot of white algarrobo. They were pounding algarrobo to make cookies with the flour, thinking that maybe their brother would come to visit them.

The boy was saying just then to the people of his camp: "Maybe I shall go over there to visit my sisters' huts."

Fox heard the youth speaking of going to visit his sisters, and decided to follow him.

When he came to where the boy's sisters were, he began to look for the woman who had the best vulva. The one with the biggest was the one he wanted. When he saw a vulva he liked, his penis rose up and he could not get it down. He was sitting down and it always wanted to rise up.

When their brother was ready they had already filled his sack with those cookies that they made with the algarrobo flour. He said to Fox: "Now we are ready; let us go."

"No, my foot has gone to sleep . . . you go!" The brother went away.

Whenever Fox saw that a woman had a small vulva, he would spit at her for he did not like her. When he saw another who had a large one, he liked her, and so his penis would rise up and he would watch her.

When the youth had gone just a short way he stopped and said: "Now my feet are asleep!"

Fox had gotten up. His penis was already hard. Then the women closed in on him and clubbed him until they killed him. They did not like what he had done with them since they did not have any clothes and were going around stark naked.

Informant: Kíki

Source: Siffredi ms.

Motif content

F112.	Journey to land of women.
F709.1.	Country of the naked.
J1117.+.	Fox as trickster. (J1117. Animal as trickster.)
Q240.+.	Lechery punished. (Q240. Sexual sins punished.)
Q422.0.1.	Punishment: beating to death.

146. The Fox and the Cariama

Fox killed a jaguar, baked it, and ate it. Cariama came by. Fox said that there was water nearby. The two of them bathed. "Who will win?" asked Fox.

They plunged into the water and emerged; they then dove into the water once more. Finally Cariama pulled out a feather and planted it in the water. He then got out, and Fox believed he was still underwater.

The bird went to look at the oven where the jaguar was, took out the meat, and carried it off. Meanwhile Fox remained in the water. It seems he finally got tired, and took out the feather. There was no cariama bird. Fox returned home and looked for the meat in the oven, but there was nothing. The bird had stolen it.

Cariama carried it away, cut it, and ate it. He then met an old man and gave him the head of the jaguar. But since Fox had magic power, he got some more meat.

Informant: Alipa

Source: Mashnshnek 1972, p. 134.

Motif content

B191.+.	Fox as magician. (B191. Animal as magician.)
H1543.	Contest in remaining under water.
J1117.+.	Bird as trickster. (J1117. Animal as trickster.)
J1118.	Clever bird.
K16.2.	Diving match: trickster eats food while dupe is under water.
K341.	Owner's interest distracted while goods are stolen.
K1800.	Deception by disguise or illusion.
K1881.	Absent person seems to be present.
L315.	Small animal overcomes large.

147. The Fox and the Jaguar

Fox found a wagon and began to follow it. There was a lot of cheese in the wagon. He met Jaguar. "Where did you get the cheese you are eating?" asked Jaguar.

"I got it from the water," said Fox.

"And how do you get it?" asked Jaguar.

"I attach a big stone to myself to get it out when the moon is full. The moon casts her reflection on the water, and there is the cheese," Fox replied.

"Are you going to get some, too?" he asked Jaguar.

"Yes, I want to eat, too," said Jaguar.

"I tie myself to a stone," Fox explained.

"Tie me up," said Jaguar.

Fox got a rope and tied a stone to it.

"Are you going to tie yourself to it, too?" asked Jaguar.

"No, I am going to push you," said Fox. He tied him up.

"Let us see," said Jaguar. "Push me in."

So Fox pushed him in. Jaguar was now in the water and began to look for the cheese. He could not find it. He began to get nervous and wanted to get out, but was unable to because the stone was heavy. He looked for the knot where the stone was tied but could not find it.

The *mojarra* fish came by: "What's up, Jaguar?" he asked.

"Fox has tricked me," replied Jaguar.

"Untie this knot." The fish untied it. Jaguar was angry. "He will not get away. I shall eat this Juan." He climbed out of the water. "Where could he have gone?" he asked himself. He followed Fox's tracks. "This is the way he went," said Jaguar.

Farther along he found him. "This time you will not get away," warned Jaguar. "I am going to eat you."

"No, Jaguar, I have a roast."

"Come with me, I am going to eat you," said Jaguar.

"No, I have a roast," said Fox. "Come, let us eat."

Jaguar obeyed and began to eat.

Fox blew up little bags and filled them full of flies.

"Be careful," Fox said to Jaguar. "When you eat the roast a lot of wind comes by, so I tie myself to a strong tree trunk, and the wind does not carry me away."

Jaguar heard the flies making a loud noise inside the bag, as if a great wind were approaching.

"The wind is coming now," said Fox.

"All right, let us tie ourselves up!" said Jaguar. "Tie me behind," he requested.

"I shall tie you up because the strong winds are coming," replied Fox. "I shall tie you up tightly."

He started to secure him. There was no wind, just the noise inside the bag, as if a great wind were passing. He tied him up. As soon as Jaguar was tied, Fox left. It was already late.

"Why is there wind?" asked Jaguar. "There is so much noise."

Fox had tied the little bag around his tail. But he was alone.

"I think he is fooling me!" said Jaguar. The hummingbird passed by. Jaguar called him over. "Come here, come here! Untie me!"

The hummingbird paid no attention and passed on by. Armadillo came by. "Armadillo, come, untie me. I am going after Juan!"

But Armadillo passed him by. He did not listen. Skunk came by. Jaguar called to him: "Skunk, come, untie me."

Skunk obeyed and untied him. "What do you have on your tail?" he asked.

Jaguar looked behind. "I thought that was the wind. Fox fooled me. But he will not escape; I shall eat him," he declared. He took off the bag and looked inside. There were flies inside it. He went in search of Fox but could not find him.

Informant: Cepillo

Source: Mashnshnek 1972, p. 134.

Summary

Fox tricks Jaguar into diving into water in search of cheese, with stone tied to his body. Struggling to get out he is aided by fish. Next, Fox attaches bag full of flies to Jaguar's tail and ties him to tree, telling him that buzzing sound is strong wind. Skunk unties him.

Motif content

B430. + .	Helpful skunk. (B430. Helpful wild beasts.)
B470.	Helpful fish.
B540.	Animal rescuer or retriever.
J1117. + .	Fox as trickster. (J1117. Animal as trickster.)
J1791.	Reflection in water thought to be the original of the thing reflected.
J1791.3.	Diving for cheese.
J1812.	Other sounds misunderstood.
J1820.	Inappropriate action from misunderstanding.
J2300.	Gullible fools.
J2413.	Foolish imitation by an animal. Tries to go beyond his powers.
K713.	Deception into allowing oneself to be fettered.
K713.1.1.	Animal allows himself to be tied to another for safety.
K1020.	Deception into disastrous attempt to procure food.
K1200.	Deception into humiliating position.
K1800.	Deception by disguise or illusion.
K1887.	Illusory sounds.

K2295.+.   Treacherous fox. (K2295. Treacherous animals.)
K2296.   Treacherous partner.

148. The Fox and the Iguana

There was *mistol*, and Fox began to gather some. When he had piled up all the *mistol* he could find, he said: "Iguana, let us make a bet."
"All right," replied Iguana.
"Who will be able to best endure hunger?" asked Fox.
"All right," replied Iguana.
"Let us go outside," suggested Fox.
"No," answered Iguana. "I am used to being inside a hole."
"All right, I shall do likewise," said Fox.
He began to gather up the *mistol* and put it in the hole. He got inside just like Iguana.
Whenever Fox got hungry, he would eat *mistol*. Iguana gathered up some fruit called *sachasandia*. He piled it up. Iguana remained in the hole until he heard thunder and felt a drizzle. Only then did he go out. Then Fox would eat the *mistol* he had stored. When he looked at what he had put away, there was very little of it left. He said: "Iguana, is this the season for fruit?"
"Not for a long time yet," replied Iguana.
"All right," said Fox, and began to eat the *mistol* he had stored.
When there was very little left, he once again asked Iguana: "Is it the fruit season yet?"
"Oh, it is still many months away," Iguana replied.
When summer arrived, Fox had no more *mistol* left. He asked Iguana: "Iguana, when will there be fruit?"
"Oh, not for a long time!" said the other.
When the trees began to bloom Iguana said: "It is still one month away." "I think I am going to die," said Fox. "It is a long way off." He had already grown thin.
When Iguana had finished the things he had stored away, he, too, was hungry. He lay down belly up, and when he turned over, it was full. Fox wanted to do the same as Iguana but could not. He grew thin. When the algarrobo was out, but was still unripe, Iguana started to go out. Fox asked Iguana: "What do you think, Iguana? Is there fruit yet?"
"Oh, it is still a long way off, Fox," replied Iguana.
The latter answered from his house, because he had already gone out. He had gone out to look for something to eat. One algarrobo was

already out, and so was the *mistol*. Some of the algarrobo and *mistol*
was already ripe. Iguana ate algarrobo. Fox did not eat anything because
he had not gone out. Fox said: "What does it look like to you, Iguana?
Is there fruit yet?"

From his house Iguana replied: "It is still a month away!"

But it was already ripe. He was lying. Fox looked at his body and
said: "I think I am going to die; I am thin."

Fox repeated his question: "What do you think, Iguana? Is there fruit?
I think I am going to die, I am so thin."

From his home Iguana replied: "It is still twenty days away."

But the algarrobo was already ripe, and so was the *mistol*. Iguana
deceived him so he would not go out.

Iguana was asleep. Fox said: "What can I do? I shall fool this Iguana."
He started to dig his way out, and he ran out quickly. He looked around
him. "How this Iguana has fooled me!"

He looked at his body and said: "I am thin. I shall eat some *mistol*."
The *mistol* was already ripe. He ate and ate. But the *mistol* fell on the
ground. He looked behind and saw that it was coming out through his
anus. He could not eat any more. "What am I going to do?" he asked
himself. "I wanted to fill myself. I shall call Nakiwó [the *moro-moro*
bee]." He started singing: "Come, come, come, Nakiwó, Nakiwó,
Nakiwó."

"Why are you calling me?" asked Nakiwó.

"Let us see; put some mud in my anus to plug it up, for I cannot eat
anymore. Everything falls out when I eat," said Fox.

So this is what Nakiwó did. He got mud and applied it to Fox's anus
to stop it up. When mud dries, it is very hard. Thus, as soon as it was
dry, Fox ate and ate and looked at his behind: "Now I am full," he said.
When Fox tried to defecate, he could not. So he called the woodpecker
over to open up his anus. The woodpecker came over and set right to
work. When he had opened it up a little, Fox started to defecate. That
is why the woodpecker has a white patch on his head.

Informant: Sentawó

Source: Mashnshnek 1972, pp. 135–136.

Summary

In hunger endurance contest between fox and iguana, latter tricks fox into
nearly starving to death. When fox finally starts to eat, food goes right through
his body. Wasp stops up his anus with mud.

Motif content

A2210.	Animal characteristics: change in ancient animal.
A2217.1.	Birds painted their present colors.

A2411.2.4.1.	Color of woodpecker.
A2412.2.+.	Why woodpecker has white spot on its head. (A2412.2. Markings on birds.)
B461.1.	Helpful woodpecker.
B481.3.	Helpful bee.
B511.+.	Bee as healer. (B511. Animal as healer.)
B511.5.	Bird heals man.
H1545.	Contest in fasting.
J1117.+.	Iguana as trickster. (J1117. Animal as trickster.)
K50.	Endurance contest won by deception.
K53.	Deceptive contest in fasting.

149. Fox, the Stupid Imitator of the Maize Parrots

One time Fox wanted to have wings. He wanted to fly up above to bring food from there to the west where the maize parrots live.

So he said to the people: "Give me wings, give me wings, for I am going to go with those parrots that eat corn!"

They gave him wings and said to him: "All right! Take off, take off!"

So Fox got up, moved his wings, and flew off, but after a short distance he fell in the middle of the dry forest. He would fall and get up again, fall and get up. Thus he went on flying at random. There is no water in that forest. Then Fox grew tired, and he left his wings. He was very thirsty and did not know what to do. He did not know where he could go to get water!

Informant: Kíki

Source: Siffredi ms.

Motif content

F1021.1.	Flight on artificial wings.
J2413.	Foolish imitation by an animal. Tries to go beyond his powers.

150. Fox and the Lamb

Fox and Lamb were going to race. Lamb knew where there was a small path, and he ran to hide there. Then he went behind Fox, who was unable to find him. "Where did you go?" asked Fox. "You have not seen me but I am here, right by the side of the road," replied Lamb.

Eventually they grew hungry, and they came to a chanar tree that had a lot of fruit. Lamb jumped, and from fifty meters away he hit the chanar tree head on. All the fruit fell to the ground, and Lamb started to eat everything. "Well, now it is your turn," he said. Fox had to do it, for he was hungry and there was nothing left. So he tried from a distance of fifty meters like Lamb, but hit the tree so awkwardly that he died.

Lamb stood there, looking down at Fox. "Well, I shall revive him," he said. He stepped on Fox, who stood up. "I was asleep," he said. "No, you were dead. You do not know how to imitate me. You had better not do it again."

Informant: Petiso

Source: Verna ms.

Motif content

E3.	Dead animal comes to life.
H1594.	Foot-racing contest.
J1117.+.	Lamb as trickster. (J1117. Animal as trickster.)
J2401.	Fatal imitation.
J2413.	Foolish imitation by an animal. Tries to go beyond his powers.
J2650.	Bungling fool.
K11.	Race won by deception.

THE MOTIF INDICES

Motif Distribution by Narrative

A. MYTHOLOGICAL MOTIFS

a. Creator A1.+.—A84. 8, 11, 24, 72.

b. Gods A181.2.—A445. 11, 30, 31, 32, 33, 37, 39, 41, 46, 56, 58, 64.

c. Demigods and culture heroes A521.—A547. 41, 42, 43, 50, 51, 52, 53, 54, 69, 70, 71, 104.

d. Cosmogony and cosmology A630.+.—A840.+. 1, 2, 3, 4, 5, 6, 7, 8, 9, 10, 12, 13, 14, 15, 21, 24, 32, 33, 37, 56, 69, 70, 71, 72, 88, 136, 137, 138, 139, 140, 141.

e. Topographical features of the earth A924.3.—A940.+. 41, 42, 43. 44.

f. World calamities A1005.—A1061.1. 16, 17, 18, 19, 20, 21, 22, 23, 24, 25, 42, 44, 45, 46, 47, 48, 49.

g. Establishment of natural order A1101.1.—A1142. 7, 11, 29, 33, 58, 69, 79, 115.

h. Creation and ordering of human life A1231.—A1654. 8, 9, 10, 11, 12, 13, 15, 16, 19, 21, 22, 24, 26, 27, 31, 33, 34, 37, 39, 40, 41, 42, 43, 44, 49, 50, 51, 52, 53, 54, 55, 56, 58, 59, 60, 80, 84, 94, 123.

i. Creation of animal life A1700.—A2160. 18, 20, 64, 67, 68, 69, 70, 71, 72, 73, 74, 75, 76, 77, 81, 84, 85, 87, 88, 89, 90, 91, 92, 94, 95, 96, 97, 98, 99, 105, 106.

j. Animal characteristics A2210.—A2571.+. 14, 26, 33, 35, 67, 69, 70, 71, 75, 76, 77, 78, 79, 80, 81, 86, 94, 99, 100, 101, 106, 148.

k. Origin of trees and plants A2600.—A2692.+. 8, 18, 23, 24, 25, 26, 27, 28, 30, 32, 33, 37, 38, 61, 62, 63, 64, 65, 66, 123.

l. Origin of plant characteristics A2700.—A2770.+. 29, 33, 34, 37.

B. ANIMALS

   a. Mythical animals B16.2.2.+.—B80.2. 18, 41, 89, 100, 101,
       102, 103, 104, 107, 108, 109, 110, 111, 115, 125, 126, 127, 128,
       136, 137, 138.
   b. Magic animals B143.1.—B191.6. 47, 98, 100, 101, 108, 123, 146.
   c. Animals with human traits B200.+.—B291.2.2. 7, 11, 12, 13,
       14, 64, 65, 66, 67, 75, 76, 77, 78, 79, 80, 81, 82, 83, 84, 86,
       93, 97, 100, 101, 104, 108, 129, 136, 137.
   d. Friendly animals B421.—B576.1.1. 12, 13, 14, 15, 17, 27, 45,
       61, 64, 65, 66, 67, 89, 92, 93, 95, 96, 97, 98, 101, 105, 106,
       108, 114, 123, 124, 129, 130, 132, 138, 147, 148.
   e. Marriage of person to animal B601.15.—B630. 129, 130, 131.
   f. Fanciful traits of animals B720.+.—B755. 100, 101.
   g. Miscellaneous animal motifs B872.—B875.1. 101, 104, 107,
       108, 109, 110.

C. TABU

   a. Tabu connected with supernatural beings C15.1.1.—C43. 124,
       136, 137, 138, 139, 140.
   b. Sex tabu C141. 106.
   c. Looking tabu C310.—C332. 20, 21, 33, 48, 124.
   d. Speaking tabu C460. 124.
   e. Miscellaneous tabus C841.9.—C898.+. 47, 106.
   f. Punishment for breaking tabu C921.—C932. 47, 136, 137,
       138, 139, 140.

D. MAGIC

   a. Transformation D12.—D682.4. 3, 5, 6, 8, 11, 15, 18, 20, 21,
       22, 24, 28, 33, 41, 42, 61, 62, 67, 69, 70, 71, 76, 77, 78, 81,
       87, 89, 90, 91, 92, 94, 95, 96, 97, 98, 99, 100, 102, 106, 110,
       111, 116, 117, 118, 121, 123, 124, 127, 128, 134, 136, 137, 138,
       139, 140, 141, 142, 143.
   b. Magic objects D906.—D1652.5. 18, 28, 32, 42, 44, 45, 48, 58,
       100, 108, 112, 121, 123, 132, 133, 136, 137, 138.
   c. Magic powers and manifestations D1711.—D2197. 5, 6, 7, 8,
       11, 15, 18, 21, 24, 26, 32, 33, 34, 35, 36, 37, 38, 42, 45, 47, 48,

58, 61, 62, 63, 64, 67, 70, 78, 82, 89, 92, 98, 100, 101, 103, 105, 106, 107, 108, 112, 113, 120, 121, 124, 128, 136, 137, 138, 139, 140, 142, 143.

E. THE DEAD

    a. Resuscitation E1.—E151. 15, 28, 33, 44, 45, 46, 47, 70, 71, 121, 124, 136, 137, 138, 139, 140, 144, 150.
    b. Ghosts and other revenants E431.13. 104.
    c. Reincarnation E631.5.1. 62.
    d. The Soul E714.+.—E781.1. 28, 63, 107, 113, 114, 136, 137.

F. MARVELS

    a. Otherworld journeys F10.—F167.1.2. 7, 9, 10, 12, 13, 14, 15, 17, 21, 24, 32, 37, 56, 68, 72, 93, 115, 133, 135, 136, 137, 138, 141, 142, 143, 145.
    b. Marvelous creatures F402.—F699.1. 3, 11, 28, 39, 40, 41, 58, 59, 62, 63, 64, 65, 66, 67, 82, 83, 89, 90, 100, 106, 110, 112, 113, 115, 116, 117, 118, 119, 120, 121, 122, 123, 124, 127, 132, 139, 140, 141, 142.
    c. Extraordinary places and things F701.—F840.+. 1, 2, 15, 18, 26, 38, 39, 42, 45, 46, 47, 48, 49, 67, 91, 92, 133, 138, 145.
    d. Extraordinary occurrences F900.+.—F1084. 18, 39, 42, 44, 47, 61, 64, 66, 67, 74, 104, 107, 108, 109, 110, 120, 123, 132, 135, 149.

G. OGRES

    a. Kinds of ogres G10.—G366.+. 61, 62, 63, 64, 65, 66, 67, 83, 89, 90, 91, 92, 93, 95, 96, 97, 98, 100, 101, 102, 103, 104, 107, 108, 109, 110, 111, 112, 113, 114, 122, 124, 126, 127, 128, 129, 131.
    b. Falling into ogre's power G421. 97, 98.
    c. Ogre defeated G500.—G530.1. 61, 62, 63, 64, 65, 66, 67, 89, 90, 91, 92, 93, 95, 96, 97, 98, 100, 101, 102, 103, 104, 113, 114, 115, 122, 126, 127, 128.
    d. Other ogre motifs G630.+.—G691.+. 66, 93, 95, 100, 101, 104.

H. TESTS

   a. Identity tests: recognition H30.+.—H105.4.+. 35, 57, 64, 65, 66, 67, 89, 90, 100.
   b. Marriage tests H481. 39, 40.
   c. Tests of cleverness H503.1.—H580. 89, 109.
   d. Tests of prowess: quests H1362.—H1397. 21, 28, 41, 63, 100, 101, 102, 103, 107, 108, 123, 132, 136, 137, 138.
   e. Other tests H1500.—H1594. 1, 2, 79, 90, 146, 148, 150.

J. THE WISE AND THE FOOLISH

   a. Acquisition and possession of wisdom (knowledge) J157. 11, 120, 128.
   b. Wise and unwise conduct J445.2.—J1050. 13, 20, 21, 28, 30, 38, 40, 41, 42, 44, 45, 46, 47, 48, 57, 62, 64, 65, 66, 67, 69, 70, 77, 78, 87, 93, 100, 104, 105, 106, 108, 113, 114, 115, 124, 125, 130, 131, 132, 138.
   c. Cleverness J1100.+.—J1144. 12, 13, 14, 26, 29, 33, 34, 35, 41, 42, 44, 45, 46, 47, 48, 49, 50, 51, 52, 53, 54, 57, 64, 65, 75, 89, 90, 91, 92, 95, 96, 97, 98, 101, 105, 106, 115, 124, 144, 145, 146, 147, 148, 150.
   d. Fools (and other unwise persons) J1700.—J2650. 33, 34, 35, 36, 42, 44, 45, 46, 47, 48, 89, 90, 118, 130, 147, 149, 150.

K. DECEPTIONS

   a. Contests won by deception K11.—K53. 146, 148, 150.
   b. Thefts and cheats K300.—K437. 12, 13, 14, 26, 146.
   c. Escape by deception K515.6.—K678. 19, 20, 21, 22, 24, 100, 115, 116, 121.
   d. Capture by deception K700.—K755. 12, 13, 14, 15, 64, 67, 69, 97, 98, 114, 132, 134, 147.
   e. Fatal deception K800.—K963. 12, 13, 64, 65, 66, 67, 89, 90, 91, 92, 93, 96, 97, 98, 100, 101, 105, 106, 107, 108, 109, 110, 115, 122, 128, 132, 134, 138.
   f. Deception into self-injury K1013.—K1020. 100, 101, 129, 147.
   g. Deception into humiliating position K1200. 147.
   h. Seduction or deceptive marriage K1311.—K1391. 35, 57, 116, 117, 118, 120.

i. Dupe's property destroyed K1461. 144.
j. Deceiver falls into own trap K1622.—K1626. 12, 13, 14, 89, 90, 91, 92.
k. Deception through shams K1800.—K1915. 45, 57, 70, 100, 119, 121, 128, 146, 147.
l. Villains and traitors K2211.—K2296. 28, 136, 138, 144, 147.

L. REVERSAL OF FORTUNE

a. Unpromising hero (heroine) L112.2. 115.
b. Triumph of the weak L315. 146.

N. CHANCE AND FATE

a. Unlucky accidents N396.—N397. 13, 89, 90.
b. Lucky accidents N440.+.—N699.6. 44, 45, 48, 51, 52, 53, 54, 137, 138, 139.
c. Helpers N810.—N845. 24, 30, 31, 32, 37, 60, 64, 65, 66, 67, 103, 104, 120, 122, 126, 127, 128, 141, 142, 143.

P. SOCIETY

a. Royalty and nobility P11.4.+. 112.
b. The family P250.1.—P272. 6, 40, 42, 43.
c. Customs P681. 80, 106.

Q. REWARDS AND PUNISHMENTS

a. Deeds punished Q211.4.—Q291. 28, 33, 67, 100, 101, 121, 142, 143, 144, 145.
b. Kinds of punishment Q411.—Q595. 28, 33, 38, 42, 44, 45, 46, 47, 49, 63, 85, 100, 101, 108, 121, 124, 129, 136, 137, 138, 139, 140, 142, 143, 144, 145.

R. CAPTIVES AND FUGITIVES

a. Captivity R4.—R13.3. 12, 13, 14, 100, 101, 102, 103, 104, 136.
b. Rescues R131.—R155.2. 40, 107, 108.

    c. Escapes and pursuits R227.1.—R228. 129, 130.
    d. Refuges and recapture R311.—R323.+. 21, 23, 24, 42, 44, 45, 46, 47, 70, 87, 100, 101, 115, 131, 135.

S. UNNATURAL CRUELTY

    a. Cruel relatives S0.—S60.+. 6, 67, 85, 87, 113, 114, 129, 130, 131.
    b. Revolting murders or mutilations S100.—S183. 12, 14, 63, 89, 90, 98, 112, 113, 114, 129, 132.
    c. Abandoned or murdered children S302. 144.

T. SEX

    a. Love T51.—T91.4. 33, 41, 57, 119, 139, 140, 141, 142.
    b. Marriage T111.—T192. 33, 41, 42, 105, 106, 116, 120, 131, 136, 137, 138, 139, 140.
    c. Illicit sexual relations T410.—T475.2.1. 20, 22, 28, 39, 42, 109, 116, 117, 118, 120, 121, 123, 139.
    d. Conception and birth T510.—T573. 10, 13, 16, 39, 42, 43, 105, 106, 119.
    e. Care of children T615.—T670. 40, 42, 43, 131.

U. THE NATURE OF LIFE

    a. Nature of life—miscellaneous U110. 115.

V. RELIGION

    a. Religious motifs—miscellaneous V514. 107.

W. TRAITS OF CHARACTER

    a. Favorable traits of character W11. 133.
    b. Unfavorable traits of character W152.—W195. 51, 52, 53, 89.

Z. MISCELLANEOUS GROUPS OF MOTIFS

    a. Unique exceptions Z310.—Z356. 18, 61, 63, 98, 113, 114.

Topical Motif Index

A. MYTHOLOGICAL MOTIFS

a. Creator A1.+.—A84.

A1.+.	Moon as creator. (A1. Identity of creator.) (8); (24).
A1.1.	Sun-god as creator. (72).
A15.1.1.	Old woman as creator. (11).
A15.3.	Old man as creator. (11).
A21.	Creator from above. (72).
A21.2.	Old man from sky as creator. (11).
A32.3.	Creator's wife. (11).
A81.	Creator goes to sky. (24).
A84.	Creator of animals. (72).

b. Gods A181.2.—A445.

A181.2.	God as cultivator. (64).
A182.3.5.	God advises mortal. (30); (32); (37).
A183.	Deity invoked. (11).
A185.3.	Deity teaches mortal. (11); (33); (37); (56).
A185.12.	Deity provides man with soul. (11).
A191.1.	Great age of the gods. (11).
A300.	God of the underworld. (30); (31); (58); (64).
A420.+.	Owner of water. (A420. God of water.) (46).
A445.	God of fish. (39); (41).

c. Demigods and culture heroes A521.—A547.

A521.	Culture hero as dupe or trickster. (42).
A522.2.3.	Hawk as culture hero. (41); (50); (51); (52); (53); (54); (69); (70); (71); (104).

A527.3.1.   Culture hero can transform self. (42).
A533.   Culture hero regulates rivers. (41); (42).
A541.   Culture hero teaches arts and crafts. (43).
A547.   Culture hero dispenses food and hospitality.
               (41); (42); (43).

d. Cosmogony and cosmology A630.+.—A840.+.

A630.+.   Animals created after initial unsuccessful
               experiment. (A630. Series of creations.) (69);
               (70); (71).
A651.1.   Series of upper worlds. (7).
A651.3.   Worlds above and below. (12); (13); (14); (15);
               (21).
A701.   Creation of the sky. (24).
A733.+.   Sun hot. (A733. Heat and light of the sun.)
               (1); (2).
A736.   Sun as human being. (72).
A736.11.   Contest between sun and moon. (1); (2).
A737.1.   Eclipse caused by monster devouring sun or
               moon. (4).
A740.   Creation of the moon. (3); (24).
A745.   Family of the moon. (3); (8); (32); (33); (37);
               (141).
A747.   Person transformed to moon. (3); (56).
A750.+.   Moon cold. (A750. Nature and condition of the
               moon.) (1); (2).
A751.   Man in the moon. (56).
A753.   Moon as a person. (8); (24); (56).
A753.2.   Moon has house. (37).
A760.+.   Stars as birds. (A760. Creation and condition
               of the stars.) (88).
A761.   Ascent to stars. People or animals ascend to the
               sky and become stars. (3); (5); (6).
A761.6.   Stars thought of as living beings. (88).
A761.6.+.   Stars are women. (A761.6. Stars thought of as
               living beings.) (137).
A762.   Star descends as human being. (9); (10); (136);
               (137); (138); (139); (140).
A762.+.   Stars descend as birds. (A762. Star descends
               as human being.) (88).

A762.2.	Mortal marries star-girl. (136); (137); (138); (139); (140).
A764.1.	Stars as children of the moon. (137).
A766.	Origin of constellations. (5); (6).
A770.	Origin of particular stars. (3).
A800.	Creation of the earth. (8); (24).
A840.+.	Earth supported by roots. (A840. Support of the earth.) (21).

e. Topographical features of the earth A924.3.—A940.+.

A924.3.	Sea released from tree-top. (42).
A930.	Origin of streams. (41); (42); (43).
A930.1.	Creator of rivers. (41); (42).
A934.4.+.	River where culture hero drags his staff. (A934.4. Rivers where god drags his staff.) (42).
A940.+.	Origin of lagoons. (A940. Origin of other bodies of water.) (44).

f. World calamities A1005.—A1061.1.

A1005.	Preservation of life during world calamity. (17); (18); (19); (20); (21); (23).
A1005.+.	Preservation of life during great calamity. (A1005. Preservation of life during world calamity.) (22).
A1006.	Renewal of world after world calamity. (16); (18); (21); (23); (24); (25).
A1006.1.	New race from single pair (or several) after world calamity. (16); (20).
A1006.2.	New race from incest. (16); (20).
A1010.	Deluge. (16); (17).
A1011.	Local deluges. (42); (44); (45); (46); (47); (48); (49).
A1018.1.	Flood as punishment for breaking tabu. (47).
A1020.	Escape from deluge. (17).
A1023.	Escape from deluge on tree. (42); (44); (45); (46); (47).
A1029.1.+.	Marvelous tree survives world-fire. (A1029.1. Marvelous tree survives deluge.) (24).

A1030.	World-fire. (19); (20); (21); (23); (24); (25).
A1030.+.	Great fire. (A1030. World-fire.) (22).
A1038.	Men hide from world-fire and renew race. (19); (20); (21).
A1060.	Earth-disturbances at end of world. (18).
A1061.1.	Earthquakes at the end of the world. (18).

g. Establishment of natural order A1101.1.—A1142.

A1101.1.	Golden age. (29); (33); (58).
A1101.2.+.	Birds were men in former age. (A1101.2. Reversal of nature in former age.) (115).
A1101.2.+.	Primeval animals human. (A1101.2. Reversal of nature in former age.) (69); (79).
A1131.	Origin of rain. (11).
A1131.3.	Rain from sea in upper world. (7).
A1141.	Origin of lightning. (7).
A1142.	Origin of thunder. (7).

h. Creation and ordering of human life A1231.—A1654.

A1231.	First man descends from sky. (16).
A1231.+.	First woman descends from sky. (A1231. First man descends from sky.) (12); (13).
A1241.3.	Man made from clay image and vivified. (9).
A1263.	Man created from part of body. (123).
A1270.	Primeval human pair. (9); (10).
A1273.1.	Incestuous first parents. (10); (16).
A1275.	Creation of first man's (woman's) mate. (9).
A1280.	First man (woman). (9); (10); (12); (13); (15); (16).
A1281.	Condition of first man (woman). (12); (13); (15).
A1282.	The mother of men. (10).
A1296.	Multiplication of man by fragmentation. (123).
A1300.	Ordering of human life. (11).
A1335.	Origin of death. (13).
A1346.	Man to earn bread by sweat of his brow. (33); (34).
A1352.	Origin of sexual intercourse. (13).
A1414.	Origin of fire. (11); (19); (50); (51); (52); (53); (54).

A1414.6. Bird as guardian of primordial fire. (19); (51); (54).

A1414.7.1. Tree as repository of fire. (19); (51).

A1415.0.2. Original fire property of one person (animal). (19); (51); (54).

A1415.0.2.+. Original fire property of certain animals. (A1415.0.2. Original fire property of one person (animal).) (50); (52); (53).

A1415.2.1. Theft of fire by bird. (50); (51); (52); (53); (54).

A1415.4. Vain attempts to circumvent theft of fire. (52); (53); (54).

A1420.+. Acquisition of honey. (A1420. Acquisition of food supply for human race.) (60).

A1420.2. Gods teach how to seek and prepare food. (11); (39); (41).

A1420.3. Creator of food items. (84).

A1423.0.1. Hoarded plants released. (26).

A1423.4. Acquisition of manioc. (31).

A1425. Origin of seed. (8); (24).

A1425.0.1. Hoarded seeds. (26).

A1426.2.1. Introduction of brewing. (58).

A1427. Acquisition of spiritous liquors. (58); (59).

A1429. Acquisition of food supply—miscellaneous. (26); (27).

A1429.+. Acquisition of fish. (A1429. Acquisition of food supply—miscellaneous.) (39); (40); (41); (42); (43); (44); (49).

A1435. Acquisition of habitations. (56).

A1438. Origin of medicine (healing). (58).

A1441. Acquisition of agriculture. (33).

A1441.4. Origin of sowing and planting. (33); (37).

A1451. Origin of pottery. (94).

A1457. Origin of fishing. (39); (40); (41); (42); (43).

A1457.3. Origin of the net for fishing. (39); (41); (43).

A1458. Origin of hunting. (11).

A1461.4. Origin of the use of the rattle. (58).

A1472. Beginning of division of labor. (11).

A1527. Custom of catching fish with nets. (39); (41); (43).

A1547.+. Origin of custom of lighting fire after death of family member. (A1547. Origin of funeral customs.) (80).

A1600.	Distribution and differentiation of peoples— general. (55).
A1611.	Origin of particular tribes. (22).
A1611.+.	Origin of the Chorote. (A1611. Origin of particular tribes.) (9); (19).
A1611.+.	Origin of the Mataco. (A1611. Origin of particular tribes.) (9).
A1611.+.	Origin of the Tapiete. (A1611. Origin of particular tribes.) (9).
A1611.+.	Origin of the Toba. (A1611. Origin of particular tribes.) (9).
A1614.4.	Origin of tribes from choices made. (55).
A1614.9.	Origin of white man. (24).
A1618.	Origin of inequalities among men. (55).
A1620.	Distribution of tribes. (21).
A1654.	Origin of priesthood (shamanism, etc.). (37); (58).

i. Creation of animal life A1700.—A2160.

A1700.	Creation of animals. (67); (68).
A1700.+.	Creation of capybara. (A1700. Creation of animals.) (81).
A1700.+.	Origin of anteater. (A1700. Creation of animals.) (75).
A1700.+.	Origin of honey bear. (A1700. Creation of animals.) (75).
A1703.+.	Sun creates useful animals. (A1703. Culture hero creates useful animals.) (72).
A1710.	Creation of animals through transformation. (69); (70); (71); (106).
A1710.+.	Creation of birds through transformation. (A1710. Creation of animals through transformation.) (99).
A1711.	Animals from transformations after deluge or world calamity. (18); (20).
A1715.+.	Bird from transformed man. (A1715. Animals from transformed man.) (87).
A1724.1.	Animals from body of slain person. (67).
A1724.1.+.	Bird from body of slain person. (A1724.1.

Animals from body of slain person.) (89); (90); (91); (92); (95); (97); (98).

A1724.1.+. Birds from body of slain monster. (A1724.1. Animals from body of slain person.) (64).

A1795. Animals drop from clouds. (88).

A1795.+. Animals drop from sky. (A1795. Animals drop from clouds.) (68).

A1795.+. Jaguar drops from sky. (A1795. Animals drop from clouds.) (74).

A1795.+. Toad drops from clouds. (A1795. Animals drop from clouds.) (84).

A1810. Creation of felidae. (74).

A1861.+. Creation of howler monkey. (A1861. Creation of monkey.) (64).

A1871.1. Origin of wild boar. (85).

A1871.2. Origin of peccary. (77).

A1895. Creation of bat. (64); (106).

A1900. Creation of birds. (64); (67); (88).

A1900.+. Origin of hummingbird. (A1900. Creation of birds.) (89); (90).

A1900.+. Origin of kihil bird. (A1900. Creation of birds.) (87).

A1900.+. Origin of ovenbird. (A1900. Creation of birds.) (94); (95); (96).

A1931. Creation of vulture. (91); (92).

A1958. Creation of owl. (97); (98).

A1964. Creation of heron. (99).

A1988. Creation of chicken. (73).

A1994. Creation of parrot. (99).

A2110. Creation of particular fishes. (84).

A2140.+. Origin of iguana. (A2140. Creation of reptiles.) (76).

A2145. Creation of snake (serpent). (105); (106).

A2160. Origin of amphibia. (84).

j. Animal characteristics A2210.—A2571.+.

A2210. Animal characteristics: change in ancient animal. (14); (26); (35); (70); (71); (76); (80); (100); (101); (106); (148).

A2213.5.	Animal characteristics from being struck. (14); (79).
A2214.	Animal characteristics from dropping ancient animal from air. (35).
A2217.	Appearance of animal from marking or painting. (80).
A2217.1.	Birds painted their present colors. (100); (101); (148).
A2218.	Animal characteristics from burning or singeing. (69); (70); (71); (106).
A2275.	Animal habit a reminiscence of former experience. (78); (81).
A2312.+.	Origin of knots on armadillo's shell. (A2312. Origin of animal shell.) (26).
A2313.+.	Why hawk's neck feathers are short. (A2313. Origin of bird's feathers.) (106).
A2335.3.2.	Why tapir has long nose. (79).
A2343.2.1.	Why parrot's beak is black. (14).
A2376.+.	How anteater got its claws. (A2376. Animal characteristics: claws and hoofs.) (69).
A2376.+.	How peccary got its hoofs. (A2376. Animal characteristics: claws and hoofs.) (69).
A2378.1.+.	Why anteater has tail. (A2378.1. Why animals have tail.) (69).
A2411.+.	Color of armadillo. (A2411. Origin of color of animal.) (80).
A2411.2.	Origin of color of bird. (100); (101).
A2411.2.4.1.	Color of woodpecker. (148).
A2412.1.+.	Markings of armadillo. (A2412.1. Markings of mammals.) (35).
A2412.2.+.	Why woodpecker has white spot on its head. (A2412.2. Markings on birds.) (148).
A2426.1.+.	Cry of fox. (A2426.1. Cries of mammals.) (33).
A2428.+.	Origin of deer's sharp hearing. (A2428. Animal's hearing.) (69).
A2431.3.	Origin of birds' nests. (99).
A2432.+.	Anteater's dwelling. (A2432. Dwelling of other animal than bird.) (69).
A2432.+.	Peccary's burrow. (A2432. Dwelling of other animal than bird.) (77).
A2432.+.	Why iguana lives in burrow. (A2432. Dwelling of other animal than bird.) (69).

A2432.+.   Why puma has no permanent dwelling. (A2432. Dwelling of other animal than bird.) (69).

A2432.+.   Wildcat's dwelling. (A2432. Dwelling of other animal than bird.) (69).

A2433.+.   Deer's haunt. (A2433. Animal's characteristic haunt.) (69).

A2433.1.   Establishment of animal haunt. (69).

A2433.2.1.+.   Why anteater lives in woods. (A2433.2.1. Animals that live in woods.) (75).

A2433.2.1.+.   Why iguana lives in woods. (A2433.2.1. Animals that live in woods.) (76).

A2433.2.1.+.   Why peccary lives in woods. (A2433.2.1. Animals that live in woods.) (69); (77).

A2433.2.1.+.   Why wild boar lives in woods. (A2433.2.1. Animals that live in woods.) (69).

A2433.2.2.+.   Why capybara lives in the water. (A2433.2.2. Animals that inhabit water.) (81).

A2433.4.+.   Why rhea lives on the plains. (A2433.4. Haunts of birds.) (69).

A2435.+.   Food of anteater. (A2435. Food of animal.) (69); (70); (71).

A2435.+.   Food of deer. (A2435. Food of animal.) (69).

A2435.+.   Food of peccary. (A2435. Food of animal.) (69).

A2435.+.   Food of puma. (A2435. Food of animal.) (69); (70); (71).

A2435.+.   Food of tapir. (A2435. Food of animal.) (69).

A2435.3.2.+.   Food of wildcat. (A2435.3.2. Food of cat.) (69); (70); (71).

A2435.3.12.+.   Food of rabbit. (A2435.3.12. Food of hare.) (70); (71).

A2435.3.14.   Food of pig. (69).

A2435.3.16.   Food of jaguar. (69); (70); (71).

A2435.4.+.   Food of rhea. (A2435.4. Food of birds.) (69).

A2435.6.+.   Food of iguana. (A2435.6. Food of fish, reptiles, etc.) (69).

A2441.2.   Cause of bird's walk. (94).

A2452.+.   Puma's occupation: hunting. (A2452. Animal's occupation: hunting.) (86).

A2461.+.   Deer's means of defense: sharp hearing. (A2461. Animal's means of defense.) (69).

A2461.+.   Peccary's means of defense: hoofs. (A2461. Animal's means of defense.) (69).

A2461.4.   Why deer run, stop, and run on again. (69).
A2470.+.   Tapir's habitual bodily movements. (A2470. Animal's habitual bodily movements.) (69).
A2481.+.   Why iguana hibernates. (A2481. Why animals hibernate.) (69).
A2491.+.   Why anteater is nocturnal. (A2491. Why certain animals avoid light.) (69).
A2491.+.   Why tapir is nocturnal. (A2491. Why certain animals avoid light.) (69).
A2491.+.   Why wildcat is nocturnal. (A2491. Why certain animals avoid light.) (69).
A2524.+.   Why peccary is pugnacious. (A2524. Why animal is pugnacious (brave, bold).) (69); (70); (71).
A2524.+.   Why tapir is pugnacious. (A2524. Why animal is pugnacious (brave, bold).) (69); (70); (71).
A2524.+.   Why wild boar is fierce. (A2524. Why animal is pugnacious (brave, bold).) (69).
A2528.+.   Why certain armadillo is strong. (A2528. Why animal is strong.) (80).
A2531.+.   Why some snakes are harmless. (A2531. Why animal is harmless.) (106).
A2532.1.   Why snakes are venomous. (106).
A2540.+.   Why jaguar scratches trees. (A2540. Other animal characteristics.) (69).
A2555.+.   Why certain armadillo is swift. (A2555. Why certain animals are swift.) (80).
A2571.   How animals received their names. (67); (69); (70); (71).
A2571.+.   How anteater received its name. (A2571. How animals received their names.) (75).
A2571.+.   How honey bear received its name. (A2571. How animals received their names.) (75).
A2571.+.   How snakes received their names. (A2571. How animals received their names.) (106).

k. Origin of trees and plants A2600.—A2692.+.

A2600.   Origin of plants. (24).
A2600.+.   Origin of sachasandia. (A2600. Origin of plants.) (30).
A2602.   Planting the earth. (8); (18); (23); (24); (37).
A2610.   Creation of plants by transformation. (28).

A2611. Plants from body of slain person or animal. (61); (62); (63); (64); (65); (66).

A2611.0.5. Parts of human or animal body transformed into plants. (28); (123).

A2611.2. Tobacco from grave of bad woman. (63).

A2611.2.+. Tobacco from ashes of bad woman. (A2611.2. Tobacco from grave of bad woman.) (61); (62); (64); (65); (66).

A2631. Origin of plant as punishment. (33).

A2680.+. Origin of brushwood. (A2680. Origin of other plant forms.) (33).

A2680.+. Origin of lianas. (A2680. Origin of other plant forms.) (28).

A2681. Origin of trees. (24); (25).

A2681.+. Origin of algarrobo tree. (A2681. Origin of trees.) (26); (27).

A2682. Origin of creepers. (123).

A2684. Origin of cultivated plants. (8); (24); (37); (38).

A2687.+. Origin of watermelon. (A2687. Origin of fruits.) (32).

A2691.2. Origin of tobacco. (61); (62); (63); (64); (65); (66).

A2692.+. Why sachasandia.is poisonous. (A2692. Origin of poisonous plants.) (30).

1. Origin of plant characteristics A2700.—A2770.+.

A2700. Origin of plant characteristics. (33); (34).

A2700.+. Origin of seasonal plant cycle. (A2700. Origin of plant characteristics.) (37).

A2752. Thorns on plants. (29).

A2770.+. Why chaguar is rooted in the ground. (A2770. Other plant characteristics.) (29).

B. ANIMALS

a. Mythical animals B16.2.2.+.—B80.2.

B16.2.2.+. Devastating jaguar. (B16.2.2. Devastating tiger.) (128).

B16.2.7. Destructive deer. (126); (127).

B16.3.	Devastating birds. (100); (101); (102); (103); (104); (125); (136); (137); (138).
B16.5.1.2.	Devastating (man-eating) sea-monster (serpent). (107); (108); (109); (110).
B16.6.+.	Devastating wasp. (B16.6. Devastating insects.) (111).
B20.+.	Deer-man. (B20. Beast-men.) (127).
B33.	Man-eating birds. (100); (101); (102); (103); (104); (136); (137); (138).
B34.	Bird of dawn. (18); (89); (100); (101).
B50.	Bird-men. (115).
B80.2.	Monster half-man, half-fish. (41).

b. Magic animals B143.1.—B191.6.

B143.1.	Bird gives warning. (98); (108); (123).
B175.	Magic fish. (47).
B191.+.	Fox as magician. (B191. Animal as magician.) (146).
B191.6.	Bird as magician. (100); (101).

c. Animals with human traits B200.+.—B291.2.2.

B200.+.	Animals in human form. (B200. Animals with human traits.) (12); (13); (14).
B200.+.	Birds in human form. (B200. Animals with human traits.) (100); (101).
B200.+.	Jaguar uses fire. (B200. Animals with human traits.) (129).
B211.3.	Speaking bird. (104).
B241.2.+.	Chief of anteaters. (B241.2. King of the various kinds of beasts.) (75).
B241.2.+.	Chief of armadillos. (B241.2. King of the various kinds of beasts.) (80).
B241.2.+.	Chief of capybaras. (B241.2. King of the various kinds of beasts.) (81).
B241.2.+.	Chief of peccaries. (B241.2. King of the various kinds of beasts.) (77); (78).
B241.2.+.	Chief of pumas. (B241.2. King of the various kinds of beasts.) (86).

B241.2.+.	Chief of tapirs. (B241.2. King of the various kinds of beasts.) (79); (82).
B241.2.+.	Chief of vizcachas. (B241.2. King of the various kinds of beasts.) (81).
B241.2.+.	Masters of the various kinds of beasts. (B241.2. King of the various kinds of beasts.) (11).
B242.+.	Chief of birds. (B242. King of birds.) (97).
B242.+.	Master of birds. (B242. King of birds.) (7).
B242.2.+.	Chiefs of the various kinds of birds. (B242.2. King of the various kinds of birds.) (93).
B242.2.2.+.	Mistress of doves. (B242.2.2. King of doves.) (83).
B244.+.	Chief of iguanas. (B244. King of reptiles.) (76).
B244.+.	Mother of caimans. (B244. King of reptiles.) (108).
B244.1.1.	Queen of watersnakes. (108).
B245.+.	Chief of amphibians. (B245. King of amphibians.) (84).
B266.	Animals fight. (7).
B291.+.	Fly as messenger. (B291. Animal as messenger.) (93); (136); (137).
B291.2.2.	Dog as messenger. (64); (65); (66); (67).

d. Friendly animals B421.—B576.1.1.

B421.	Helpful dog. (64); (65); (66); (67).
B430.+.	Helpful skunk. (B430. Helpful wild beasts.) (147).
B435.1.	Helpful fox. (27); (114).
B450.	Helpful birds. (45); (64); (123); (132).
B455.4.	Helpful hawk. (15); (89); (92); (93); (95); (96); (97); (98); (101); (105); (106); (124).
B461.1.	Helpful woodpecker. (108); (148).
B469.9.	Helpful parrot. (61).
B470.	Helpful fish. (147).
B476.	Helpful eel. (61).
B481.3.	Helpful bee. (148).
B483.1.	Helpful fly. (66); (67).
B491.1.	Helpful serpent. (108).
B511.+.	Bee as healer. (B511. Animal as healer.) (148).
B511.5.	Bird heals man. (148).

B515.+.	Resuscitation by hawk. (B515. Resuscitation by animals.) (124).
B521.3.	Animals warn against attack. (98).
B524.2.	Animals overcome man's adversary by strategy. (105); (106); (114); (132).
B527.	Animal saves man from death by drowning. (17).
B531.	Animals provide food for men. (27); (129); (130).
B540.	Animal rescuer or retriever. (124); (147).
B542.1.	Bird flies with man to safety. (61).
B546.	Animal searches for dead man. (124).
B552.	Man carried by bird. (61); (138).
B560.	Animals advise men. (114).
B563.	Animals direct man on journey. (108).
B563.2.	Birds point out road to hero. (123).
B563.6.	Birds as scouts. (64).
B576.1.1.	Guardian animals evaded. (12); (13); (14).

e. Marriage of person to animal B601.15.—B630.

B601.15.	Marriage to jaguar. (129); (130); (131).
B630.	Offspring of marriage to animal. (131).

f. Fanciful traits of animals B720.+.—B755.

B720.+.	Eagle with multicolored blood. (B720. Fanciful bodily members of animals.) (100).
B755.	Animal calls the dawn. (100); (101).

g. Miscellaneous animal motifs B872.—B875.1.

B872.	Giant birds. (101); (104).
B875.1.	Giant serpent. (107); (108); (109); (110).

C. TABU

a. Tabu connected with supernatural beings C15.1.1.—C43.

C15.1.1.	Wish for star wife realized. (136); (137); (138); (139).

C30.   Tabu: offending supernatural relative. (136); (137); (138); (139); (140).

C43.   Tabu: offending wood-spirit. (124).

b. Sex tabu C141.

C141.   Tabu: going forth during menses. (106).

c. Looking tabu C310.—C332.

C310.   Tabu: looking at certain person or thing. (48).
C311.1.   Tabu: seeing supernatural creatures. (124).
C330.   Tabu: looking in certain direction. (21).
C331.   Tabu: looking back. (33).
C332.   Tabu: looking around. (20).

d. Speaking tabu C460.

C460.   Laughing tabu. (124).

e. Miscellaneous tabus C841.9.—C898.+.

C841.9.   Tabu: killing certain fish. (47).
C898.+.   Tabu: widow not to go outside. (C898. Tabus concerned with mourning.) (106).

f. Punishment for breaking tabu C921.—C932.

C921.   Immediate death for breaking tabu. (136); (137); (138); (139); (140).
C923.   Death by drowning for breaking tabu. (47).
C932.   Loss of wife (husband) for breaking tabu. (136); (139).

D. MAGIC

a. Transformation D12.—D682.4.

D12.   Transformation: man to woman. (116); (117); (118).
D52.   Magic change to different appearance. (143).

D52.2.	Ugly man becomes handsome. (141); (142).
D57.	Change in person's color. (110).
D91.	Transformation: normal man to cannibal. (62); (67).
D94.	Transformation: man to ogre. (62).
D100.	Transformation: man to animal. (11); (20); (24); (69); (124).
D100.+.	Transformation: man to armadillo. (D100. Transformation: man to animal.) (116); (117); (121).
D100.+.	Transformation: woman to anteater. (D100. Transformation: man to animal.) (22).
D100.+.	Transformation: woman to bat. (D100. Transformation: man to animal.) (106).
D114.1.1.	Transformation: man to deer. (127).
D114.3.1.	Transformation: man to peccary. (18); (70); (77); (78).
D141.	Transformation: man to dog. (41).
D150.	Transformation: man to bird. (18); (21); (22); (87); (99); (100); (134).
D150.+.	Transformation: woman to bird. (D150. Transformation: man to bird.) (94).
D152.2.	Transformation: man to eagle. (102).
D173.	Transformation: man to eel. (61).
D186.1.	Transformation: man to butterfly. (100).
D197.1.	Transformation: man to iguana. (18); (76).
D212.	Transformation: man (woman) to flower. (100).
D215.	Transformation: man to tree. (42).
D293.	Transformation: man to star. (5); (6).
D293.+.	Transformation: woman to star. (D293. Transformation: man to star.) (3).
D350.+.	Transformation: parakeet to person. (D350. Transformation: bird to person.) (15).
D380.+.	Transformation: wasp to person. (D380. Transformation: insect to person.) (111).
D410.+.	Transformation: vizcacha to capybara. (D410. Transformation: one animal to another.) (81).
D437.	Transformation: part of animal or person to person. (123).
D437.+.	Transformation: intestines to person. (D437. Transformation: part of animal or person to person.) (28).

D439.5.2.	Transformation: star to person. (136); (137); (138); (139); (140).
D440.+.	Transformation: star to bird. (D440. Transformation: object to animal.) (137).
D441.6.1.+.	Transformation: ashes into birds. (D441.6.1. Transformation: ashes into animals.) (89); (90); (91); (92); (95); (96); (97); (98).
D451.+.	Transformation: maize to brushwood. (D451. Transformation of vegetable form.) (33).
D451.8.+.	Transformation: leaf to beans. (D451.8. Transformation: leaf to another object.) (139); (140).
D457.+.	Transformation: intestines to lianas. (D457. Transformed parts of person or animal to object.) (28).
D489.+.	Penis made larger. (D489. Objects made larger —miscellaneous.) (117); (118).
D489.+.	Small earth made to grow large. (D489. Objects made larger—miscellaneous.) (8).
D520.+.	Transformation by calling out. (D520. Transformation through power of the word.) (94).
D551.+.	Transformation by eating ashes. (D551. Transformation by eating.) (134).
D560.+.	Transformation by spitting. (D560. Transformation by various means.) (139); (140).
D576.	Transformation by being burned. (69); (70); (71).
D610.	Repeated transformation. (124).
D631.1.1.	Person changes appearance at will. (61); (100); (116); (117); (121); (124); (127); (128); (134).
D631.3.	Size of object changed at will. (8).
D642.	Transformation to escape difficult situation. (61).
D642.1.	Transformation to escape from captivity. (124).
D642.2.	Transformation to escape death. (87); (89); (100); (124).
D642.5.	Transformation to escape notice. (89).
D642.7.	Transformation to elude pursuers. (127).
D651.1.	Transformation to kill enemy. (102).
D655.	Transformation to receive food. (41).
D657.	Transformation to steal. (41).
D658.3.	Transformation of sex to seduce. (116); (117); (118).

D671.	Transformation flight. (100).
D681.	Gradual transformation. (81).
D682.	Partial transformation. (41).
D682.4.	Partial transformation—color changed. (110).

b. Magic objects D906.—D1652.5.

D906.	Magic wind. (108).
D921.	Magic lake (pond). (108).
D950.	Magic tree. (100).
D961.1.	Garden produced by magic. (137).
D1002.	Magic excrements. (28).
D1002.1.	Magic urine. (136); (137); (138).
D1030.1.	Food supplied by magic. (44); (48).
D1065.5.	Magic sandals. (28).
D1071.0.1.	Jewels produced by magic. (137); (138).
D1171.	Magic vessel. (44).
D1212.	Magic rattle. (58).
D1254.	Magic staff. (42).
D1335.2.	Magic strength-giving drink. (112).
D1349.1.6.	Tiny amount of food magically satisfies. (32).
D1380.2.	Tree (plant) protects. (100).
D1393.1.	Tree opens and conceals fugitive. (100).
D1454.+.	Crystals from urine. (D1454. Parts of human body furnish treasure.) (136).
D1454.+.	Jewels from urine. (D1454. Parts of human body furnish treasure.) (137); (138).
D1472.1.19.	Magic food-basket (vessel) supplies food. (44).
D1500.1.24.	Magic healing song. (58).
D1500.4.+.	Magic intestinal wind causes disease. (D1500.4. Magic object causes disease.) (132).
D1549.3.8.+.	Staff stuck in river bed stops water. (D1549.3.8. Spear stuck in river bed stops water.) (42).
D1556.	Self-opening tree-trunk. (100).
D1600.	Automatic object. (28).
D1602.	Self-returning magic object. (28).
D1602.+.	Self-returning sandal. (D1602. Self-returning magic object.) (123).
D1610.2.	Speaking tree. (100).
D1619.+.	Sky speaks. (D1619. Miscellaneous speaking objects.) (18).
D1643.	Object travels by itself. (28); (121).
D1652.1.	Inexhaustible food. (45).

D1652.1.10. Inexhaustible fish. (44); (48).
D1652.5. Inexhaustible vessel. (44); (133).

c. Magic powers and manifestations D1711.—D2197.

D1711. Magician. (11); (48); (58).
D1711.0.1. Magician's apprentice. (58).
D1711.0.3. Means of becoming magician. (58).
D1720. Acquisition of magic powers. (67); (142); (143).
D1726. Magic power from deity. (58).
D1765. Magic results produced by command. (48); (121).
D1781.+. Knowledge from singing. (D1781. Magic results from singing.) (103).
D1810. Magic knowledge. (8); (21); (89); (92); (98); (101); (103); (124).
D1810.0.1. Omniscience of a god. (33).
D1810.0.2. Magic knowledge of magician. (128).
D1810.8.1. Truth given in vision. (107).
D1810.8.2. Information received through dream. (120); (128).
D1810.8.2.3. Murder made known in a dream. (138).
D1810.8.3. Warning in dreams. (78); (120).
D1810.8.3.1.1. Dream warns of illness or injury. (78).
D1810.8.3.2. Dream warns of danger which will happen in near future. (78).
D1812.3.3. Future revealed in dream. (18).
D1812.3.3.11. Death of another revealed in dream. (138).
D1814.2. Advice from dream. (18).
D1819.1. Magic knowledge of another's thoughts. (136).
D1830. Magic strength. (112).
D1840. Magic invulnerability. (62).
D1841.3. Burning magically evaded. (62).
D2060. Death or bodily injury by magic. (15); (58); (142); (143).
D2061. Magic murder. (63).
D2061.2.+. Murder by throwing earth over victim. (D2061.2. Means employed in magic murder.) (63).
D2070. Bewitching. (113).
D2072. Magic paralysis. (67).
D2074. Attracting by magic. (121).
D2074.1. Animals magically called. (124).

D2081.	Land made magically sterile. (33).
D2089.6.	House destroyed by magic. (67).
D2105.	Provisions magically furnished. (15).
D2106.	Magic multiplication of objects. (33).
D2106.1.2.	Animals miraculously multiplied. (45); (48).
D2135.	Magic air journey. (5); (6).
D2135.0.3.	Magic ability to fly. (103).
D2136.	Objects magically moved. (121).
D2142.1.	Wind produced by magic. (67); (100).
D2143.1.	Rain produced by magic. (7); (24); (37); (38).
D2146.	Magic control of night and day. (100); (101).
D2146.2.1.	Night produced by magic. (70).
D2146.2.2.	Night magically lengthened. (100); (101).
D2148.	Earth magically caused to quake. (64).
D2150.+.	Partially eaten fruit made whole again. (D2150. Miscellaneous magic manifestations.) (32); (37).
D2151.	Magic control of waters. (45); (47); (48).
D2151.0.2.	Waters made to dry up. (107); (108).
D2151.2.	Magic control of rivers. (42).
D2157.	Magic control of soil and crops. (64).
D2157.2.	Magic quick growth of crops. (8); (33); (34); (35); (36); (38); (136); (137).
D2157.4.	Miraculous speedy growth of a tree. (26).
D2158.	Magic control of fires. (105); (106).
D2161.	Magic healing power. (11); (58).
D2161.3.1.1.	Eyes torn out magically replaced. (136); (137).
D2165.	Escapes by magic. (61).
D2178.+.	Maize plants produced by magic. (D2178. Objects produced by magic.) (63).
D2178.+.	Vegetables produced by magic. (D2178. Objects produced by magic.) (136); (139); (140).
D2178.4.	Animals created by magic. (100).
D2197.	Magic dominance over animals. (70); (82).

E. THE DEAD

a. Resuscitation E1.—E151.

| E1. | Person comes to life. (28); (33); (44); (45); (46); (47); (121); (124); (136); (137); (138); (139); (140); (144). |

E3.	Dead animal comes to life. (15); (70); (71); (150).
E30.	Resuscitation by arrangement of members. (124); (137); (138).
E32.0.1.	Eaten person resuscitated. (124); (136); (137); (138).
E35.	Resuscitation from fragments of body. (136); (137).
E42.	Resuscitation from ashes of dead man. (121).
E50.+.	Resuscitation by sprinkling earth. (E50. Resuscitation by magic.) (15); (136); (137); (138); (139); (140).
E121.	Resuscitation by supernatural person. (136); (137); (138); (139); (140).
E151.	Repeated resuscitation. (33); (44).

b. Ghosts and other revenants E431.13.

| E431.13. | Corpse burned to prevent return. (104). |

c. Reincarnation E631.5.1.

| E631.5.1. | Reincarnation as tobacco plant. (62). |

d. The Soul E714.+.—E781.1.

E714.+.	Ogre's heart (life) in foot. (E714. Soul (or life) kept in special part of body.) (113); (114).
E714.4.	Soul (life) in the heart. (63).
E721.	Soul journeys from the body. (107).
E780.	Vital bodily members. (28).
E781.	Eyes successfully replaced. (136); (137).
E781.1.	Substituted eyes. Lost eyes are replaced by those of another person or animal. (137).

F. MARVELS

a. Otherworld journeys F10.—F167.1.2.

| F10. | Journey to upper world. (17); (37); (68); (135); (136); (137); (138); (141). |

F10.1.   Return from upper world. (68); (137); (138); (141).
F11.3.   Man goes to heaven for limited time. (68); (137); (138).
F12.   Journey to see deity. (37).
F15.   Visit to star-world. (68); (137); (138).
F16.   Visit to land of moon. (32); (37); (141); (142); (143).
F30.   Inhabitant of upper world visits earth. (7); (9); (10); (12); (13); (14); (15); (56); (72); (93).
F51.   Sky-rope. (10); (12); (13); (14).
F53.   Ascent to upper world on arrow chain. (115).
F54.   Tree to upper world. (15); (24).
F62.2.   Birds carry person from upper world. (138).
F80.   Journey to lower world. (21).
F111.   Journey to earthly paradise. (133).
F112.   Journey to land of women. (145).
F113.   Land of men. (12); (13).
F162.6.   Lakes in otherworld. (7).
F166.11.   Abundant food in otherworld. (37); (68).
F167.+.   Women live in the sky. (F167. Inhabitants of otherworld.) (12); (13).
F167.+.   Women live in upper world. (F167. Inhabitants of otherworld.) (14).
F167.1.   Animals in otherworld. (68); (137).
F167.1.2.   Birds in otherworld. (7); (15).

b. Marvelous creatures F402.—F699.1.

F402.   Evil spirits. (59).
F402.1.5.   Demon causes disease. (83).
F402.1.5.1.+.   Demons carry off man's soul. (F402.1.5.1. Demons seek to carry off king's soul.) (83).
F402.1.10.   Spirit pursues person. (83).
F402.1.11.   Spirit causes death. (83).
F402.1.15.+.   Demon suitors of boy. (F402.1.15. Demon suitors of girl.) (83).
F402.6.4.1.   Spirits live in caves. (83).
F403.2.   Spirits help mortal. (11); (58).
F403.2.2.1.   Familiar spirit in animal form. (127).
F403.2.2.1.+.   Tapir as shaman's spirit helper. (F403.2.2.1.

	Familiar spirit in animal form.) (82).
F403.2.3.2.	Spirit gives warning. (83).
F412.1.+.	Invisible spirit laughs. (F412.1. Invisible spirit speaks.) (83).
F441.	Wood-spirit. (64); (124).
F441.5.2.	Wood-spirit gigantic. (124).
F515.2.2.	Person with very long fingernails. (62); (67); (113).
F518.	Persons with tails. (62); (64); (65); (66).
F521.1.	Man covered with hair. (132).
F527.1.	Red person. (110).
F531.	Giant. (118); (121); (122); (123).
F531.1.6.3.	Giants with shaggy hair on their bodies. (124).
F531.1.6.3.1.	Giant (giantess) with particularly long hair. (124).
F531.4.5.1.+.	Giant with club as weapon. (F531.4.5.1. Giant with iron club as weapon.) (122).
F531.6.5.2.	Giants large or small at will. (118).
F541.	Remarkable eyes. (132).
F541.6.2.	Person has red eye. (62).
F544.3.+.	Large teeth. (F544.3. Remarkable teeth.) (64).
F544.3.5.	Remarkably long teeth. (62).
F547.3.1.	Long penis. (67); (116); (117); (118); (120).
F548.0.1.	Pointed leg. (89); (90).
F559.3.	Extraordinary excrement. (28).
F559.7.+.	Heart in ankle. (F559.7. Remarkable heart.) (63).
F560.+.	Asleep by day, awake by night. (F560. Unusual manner of life.) (132).
F575.1.	Remarkably beautiful woman. (39); (40); (41); (106).
F575.2.	Handsome man. (3); (89).
F576.	Extraordinary ugliness. (139); (140); (141); (142).
F610.	Remarkably strong man. (112).
F642.4.	Person sees equally well by night or day. (132).
F661.	Skillful marksman. (83).
F661.7.3.	One arrow shot into end of last one to make rope of arrows. (115).
F679.5.	Skillful hunter. (83); (100).
F688.	Man with marvelous voice. (89).
F699.1.	Marvelous dancer. (119).

c. Extraordinary places and things F701.—F840.+.

F701.	Land of plenty. (38); (133).
F709.1.	Country of the naked. (145).
F713.	Extraordinary pond (lake). (45); (46); (47); (48).
F721.1.	Underground passages. (39).
F771.	Extraordinary castle (house, palace). (67).
F791.1.	Sky lowers on people. (18).
F800.	Extraordinary rocks and stones. (91); (92).
F811.	Extraordinary tree. (15); (26); (39); (42); (49).
F811.+.	Tree containing water and fish. (F811. Extraordinary tree.) (39); (42); (49).
F811.5.3.	Fish-producing tree. (39); (42); (49).
F811.20.	Bleeding tree. (42).
F827.	Extraordinary ornaments. (138).
F840.+.	Extraordinary ornaments. (138).
F840.+.	Extraordinary cold path. (F840. Other extraordinary objects and places.) (1); (2).
F840.+.	Extraordinary hot path. (F840. Other extraordinary objects and places.) (1); (2).

d. Extraordinary occurrences F900.+.—F1084.

F900.+.	Crawling through the body of another. (F900. Extraordinary occurrences.) (66); (67).
F911.	Person (animal) swallowed without killing. (107); (108); (109); (110).
F911.7.	Serpent swallows man. (107); (108); (109); (110).
F912.2.	Victim kills swallower from within by cutting. (107); (108); (109); (110).
F921.	Swallowed person becomes bald. (108); (110).
F921.1.+.	Swallowed person becomes soft. (F921.1. Swallowed person becomes boneless.) (108).
F942.	Man sinks into earth. (18); (64).
F960.2.5.2.+.	Earthquake at ogre's death. (F960.2.5.2. Earthquake at witch's death.) (67).
F969.4.	Extraordinary earthquake. (67).
F980.+.	Jaguar gives birth to other felines. (F980. Extraordinary occurrences concerning animals.) (74).

F986.	Extraordinary occurrences concerning fishing. (39); (42); (44); (47).
F989.15.	Hunt for extraordinary (magic) animal. (135).
F1009.	Inanimate object acts as if living. (123).
F1021.	Extraordinary flights through air. (135).
F1021.1.	Flight on artificial wings. (135); (149).
F1034.	Person concealed in another's body. (61).
F1041.+.	Burning intestinal wind. (F1041. Extraordinary physical reactions of persons.) (108); (109).
F1068.	Realistic dream. (120).
F1082.	Person changes color. (110).
F1084.	Furious battle. (104); (132).

G. OGRES

a. Kinds of ogres G10.—G366.+.

G10.	Cannibalism. (112).
G11.6.	Man-eating woman. (61); (62); (63); (64); (66); (113); (114).
G11.6.4.	Woman devours her husband. (113); (114).
G11.10.	Cannibalistic spirits. (124).
G30.	Person becomes cannibal. (62); (67); (89); (90); (113).
G36.	Taste of human flesh leads to habitual cannibalism. (89).
G51.	Person eats own flesh. (89); (90).
G61.1.	Child recognizes relative's flesh when it is served to be eaten. (63); (129).
G71.+.	Animal son eats human mother. (G71. Unnatural children eat parent.) (131).
G72.+.	Unnatural mother eats children. (G72. Unnatural parents eat children.) (113); (114).
G72.1.	Woman plans to eat her children. (63).
G81.	Unwitting marriage to cannibal. (63).
G121.+.	Blind ogre. (G121. Blind giant ogre.) (92).
G302.3.3.+.	Demon in form of white woman. (G302.3.3. Demon in form of old woman.) (83).
G302.7.1.	Sexual relations between man and demons. (83).

G310.	Ogres with characteristic methods. (64); (65); (67); (91); (92); (93); (95); (96); (97); (98); (122); (126); (127); (128).
G310.+.	Headhunter. (G310. Ogres with characteristic methods.) (112).
G310.+.	Ogre kills by squeezing testicles. (G310. Ogres with characteristic methods.) (63).
G312.	Cannibal ogre. (61); (62); (63); (64); (66); (67); (89); (90); (91); (92); (93).
G321.2.	Ogress at a spot along the road takes toll of lives. (95).
G341.1.	Ogre with sharpened leg. (89); (90).
G346.	Devastating monster. (61); (62); (63); (64); (65); (66); (67); (89); (90); (104); (122); (126); (128).
G350.+.	Deer as ogre. (G350. Animal ogres.) (126).
G350.+.	Deer-man as ogre. (G350. Animal ogres.) (127).
G350.+.	Jaguar-man as ogre. (G350. Animal ogres.) (128).
G350.+.	Wasp as ogre. (G350. Animal ogres.) (111).
G353.1.	Cannibal bird as ogre. (100); (101); (102); (103); (104).
G354.1.	Snake as ogre. (107); (108); (109); (110).
G360.	Ogres with monstrous features. (62); (64); (67).
G366.+.	Ogre with cavities in his body. (G366. Ogre monstrous as to trunk.) (91); (93).

b. Falling into ogre's power G421.

G421.	Ogre traps victim. (97); (98).

c. Ogre defeated G500.—G530.1.

G500.	Ogre defeated. (126).
G510.4.	Hero overcomes devastating animal. (100); (101); (102); (103).
G512.	Ogre killed. (61); (64); (65); (67); (89); (90); (93); (101); (115); (122); (127).
G512.1.2.	Ogre decapitated. (100).
G512.3.	Ogre burned to death. (62); (66); (91); (92); (95); (96); (97); (98).

G512.3.2.	Ogre burned in his own oven. (95).
G512.8.	Ogre killed by striking. (63); (104); (113); (114); (128).
G512.8.1.	Ogre killed by striking with club. (102).
G514.3.	Ogre caught in noose and killed. (114).
G530.1.	Help from ogre's wife (mistress). (100).

d. Other ogre motifs G630.+.—G691.+.

G630.+.	Bird ogre lives in sky. (G630. Characteristics of ogres.) (100); (101).
G630.+.	Ogre lives in sky. (G630. Characteristics of ogres.) (93).
G630.+.	Ogre lives underground. (G630. Characteristics of ogres.) (66).
G637.	Ogres live in trees. (95).
G691.+.	Bones of victims in front of ogre's house. (G691. Bodies of victims in front of ogre's house.) (100); (104).

H. TESTS

a. Identity tests: recognition H30.+.—H105.4.+.

H30.+.	Recognition by smell. (H30. Recognition through personal peculiarities.) (35); (57).
H30.+.	Recognition by sounds. (H30. Recognition through personal peculiarities.) (67).
H38.+.	Person's identity betrayed by habitual conversation. (H38. Person's rank betrayed by habitual conversation.) (89); (90).
H50.+.	Recognition by teeth. (H50. Recognition by bodily marks or physical attributes.) (57).
H84.	Tokens of exploits. (64); (65); (66); (67); (100).
H105.	Parts of slain animals as token of slaying. (100).
H105.4.+.	Penis of monster as token (proof) of slaying. (H105.4. Head of monster as token (proof) of slaying.) (67).

H105.4.+.   Tail of monster as token (proof) of slaying.
              (H105.4. Head of monster as token (proof) of
              slaying.) (64); (65); (66).

b. Marriage tests H481.

H481.   Infant picks out his unknown father. (39); (40).

c. Tests of cleverness H503.1.—H580.

H503.1.   Song duel. Contest in singing. (89).
H580.   Enigmatic statements. (109).

d. Tests of prowess: quests H1362.—H1397.

H1362.   Quest for devastating animals. (100); (101);
              (102); (103).
H1371.1.   Quest for the world's end. (21).
H1381.3.1.   Quest for bride. (41).
H1385.   Quest for lost persons. (21).
H1385.3.   Quest for vanished wife (mistress). (28); (136);
              (137); (138).
H1385.8.   Quest for lost brother(s). (107); (108).
H1385.9.   Quest for lost (stolen) family. (123).
H1397.   Quest for enemies. (63); (132).

e. Other tests H1500.—H1594.

H1500.   Tests of endurance. (1); (2).
H1511.   Heat test. Attempt to kill hero by burning him
              in fire. (1); (2).
H1512.   Cold test. (1); (2).
H1540.+.   Contest: staying awake. (H1540. Contests in
              endurance.) (90).
H1541.   Contest in enduring cold. (1); (2).
H1542.   Contest in enduring heat. (1); (2).
H1543.   Contest in remaining under water. (146).
H1545.   Contest in fasting. (148).

H1562.	Test of strength. (79).
H1594.	Foot-racing contest. (150).

J. THE WISE AND THE FOOLISH

a. Acquisition and possession of wisdom (knowledge) J157.

J157.	Wisdom (knowledge) from dream. (11); (120); (128).

b. Wise and unwise conduct J445.2.—J1050.

J445.2.	Foolish marriage of old man and young girl. (87).
J514.	One should not be too greedy. (45).
J580.	Wisdom of caution. (20); (21); (42); (62); (78); (93); (104); (105); (106).
J581.	Foolishness of noise-making when enemies overhear. (124).
J585.	Caution in eating. (40); (41); (44).
J613.	Wise fear of the weak for the strong. (64); (65); (66); (67); (108); (113); (114); (115); (125); (130); (131).
J620.	Forethought in prevention of others' plans. (42).
J640.	Avoidance of others' power. (28); (113); (114); (115); (131); (132).
J641.	Escaping before enemy can strike. (57); (64); (65); (66); (67); (77); (87); (115); (132).
J647.	Avoiding enemy's revenge. (93).
J652.	Inattention to warnings. (13); (46); (47); (48); (100); (108); (124); (138).
J670.	Forethought in defenses against others. (64); (65); (66); (67); (70); (77); (78); (104); (105); (106).
J710.	Forethought in provision for food. (20); (38); (69).
J711.	In time of plenty provide for want. (69).
J1050.	Attention to warnings. (30); (78).

c. Cleverness J1100.+.—J1144.

J1100.+.	Clever dog. (J1100. Cleverness.) (64); (65).
J1100.+.	Clever honey bear. (J1100. Cleverness.) (75).
J1113.	Clever boy. (41); (124).
J1117.+.	Bird as trickster. (J1117. Animal as trickster.) (53); (146).
J1117.+.	Fox as trickster. (J1117. Animal as trickster.) (26); (29); (33); (34); (35); (42); (44); (45); (46); (47); (48); (49); (57); (144); (145); (147).
J1117.+.	Iguana as trickster. (J1117. Animal as trickster.) (148).
J1117.+.	Lamb as trickster. (J1117. Animal as trickster.) (150).
J1118.	Clever bird. (50); (51); (52); (53); (54); (89); (90); (91); (92); (95); (96); (97); (98); (101); (105); (106); (115); (146).
J1144.	Eaters of stolen food detected. (12); (13); (14).

d. Fools (and other unwise persons) J1700.—J2650.

J1700.	Fools. (35); (36).
J1790.	Shadow mistaken for substance. (130).
J1791.	Reflection in water thought to be the original of the thing reflected. (147).
J1791.3.	Diving for cheese. (147).
J1810.	Physical phenomena misunderstood. (42); (44); (45); (46); (47).
J1812.	Other sounds misunderstood. (147).
J1820.	Inappropriate action from misunderstanding. (147).
J1820.+.	Attempted rape of man disguised as woman. (J1820. Inappropriate action from misunderstanding.) (118).
J2300.	Gullible fools. (147).
J2400.	Foolish imitation. (33); (34); (42); (44); (48).
J2401.	Fatal imitation. (150).
J2413.	Foolish imitation by an animal. Tries to go beyond his powers. (147); (149); (150).
J2424.	The sharpened leg. (89); (90).
J2650.	Bungling fool. (45); (46); (150).

K. DECEPTIONS

a. Contests won by deception K11.—K53.

K11.	Race won by deception. (150).
K16.2.	Diving match: trickster eats food while dupe is under water. (146).
K50.	Endurance contest won by deception. (148).
K53.	Deceptive contest in fasting. (148).

b. Thefts and cheats K300.—K437.

K300.	Thefts and cheats—general. (12); (13); (14).
K341.	Owner's interest distracted while goods are stolen. (146).
K341.2.2.	Thief shams sickness and steals. (26).
K400.	Thief escapes detection. (13); (14).
K437.	Robber overcome. (12); (13); (14).

c. Escape by deception K515.6.—K678.

K515.6.	Escape by hiding in the earth. (19); (20); (21); (22); (24); (116); (121).
K649.1.	Confederate hides fugitive. (100).
K678.	Cutting rope to kill ogre who is climbing the rope to kill his victim. (115).

d. Capture by deception K700.—K755.

K700.	Capture by deception. (15); (69); (97); (134).
K713.	Deception into allowing oneself to be fettered. (147).
K713.1.1.	Animal allows himself to be tied to another for safety. (147).
K730.	Victim trapped. (12); (13); (14); (15); (64); (67); (114); (134).
K735.	Capture in pitfall. (69); (98); (132).
K755.	Capture by masking as another. (134).

e. Fatal deception K800.—K963.

K800.	Killing or maiming by deception. (89); (90); (91); (92); (93); (100); (101).
K810.	Fatal deception into trickster's power. (89); (90); (91); (92); (93); (97); (132); (134).
K812.	Victim burned in his own house (or hiding place). (96); (97); (98).
K815.	Victim lured by kind words approaches trickster and is killed. (93); (98).
K825.	Victim persuaded to hold out his tongue: cut off. (101).
K825.+.	Victim persuaded to hold out his tongue: bit by snake. (K825. Victim persuaded to hold out his tongue: cut off.) (100).
K827.	Dupe persuaded to relax vigilance: seized. (93).
K839.2.	Victim lured into approach by false token. (64); (89); (90).
K910.	Murder by strategy. (64); (65); (66); (67); (89); (90); (91); (92); (100); (101); (105); (106).
K911.3.	Sleep feigned to kill enemy. (128).
K930.	Treacherous murder of enemy's children or charges. (100); (101).
K952.	Animal (monster) killed from within. (107); (108); (109); (110).
K955.	Murder by burning. (105); (106).
K959.2.	Murder in one's sleep. (122); (138).
K959.4.	Murder from behind. (89); (90); (132).
K963.	Rope cut and victim dropped. (12); (13); (115).

f. Deception into self-injury K1013.—K1020.

K1013.	False beauty-doctor. (100); (101); (129).
K1020.	Deception into disastrous attempt to procure food. (147).

g. Deception into humiliating position K1200.

K1200.	Deception into humiliating position. (147).

h. Seduction or deceptive marriage K1311.—K1391.

> K1311. Seduction by masking as woman's husband. (35).
> K1315. Seduction by impostor. (57).
> K1321. Seduction by man disguising as woman. (116); (117); (118).
> K1340. Entrance into girl's (man's) room (bed) by trick. (117); (118).
> K1391. Long distance sexual intercourse. (116); (120).

i. Dupe's property destroyed K1461.

> K1461. Caring for the child: child killed. (144).

j. Deceiver falls into own trap K1622.—K1626.

> K1622. Thief climbing rope discovered and rope cut. (12); (13); (14).
> K1626. Would-be killers killed. (89); (90); (91); (92).

k. Deception through shams K1800.—K1915.

> K1800. Deception by disguise or illusion. (70); (146); (147).
> K1810. Deception by disguise. (119).
> K1860. Deception by feigned death (sleep). (121).
> K1868. Deception by pretending sleep. (45); (128).
> K1881. Absent person seems to be present. (146).
> K1887. Illusory sounds. (147).
> K1892. Deception by hiding. (100).
> K1915. The false bridegroom. (57).

l. Villains and traitors K2211.—K2296.

> K2211. Treacherous brother. (28).
> K2295.+. Treacherous bird. (K2295. Treacherous animals.) (136); (138).

K2295.+.   Treacherous fox. (K2295. Treacherous animals.)
                (144); (147).
K2296.   Treacherous partner. (147).

L. REVERSAL OF FORTUNE

   a. Unpromising hero (heroine) L112.2.

     L112.2.   Very small hero. (115).

   b. Triumph of the weak L315.

     L315.   Small animal overcomes large. (146).

N. CHANCE AND FATE

   a. Unlucky accidents N396.—N397.

     N396.   The sleeping guard. (13).
     N397.   Accidental self-injury. (89); (90).

   b. Lucky accidents N440.+.—N699.6.

     N440.+.   Secret learned. (N440. Valuable secrets learned.)
                (44); (45); (51); (52); (53); (54).
     N450.   Secrets overheard. (48).
     N455.   Overheard (human) conversation. (45).
     N699.6.   Overheard wish is realized. (137); (138); (139).

   c. Helpers N810.—N845.

     N810.   Supernatural helpers. (122).
     N817.0.1.   God as helper. (30); (31).

N818.1.+. Moon as helper. (N818.1. Sun as helper.) (24);
           (32); (37); (141); (142); (143).
N825.2.   Old man helper. (60); (65).
N845.   Magician as helper. (64); (66); (67); (103); (104);
           (120); (126); (127); (128).

P. SOCIETY

a. Royalty and nobility P11.4.+.

   P11.4.+.   Chief chosen on basis of strength. (P11.4. King
               chosen on basis of strength and exploits.) (112).

b. The family P250.1.—P272.

   P250.1.   Elder children to protect younger. (6).
   P272.   Foster mother. (40); (42); (43).

c. Customs P681.

   P681.   Mourning customs. (80); (106).

Q. REWARDS AND PUNISHMENTS

a. Deeds punished Q211.4.—Q291.

   Q211.4.   Murder of children punished. (144).
   Q212.   Theft punished. (33); (121).
   Q240.+.   Lechery punished. (Q240. Sexual sins punished.)
              (145).
   Q242.3.   Punishment for man who makes advances to
              sister-in-law. (28).
   Q280.   Unkindness punished. (100); (101); (142); (143).
   Q291.   Hard-heartedness punished. (67).

b. Kinds of punishment Q411.—Q595.

Q411.	Death as punishment. (124); (129); (136); (137); (138); (139); (140); (142); (143).
Q411.6.	Death as punishment for murder. (63); (138); (144).
Q411.7.	Death as punishment for ravisher. (121).
Q422.0.1.	Punishment: beating to death. (33); (63); (121); (138); (145).
Q424.	Punishment: strangling. (85).
Q428.	Punishment: drowning. (42); (44); (45); (46); (47); (49).
Q432.	Punishment: ejectment. (33); (45).
Q450.	Cruel punishments. (28).
Q450.+.	Punishment: bodily orifices stopped up. (Q450. Cruel punishments.) (144).
Q451.7.	Blinding as punishment. (121).
Q453.+.	Punishment: being stung by wasps. (Q453. Punishment: being bitten by animal.) (121).
Q470.	Humiliating punishments. (85).
Q550.	Miraculous punishments. (33).
Q550.+.	Rain as punishment. (Q550. Miraculous punishments.) (38).
Q551.3.2.3.	Punishment: transformation into frog. (38).
Q551.3.2.3.+.	Punishment: transformation into toad. (Q551.3.2.3. Punishment: transformation into frog.) (38).
Q552.3.4.	Food magically disappears. (33).
Q552.19.	Miraculous drowning as punishment. (108).
Q552.20.1.	Miraculous darkness as punishment. (100); (101).
Q580.	Punishment fitted to crime. (28).
Q595.	Loss or destruction of property as punishment. (33).

R. CAPTIVES AND FUGITIVES

a. Captivity R4.—R13.3.

R4.	Surprise capture. (12); (13); (14).
R13.3.	Person carried off by bird. (100); (101); (102); (103); (104); (136).

b. Rescues R131.—R155.2.

R131.   Exposed or abandoned child rescued. (40).
R155.2.   Elder brother rescues younger. (107); (108).

c. Escapes and pursuits R227.1.—R228.

R227.1.   Wife flees from animal husband. (129).
R228.   Children leave home because their parents
           refuse them food. (129); (130).

d. Refuges and recapture R311.—R323.+.

R311.   Tree refuge. (42); (44); (45); (46); (47); (70);
           (87); (100); (101); (131); (135).
R316.1.   Refuge on island. (23).
R323.   Refuge in upper world. (24); (115); (135).
R323.+.   Refuge in lower world. (R323. Refuge in upper
           world.) (21).

S. UNNATURAL CRUELTY

a. Cruel relatives S0.—S60.+.

S0.   Cruel relative. (67); (129).
S12.   Cruel mother. (6); (130).
S12.2.   Cruel mother kills child. (85); (113); (114).
S12.4.+.   Cruel mother blinds daughter. (S12.4. Cruel
           mother blinds son.) (114).
S12.6.   Cruel mother refuses children food. (129);
           (130).
S21.   Cruel son. (131).
S60.+.   Cruel wife. (S60. Cruel spouse.) (87).

b. Revolting murders or mutilations S100.—S183.

S100.   Revolting murders or mutilations. (132).
S113.2.   Murder by suffocation. (98).

S115.	Murder by stabbing. (89); (90).
S139.2.1.1.	Head of murdered man taken along as trophy. (112); (113).
S139.2.2.	Other indignities to corpse. (63).
S160.1.	Self-mutilation. (89); (90).
S165.	Mutilation: putting out eyes. (12); (14); (114); (129).
S176.	Mutilation: sex organs cut off. (63).
S183.	Frightful meal. (113); (114).

  c. Abandoned or murdered children S302.

S302.	Children murdered. (144).

T. SEX

  a. Love T51.—T91.4.

T51.	Wooing by emissary. (41); (57).
T55.	Girl as wooer. (33); (57); (119).
T75.0.1.	Suitors ill-treated. (139); (140); (141); (142).
T91.4.	Age and youth in love. (41).

  b. Marriage T111.—T192.

T111.	Marriage of mortal and supernatural being. (41); (42).
T111.1.2.	Man marries the daughter of a god. (33).
T111.2.	Woman from sky-world marries mortal man. (136); (137); (138); (139); (140).
T121.	Unequal marriage. (41).
T131.1.2.	Father's consent to son's (daughter's) marriage necessary. (33).
T173.	Murderous bride. (105); (106).
T182.	Death from intercourse. (105); (106); (116); (120).
T192.	Marriage by force. (131).

c. Illicit sexual relations T410.—T475.2.1.

T410.	Incest. (28); (121); (123).
T411.	Father-daughter incest. (20).
T415.	Brother-sister incest. (22).
T415.5.	Brother-sister marriage. (22).
T417.1.	Mother-in-law seduces son-in-law. (109).
T425.	Brother-in-law seduces (seeks to seduce) sister-in-law. (28); (121); (123).
T425.+.	Brother-in-law marries sister-in-law. (T425. Brother-in-law seduces (seeks to seduce) sister-in-law.) (42).
T471.	Rape. (116); (117); (118); (120); (121).
T475.	Unknown (clandestine) paramour. (39); (139).
T475.2.1.	Intercourse with sleeping girl. (118).

d. Conception and birth T510.—T573.

T510.	Miraculous conception. (105); (106).
T517.	Conception from extraordinary intercourse. (39); (42); (43).
T517.1.	Conception from hand or foot. (42); (43).
T532.+.	Conception from sand in vagina. (T532. Conception from other contacts.) (10).
T532.1.+.	Conception from snakeskin in vagina. (T532.1. Conception from contact with magic object.) (105); (106).
T532.5.1.	Conception from touching another's garment. (119).
T541.+.	Birth from hand. (T541. Birth from unusual part of person's body.) (16); (42); (43).
T554.7.	Woman gives birth to a snake. (105); (106).
T573.	Short pregnancy. (13); (39); (42).

e. Care of children T615.—T670.

T615.	Supernatural growth. (42); (131).
T670.	Adoption of children. (40); (42); (43).

U. THE NATURE OF LIFE

    a. Nature of life—miscellaneous U110.

        U110.   Appearances deceive. (115).

V. RELIGION

    a. Religious motifs—miscellaneous V514.

        V514.   Non-religious visions. (107).

W. TRAITS OF CHARACTER

    a. Favorable traits of character W11.

        W11.   Generosity. (133).

    b. Unfavorable traits of character W152.—W195.

        W152.   Stinginess. (51); (52); (53).
        W188.   Contentiousness. (89).
        W195.   Envy. (89).

Z. MISCELLANEOUS GROUPS OF MOTIFS

    a. Unique exceptions Z310.—Z356.

        Z310.   Unique vulnerability. (63).
        Z310.+.   Eyes only vulnerable spot. (Z310. Unique vulnerability.) (61).
        Z311.   Achilles heel. Invulnerability except in one spot. (113); (114).
        Z356.   Unique survivor. (18); (61); (98).

Alphabetical Motif Index

ABANDONED.—Exposed or abandoned child rescued R131. (40).

ABILITY. — Magic ability to fly D2135.0.3. (103).

ABOVE. — Creator from above A21. (72); worlds above and below A651.3. (12); (13); (14); (15); (21).

ABSENT person seems to be present K1881. (146).

ABUNDANT food in otherworld F166.11. (37); (68).

ACCIDENTAL self-injury N397. (89); (90).

ACHILLES heel. Invulnerability except in one spot Z311. (113); (114).

ACQUISITION of agriculture A1441. (33); of fish A1429.+. (39); (40); (41); (42); (43); (44); (49); of food supply—miscellaneous A1429. (26); (27); of habitations A1435. (56); of honey A1420.+. (60); of magic powers D1720. (67); (142); (143); of manioc A1423.4. (31); of spiritous liquors A1427. (58); (59).

ACT. — Inanimate object acts as if living F1009. (123).

ACTION. — Inappropriate action from misunderstanding J1820. (147).

ADOPTION of children T670. (40); (42); (43).

ADVANCES. — Punishment for man who makes advances to sister-in-law Q242.3. (28).

ADVERSARY. — Animals overcome man's adversary by strategy B524.2. (105); (106); (114); (132).

ADVICE from dream D1814.2. (18).

ADVISE. — Animals advise men B560. (114); god advises mortal A182.3.5. (30); (32); (37).

AGE and youth in love T91.4. (41). — Birds were men in former age A1101.2.+. (115); golden age A1101.1. (29); (33); (58); great age of the gods A191.1. (11).

AGRICULTURE. — Acquisition of agriculture A1441. (33).

AIR. — Animal characteristics from dropping ancient animal from air A2214. (35); extraordinary flights through air F1021. (135); magic air journey D2135. (5); (6).

ALGARROBO. — Origin of algarrobo tree A2681.+. (26); (27).

ALLOW. — Animal allows himself to be tied to another for safety K713.1.1. (147).

ALLOWING. — Deception into allowing oneself to be fettered K713. (147).

AMOUNT. — Tiny amount of food magically satisfies D1349.1.6. (32).

AMPHIBIA. — Origin of amphibia A2160. (84).

AMPHIBIANS. — Chief of amphibians B245.+. (84).

ANCIENT. — Animal characteristics: change in ancient animal A2210. (14); (26); (35); (70); (71); (76); (80); (100); (101); (106); (148); animal characteristics from dropping ancient animal from air A2214. (35).

ANIMAL allows himself to be tied to another for safety K713.1.1. (147); calls the dawn B755. (100); (101); characteristics: change in ancient animal A2210. (14); (26); (35); (70); (71); (76); (80); (100); (101); (106); (148); characteristics from being struck A2213.5. (14); (79); characteristics from burning or singeing A2218. (69); (70); (71); (106); characteristics from dropping ancient animal from air A2214. (35); habit a reminiscence of former experience A2275. (78); (81); (monster) killed from within K952. (107); (108); (109); (110); rescuer or retriever B540. (124); (147); saves man from death by drowning B527. (17); searches for dead man B546. (124); son eats human mother G71.+. (131). — Appearance of animal from marking or painting A2217. (80); dead animal comes to life E3. (15); (70); (71); (150); establishment of animal haunt A2433.1. (69); familiar spirit in animal form F403.2.2.1. (127); foolish imitation by an animal. Tries to go beyond his powers J2413. (147); (149); (150); hero overcomes devastating animal G510.4. (100); (101); (102); (103); hunt for extraordinary (magic) animal F989.15. (135); offspring of marriage to animal B630. (131); original fire property of one person (animal) A1415.0.2. (19); (51); (54); parts of human or animal body transformed into plants A2611.0.5. (28); (123); person (animal) swallowed without killing F911. (107); (108); (109); (110); plants from body of slain person or animal A2611. (61); (62); (63); (64); (65); (66); small animal overcomes large L315. (146); substituted eyes. Lost eyes are replaced by those of another person or animal E781.1. (137); transformation: man to animal D100. (11); (20); (24); (69); (124); transformation: part of animal or person to person D437. (123); wife flees from animal husband R227.1. (129).

ANIMALS advise men B560. (114); created after initial unsuccessful experiment A630.+. (69); (70); (71); created by magic D2178.4. (100); direct man on journey B563. (108); drop from clouds A1795. (88); drop from sky A1795.+. (68); fight B266. (7); from body of slain person A1724.1. (67); from transformations after deluge or world calamity A1711. (18); (20); in human form B200.+. (12); (13); (14); in otherworld F167.1. (68); (137); magically called D2074.1. (124); miraculously multiplied D2106.1.2. (45); (48); overcome man's adversary by strategy B524.2. (105); (106); (114); (132); provide food for men B531. (27); (129); (130); warn against attack B521.3. (98). — Ascent to stars. People or animals ascend to the sky and become stars A761. (3); (5); (6); creation of animals A1700. (67); (68); creation of animals through transformation A1710. (69); (70); (71); (106); creator of animals A84. (72); guardian animals evaded B576.1.1. (12); (13); (14); how animals received their names A2571. (67); (69); (70); (71); magic dominance over animals D2197. (70); (82); original fire property of certain animals A1415.0.2.+. (50); (52); (53); parts of slain animals as token of slaying H105. (100); primeval animals human A1101.2.+. (69); (79); quest for devastating animals H1362. (100); (101); (102); (103); sun creates useful animals A1703.+. (72).

ANKLE. — Heart in ankle F559.7.+. (63).

ANTEATER. — Anteater's dwelling A2432.+. (69); food of anteater A2435.+. (69); (70); (71); how anteater got its claws A2376.+. (69); how anteater received its name A2571.+. (75); origin of anteater A1700.+. (75); transformation: woman to anteater D100.+. (22); why anteater has tail A2378.1.+. (69); why anteater is nocturnal A2491.+. (69); why anteater lives in woods A2433.2.1.+. (75).

ANTEATERS. — Chief of anteaters B241.+. (75).

APPEARANCE of animal from marking or painting A2217. (80). — Magic change to different appearance D52. (143); person changes appearance at will D631.1.1. (61); (100); (116); (117); (121); (124); (127); (128); (134).

APPEARANCES deceive U110. (115).

APPRENTICE. — Magician's apprentice D1711.0.1. (58).

APPROACH. — Victim lured by kind words approaches trickster and is killed K815. (93); (98); victim lured into approach by false token K839.2. (64); (89); (90).

ARMADILLO. — Color of armadillo A2411.+. (80); markings of armadillo A2412.1.+. (35); origin of knots on armadillo's shell A2312.+. (26); transformation: man to armadillo D100.+. (116); (117); (121); why certain armadillo is strong A2528.+. (80); why certain armadillo is swift A2555.+. (80).

ARMADILLOS. — Chief of armadillos B241.2.+. (80).

AROUND. — Tabu: looking around C332. (20).

ARRANGEMENT. — Resuscitation by arrangement of members E30. (124); (137); (138).

ARROW. — Ascent to upper world on arrow chain F53. (115); one arrow shot into end of last one to make rope of arrows F661.7.3. (115).

ARROWS. — One arrow shot into end of last one to make rope of arrows F661.7.3. (115).

ARTIFICIAL. — Flight on artificial wings F1021.1. (135); (149).

ARTS. — Culture hero teaches arts and crafts A541. (43).

ASCEND. — Ascent to stars. People or animals ascend to the sky and become stars A761. (3); (5); (6).

ASCENT to stars. People or animals ascend to the sky and become stars A761. (3); (5); (6); to upper world on arrow chain F53. (115).

ASHES. — Resuscitation from ashes of dead man E42. (121); tobacco from ashes of bad woman A2611.2.+. (61); (62); (64); (65); (66); transformation: ashes into birds D441.6.1.+. (89); (90); (91); (92); (95); (96); (97); (98); transformation by eating ashes D551.+. (134).

ASLEEP by day, awake by night F560.+. (132).

ATTACK. — Animals warn against attack B521.3. (98).

ATTEMPT. — Deception into disastrous attempt to procure food K1020. (147); heat test. Attempt to kill hero by burning him in fire H1511. (1); (2).

ATTEMPTED rape of man disguised as woman J1820.+. (118).

ATTEMPTS. — Vain attempts to circumvent theft of fire A1415.4. (52); (53); (54).

ATTENTION to warnings J1050. (30); (78).

ATTRACTING by magic D2074. (121).

AUTOMATIC object D1600. (28).

AVOIDANCE of others' power J640. (28); (113); (114); (115); (131); (132).

AVOIDING enemy's revenge J647. (93).

AWAKE. — Asleep by day, awake by night F560.+. (132); contest: staying awake H1540.+. (90).

BAD. — Tobacco from ashes of bad woman A2611.2.+. (61); (62); (64); (65); (66); tobacco from grave of bad woman A2611.2. (63).

BALD. — Swallowed person becomes bald F921. (108); (110).

BASKET. — Magic food-basket (vessel) supplies food D1472.1.19. (44).

BAT. — Creation of bat A1895. (64); (106); transformation: woman to bat D100.+. (106).

BATTLE. — Furious battle F1084. (104); (132).

BEAK. — Why parrot's beak is black A2343.2.1. (14).

BEANS. — Transformation: leaf to beans D451.8.+. (139); (140).

BEAR. — Clever honey bear J1100.+. (75); how honey bear received its name A2571.+. (75); origin of honey bear A1700.+. (75).

BEASTS. — Masters of the various kinds of beasts B241.2.+. (11).

BEATING. — Punishment: beating to death Q422.0.1. (33); (63); (121); (138); (145).

BEAUTIFUL. — Remarkably beautiful woman F575.1. (39); (40); (41); (106).

BEAUTY. — False beauty-doctor K1013. (100); (101); (129).

BECOME. — Ascent to stars. People or animals ascend to the sky and become stars A761. (3); (5); (6); person becomes cannibal G30. (62); (67); (89); (90); (113); swallowed person becomes bald F921. (108); (110); swallowed person becomes soft F921.1.+. (108); ugly man becomes handsome D52.2. (141); (142).

BECOMING. — Means of becoming magician D1711.0.3. (58).

BED. — Entrance into girl's (man's) room (bed) by trick K1340. (117); (118); staff stuck in river bed stops water D1549.3.8.+. (42).

BEE as healer B511.+. (148). — Helpful bee B481.3. (148).

BEGINNING of division of labor A1472. (11).

BEHIND. — Murder from behind K959.4. (89); (90); (132).

BEING. — Marriage of mortal and supernatural being T111. (41); (42); star descends as human being A762. (9); (10); (136); (137); (138); (139); (140); sun as human being A736. (72).

BEINGS. — Stars thought of as living beings A761.6. (88).

BELOW. — Worlds above and below A651.3. (12); (13); (14); (15); (21).

BETRAYED. — Person's identity betrayed by habitual conversation H38.+. (89); (90).

BEWITCHING D2070. (113).

BEYOND. — Foolish imitation by an animal. Tries to go beyond his powers J2413. (147); (149); (150).

BIRD as guardian of primordial fire A1414.6. (19); (51); (54); as magician B191.6. (100); (101); as trickster J1117.+. (53); (146); flies with man to safety B542.1. (61); from body of slain person A1724.1.+. (89); (90); (91); (92); (95); (97); (98); from transformed man A1715.+. (87); gives warning B143.1. (98); (108); (123); heals man B511.5. (148); men B50. (115); of dawn B34. (18); (89); (100); (101); ogre lives in sky G630.+. (100); (101). — Cannibal bird as ogre G353.1. (100); (101); (102); (103); (104); cause of bird's walk A2441.2. (94); clever bird J1118. (50); (51); (52);

(53); (54); (89); (90); (91); (92); (95); (96); (97); (98); (101); (105); (106); (115); (146); man carried by bird B552. (61); (138); origin of color of bird A2411.2. (100); (101); origin of kihil bird A1900.+. (87); person carried off by bird R13.3. (100); (101); (102); (103); (104); (136); speaking bird B211.3. (104); theft of fire by bird A1415.2.1. (50); (51); (52); (53); (54); transformation: man to bird D150. (18); (21); (22); (87); (99); (100); (134); transformation: star to bird D440.+. (137); transformation: woman to bird D150.+. (94); treacherous bird K2295.+. (136); (138).

BIRDS as scouts B563.6. (64); carry person from upper world F62.2. (138); from body of slain monster A1724.1.+. (64); in human form B200.+. (100); (101); in otherworld F167.1.2. (7); (15); painted their present colors A2217.1. (100); (101); (148); point out road to hero B563.2. (123); were men in former age A1101.2.+. (115). — Chief of birds B242.+. (97); chiefs of the various kinds of birds B242.2.+. (93); creation of birds A1900. (64); (67); (88); creation of birds through transformation A1710.+. (99); devastating birds B16.3. (100); (101); (102); (103); (104); (125); (136); (137); (138); giant birds B872. (101); (104); helpful birds B450. (45); (64); (123); (132); man-eating birds B33. (100); (101); (102); (103); (104); (136); (137); (138); master of birds B242.+. (7); origin of birds' nests A2431.3. (99); stars as birds A760.+. (88); stars descend as birds A762.+. (88); transformation: ashes into birds D441.6.1.+. (89); (90); (91); (92); (95); (96); (97); (98).

BIRTH from hand T541.+. (16); (42); (43). — Jaguar gives birth to other felines F980.+. (74); woman gives birth to a snake T554.7. (105); (106).

BIT. — Victim persuaded to hold out his tongue: bit by snake K825.+. (100).

BLACK. — Why parrot's beak is black A2343.2.1. (14).

BLEEDING tree F811.20. (42).

BLIND ogre G121.+. (92). — Cruel mother blinds daughter S12.4.+. (114).

BLINDING as punishment Q451.7. (121).

BLOOD. — Eagle with multicolored blood B720.+. (100).

BOAR. — Origin of wild boar A1871.1. (85); why wild boar is fierce A2524.+. (69); why wild boar lives in woods A2433.2.1.+. (69).

BODIES. — Giants with shaggy hair on their bodies F531.1.6.3. (124).

BODILY. — Death or bodily injury by magic D2060. (15); (58); (142); (143); punishment: bodily orifices stopped up Q450.+. (144); tapir's habitual bodily movements A2470.+. (69); vital bodily members E780. (28).

BODY. — Animals from body of slain person A1724.1. (67); bird from body of slain person A1724.1.+. (89); (90); (91); (92); (95); (97); (98); birds from body of slain monster A1724.1.+. (64); crawling through the body of another F900.+. (66); (67); man created from part of body A1263. (123); ogre with cavities in his body G366.+. (91); (93); parts of human or animal body transformed into plants A2611.0.5. (28); (123); person concealed in another's body F1034. (61); plants from body of slain person or animal A2611. (61); (62); (63); (64); (65); (66); resuscitation from fragments of body E35. (136); (137); soul journeys from the body E721. (107).

BONES of victims in front of ogre's house G691.+. (100); (104).

BOY. — Clever boy J1113. (41); (124); demon suitors of boy F402.1.15.+. (83).

BREAD. — Man to earn bread by sweat of his brow A1346. (33); (34).

BREAKING. — Death by drowning for breaking tabu C923. (47); flood as punishment for breaking tabu A1018.1. (47); immediate death for breaking tabu C921. (136); (137); (138); (139); (140); loss of wife (husband) for breaking tabu C932. (136); (139).

BREWING. — Introduction of brewing A1426.2.1. (58).

BRIDE. — Murderous bride T173. (105); (106); quest for bride H1381.3.1. (41).

BRIDEGROOM. — The false bridegroom K1915. (57).

BROTHER-in-law marries sister-in-law T425.+. (42); -in-law seduces (seeks to seduce) sister-in-law T425. (28); (121); (123); -sister incest T415. (22); -sister marriage T415.5. (22). — Elder brother rescues younger R155.2. (107); (108); quest for lost brother(s) H1385.8. (107); (108); treacherous brother K2211. (28).

BROW. — Man to earn bread by sweat of his brow A1346. (33); (34).

BRUSHWOOD. — Origin of brushwood A2680.+. (33); transformation: maize to brushwood D451.+. (33).

BUNGLING fool J2650. (45); (46); (150).

BURNED. — Corpse burned to prevent return E431.13. (104); ogre burned in his own oven G512.3.2. (95); ogre burned to death G512.3. (62); (66); (91); (92); (95); (96); (97); (98); transformation by being burned D576. (69); (70); (71); victim burned in his own house (or hiding place) K812. (96); (97); (98).

BURNING intestinal wind F1041.+. (108); (109); magically evaded D1841.3. (62). — Animal characteristics from burning or singeing A2218. (69); (70); (71); (106); heat test. Attempt to kill hero by burning him in fire H1511. (1); (2); murder by burning K955. (105); (106).

BURROW. — Peccary's burrow A2432.+. (77); why iguana lives in burrow A2432.+. (69).

BUTTERFLY. — Transformation: man to butterfly D186.1. (100).

CAIMANS. — Mother of caimans B244.+. (108).

CALAMITY. — Animals from transformations after deluge or world calamity A1711. (18); (20); new race from single pair (or several) after world calamity A1006.1. (16); (20); preservation of life during great calamity A1005.+. (22); preservation of life during world calamity A1005. (17); (18); (19); (20); (21); (23); renewal of world after world calamity A1006. (16); (18); (21); (23); (24); (25).

CALL. — Animal calls the dawn B755. (100); (101).

CALLED. — Animals magically called D2074.1. (124).

CALLING. — Transformation by calling out D520.+. (94).

CANNIBAL bird as ogre G353.1. (100); (101); (102); (103); (104); ogre G312. (61); (62); (63); (64); (66); (67); (89); (90); (91); (92); (93). — Person becomes cannibal G30. (62); (67); (89); (90); (113); transformation: normal man to cannibal D91. (62); (67); unwitting marriage to cannibal G81. (63).

CANNIBALISM G10. (112). — Taste of human flesh leads to habitual cannibalism G36. (89).

CANNIBALISTIC spirits G11.10. (124).

CAPTIVITY. — Transformation to escape from captivity D642.1. (124).

CAPTURE by deception K700. (15); (69); (97); (134); by masking as another K755. (134); in pitfall K735. (69); (98); (132). — Surprise capture R4. (12); (13); (14).

CAPYBARA. — Creation of capybara A1700.+. (81); transformation: vizcacha to capybara D410.+. (81); why capybara lives in the water A2433.2.2.+. (81).

CAPYBARAS. — Chief of capybaras B241.2.+. (81).

CARING for the child: child killed K1461. (144).

CARRIED. — Man carried by bird B552. (61); (138); person carried off by bird R13.3. (100); (101); (102); (103); (104); (136).

CARRY. — Birds carry person from upper world F62.2. (138); demons carry off man's soul F402.1.5.1.+. (83).

CATCHING. — Custom of catching fish with nets A1527. (39); (41); (43).

CAUGHT. — Ogre caught in noose and killed G514.3. (114).

CAUSE of bird's walk A2441.2. (94). — Demon causes disease F402.1.5. (83); magic intestinal wind causes disease D1500.4.+. (132); spirit causes death F402.1.11. (83).

CAUSED. — Earth magically caused to quake D2148. (64); eclipse caused by monster devouring sun or moon A737.1. (4).

CAUTION in eating J585. (40); (41); (44). — Wisdom of caution J580. (20); (21); (42); (62); (78); (93); (104); (105); (106).

CAVES. — Spirits live in caves F402.6.4.1. (83).

CAVITIES. — Ogre with cavities in his body G366. +. (91); (93).

CHAGUAR. — Why chaguar is rooted in the ground A2770. +. (29).

CHAIN. — Ascent to upper world on arrow chain F53. (115).

CHANGE in person's color D57. (110). — Animal characteristics: change in ancient animal A2210. (14); (26); (35); (70); (71); (76); (80); (100); (101); (106); (148); magic change to different appearance D52. (143); person changes appearance at will D631.1.1. (61); (100); (116); (117); (121); (124); (127); (128); (134); person changes color F1082. (110).

CHANGED. — Partial transformation — color changed D682.4. (110); size of object changed at will D631.3. (8).

CHARACTERISTIC. — Ogres with characteristic methods G310. (64); (65); (67); (91); (92); (93); (95); (96); (97); (98); (122); (126); (127); (128).

CHARACTERISTICS. — Animal characteristics: change in ancient animal A2210. (14); (26); (35); (70); (71); (76); (80); (100); (101); (106); (148); animal characteristics from being struck A2213.5. (14); (79); animal characteristics from burning or singeing A2218. (69); (70); (71); (106); animal characteristics from dropping ancient animal from air A2214. (35); origin of plant characteristics A2700. (33); (34).

CHARGES. — Treacherous murder of enemy's children or charges K930. (100); (101).

CHEATS. — Thefts and cheats — general K300. (12); (13); (14).

CHEESE. — Diving for cheese J1791.3. (147).

CHICKEN. — Creation of chicken A1988. (73).

CHIEF chosen on basis of strength P11.4. +. (112); of amphibians B245. +. (84); of anteaters B241. +. (75); of armadillos B241.2. +. (80); of birds B242. +. (97); of capybaras B241.2. +. (81); of iguanas B244. +. (76); of peccaries B241.2. +. (77); (78); of pumas B241.2. +. (86); of tapirs B241.2. +. (79); (82); of vizcachas B241.2. +. (81).

CHIEFS of the various kinds of birds B242.2. +. (93).

CHILD recognizes relative's flesh when it is served to be eaten G61.1. (63); (129). — Caring for the child: child killed K1461. (144); cruel mother kills child S12.2. (85); (113); (114); exposed or abandoned child rescued R131. (40).

CHILDREN leave home because their parents refuse them food R228. (129); (130); murdered S302. (144). — Adoption of children T670. (40); (42); (43); cruel mother refuses children food S12.6. (129); (130); elder children to protect younger P250.1. (6); murder of children punished Q211.4. (144); stars as children of the moon A764.1. (137); treacherous murder of enemy's children or charges

K930. (100); (101); unnatural mother eats children G72.+. (113); (114); woman plans to eat her children G72.1. (63).

CHOICES. — Origin of tribes from choices made A1614.4. (55).

CHOROTE. — Origin of the Chorote A1611.+. (9); (19).

CHOSEN. — Chief chosen on basis of strength P11.4.+. (112).

CIRCUMVENT. —Vain attempts to circumvent theft of fire A1415.4. (52); (53); (54).

CLANDESTINE. — Unknown (clandestine) paramour T475. (39); (139).

CLAWS. — How anteater got its claws A2376.+. (69).

CLAY. — Man made from clay image and vivified A1241.3. (9).

CLEVER bird J1118. (50); (51); (52); (53); (54); (89); (90); (91); (92); (95); (96); (97); (98); (101); (105); (106); (115); (146); boy J1113. (41); (124); dog J1100.+. (64); (65); honey bear J1100.+. (75).

CLIMBING. — Cutting rope to kill ogre who is climbing the rope to kill his victim K678. (115); thief climbing rope discovered and rope cut K1622. (12); (13); (14).

CLOUDS. — Animals drop from clouds A1795. (88); toad drops from clouds A1795.+. (84).

CLUB. — Giant with club as weapon F531.4.5.1.+. (122); ogre killed by striking with club G512.8.1. (102).

COLD test H1512. (1); (2). — Contest in enduring cold H1541. (1); (2); extraordinary cold path F840.+. (1); (2); moon cold A750.+. (1); (2).

COLOR of armadillo A2411.+. (80); of woodpecker A2411.2.4.1. (148). — Change in person's color D57. (110); origin of color of bird A2411.2. (100); (101); partial transformation — color changed D682.4. (110); person changes color F1082. (110).

COLORS. — Birds painted their present colors A2217.1. (100); (101); (148).

COMMAND. — Magic results produced by command D1765. (48); (121).

CONCEAL. — Tree opens and conceals fugitive D1393.1. (100).

CONCEALED. — Person concealed in another's body F1034. (61).

CONCEPTION from extraordinary intercourse T517. (39); (42); (43); from hand or foot T517.1. (42); (43); from sand in vagina T532.+. (10); from snakeskin in vagina T532.1.+. (105); (106); from touching another's garment T532.5.1. (119). — Miraculous conception T510. (105); (106).

CONDITION of first man (woman) A1281. (12); (13); (15).

CONFEDERATE hides fugitive K649.1. (100).

CONSENT. — Father's consent to son's (daughter's) marriage necessary T131.1.2. (33).

CONSTELLATIONS. — Origin of constellations A766. (5); (6).

CONTAINING. — Tree containing water and fish F811.+. (39); (42); (49).

CONTENTIOUSNESS W188. (89).

CONTEST between sun and moon A736.11. (1); (2); in enduring cold H1541. (1); (2); in enduring heat H1542. (1); (2); in fasting H1545. (148); in remaining under water H1543. (146); staying awake H1540.+. (90). — Deceptive contest in fasting K53. (148); endurance contest won by deception K50. (148); foot-racing contest H1594. (150); song duel. Contest in singing H503.1. (89).

CONTROL. — Magic control of fires D2158. (105); (106); magic control of night and day D2146. (100); (101); magic control of rivers D2151.2. (42); magic control of soil and crops D2157. (64); magic control of waters D2151. (45); (47); (48).

CONVERSATION. — Overheard (human) conversation N455. (45); person's identity betrayed by habitual conversation H38.+. (89); (90).

CORPSE burned to prevent return E431.13. (104). — Other indignities to corpse S139.2.2. (63).

COUNTRY of the naked F709.1. (145).

COVERED. — Man covered with hair F521.1. (132).

CRAFTS. — Culture hero teaches arts and crafts A541. (43).

CRAWLING through the body of another F900.+. (66); (67).

CREATE. — Sun creates useful animals A1703.+. (72).

CREATED. — Animals created after initial unsuccessful experiment A630.+. (69); (70); (71); animals created by magic D2178.4. (100); man created from part of body A1263. (123).

CREATION of animals A1700. (67); (68); of animals through transformation A1710. (69); (70); (71); (106); of bat A1895. (64); (106); of birds A1900. (64); (67); (88); of birds through transformation A1710.+. (99); of capybara A1700.+. (81); of chicken A1988. (73); of felidae A1810. (74); of first man's (woman's) mate A1275. (9); of heron A1964. (99); of howler monkey A1861.+. (64); of owl A1958. (97); (98); of parrot A1994. (99); of particular fishes A2110. (84); of plants by transformation A2610. (28); of snake (serpent) A2145. (105); (106); of the earth A800. (8); (24); of the moon A740. (3); (24); of the sky A701. (24); of vulture A1931. (91); (92).

CREATOR from above A21. (72); goes to sky A81. (24); of animals A84. (72); of food items A1420.3. (84); of rivers A930.1. (41); (42). — Creator's wife A32.3. (11); moon as creator A1.+. (8); (24); old man as creator A15.3. (11); old man from sky as creator A21.2. (11); old woman as creator A15.1.1. (11); sun-god as creator A1.1. (72).

CREATURES. — Tabu: seeing supernatural creatures C311.1. (124).

CREEPERS. — Origin of creepers A2682. (123).

CRIME. — Punishment fitted to crime Q580. (28).

CROPS. — Magic control of soil and crops D2157. (64); magic quick growth of crops D2157.2. (8); (33); (34); (35); (36); (38); (136); (137).

CRUEL mother S12. (6); (130); mother blinds daughter S12.4. +. (114); mother kills child S12.2. (85); (113); (114); mother refuses children food S12.6. (129); (130); punishments Q450. (28); relative S0. (67); (129); son S21. (131); wife S60. +. (87).

CRY of fox A2426.1. +. (33).

CRYSTALS from urine D1454. +. (136).

CULTIVATED. — Origin of cultivated plants A2684. (8); (24); (37); (38).

CULTIVATOR. — God as cultivator A181.2. (64).

CULTURE hero as dupe or trickster A521. (42); hero can transform self A527.3.1. (42); hero dispenses food and hospitality A547. (41); (42); (43); hero regulates rivers A533. (41); (42); hero teaches arts and crafts A541. (43). — Hawk as culture hero A522.2.3. (41); (50); (51); (52); (53); (54); (69); (70); (71); (104); river where culture hero drags his staff A934.4. +. (42).

CUSTOM of catching fish with nets A1527. (39); (41); (43). — Origin of custom of lighting fire after death of family member A1547. +. (80).

CUSTOMS. — Mourning customs P681. (80); (106).

CUT. — Mutilation: sex organs cut off S176. (63); rope cut and victim dropped K963. (12); (13); (115); thief climbing rope discovered and rope cut K1622. (12); (13); (14); victim persuaded to hold out his tongue: cut off K825. (101).

CUTTING rope to kill ogre who is climbing the rope to kill his victim K678. (115). — Victim kills swallower from within by cutting F912.2. (107); (108); (109); (110).

CYCLE. — Origin of seasonal plant cycle A2700. +. (37).

DANCER. — Marvelous dancer F699.1. (119).

DANGER. — Dream warns of danger which will happen in near future D1810.8.3.2. (78).

DARKNESS. — Miraculous darkness as punishment Q552.20.1. (100); (101).

DAUGHTER. — Cruel mother blinds daughter S12.4. +. (114); father-daughter incest T411. (20); father's consent to son's (daughter's) marriage necessary T131.1.2. (33); man marries the daughter of a god T111.1.2. (33).

DAWN. — Animal calls the dawn B755. (100); (101); bird of dawn B34. (18); (89); (100); (101).

DAY. — Asleep by day, awake by night F560.+. (132); magic control of night and day D2146. (100); (101); person sees equally well by night or day F642.4. (132).

DEAD animal comes to life E3. (15); (70); (71); (150). — Animal searches for dead man B546. (124); resuscitation from ashes of dead man E42. (121).

DEATH as punishment Q411. (124); (129); (136); (137); (138); (139); (140); (142); (143); as punishment for murder Q411.6. (63); (138); (144); as punishment for ravisher Q411.7. (121); by drowning for breaking tabu C923. (47); from intercourse T182. (105); (106); (116); (120); of another revealed in dream D1812.3.3.11. (138); or bodily injury by magic D2060. (15); (58); (142); (143). — Animal saves man from death by drowning B527. (17); deception by feigned death (sleep) K1860. (121); earthquake at ogre's death F960.2.5.2.+. (67); immediate death for breaking tabu C921. (136); (137); (138); (139); (140); ogre burned to death G512.3. (62); (66); (91); (92); (95); (96); (97); (98); origin of custom of lighting fire after death of family member A1547.+. (80); origin of death A1335. (13); punishment: beating to death Q422.0.1. (33); (63); (121); (138); (145); spirit causes death F402.1.11. (83); transformation to escape death D642.2. (87); (89); (100); (124).

DECAPITATED. — Ogre decapitated G512.1.2. (100).

DECEIVE. — Appearances deceive U110. (115).

DECEPTION by disguise K1810. (119); by disguise or illusion K1800. (70); (146); (147); by feigned death (sleep) K1860. (121); by hiding K1892. (100); by pretending sleep K1868. (45); (128); into allowing oneself to be fettered K713. (147); into disastrous attempt to procure food K1020. (147); into humiliating position K1200. (147). — Capture by deception K700. (15); (69); (97); (134); endurance contest won by deception K50. (148); fatal deception into trickster's power K810. (89); (90); (91); (92); (93); (97); (132); (134); killing or maiming by deception K800. (89); (90); (91); (92); (93); (100); (101); race won by deception K11. (150).

DECEPTIVE contest in fasting K53. (148).

DEER as ogre G350.+. (126); -man B20.+. (127); -man as ogre G350.+. (127). — Deer's haunt A2433.+. (69); deer's means of defense: sharp hearing A2461.+. (69); destructive deer B16.2.7. (126); (127); food of deer A2435.+. (69); origin of deer's sharp hearing A2428.+. (69); transformation: man to deer D114.1.1. (127); why deer run, stop, and run on again A2461.4. (69).

DEFEATED. — Ogre defeated G500. (126).

DEFENSE. — Deer's means of defense: sharp hearing A2461.+. (69);

peccary's means of defense: hoofs A2461.+. (69).

DEFENSES. — Forethought in defenses against others J670. (64); (65); (66); (67); (70); (77); (78); (104); (105); (106).

DEITY invoked A183. (11); provides man with soul A185.12. (11); teaches mortal A185.3. (11); (33); (37); (56). — Journey to see deity F12. (37); magic power from deity D1726. (58).

DELUGE A1010. (16); (17). — Animals from transformations after deluge or world calamity A1711. (18); (20); escape from deluge A1020. (17); escape from deluge on tree A1023. (42); (44); (45); (46); (47).

DELUGES. — Local deluges A1011. (42); (44); (45); (46); (47); (48); (49).

DEMON causes disease F402.1.5. (83); in form of white woman G302.3.3.+. (83); suitors of boy F402.1.15.+. (83).

DEMONS carry off man's soul F402.1.5.1.+. (83). — Sexual relations between man and demons G302.7.1. (83).

DESCEND. — First man descends from sky A1231. (16); first woman descends from sky A1231.+. (12); (13); star descends as human being A762. (9); (10); (136); (137); (138); (139); (140); stars descend as birds A762.+. (88).

DESTROYED. — House destroyed by magic D2089.6. (67).

DESTRUCTION. — Loss or destruction of property as punishment Q595. (33).

DESTRUCTIVE deer B16.2.7. (126); (127).

DETECTED. — Eaters of stolen food detected J1144. (12); (13); (14).

DETECTION. — Thief escapes detection K400. (13); (14).

DEVASTATING birds B16.3. (100); (101); (102); (103); (104); (125); (136); (137); (138); jaguar B16.2.2.+. (128); (man-eating) sea-monster (serpent) B16.5.1.2. (107); (108); (109); (110); monster G346. (61); (62); (63); (64); (65); (66); (67); (89); (90); (104); (122); (126); (128); wasp B16.6.+. (111). — Hero overcomes devastating animal G510.4. (100); (101); (102); (103); quest for devastating animals H1362. (100); (101); (102); (103).

DEVOUR. — Woman devours her husband G11.6.4. (113); (114).

DEVOURING. — Eclipse caused by monster devouring sun or moon A737.1. (4).

DIFFERENT. — Magic change to different appearance D52. (143).

DIFFERENTIATION. — Distribution and differentiation of peoples — general A1600. (55).

DIFFICULT. — Transformation to escape difficult situation D642. (61).

DIRECT. — Animals direct man on journey B563. (108).

DIRECTION. — Tabu: looking in certain direction C330. (21).

DISAPPEAR. — Food magically disappears Q552.3.4. (33).

DISASTROUS. — Deception into disastrous attempt to procure food K1020. (147).

DISCOVERED. — Thief climbing rope discovered and rope cut K1622. (12); (13); (14).

DISEASE. — Demon causes disease F402.1.5. (83); magic intestinal wind causes disease D1500.4.+. (132).

DISGUISE. — Deception by disguise K1810. (119); deception by disguise or illusion K1800. (70); (146); (147).

DISGUISED. — Attempted rape of man disguised as woman J1820.+. (118).

DISGUISING. — Seduction by man disguising as woman K1321. (116); (117); (118).

DISPENSE. — Culture hero dispenses food and hospitality A547. (41); (42); (43).

DISTANCE. — Long distance sexual intercourse K1391. (116); (120).

DISTRACTED. — Owner's interest distracted while goods are stolen K341. (146).

DISTRIBUTION and differentiation of peoples — general A1600. (55); of tribes A1620. (21).

DISTURBANCES. — Earth-disturbances at end of world A1060. (18).

DIVING for cheese J1791.3. (147); match: trickster eats food while dupe is under water K16.2. (146).

DIVISION. — Beginning of division of labor A1472. (11).

DOCTOR. — False beauty-doctor K1013. (100); (101); (129).

DOG as messenger B291.2.2. (64); (65); (66); (67). — Clever dog J1100.+. (64); (65); helpful dog B421. (64); (65); (66); (67); transformation: man to dog D141. (41).

DOMINANCE. — Magic dominance over animals D2197. (70); (82).

DOVES. — Mistress of doves B242.2.2.+. (83).

DRAG. — River where culture hero drags his staff A934.4.+. (42).

DREAM warns of danger which will happen in near future D1810.8.3.2. (78); warns of illness or injury D1810.8.3.1.1. (78). — Advice from dream D1814.2. (18); death of another revealed in dream D1812.3.3.11. (138); future revealed in dream D1812.3.3. (18); information received through dream D1810.8.2. (120); (128); murder made known in a dream D1810.8.2.3. (138); realistic dream F1068. (120); wisdom (knowledge) from dream J157. (11); (120); (128).

DREAMS. — Warning in dreams D1810.8.3. (78); (120).

DRINK. — Magic strength-giving drink D1335.2. (112).

DROP. — Animals drop from clouds A1795. (88); animals drop from sky A1795.+. (68); jaguar drops from sky A1795.+. (74); toad drops from clouds A1795.+. (84).

DROPPED. — Rope cut and victim dropped K963. (12); (13); (115).

DROPPING. — Animal characteristics from dropping ancient animal from air A2214. (35).

DROWNING. — Animal saves man from death by drowning B527. (17); death by drowning for breaking tabu C923. (47); miraculous drowning as punishment Q552.19. (108); punishment: drowning Q428. (42); (44); (45); (46); (47); (49).

DRY. — Waters made to dry up D2151.0.2. (107); (108).

DUEL. — Song duel. Contest in singing H503.1. (89).

DUPE persuaded to relax vigilance: seized K827. (93). — Culture hero as dupe or trickster A521. (42); diving match: trickster eats food while dupe is under water K16.2. (146).

DWELLING. — Anteater's dwelling A2432.+. (69); why puma has no permanent dwelling A2432.+. (69); wildcat's dwelling A2432.+. (69).

EAGLE with multicolored blood B720.+. (100). — Transformation: man to eagle D152.2. (102).

EARN. — Man to earn bread by sweat of his brow A1346. (33); (34).

EARTH-disturbances at end of world A1060. (18); magically caused to quake D2148. (64); supported by roots A840.+. (21). — Creation of the earth A800. (8); (24); escape by hiding in the earth K515.6. (19); (20); (21); (22); (24); (116); (121); inhabitant of upper world visits earth F30. (7); (9); (10); (12); (13); (14); (15); (56); (72); (93); man sinks into earth F942. (18); (64); murder by throwing earth over victim D2061.2.+. (63); planting the earth A2602. (8); (18); (23); (24); (37); resuscitation by sprinkling earth E50.+. (15); (136); (137); (138); (139); (140); small earth made to grow large D489.+. (8).

EARTHLY. — Journey to earthly paradise F111. (133).

EARTHQUAKE at ogre's death F960.2.5.2.+. (67). — Extraordinary earthquake F969.4. (67).

EARTHQUAKES at the end of the world A1061.1. (18).

EAT. — Animal son eats human mother G71.+. (131); diving match: trickster eats food while dupe is under water K16.2. (146); person eats own flesh G51. (89); (90); unnatural mother eats children G72.+. (113); (114); woman plans to eat her children G72.1. (63).

EATEN person resuscitated E32.0.1. (124); (136); (137); (138). — Child recognizes relative's flesh when it is served to be eaten G61.1. (63); (129); partially eaten fruit made whole again D2150.+. (32); (37).

EATERS of stolen food detected J1144. (12); (13); (14).

EATING. — Caution in eating J585. (40); (41); (44); devastating (man-eating) sea-monster (serpent) B16.5.1.2. (107); (108); (109); (110); man-eating birds B33. (100); (101); (102); (103); (104); (136); (137);

(138); man-eating woman G11.6. (61); (62); (63); (64); (66); (113); (114); transformation by eating ashes D551. + . (134).

ECLIPSE caused by monster devouring sun or moon A737.1. (4).

EEL. — Helpful eel B476. (61); transformation: man to eel D173. (61).

EJECTMENT. — Punishment: ejectment Q432. (33); (45).

ELDER brother rescues younger R155.2. (107); (108); children to protect younger P250.1. (6).

ELUDE. — Transformation to elude pursuers D642.7. (127).

EMISSARY. — Wooing by emissary T51. (41); (57).

END. — Earth-disturbances at end of world A1060. (18); earthquakes at the end of the world A1061.1. (18); one arrow shot into end of last one to make rope of arrows F661.7.3. (115); quest for the world's end H1371.1. (21).

ENDURANCE contest won by deception K50. (148). — Tests of endurance H1500. (1); (2).

ENDURING. — Contest in enduring cold H1541. (1); (2); contest in enduring heat H1542. (1); (2).

ENEMIES. — Foolishness of noise-making when enemies overhear J581. (124); quest for enemies H1397. (63); (132).

ENEMY. — Avoiding enemy's revenge J647. (93); escaping before enemy can strike J641. (57); (64); (65); (66); (67); (77); (87); (115); (132); sleep feigned to kill enemy K911.3. (128); transformation to kill enemy D651.1. (102); treacherous murder of enemy's children or charges K930. (100); (101).

ENIGMATIC statements H580. (109).

ENTRANCE into girl's (man's) room (bed) by trick K1340. (117); (118).

ENVY W195. (89).

EQUALLY. — Person sees equally well by night or day F642.4. (132).

ESCAPE by hiding in the earth K515.6. (19); (20); (21); (22); (24); (116); (121); from deluge A1020. (17); from deluge on tree A1023. (42); (44); (45); (46); (47). — Thief escapes detection K400. (13); (14); transformation to escape death D642.2. (87); (89); (100); (124); transformation to escape difficult situation D642. (61); transformation to escape from captivity D642.1. (124); transformation to escape notice D642.5. (89).

ESCAPES by magic D2165. (61).

ESCAPING before enemy can strike J641. (57); (64); (65); (66); (67); (77); (87); (115); (132).

ESTABLISHMENT of animal haunt A2433.1. (69).

EVADED. — Burning magically evaded D1841.3. (62); guardian animals evaded B576.1.1. (12); (13); (14).

EVIL spirits F402. (59).

EXCREMENT. — Extraordinary excrement F559.3. (28).

EXCREMENTS. — Magic excrements D1002. (28).

EXPERIENCE. — Animal habit a reminiscence of former experience A2275. (78); (81).

EXPERIMENT. — Animals created after initial unsuccessful experiment A630.+. (69); (70); (71).

EXPLOITS. — Tokens of exploits H84. (64); (65); (66); (67); (100).

EXPOSED or abandoned child rescued R131. (40).

EXTRAORDINARY castle (house, palace) F771. (67); cold path F840.+. (1); (2); earthquake F969.4. (67); excrement F559.3. (28); flights through air F1021. (135); hot path F840.+. (1); (2); occurrences concerning fishing F986. (39); (42); (44); (47); ornaments F827. (138); pond (lake) F713. (45); (46); (47); (48); rocks and stones F800. (91); (92); tree F811. (15); (26); (39); (42); (49); ugliness F576. (139); (140); (141); (142). — Conception from extraordinary intercourse T517. (39); (42); (43); hunt for extraordinary (magic) animal F989.15. (135).

EYE. — Person has red eye F541.6.2. (62).

EYES only vulnerable spot Z310.+. (61); successfully replaced E781. (136); (137); torn out magically replaced D2161.3.1.1. (136); (137). —Mutilation: putting out eyes S165. (12); (14); (114); (129); remarkable eyes F541. (132); substituted eyes. Lost eyes are replaced by those of another person or animal E781.1. (137).

FALSE beauty-doctor K1013. (100); (101); (129). — The false bridegroom K1915. (57); victim lured into approach by false token K839.2. (64); (89); (90).

FAMILIAR spirit in animal form F403.2.2.1. (127).

FAMILY of the moon A745. (3); (8); (32); (33); (37); (141). — Origin of custom of lighting fire after death of family member A1547.+. (80); quest for lost (stolen) family H1385.9. (123).

FASTING. — Contest in fasting H1545. (148); deceptive contest in fasting K53. (148).

FATAL deception into trickster's power K810. (89); (90); (91); (92); (93); (97); (132); (134); imitation J2401. (150).

FATHER-daughter incest T411. (20). — Father's consent to son's (daughter's) marriage necessary T131.1.2. (33); infant picks out his unknown father H481. (39); (40).

FEAR. — Wise fear of the weak for the strong J613. (64); (65); (66); (67); (108); (113); (114); (115); (125); (130); (131).

FEATHERS. — Why hawk's neck feathers are short A2313.+. (106).

FEATURES. — Ogres with monstrous features G360. (62); (64); (67).

FEIGNED. — Deception by feigned death (sleep) K1860. (121); sleep feigned to kill enemy K911.3. (128).

FELIDAE. — Creation of felidae A1810. (74).

FELINES. — Jaguar gives birth to other felines F980.+. (74).

FETTERED. — Deception into allowing oneself to be fettered K713. (147).

FIERCE. — Why wild boar is fierce A2524.+. (69).

FIGHT. — Animals fight B266. (7).

FINGERNAILS. — Person with very long fingernails F515.2.2. (62); (67); (113).

FIRE. — Bird as guardian of primordial fire A1414.6. (19); (51); (54); great fire A1030.+. (22); heat test. Attempt to kill hero by burning him in fire H1511. (1); (2); jaguar uses fire B200.+. (129); marvelous tree survives world-fire A1029.1.+. (24); men hide from world-fire and renew race A1038. (19); (20); (21); origin of custom of lighting fire after death of family member A1547.+. (80); origin of fire A1414. (11); (19); (50); (51); (52); (53); (54); original fire property of certain animals A1415.0.2.+. (50); (52); (53); original fire property of one person (animal) A1415.0.2. (19); (51); (54); theft of fire by bird A1415.2.1. (50); (51); (52); (53); (54); tree as repository of fire A1414.7.1. (19); (51); vain attempts to circumvent theft of fire A1415.4. (52); (53); (54); world-fire A1030. (19); (20); (21); (23); (24); (25).

FIRES. — Magic control of fires D2158. (105); (106).

FIRST man descends from sky A1231. (16); man (woman) A1280. (9); (10); (12); (13); (15); (16); woman descends from sky A1231.+. (12); (13). — Condition of first man (woman) A1281. (12); (13); (15); creation of first man's (woman's) mate A1275. (9); incestuous first parents A1273.1. (10); (16).

FISH-producing tree F811.5.3. (39); (42); (49). — Acquisition of fish A1429.+. (39); (40); (41); (42); (43); (44); (49); custom of catching fish with nets A1527. (39); (41); (43); god of fish A445. (39); (41); helpful fish B470. (147); inexhaustible fish D1652.1.10. (44); (48); magic fish B175. (47); monster half-man, half-fish B80.2. (41); tabu: killing certain fish C841.9. (47); tree containing water and fish F811.+. (39); (42); (49).

FISHES. — Creation of particular fishes A2110. (84).

FISHING. — Extraordinary occurrences concerning fishing F986. (39); (42); (44); (47); origin of fishing A1457. (39); (40); (41); (42); (43); origin of the net for fishing A1457.3. (39); (41); (43).

FITTED. — Punishment fitted to crime Q580. (28).

FLEE. — Wife flees from animal husband R227.1. (129).

FLESH. — Child recognizes relative's flesh when it is served to be eaten G61.1. (63); (129); person eats own flesh G51. (89); (90); taste of human flesh leads to habitual cannibalism G36. (89).

FLIGHT on artificial wings F1021.1. (135); (149). — Transformation flight D671. (100).

FLIGHTS. — Extraordinary flights through air F1021. (135).

FLOOD as punishment for breaking tabu A1018.1. (47).

FLOWER. — Transformation: man (woman) to flower D212. (100).

FLY (= insect) as messenger B291.+. (93); (136); (137). — Helpful fly B483.1. (66); (67).

FLY (= movement through air). — Bird flies with man to safety B542.1. (61); magic ability to fly D2135.0.3. (103).

FOOD magically disappears Q552.3.4. (33); of anteater A2435.+. (69); (70); (71); of deer A2435.+. (69); of iguana A2435.6.+. (69); of jaguar A2435.3.16. (69); (70); (71); of peccary A2435.+. (69); of pig A2435.3.14. (69); of puma A2435.+. (69); (70); (71); of rabbit A2435.3.12.+. (70); (71); of rhea A2435.4.+. (69); of tapir A2435.+. (69); of wildcat A2435.3.2.+. (69); (70); (71); supplied by magic D1030.1. (44); (48). — Abundant food in otherworld F166.11. (37); (68); animals provide food for men B531. (27); (129); (130); acquisition of food supply — miscellaneous A1429. (26); (27); children leave home because their parents refuse them food R228. (129); (130); creator of food items A1420.3. (84); cruel mother refuses children food S12.6. (129); (130); culture hero dispenses food and hospitality A547. (41); (42); (43); deception into disastrous attempt to procure food K1020. (147); diving match: trickster eats food while dupe is under water K16.2. (146); eaters of stolen food detected J1144. (12); (13); (14); forethought in provision for food J710. (20); (38); (69); gods teach how to seek and prepare food A1420.2. (11); (39); (41); inexhaustible food D1652.1. (45); magic food-basket (vessel) supplies food D1472.1.19. (44); tiny amount of food magically satisfies D1349.1.6. (32); transformation to receive food D655. (41).

FOOL. — Bungling fool J2650. (45); (46); (150).

FOOLISH imitation J2400. (33); (34); (42); (44); (48); imitation by an animal. Tries to go beyond his powers J2413. (147); (149); (150); marriage of old man and young girl J445.2. (87).

FOOLISHNESS of noise-making when enemies overhear J581. (124).

FOOLS J1700. (35); (36). — Gullible fools J2300. (147).

FOOT-racing contest H1594. (150). — Conception from hand or foot T517.1. (42); (43); ogre's heart (life) in foot E714.+. (113); (114).

FORCE. — Marriage by force T192. (131).

FORETHOUGHT in defenses against others J670. (64); (65); (66); (67); (70); (77); (78); (104); (105); (106); in prevention of others' plans J620. (42); in provision for food J710. (20); (38); (69).

FORM. — Animals in human form B200.+. (12); (13); (14); birds in human form B200.+. (100); (101); demon in form of white woman G302.3.3.+. (83); familiar spirit in animal form F403.2.2.1. (127).

FOSTER mother P272. (40); (42); (43).

FOX as magician B191.+. (146); as trickster J1117+. (26); (29); (33); (34); (35); (42); (44); (45); (46); (47); (48); (49); (57); (144); (145); (147). — Cry of fox A2426.1.+. (33); helpful fox B435.1. (27); (114); treacherous fox K2295.+. (144); (147).

FRAGMENTATION. — Multiplication of man by fragmentation A1296. (123).

FRAGMENTS. — Resuscitation from fragments of body E35. (136); (137).

FRIGHTFUL meal S183. (113); (114).

FROG. — Punishment: transformation into frog Q551.3.2.3. (38).

FRONT. — Bones of victims in front of ogre's house G691.+. (100); (104).

FRUIT. — Partially eaten fruit made whole again D2150.+. (32); (37).

FUGITIVE. — Confederate hides fugitive K649.1. (100); tree opens and conceals fugitive D1393.1. (100).

FURIOUS battle F1084. (104); (132).

FURNISHED. — Provisions magically furnished D2105. (15).

FUTURE revealed in dream D1812.3.3. (18). — Dream warns of danger which will happen in near future D1810.8.3.2. (78).

GARDEN produced by magic D961.1. (137).

GARMENT. — Conception from touching another's garment T532.5.1. (119).

GENEROSITY W11. (133).

GIANT F531. (118); (121); (122); (123); birds B872. (101); (104); (giantess) with particularly long hair F531.1.6.3.1. (124); serpent B875.1. (107); (108); (109); (110); with club as weapon F531.4.5.1.+. (122).

GIANTESS. — Giant (giantess) with particularly long hair F531.1.6.3.1. (124).

GIANTS large or small at will F531.6.5.2. (118); with shaggy hair on their bodies F531.1.6.3. (124).

GIGANTIC. — Wood-spirit gigantic F441.5.2. (124).

GIRL as wooer T55. (33); (57); (119). — Entrance into girl's (man's) room (bed) by trick K1340. (117); (118); foolish marriage of old man and young girl J445.2. (87); intercourse with sleeping girl T475.2.1. (118); mortal marries star-girl A762.2. (136); (137); (138); (139); (140).

GIVE. — Bird gives warning B143.1. (98); (108); (123); jaguar gives

birth to other felines F980.+. (74); spirit gives warning F403.2.3.2.
(83); woman gives birth to a snake T554.7. (105); (106).

GIVEN. — Truth given in vision D1810.8.1. (107).

GIVING. — Magic strength-giving drink D1335.2. (112).

GOD advises mortal A182.3.5. (30); (32); (37); as cultivator A181.2.
(64); as helper N817.0.1. (30); (31); of fish A445. (39); (41); of the
underworld A300. (30); (31); (58); (64). — Man marries the
daughter of a god T111.1.2. (33); omniscience of a god D1810.0.1.
(33); sun-god as creator A1.1. (72).

GODS teach how to seek and prepare food A1420.2. (11); (39); (41).
— Great age of the gods A191.1. (11).

GOLDEN age A1101.1. (29); (33); (58).

GRADUAL transformation D681. (81).

GRAVE. — Tobacco from grave of bad woman A2611.2. (63).

GREAT age of the gods A191.1. (11); fire A1030.+. (22). — Preservation of life during great calamity A1005.+. (22).

GREEDY. — One should not be too greedy J514. (45).

GROUND. — Why chaguar is rooted in the ground A2770.+. (29).

GROW. — Small earth made to grow large D489.+. (8).

GROWTH. — Magic quick growth of crops D2157.2. (8); (33); (34);
(35); (36); (38); (136); (137); miraculous speedy growth of a tree
D2157.4. (26); supernatural growth T615. (42); (131).

GUARD. — The sleeping guard N396. (13).

GUARDIAN animals evaded B576.1.1. (12); (13); (14). — Bird as
guardian of primordial fire A1414.6. (19); (51); (54).

GULLIBLE fools J2300. (147).

HABIT. — Animal habit a reminiscence of former experience A2275.
(78); (81).

HABITATIONS. — Acquisition of habitations A1435. (56).

HABITUAL. — Person's identity betrayed by habitual conversation
H38.+. (89); (90); tapir's habitual bodily movements A2470.+.
(69); taste of human flesh leads to habitual cannibalism G36. (89).

HAIR. — Giant (giantess) with particularly long hair F531.1.6.3.1.
(124); giants with shaggy hair on their bodies F531.1.6.3. (124);
man covered with hair F521.1. (132).

HALF. — Monster half-man, half-fish B80.2. (41).

HAND. — Birth from hand T541.+. (16); (42); (43); conception from
hand or foot T517.1. (42); (43).

HANDSOME man F575.2. (3); (89). — Ugly man becomes handsome
D52.2. (141); (142).

HAPPEN. — Dream warns of danger which will happen in near
future D1810.8.3.2. (78).

HARD-heartedness punished Q291. (67).

HARMLESS. — Why some snakes are harmless A2531.+. (106).
HAUNT. — Deer's haunt A2433.+. (69); establishment of animal haunt A2433.1. (69).
HAWK as culture hero A522.2.3. (41); (50); (51); (52); (53); (54); (69); (70); (71); (104). — Helpful hawk B455.4. (15); (89); (92); (93); (95); (96); (97); (98); (101); (105); (106); (124); resuscitation by hawk B515.+. (124); why hawk's neck feathers are short A2313.+. (106).
HEAD of murdered man taken along as trophy S139.2.1.1. (112); (113). — Why woodpecker has white spot on its head A2412.2.+. (148).
HEADHUNTER G310.+. (112).
HEAL. — Bird heals man B511.5. (148).
HEALER. — Bee as healer B511.+. (148).
HEALING. — Magic healing power D2161. (11); (58); magic healing song D1500.1.24. (58); origin of medicine (healing) A1438. (58).
HEARING. — Deer's means of defense: sharp hearing A2461.+. (69); origin of deer's sharp hearing A2428.+. (69).
HEART in ankle F559.7.+. (63). — Ogre's heart (life) in foot E714.+. (113); (114); soul (life) in the heart E714.4. (63).
HEAT test. Attempt to kill hero by burning him in fire H1511. (1); (2). — Contest in enduring heat H1542. (1); (2).
HEAVEN. — Man goes to heaven for limited time F11.3. (68); (137); (138).
HEEL. — Achilles heel. Invulnerability except in one spot Z311. (113); (114).
HELP from ogre's wife (mistress) G530.1. (100). — Spirits help mortal F403.2. (11); (58).
HELPER. — God as helper N817.0.1. (30); (31); magician as helper N845. (64); (66); (67); (103); (104); (120); (126); (127); (128); moon as helper N818.1.+. (24); (32); (37); (141); (142); (143); old man helper N825.2. (60); (65); tapir as shaman's spirit helper F403.2.2.1.+. (82).
HELPERS. — Supernatural helpers N810. (122).
HELPFUL bee B481.3. (148); birds B450. (45); (64); (123); (132); dog B421. (64); (65); (66); (67); eel B476. (61); fish B470. (147); fly B483.1. (66); (67); fox B435.1. (27); (114); hawk B455.4. (15); (89); (92); (93); (95); (96); (97); (98); (101); (105); (106); (124); parrot B469.9. (61); serpent B491.1. (108); skunk B430.+. (147); woodpecker B461.1. (108); (148).
HERO overcomes devastating animal G510.4. (100); (101); (102); (103). — Birds point out road to hero B563.2. (123); culture hero as dupe or trickster A521. (42); culture hero can transform self

A527.3.1. (42); culture hero dispenses food and hospitality A547. (41); (42); (43); culture hero regulates rivers A533. (41); (42); culture hero teaches arts and crafts A541. (43); hawk as culture hero A522.2.3. (41); (50); (51); (52); (53); (54); (69); (70); (71); (104); heat test. Attempt to kill hero by burning him in fire H1511. (1); (2); river where culture hero drags his staff A934.4.+. (42); very small hero L112.2. (115).

HERON. — Creation of heron A1964. (99).

HIBERNATE. — Why iguana hibernates A2481.+. (69).

HIDE. — Confederate hides fugitive K649.1. (100); men hide from world-fire and renew race A1038. (19); (20); (21).

HIDING. — Deception by hiding K1892. (100); escape by hiding in the earth K515.6. (19); (20); (21); (22); (24); (116); (121); victim burned in his own house (or hiding place) K812. (96); (97); (98).

HOARDED plants released A1423.0.1. (26); seeds A1425.0.1. (26).

HOLD. — Victim persuaded to hold out his tongue: bit by snake K825.+. (100); victim persuaded to hold out his tongue: cut off K825. (101).

HOME. — Children leave home because their parents refuse them food R228. (129); (130).

HONEY. — Acquisition of honey A1420.+. (60); clever honey bear J1100.+. (75); how honey bear received its name A2571.+. (75); origin of honey bear A1700.+. (75).

HOOFS. — How peccary got its hoofs A2376.+. (69); peccary's means of defense: hoofs A2461.+. (69).

HOSPITALITY. — Culture hero dispenses food and hospitality A547. (41); (42); (43).

HOT. — Extraordinary hot path F840.+. (1); (2); sun hot A733.+. (1); (2).

HOUSE destroyed by magic D2089.6. (67). — Bones of victims in front of ogre's house G691.+. (100); (104); extraordinary castle (house, palace) F771. (67); moon has house A753.2. (37); victim burned in his own house (or hiding place) K812. (96); (97); (98).

HOWLER. — Creation of howler monkey A1861.+. (64).

HUMAN. — Animal son eats human mother G71.+. (131); animals in human form B200.+. (12); (13); (14); birds in human form B200.+. (100); (101); ordering of human life A1300. (11); overheard (human) conversation N455. (45); parts of human or animal body transformed into plants A2611.0.5. (28); (123); primeval animals human A1101.2.+. (69); (79); primeval human pair A1270. (9); (10); star descends as human being A762. (9); (10); (136); (137); (138); (139); (140); sun as human being A736. (72); taste of human flesh leads to habitual cannibalism G36. (89).

HUMILIATING punishments Q470. (85). — Deception into humiliating position K1200. (147).

HUMMINGBIRD. — Origin of hummingbird A1900.+. (89); (90).

HUNT for extraordinary (magic) animal F989.15. (135).

HUNTER. — Skillful hunter F679.5. (83); (100).

HUNTING. — Origin of hunting A1458. (11); puma's occupation: hunting A2452.+. (86).

HUSBAND. — Loss of wife (husband) for breaking tabu C932. (136); (139); seduction by masking as woman's husband K1311. (35); wife flees from animal husband R227.1. (129); woman devours her husband G11.6.4. (113); (114).

IDENTITY. — Person's identity betrayed by habitual conversation H38.+. (89); (90).

IGUANA as trickster J1117.+. (148). — Food of iguana A2435.6.+. (69); origin of iguana A2140.+. (76); transformation: man to iguana D197.1. (18); (76); why iguana hibernates A2481.+. (69); why iguana lives in burrow A2432.+. (69); why iguana lives in woods A2433.2.1.+. (76).

IGUANAS. — Chief of iguanas B244.+. (76).

ILL. — Suitors ill-treated T75.0.1. (139); (140); (141); (142).

ILLNESS. — Dream warns of illness or injury D1810.8.3.1.1. (78).

ILLUSION. — Deception by disguise or illusion K1800. (70); (146); (147).

ILLUSORY sounds K1887. (147).

IMAGE. — Man made from clay image and vivified A1241.3. (9).

IMITATION. — Fatal imitation J2401. (150); foolish imitation J2400. (33); (34); (42); (44); (48); foolish imitation by an animal. Tries to go beyond his powers J2413. (147); (149); (150).

IMMEDIATE death for breaking tabu C921. (136); (137); (138); (139); (140).

IMPOSTOR. — Seduction by impostor K1315. (57).

INANIMATE object acts as if living F1009. (123).

INAPPROPRIATE action from misunderstanding J1820. (147).

INATTENTION to warnings J652. (13); (46); (47); (48); (100); (108); (124); (138).

INCEST T410. (28); (121); (123). — Brother-sister incest T415. (22); father-daughter incest T411. (20); new race from incest A1006.2. (16); (20).

INCESTUOUS first parents A1273.1. (10); (16).

INDIGNITIES. — Other indignities to corpse S139.2.2. (63).

INEQUALITIES. — Origin of inequalities among men A1618. (55).

INEXHAUSTIBLE fish D1652.1.10. (44); (48); food D1652.1. (45); vessel D1652.5. (44); (133).

INFANT picks out his unknown father H481. (39); (40).

INFORMATION received through dream D1810.8.2. (120); (128).

INHABITANT of upper world visits earth F30. (7); (9); (10); (12); (13); (14); (15); (56); (72); (93).

INITIAL. — Animals created after initial unsuccessful experiment A630.+. (69); (70); (71).

INJURY. — Accidental self-injury N397. (89); (90); death or bodily injury by magic D2060. (15); (58); (142); (143); dream warns of illness or injury D1810.8.3.1.1. (78).

INTERCOURSE with sleeping girl T475.2.1. (118). — Conception from extraordinary intercourse T517. (39); (42); (43); death from intercourse T182. (105); (106); (116); (120); long distance sexual intercourse K1391. (116); (120); origin of sexual intercourse A1352. (13).

INTEREST. — Owner's interest distracted while goods are stolen K341. (146).

INTESTINAL. — Burning intestinal wind F1041.+. (108); (109); magic intestinal wind causes disease D1500.4.+. (132).

INTESTINES. — Transformation: intestines to lianas D457.+. (28); transformation: intestines to person D437.+. (28).

INTRODUCTION of brewing A1426.2.1. (58).

INVISIBLE spirit laughs F412.1.+. (83).

INVOKED. — Deity invoked A183. (11).

INVULNERABILITY. — Achilles heel. Invulnerability except in one spot Z311. (113); (114); magic invulnerabilty D1840. (62).

ISLAND. — Refuge on island R316.1. (23).

JAGUAR drops from sky A1795.+. (74); gives birth to other felines F980.+. (74); -man as ogre G350.+. (128); uses fire B200.+. (129). — Devastating jaguar B16.2.2.+. (128); food of jaguar A2435.3.16. (69); (70); (71); marriage to jaguar B601.15. (129); (130); (131); why jaguar scratches trees A2540.+. (69).

JEWELS from urine D1454.+. (137); (138); produced by magic D1071.0.1. (137); (138).

JOURNEY to earthly paradise F111. (133); to land of women F112. (145); to lower world F80. (21); to see deity F12. (37); to upper world F10. (17); (37); (68); (135); (136); (137); (138); (141). — Animals direct man on journey B563. (108); magic air journey D2135. (5); (6).

JOURNEYS. — Soul journeys from the body E721. (107).

KIHIL. — Origin of kihil bird A1900.+. (87).

KILL. — Cruel mother kills child S12.2. (85); (113); (114); cutting rope to kill ogre who is climbing the rope to kill his victim K678. (115); heat test. Attempt to kill hero by burning him in fire H1511.

(1); (2); ogre kills by squeezing testicles G310.+. (63); sleep feigned to kill enemy K911.3. (128); transformation to kill enemy D651.1. (102); victim kills swallower from within by cutting F912.2. (107); (108); (109); (110).

KILLED. — Animal (monster) killed from within K952. (107); (108); (109); (110); caring for the child: child killed K1461. (144); ogre caught in noose and killed G514.3. (114); ogre killed G512. (61); (64); (65); (67); (89); (90); (93); (101); (115); (122); (127); ogre killed by striking G512.8. (63); (104); (113); (114); (128); ogre killed by striking with club G512.8.1. (102); victim lured by kind words approaches trickster and is killed K815. (93); (98); would-be killers killed K1626. (89); (90); (91); (92).

KILLERS. — Would-be killers killed K1626. (89); (90); (91); (92).

KILLING or maiming by deception K800. (89); (90); (91); (92); (93); (100); (101). — Person (animal) swallowed without killing F911. (107); (108); (109); (110); tabu: killing certain fish C841.9. (47).

KIND. — Victim lured by kind words approaches trickster and is killed K815. (93); (98).

KINDS. — Chiefs of the various kinds of birds B242.2.+. (93); masters of the various kinds of beasts B241.2.+. (11).

KNOTS. — Origin of knots on armadillo's shell A2312.+. (26).

KNOWLEDGE from singing D1781.+. (103). — Magic knowledge D1810. (8); (21); (89); (92); (98); (101); (103); (124); magic knowledge of another's thoughts D1819.1. (136); magic knowledge of magician D1810.0.2. (128); wisdom (knowledge) from dream J157. (11); (120); (128).

KNOWN. — Murder made known in a dream D1810.8.2.3. (138).

LABOR. — Beginning of division of labor A1472. (11).

LAGOONS. — Origin of lagoons A940.+. (44).

LAKE. — Extraordinary pond (lake) F713. (45); (46); (47); (48); magic lake (pond) D921. (108).

LAKES in otherworld F162.6. (7).

LAMB as trickster J1117.+. (150).

LAND made magically sterile D2081. (33); of men F113. (12); (13); of plenty F701. (38); (133). — Journey to land of women F112. (145); visit to land of moon F16. (32); (37); (141); (142); (143).

LARGE teeth F544.3.+. (64). — Giants large or small at will F531.6.5.2. (118); small animal overcomes large L315. (146); small earth made to grow large D489.+. (8).

LARGER. — Penis made larger D489.+. (117); (118).

LAST. — One arrow shot into end of last one to make rope of arrows F661.7.3. (115).

LAUGH. — Invisible spirit laughs F412.1.+. (83).

LAUGHING tabu C460. (124).

LEAD. — Taste of human flesh leads to habitual cannibalism G36. (89).

LEAF. — Transformation: leaf to beans D451.8.+. (139); (140).

LEARNED. — Secret learned N440.+. (44); (45); (51); (52); (53); (54).

LEAVE. — Children leave home because their parents refuse them food R228. (129); (130).

LECHERY punished Q240.+. (145).

LEG. — Ogre with sharpened leg G341.1. (89); (90); pointed leg F548.0.1. (89); (90); the sharpened leg J2424. (89); (90).

LENGTHENED. — Night magically lengthened D2146.2.2. (100); (101).

LIANAS. — Origin of lianas A2680.+. (28); transformation: intestines to lianas D457.+. (28).

LIFE. — Dead animal comes to life E3. (15); (70); (71); (150); ogre's heart (life) in foot E714.+. (113); (114); ordering of human life A1300. (11); person comes to life E1. (28); (33); (44); (45); (46); (47); (121); (124); (136); (137); (138); (139); (140); (144); preservation of life during great calamity A1005.+. (22); preservation of life during world calamity A1005. (17); (18); (19); (20); (21); (23); soul (life) in the heart E714.4. (63).

LIGHTING. — Origin of custom of lighting fire after death of family member A1547.+. (80).

LIGHTNING. — Origin of lightning A1141. (7).

LIQUORS. — Acquisition of spiritous liquors A1427. (58); (59).

LIVE. — Bird ogre lives in sky G630.+. (100); (101); ogre lives in sky G630.+. (93); ogre lives underground G630.+. (66); ogres live in trees G637. (95); spirits live in caves F402.6.4.1. (83); why anteater lives in woods A2433.2.1.+. (75); why capybara lives in the water A2433.2.2.+. (81); why iguana lives in burrow A2432.+. (69); why iguana lives in woods A2433.2.1.+. (76); why peccary lives in woods A2433.2.1.+. (69); (77); why rhea lives on the plains A2433.4.+. (69); why wild boar lives in woods A2433.2.1.+. (69); women live in the sky F167.+. (12); (13); women live in upper world F167.+. (14).

LIVES. — Ogress at a spot along the road takes toll of lives G321.2. (95).

LIVING. — Inanimate object acts as if living F1009. (123); stars thought of as living beings A761.6. (88).

LOCAL deluges A1011. (42); (44); (45); (46); (47); (48); (49).

LONG distance sexual intercourse K1391. (116); (120); penis F547.3.1. (67); (116); (117); (118); (120). — Giant (giantess) with particularly

long hair F531.1.6.3.1. (124); person with very long fingernails
F515.2.2. (62); (67); (113); remarkably long teeth F544.3.5. (62);
why tapir has long nose A2335.3.2. (79).
LOOKING. — Tabu: looking around C332. (20); tabu: looking at
certain person or thing C310. (48); tabu: looking back C331.
(33); tabu: looking in certain direction C330. (21).
LOSS of wife (husband) for breaking tabu C932. (136); (139); or
destruction of property as punishment Q595. (33).
LOST. — Quest for lost (stolen) family H1385.9. (123); quest for
lost brother(s) H1385.8. (107); (108); quest for lost persons H1385.
(21); substituted eyes. Lost eyes are replaced by those of another
person or animal E781.1. (137).
LOVE. — Age and youth in love T91.4. (41).
LOWER. — Journey to lower world F80. (21); refuge in lower world
R323.+. (21); sky lowers on people F791.1. (18).
LURED. — Victim lured by kind words approaches trickster and is
killed K815. (93); (98); victim lured into approach by false token
K839.2. (64); (89); (90).
MAGIC ability to fly D2135.0.3. (103); air journey D2135. (5); (6);
change to different appearance D52. (143); control of fires D2158.
(105); (106); control of night and day D2146. (100); (101); control
of rivers D2151.2. (42); control of soil and crops D2157. (64);
control of waters D2151. (45); (47); (48); dominance over animals
D2197. (70); (82); excrements D1002. (28); fish B175. (47); food-
basket (vessel) supplies food D1472.1.19. (44); healing power
D2161. (11); (58); healing song D1500.1.24. (58); intestinal wind
causes disease D1500.4.+. (132); invulnerability D1840. (62);
knowledge D1810. (8); (21); (89); (92); (98); (101); (103); (124);
knowledge of another's thoughts D1819.1. (136); knowledge of
magician D1810.0.2. (128); lake (pond) D921. (108); multiplication
of objects D2106. (33); murder D2061. (63); paralysis D2072. (67);
power from deity D1726. (58); quick growth of crops D2157.2.
(8); (33); (34); (35); (36); (38); (136); (137); rattle D1212. (58);
results produced by command D1765. (48); (121); sandals D1065.5.
(28); staff D1254. (42); strength D1830. (112); strength-giving
drink D1335.2. (112); tree D950. (100); urine D1002.1. (136);
(137); (138); vessel D1171. (44); wind D906. (108). — Acquisition
of magic powers D1720. (67); (142); (143); animals created by
magic D2178.4. (100); attracting by magic D2074. (121); death or
bodily injury by magic D2060. (15); (58); (142); (143); escapes by
magic D2165. (61); food supplied by magic D1030.1. (44); (48);
garden produced by magic D961.1. (137); house destroyed by

magic D2089.6. (67); hunt for extraordinary (magic) animal F989.15. (135); jewels produced by magic D1071.0.1. (137); (138); maize plants produced by magic D2178.+. (63); night produced by magic D2146.2.1. (70); rain produced by magic D2143.1. (7); (24); (37); (38); self-returning magic object D1602. (28); vegetables produced by magic D2178.+. (136); (139); (140); wind produced by magic D2142.1. (67); (100).

MAGICALLY. — Animals magically called D2074.1. (124); burning magically evaded D1841.3. (62); earth magically caused to quake D2148. (64); eyes torn out magically replaced D2161.3.1.1. (136); (137); food magically disappears Q552.3.4. (33); land made magically sterile D2081. (33); night magically lengthened D2146.2.2. (100); (101); objects magically moved D2136. (121); provisions magically furnished D2105. (15); tiny amount of food magically satisfies D1349.1.6. (32).

MAGICIAN D1711. (11); (48); (58); as helper N845. (64); (66); (67); (103); (104); (120); (126); (127); (128). — Bird as magician B191.6. (100); (101); fox as magician B191.+. (146); magic knowledge of magician D1810.0.2. (128); magician's apprentice D1711.0.1. (58); means of becoming magician D1711.0.3. (58).

MAIMING. — Killing or maiming by deception K800. (89); (90); (91); (92); (93); (100); (101).

MAIZE plants produced by magic D2178.+. (63). — Transformation: maize to brushwood D451.+. (33).

MAN carried by bird B552. (61); (138); covered with hair F521.1. (132); created from part of body A1263. (123); -eating birds B33. (100); (101); (102); (103); (104); (136); (137); (138); -eating woman G11.6. (61); (62); (63); (64); (66); (113); (114); goes to heaven for limited time F11.3. (68); (137); (138); in the moon A751. (56); made from clay image and vivified A1241.3. (9); marries the daughter of a god T111.1.2. (33); sinks into earth F942. (18); (64); to earn bread by sweat of his brow A1346. (33); (34); with marvelous voice F688. (89). — Animal saves man from death by drowning B527. (17); animal searches for dead man B546. (124); animals direct man on journey B563. (108); animals overcome man's adversary by strategy B524.2. (105); (106); (114); (132); attempted rape of man disguised as woman J1820.+. (118); bird flies with man to safety B542.1. (61); bird from transformed man A1715.+. (87); bird heals man B511.5. (148); condition of first man (woman) A1281. (12); (13); (15); creation of first man's (woman's) mate A1275. (9); deer-man B20.+. (127); deer-man as ogre G350.+. (127); deity provides man with soul A185.12. (11);

demons carry off man's soul F402.1.5.1.+. (83); devastating (man-eating) sea-monster (serpent) B16.5.1.2. (107); (108); (109); (110); entrance into girl's (man's) room (bed) by trick K1340. (117); (118); first man (woman) A1280. (9); (10); (12); (13); (15); (16); first man descends from sky A1231. (16); foolish marriage of old man and young girl J445.2. (87); handsome man F575.2. (3); (89); head of murdered man taken along as trophy S139.2.1.1. (112); (113); jaguar-man as ogre G350.+. (128); monster half-man, half-fish B80.2. (41); multiplication of man by fragmentation A1296. (123); old man as creator A15.3. (11); old man from sky as creator A21.2. (11); old man helper N825.2. (60); (65); origin of white man A1614.9. (24); punishment for man who makes advances to sister-in-law Q242.3. (28); remarkably strong man F610. (112); resuscitation from ashes of dead man E42. (121); seduction by man disguising as woman K1321. (116); (117); (118); serpent swallows man F911.7. (107); (108); (109); (110); sexual relations between man and demons G302.7.1. (83); transformation: man to animal D100. (11); (20); (24); (69); (124); transformation: man to armadillo D100.+. (116); (117); (121); transformation: man to bird D150. (18); (21); (22); (87); (99); (100); (134); transforma-tion: man to butterfly D186.1. (100); transformation: man to deer D114.1.1. (127); transformation: man to dog D141. (41); transformation: man to eagle D152.2. (102); transformation: man to eel D173. (61); transformation: man to iguana D197.1. (18); (76); transformation: man to ogre D94. (62); transformation: man to peccary D114.3.1. (18); (70); (77); (78); transformation: man to star D293. (5); (6); transformation: man to tree D215. (42); transformation: man to woman D12. (116); (117); (118); trans-formation: man (woman) to flower D212. (100); transformation: normal man to cannibal D91. (62); (67); ugly man becomes hand-some D52.2. (141); (142); woman from sky-world marries mortal man T111.2. (136); (137); (138); (139); (140).

MANIOC. — Acquisition of manioc A1423.4. (31).
MARKING. — Appearance of animal from marking or painting A2217. (80).
MARKINGS of armadillo A2412.1.+. (35).
MARKSMAN. — Skillful marksman F661. (83).
MARRIAGE by force T192. (131); of mortal and supernatural being T111. (41); (42); to jaguar B601.15. (129); (130); (131). — Brother-sister marriage T415.5. (22); father's consent to son's (daughter's) marriage necessary T131.1.2. (33); foolish marriage of old man and young girl J445.2. (87); offspring of marriage to animal

B630. (131); unequal marriage T121. (41); unwitting marriage to cannibal G81. (63).

MARRY. — Brother-in-law marries sister-in-law T425.+. (42); man marries the daughter of a god T111.1.2. (33); mortal marries star-girl A762.2. (136); (137); (138); (139); (140); woman from sky-world marries mortal man T111.2. (136); (137); (138); (139); (140).

MARVELOUS dancer F699.1. (119); tree survives world-fire A1029.1.+. (24). — Man with marvelous voice F688. (89).

MASKING. — Capture by masking as another K755. (134); seduction by masking as woman's husband K1311. (35).

MASTER of birds B242.+. (7).

MASTERS of the various kinds of beasts B241.2.+. (11).

MATACO. — Origin of the Mataco A1611.+. (9).

MATCH. — Diving match: trickster eats food while dupe is under water K16.2. (146).

MATE. — Creation of first man's (woman's) mate A1275. (9).

MEAL. — Frightful meal S183. (113); (114).

MEANS of becoming magician D1711.0.3. (58). — Deer's means of defense: sharp hearing A2461.+. (69); peccary's means of defense: hoofs A2461.+. (69).

MEDICINE. — Origin of medicine (healing) A1438. (58).

MEMBER. — Origin of custom of lighting fire after death of family member A1547.+. (80).

MEMBERS. — Resuscitation by arrangement of members E30. (124); (137); (138); vital bodily members E780. (28).

MEN hide from world-fire and renew race A1038. (19); (20); (21). — Animals advise men B560. (114); animals provide food for men B531. (27); (129); (130); bird-men B50. (115); birds were men in former age A1101.2.+. (115); land of men F113. (12); (13); origin of inequalities among men A1618. (55); the mother of men A1282. (10).

MENSES. — Tabu: going forth during menses C141. (106).

MESSENGER. — Dog as messenger B291.2.2. (64); (65); (66); (67); fly as messenger B291.+. (93); (136); (137).

METHODS. — Ogres with characteristic methods G310. (64); (65); (67); (91); (92); (93); (95); (96); (97); (98); (122); (126); (127); (128).

MIRACULOUS conception T510. (105); (106); darkness as punishment Q552.20.1. (100); (101); drowning as punishment Q552.19. (108); punishments Q550. (33); speedy growth of a tree D2157.4. (26).

MIRACULOUSLY. — Animals miraculously multiplied D2106.1.2. (45); (48).

MISTAKEN. — Shadow mistaken for substance J1790. (130).

MISTRESS of doves B242.2.2.+. (83). — Help from ogre's wife (mistress) G530.1. (100); quest for vanished wife (mistress) H1385.3. (28); (136); (137); (138).

MISUNDERSTANDING. — Inappropriate action from misunderstanding J1820. (147).

MISUNDERSTOOD. — Other sounds misunderstood J1812. (147); physical phenomena misunderstood J1810. (42); (44); (45); (46); (47).

MONKEY. — Creation of howler monkey A1861.+. (64).

MONSTER half-man, half-fish B80.2. (41). — Animal (monster) killed from within K952. (107); (108); (109); (110); birds from body of slain monster A1724.1.+. (64); devastating (man-eating) sea-monster (serpent) B16.5.1.2. (107); (108); (109); (110); devastating monster G346. (61); (62); (63); (64); (65); (66); (67); (89); (90); (104); (122); (126); (128); eclipse caused by monster devouring sun or moon A737.1. (4); penis of monster as token (proof) of slaying H105.4.+. (67); tail of monster as token (proof) of slaying H105.4.+. (64); (65); (66).

MONSTROUS. — Ogres with monstrous features G360. (62); (64); (67).

MOON as a person A753. (8); (24); (56); as creator A1.+. (8); (24); as helper N818.1.+. (24); (32); (37); (141); (142); (143); cold A750.+. (1); (2); has house A753.2. (37). — Contest between sun and moon A736.11. (1); (2); creation of the moon A740. (3); (24); eclipse caused by monster devouring sun or moon A737.1. (4); family of the moon A745. (3); (8); (32); (33); (37); (141); man in the moon A751. (56); person transformed to moon A747. (3); (56); stars as children of the moon A764.1. (137); visit to land of moon F16. (32); (37); (141); (142); (143).

MORTAL marries star-girl A762.2. (136); (137); (138); (139); (140). — Deity teaches mortal A185.3. (11); (33); (37); (56); god advises mortal A182.3.5. (30); (32); (37); marriage of mortal and supernatural being T111. (41); (42); spirits help mortal F403.2. (11); (58); woman from sky-world marries mortal man T111.2. (136); (137); (138); (139); (140).

MOTHER-in-law seduces son-in-law T417.1. (109); of caimans B244.+. (108). — Animal son eats human mother G71.+. (131); cruel mother S12. (6); (130); cruel mother blinds daughter S12.4.+. (114); cruel mother kills child S12.2. (85); (113); (114); cruel mother refuses children food S12.6. (129); (130); foster mother P272. (40); (42); (43); the mother of men A1282. (10); unnatural mother eats children G72.+. (113); (114).

MOURNING customs P681. (80); (106).

MOVED. — Objects magically moved D2136. (121).

MOVEMENTS. — Tapir's habitual bodily movements A2470.+. (69).

MULTICOLORED. — Eagle with multicolored blood B720.+. (100).

MULTIPLICATION of man by fragmentation A1296. (123). — Magic multiplication of objects D2106. (33).

MULTIPLIED. — Animals miraculously multiplied D2106.1.2. (45); (48).

MURDER by burning K955. (105); (106); by stabbing S115. (89); (90); by strategy K910. (64); (65); (66); (67); (89); (90); (91); (92); (100); (101); (105); (106); by suffocation S113.2. (98); by throwing earth over victim D2061.2.+. (63); from behind K959.4. (89); (90); (132); in one's sleep K959.2. (122); (138); made known in a dream D1810.8.2.3. (138); of children punished Q211.4. (144). — Death as punishment for murder Q411.6. (63); (138); (144); magic murder D2061. (63); treacherous murder of enemy's children or charges K930. (100); (101).

MURDERED. — Children murdered S302. (144); head of murdered man taken along as trophy S139.2.1.1. (112); (113).

MURDEROUS bride T173. (105); (106).

MURDERS. — Revolting murders or mutilations S100. (132).

MUTILATION: putting out eyes S165. (12); (14); (114); (129); sex organs cut off S176. (63). — Self-mutilation S160.1. (89); (90).

MUTILATIONS. — Revolting murders or mutilations S100. (132).

NAKED. — Country of the naked F709.1. (145).

NAME. — How anteater received its name A2571.+. (75); how honey bear received its name A2571.+. (75).

NAMES. — How animals received their names A2571. (67); (69); (70); (71); how snakes received their names A2571.+. (106).

NECESSARY. — Father's consent to son's (daughter's) marriage necessary T131.1.2. (33).

NECK. — Why hawk's neck feathers are short A2313.+. (106).

NESTS. — Origin of birds' nests A2431.3. (99).

NET. — Origin of the net for fishing A1457.3. (39); (41); (43).

NETS. — Custom of catching fish with nets A1527. (39); (41); (43).

NEW race from incest A1006.2. (16); (20); race from single pair (or several) after world calamity A1006.1. (16); (20).

NIGHT magically lengthened D2146.2.2. (100); (101); produced by magic D2146.2.1. (70). — Asleep by day, awake by night F560.+ (132); magic control of night and day D2146. (100); (101); person sees equally well by night or day F642.4. (132).

NOCTURNAL. — Why anteater is nocturnal A2491.+. (69); why tapir is nocturnal A2491.+. (69); why wildcat is nocturnal A2491.+. (69).

NOISE. — Foolishness of noise-making when enemies overhear J581. (124).

NOOSE. — Ogre caught in noose and killed G514.3. (114).

NORMAL. — Transformation: normal man to cannibal D91. (62); (67).

NOSE. — Why tapir has long nose A2335.3.2. (79).

NOTICE. — Transformation to escape notice D642.5. (89).

OBJECT travels by itself D1643. (28); (121). — Automatic object D1600. (28); inanimate object acts as if living F1009. (123); self-returning magic object D1602. (28); size of object changed at will D631.3. (8).

OBJECTS magically moved D2136. (121). — Magic multiplication of objects D2106. (33).

OCCUPATION. — Puma's occupation: hunting A2452.+. (86).

OCCURRENCES. — Extraordinary occurrences concerning fishing F986. (39); (42); (44); (47).

OFFENDING. — Tabu: offending supernatural relative C30. (136); (137); (138); (139); (140); tabu: offending wood-spirit C43. (124).

OFFSPRING of marriage to animal B630. (131).

OGRE burned in his own oven G512.3.2. (95); burned to death G512.3. (62); (66); (91); (92); (95); (96); (97); (98); caught in noose and killed G514.3. (114); decapitated G512.1.2. (100); defeated G500. (126); killed G512. (61); (64); (65); (67); (89); (90); (93); (101); (115); (122); (127); killed by striking G512.8. (63); (104); (113); (114); (128); killed by striking with club G512.8.1. (102); kills by squeezing testicles G310.+. (63); lives in sky G630.+. (93); lives underground G630.+. (66); traps victim G421. (97); (98); with cavities in his body G366.+. (91); (93); with sharpened leg G341.1. (89); (90). — Bird ogre lives in sky G630.+. (100); (101); blind ogre G121.+. (92); bones of victims in front of ogre's house G691.+. (100); (104); cannibal bird as ogre G353.1. (100); (101); (102); (103); (104); cannibal ogre G312. (61); (62); (63); (64); (66); (67); (89); (90); (91); (92); (93); cutting rope to kill ogre who is climbing the rope to kill his victim K678. (115); deer as ogre G350.+. (126); deer-man as ogre G350.+. (127); earthquake at ogre's death F960.2.5.2.+. (67); help from ogre's wife (mistress) G530.1. (100); jaguar-man as ogre G350.+. (128); ogre's heart (life) in foot E714.+. (113); (114); snake as ogre G354.1. (107); (108); (109); (110); transformation: man to ogre D94. (62); wasp as ogre G350.+. (111).

OGRES live in trees G637. (95); with characteristic methods G310. (64); (65); (67); (91); (92); (93); (95); (96); (97); (98); (122); (126); (127); (128); with monstrous features G360. (62); (64); (67).

OGRESS at a spot along the road takes toll of lives G321.2. (95).

OLD man as creator A15.3. (11); man from sky as creator A21.2. (11); man helper N825.2. (60); (65); woman as creator A15.1.1. (11);.

—Foolish marriage of old man and young girl J445.2. (87).

OMNISCIENCE of a god D1810.0.1. (33).

ONE. — Achilles heel. Invulnerability except in one spot Z311. (113); (114); original fire property of one person (animal) A1415.0.2. (19); (51); (54).

OPEN. — Tree opens and conceals fugitive D1393.1. (100).

OPENING. — Self-opening tree-trunk D1556. (100).

ORDERING of human life A1300. (11).

ORGANS. — Mutilation: sex organs cut off S176. (63).

ORIFICES. — Punishment: bodily orifices stopped up Q450.+. (144).

ORIGIN of algarrobo tree A2681.+. (26); (27); of amphibia A2160. (84); of anteater A1700.+. (75); of birds' nests A2431.3. (99); of brushwood A2680.+. (33); of color of bird A2411.2. (100); (101); of constellations A766. (5); (6); of creepers A2682. (123); of cultivated plants A2684. (8); (24); (37); (38); of custom of lighting fire after death of family member A1547.+. (80); of death A1335. (13); of deer's sharp hearing A2428.+. (69); of fire A1414. (11); (19); (50); (51); (52); (53); (54); of fishing A1457. (39); (40); (41); (42); (43); of honey bear A1700.+. (75); of hummingbird A1900.+. (89); (90); of hunting A1458. (11); of iguana A2140.+. (76); of inequalities among men A1618. (55); of kihil bird A1900.+. (87); of knots on armadillo's shell A2312.+. (26); of lagoons A940.+. (44); of lianas A2680.+. (28); of lightning A1141. (7); of medicine (healing) A1438. (58); of ovenbird A1900.+. (94); (95); (96); of particular stars A770. (3); of particular tribes A1611. (22); of peccary A1871.2. (77); of plant as punishment A2631. (33); of plant characteristics A2700. (33); (34); of plants A2600. (24); of pottery A1451. (94); of priesthood (shamanism, etc.) A1654. (37); (58); of rain A1131. (11); of sachasandia A2600.+. (30); of seasonal plant cycle A2700.+. (37); of seed A1425. (8); (24); of sexual intercourse A1352. (13); of sowing and planting A1441.4. (33); (37); of streams A930. (41); (42); (43); of the net for fishing A1457.3. (39); (41); (43); of the use of the rattle A1461.4. (58); of the Chorote A1611.+. (9); (19); of the Mataco A1611.+. (9); of the Tapiete A1611.+. (9); of the Toba A1611.+. (9); of thunder A1142. (7); of tobacco A2691.2. (61); (62); (63); (64); (65); (66); of trees A2681. (24); (25); of tribes from choices made A1614.4. (55); of watermelon A2687.+. (32); of white man A1614.9. (24); of wild boar A1871.1. (85).

ORIGINAL fire property of certain animals A1415.0.2.+. (50); (52); (53); fire property of one person (animal) A1415.0.2. (19); (51); (54). — Reflection in water thought to be the original of the thing reflected J1791. (147).

ORNAMENTS. — Extraordinary ornaments F827. (138).

OTHERWORLD. — Abundant food in otherworld F166.11. (37); (68); animals in otherworld F167.1. (68); (137); birds in otherworld F167.1.2. (7); (15); lakes in otherworld F162.6. (7).

OUTSIDE. — Tabu: widow not to go outside C898. +. (106).

OVEN. — Ogre burned in his own oven G512.3.2. (95).

OVENBIRD. — Origin of ovenbird A1900. +. (94); (95); (96).

OVERCOME. — Animals overcome man's adversary by strategy B524.2. (105); (106); (114); (132); hero overcomes devastating animal G510.4. (100); (101); (102); (103); robber overcome K437. (12); (13); (14); small animal overcomes large L315. (146).

OVERHEAR. — Foolishness of noise-making when enemies overhear J581. (124).

OVERHEARD (human) conversation N455. (45); wish is realized N699.6. (137); (138); (139). — Secrets overheard N450. (48).

OWL. — Creation of owl A1958. (97); (98).

OWN. — Ogre burned in his own oven G512.3.2. (95); person eats own flesh G51. (89); (90); victim burned in his own house (or hiding place) K812. (96); (97); (98).

OWNER of water A420. +. (46). — Owner's interest distracted while goods are stolen K341. (146).

PAINTED. — Birds painted their present colors A2217.1. (100); (101); (148).

PAINTING. — Appearance of animal from marking or painting A2217. (80).

PAIR. — New race from single pair (or several) after world calamity A1006.1. (16); (20); primeval human pair A1270. (9); (10).

PARADISE. — Journey to earthly paradise F111. (133).

PARAKEET. — Transformation: parakeet to person D350. +. (15).

PARALYSIS. — Magic paralysis D2072. (67).

PARAMOUR. — Unknown (clandestine) paramour T475. (39); (139).

PARENTS. — Children leave home because their parents refuse them food R228. (129); (130); incestuous first parents A1273.1. (10); (16).

PARROT. — Creation of parrot A1994. (99); helpful parrot B469.9. (61); why parrot's beak is black A2343.2.1. (14).

PART. — Man created from part of body A1263. (123); transformation: part of animal or person to person D437. (123).

PARTIAL transformation D682. (41); transformation — color changed D682.4. (110).

PARTIALLY eaten fruit made whole again D2150. +. (32); (37).

PARTNER. — Treacherous partner K2296. (147).

PARTS of human or animal body transformed into plants A2611.0.5. (28); (123); of slain animals as token of slaying H105. (100).

PASSAGES. — Underground passages F721.1. (39).

PATH. — Extraordinary cold path F840.+. (1); (2); extraordinary hot path F840.+. (1); (2).

PECCARIES. — Chief of peccaries B241.2.+. (77); (78).

PECCARY. — Food of peccary A2435.+. (69); how peccary got its hoofs A2376.+. (69); origin of peccary A1871.2. (77); peccary's burrow A2432.+. (77); peccary's means of defense: hoofs A2461.+. (69); transformation: man to peccary D114.3.1. (18); (70); (77); (78); why peccary is pugnacious A2524.+. (69); (70); (71); why peccary lives in woods A2433.2.1.+. (69); (77).

PENIS made larger D489.+. (117); (118); of monster as token (proof) of slaying H105.4.+. (67). — Long penis F547.3.1. (67); (116); (117); (118); (120).

PEOPLE. — Ascent to stars. People or animals ascend to the sky and become stars A761. (3); (5); (6); sky lowers on people F791.1. (18).

PEOPLES. — Distribution and differentiation of peoples—general A1600. (55).

PERMANENT. — Why puma has no permanent dwelling A2432.+. (69).

PERSON (animal) swallowed without killing F911. (107); (108); (109); (110); becomes cannibal G30. (62); (67); (89); (90); (113); carried off by bird R13.3. (100); (101); (102); (103); (104); (136); changes appearance at will D631.1.1. (61); (100); (116); (117); (121); (124); (127); (128); (134); changes color F1082. (110); comes to life E1. (28); (33); (44); (45); (46); (47); (121); (124); (136); (137); (138); (139); (140); (144); concealed in another's body F1034. (61); eats own flesh G51. (89); (90); has red eye F541.6.2. (62); sees equally well by night or day F642.4. (132); transformed to moon A747. (3); (56); with very long fingernails F515.2.2. (62); (67); (113). — Absent person seems to be present K1881. (146); animals from body of slain person A1724.1. (67); bird from body of slain person A1724.1.+. (89); (90); (91); (92); (95); (97); (98); birds carry person from upper world F62.2. (138); change in person's color D57. (110); eaten person resuscitated E32.0.1. (124); (136); (137); (138); moon as a person A753. (8); (24); (56); original fire property of one person (animal) A1415.0.2. (19); (51); (54); person's identity betrayed by habitual conversation H38.+. (89); (90); plants from body of slain person or animal A2611. (61); (62); (63); (64); (65); (66); red person F527.1. (110); resuscitation by supernatural person E121. (136); (137); (138); (139); (140); spirit pursues person F402.1.10. (83); substituted eyes. Lost eyes are replaced by those of another person or animal E781.1. (137); swallowed person becomes bald F921.

(108); (110); swallowed person becomes soft F921.1.+. (108); tabu: looking at certain person or thing C310. (48); transformation: intestines to person D437.+. (28); transformation: parakeet to person D350.+. (15); transformation: part of animal or person to person D437. (123); transformation: star to person D439.5.2. (136); (137); (138); (139); (140); transformation: wasp to person D380.+. (111).

PERSONS with tails F518. (62); (64); (65); (66). — Quest for lost persons H1385. (21).

PERSUADED. — Dupe persuaded to relax vigilance: seized K827. (93); victim persuaded to hold out his tongue: bit by snake K825.+. (100); victim persuaded to hold out his tongue: cut off K825. (101).

PHENOMENA. — Physical phenomena misunderstood J1810. (42); (44); (45); (46); (47).

PHYSICAL phenomena misunderstood J1810. (42); (44); (45); (46); (47).

PICK. — Infant picks out his unknown father H481. (39); (40).

PIG. — Food of pig A2435.3.14. (69).

PITFALL. — Capture in pitfall K735. (69); (98); (132).

PLAINS. — Why rhea lives on the plains A2433.4.+. (69).

PLAN. — Woman plans to eat her children G72.1. (63).

PLANS. — Forethought in prevention of others' plans J620. (42).

PLANT. — Origin of plant as punishment A2631. (33); origin of plant characteristics A2700. (33); (34); origin of seasonal plant cycle A2700.+. (37); reincarnation as tobacco plant E631.5.1. (62); tree (plant) protects D1380.2. (100).

PLANTING the earth A2602. (8); (18); (23); (24); (37). — Origin of sowing and planting A1441.4. (33); (37).

PLANTS from body of slain person or animal A2611. (61); (62); (63); (64); (65); (66). — Creation of plants by transformation A2610. (28); hoarded plants released A1423.0.1. (26); maize plants produced by magic D2178.+. (63); origin of cultivated plants A2684. (8); (24); (37); (38); origin of plants A2600. (24); parts of human or animal body transformed into plants A2611.0.5. (28); (123); thorns on plants A2752. (29).

PLENTY. — In time of plenty provide for want J711. (69); land of plenty F701. (38); (133).

POINT. — Birds point out road to hero B563.2. (123).

POINTED leg F548.0.1. (89); (90).

POISONOUS. — Why sachasandia is poisonous A2692.+. (30).

POND. — Extraordinary pond (lake) F713. (45); (46); (47); (48); magic lake (pond) D921. (108).

POSITION. — Deception into humiliating position K1200. (147).

POTTERY. — Origin of pottery A1451. (94).
POWER. — Avoidance of others' power J640. (28); (113); (114); (115);
   (131); (132); fatal deception into trickster's power K810. (89); (90);
   (91); (92); (93); (97); (132); (134); magic healing power D2161. (11);
   (58); magic power from deity D1726. (58).
POWERS. — Acquisition of magic powers D1720. (67); (142); (143);
   foolish imitation by an animal. Tries to go beyond his powers
   J2413. (147); (149); (150).
PREGNANCY. — Short pregnancy T573. (13); (39); (42).
PREPARE. — Gods teach how to seek and prepare food A1420.2. (11);
   (39); (41).
PRESENT. — Absent person seems to be present K1881. (146); birds
   painted their present colors A2217.1. (100); (101); (148).
PRESERVATION of life during great calamity A1005.+. (22); of life
   during world calamity A1005. (17); (18); (19); (20); (21); (23).
PRETENDING. — Deception by pretending sleep K1868. (45); (128).
PREVENT. — Corpse burned to prevent return E431.13. (104).
PREVENTION. — Forethought in prevention of others' plans J620. (42).
PRIMEVAL animals human A1101.2.+. (69); (79); human pair A1270.
   (9); (10).
PRIMORDIAL. — Bird as guardian of primordial fire A1414.6. (19);
   (51); (54).
PROCURE. — Deception into disastrous attempt to procure food K1020.
   (147).
PRODUCED. — Garden produced by magic D961.1. (137); jewels
   produced by magic D1071.0.1. (137); (138); magic results produced
   by command D1765. (48); (121); maize plants produced by magic
   D2178.+. (63); night produced by magic D2146.2.1. (70); rain
   produced by magic D2143.1. (7); (24); (37); (38); vegetables produced by magic D2178.+. (136); (139); (140); wind produced by
   magic D2142.1. (67); (100).
PRODUCING. — Fish-producing tree F811.5.3. (39); (42); (49).
PROOF. — Penis of monster as token (proof) of slaying H105.4.+.
   (67); tail of monster as token (proof) of slaying H105.4.+. (64);
   (65); (66).
PROPERTY. — Loss or destruction of property as punishment Q595.
   (33); original fire property of certain animals A1415.0.2.+. (50);
   (52); (53); original fire property of one person (animal) A1415.0.2.
   (19); (51); (54).
PROTECT. — Elder children to protect younger P250.1. (6); tree (plant)
   protects D1380.2. (100).

PROVIDE. — Animals provide food for men B531. (27); (129); (130); deity provides man with soul A185.12. (11); in time of plenty provide for want J711. (69).

PROVISION. — Forethought in provision for food J710. (20); (38); (69).

PROVISIONS magically furnished D2105. (15).

PUGNACIOUS. — Why peccary is pugnacious A2524.+. (69); (70); (71); why tapir is pugnacious A2524.+. (69); (70); (71).

PUMA. — Food of puma A2435.+. (69); (70); (71); puma's occupation: hunting A2452.+. (86); why puma has no permanent dwelling A2432.+. (69).

PUMAS. — Chief of pumas B241.2.+. (86).

PUNISHED. — Hard-heartedness punished Q291. (67); lechery punished Q240.+. (145); murder of children punished Q211.4. (144); theft punished Q212. (33); (121); unkindness punished Q280. (100); (101); (142); (143).

PUNISHMENT: beating to death Q422.0.1. (33); (63); (121); (138); (145); being stung by wasps Q453.+. (121); bodily orifices stopped up Q450.+. (144); drowning Q428. (42); (44); (45); (46); (47); (49); ejectment Q432. (33); (45); fitted to crime Q580. (28); for man who makes advances to sister-in-law Q242.3. (28); strangling Q424. (85); transformation into frog Q551.3.2.3. (38); transformation into toad Q551.3.2.3.+. (38). — Blinding as punishment Q451.7. (121); death as punishment Q411. (124); (129); (136); (137); (138); (139); (140); (142); (143); death as punishment for murder Q411.6. (63); (138); (144); death as punishment for ravisher Q411.7. (121); flood as punishment for breaking tabu A1018.1. (47); loss or destruction of property as punishment Q595. (33); miraculous darkness as punishment Q552.20.1. (100); (101); miraculous drowning as punishment Q552.19. (108); origin of plant as punishment A2631. (33); rain as punishment Q550.+. (38).

PUNISHMENTS. — Cruel punishments Q450. (28); humiliating punishments Q470. (85); miraculous punishments Q550. (33).

PURSUE. — Spirit pursues person F402.1.10. (83).

PURSUERS. — Transformation to elude pursuers D642.7. (127).

QUAKE. — Earth magically caused to quake D2148. (64).

QUEEN of watersnakes B244.1.1. (108).

QUEST for bride H1381.3.1. (41); for devastating animals H1362. (100); (101); (102); (103); for enemies H1397. (63); (132); for lost (stolen) family H1385.9. (123); for lost brother(s) H1385.8. (107); (108); for lost persons H1385. (21); for the world's end H1371.1. (21); for vanished wife (mistress) H1385.3. (28); (136); (137); (138).

QUICK. — Magic quick growth of crops D2157.2. (8); (33); (34); (35); (36); (38); (136); (137).

RABBIT. — Food of rabbit A2435.3.12.+. (70); (71).

RACE (= people). — Men hide from world-fire and renew race A1038. (19); (20); (21); new race from incest A1006.2. (16); (20); new race from single pair (or several) after world calamity A1006.1. (16); (20).

RACE (= speed contest) won by deception K11. (150).

RACING. — Foot-racing contest H1594. (150).

RAIN as punishment Q550.+. (38); from sea in upper world A1131.3. (7); produced by magic D2143.1. (7); (24); (37); (38). — Origin of rain A1131. (11).

RAPE T471. (116); (117); (118); (120); (121). — Attempted rape of man disguised as woman J1820.+. (118).

RATTLE. — Magic rattle D1212. (58); origin of the use of the rattle A1461.4. (58).

RAVISHER. — Death as punishment for ravisher Q411.7. (121).

REALISTIC dream F1068. (120).

REALIZED. — Overheard wish is realized N699.6. (137); (138); (139); wish for star wife realized C15.1.1. (136); (137); (138); (139).

RECEIVE. — Transformation to receive food D655. (41).

RECEIVED. — How animals received their names A2571. (67); (69); (70); (71); how anteater received its name A2571.+. (75); how honey bear received its name A2571.+. (75); how snakes received their names A2571.+. (106); information received through dream D1810.8.2. (120); (128).

RECOGNITION by smell H30.+. (35); (57); by sounds H30.+. (67); by teeth H50.+. (57).

RECOGNIZE. — Child recognizes relative's flesh when it is served to be eaten G61.1. (63); (129).

RED person F527.1. (110). — Person has red eye F541.6.2. (62).

REFLECTED. — Reflection in water thought to be the original of the thing reflected J1791. (147).

REFLECTION in water thought to be the original of the thing reflected J1791. (147).

REFUGE in lower world R323.+. (21); in upper world R323. (24); (115); (135); on island R316.1. (23). — Tree refuge R311. (42); (44); (45); (46); (47); (70); (87); (100); (101); (131); (135).

REFUSE. — Children leave home because their parents refuse them food R228. (129); (130); cruel mother refuses children food S12.6. (129); (130).

REGULATE. — Culture hero regulates rivers A533. (41); (42).

REINCARNATION as tobacco plant E631.5.1. (62).

RELATIONS. — Sexual relations between man and demons G302.7.1. (83).

RELATIVE. — Child recognizes relative's flesh when it is served to be eaten G61.1. (63); (129); cruel relative S0. (67); (129); tabu: offending supernatural relative C30. (136); (137); (138); (139); (140).

RELAX. — Dupe persuaded to relax vigilance: seized K827. (93).

RELEASED. — Hoarded plants released A1423.0.1. (26); sea released from tree-top A924.3. (42).

RELIGIOUS. — Non-religious visions V514. (107).

REMAINING. — Contest in remaining under water H1543. (146).

REMARKABLE eyes F541. (132).

REMARKABLY beautiful woman F575.1. (39); (40); (41); (106); long teeth F544.3.5. (62); strong man F610. (112).

REMINISCENCE. — Animal habit a reminiscence of former experience A2275. (78); (81).

RENEW. — Men hide from world-fire and renew race A1038. (19); (20); (21).

RENEWAL of world after world calamity A1006. (16); (18); (21); (23); (24); (25).

REPEATED resuscitation E151. (33); (44); transformation D610. (124).

REPLACED. — Eyes successfully replaced E781. (136); (137); eyes torn out magically replaced D2161.3.1.1. (136); (137); substituted eyes. Lost eyes are replaced by those of another person or animal E781.1. (137).

REPOSITORY. — Tree as repository of fire A1414.7.1. (19); (51).

RESCUE. — Elder brother rescues younger R155.2. (107); (108).

RESCUED. — Exposed or abandoned child rescued R131. (40).

RESCUER. — Animal rescuer or retriever B540. (124); (147).

RESULTS. — Magic results produced by command D1765. (48); (121).

RESUSCITATED. — Eaten person resuscitated E32.0.1. (124); (136); (137); (138).

RESUSCITATION by arrangement of members E30. (124); (137); (138); by hawk B515.+. (124); by sprinkling earth E50.+. (15); (136); (137); (138); (139); (140); by supernatural person E121. (136); (137); (138); (139); (140); from ashes of dead man E42. (121); from fragments of body E35. (136); (137). — Repeated resuscitation E151. (33); (44).

RETRIEVER. — Animal rescuer or retriever B540. (124); (147).

RETURN from upper world F10.1. (68); (137); (138); (141). — Corpse burned to prevent return E431.13. (104).

RETURNING. — Self-returning magic object D1602. (28); self-returning sandal D1602.+. (123).

REVEALED. — Death of another revealed in dream D1812.3.3.11. (138); future revealed in dream D1812.3.3. (18).

REVENGE. — Avoiding enemy's revenge J647. (93).

REVOLTING murders or mutilations S100. (132).

RHEA. — Food of rhea A2435.4.+. (69); why rhea lives on the plains A2433.4.+. (69).

RIVER where culture hero drags his staff A934.4.+. (42). — Staff stuck in river bed stops water D1549.3.8.+. (42).

RIVERS. — Creator of rivers A930.1. (41); (42); culture hero regulates rivers A533. (41); (42); magic control of rivers D2151.2. (42).

ROAD. — Birds point out road to hero B563.2. (123); ogress at a spot along the road takes toll of lives G321.2. (95).

ROBBER overcome K437. (12); (13); (14).

ROCKS. — Extraordinary rocks and stones F800. (91); (92).

ROOM. — Entrance into girl's (man's) room (bed) by trick K1340. (117); (118).

ROOTED. — Why chaguar is rooted in the ground A2770.+. (29).

ROOTS. — Earth supported by roots A840.+. (21).

ROPE cut and victim dropped K963. (12); (13); (115). — Cutting rope to kill ogre who is climbing the rope to kill his victim K678. (115); one arrow shot into end of last one to make rope of arrows F661.7.3. (115); sky-rope F51. (10); (12); (13); (14); thief climbing rope discovered and rope cut K1622. (12); (13); (14).

RUN. — Why deer run, stop, and run on again A2461.4. (69).

SACHASANDIA. — Origin of sachasandia A2600.+. (30); why sachasandia is poisonous A2692.+. (30).

SAFETY. — Animal allows himself to be tied to another for safety K713.1.1. (147); bird flies with man to safety B542.1. (61).

SAND. — Conception from sand in vagina T532.+. (10).

SANDAL. — Self-returning sandal D1602.+. (123).

SANDALS. — Magic sandals D1065.5. (28).

SATISFY. — Tiny amount of food magically satisfies D1349.1.6. (32).

SAVE. — Animal saves man from death by drowning B527. (17).

SCOUTS. — Birds as scouts B563.6. (64).

SCRATCH. — Why jaguar scratches trees A2540.+. (69).

SEA released from tree-top A924.3. (42). — Devastating (man-eating) sea-monster (serpent) B16.5.1.2. (107); (108); (109); (110); rain from sea in upper world A1131.3. (7).

SEARCH. — Animal searches for dead man B546. (124).

SEASONAL. — Origin of seasonal plant cycle A2700.+. (37).

SECRET learned N440.+. (44); (45); (51); (52); (53); (54).

SECRETS overheard N450. (48).

SEDUCE. — Brother-in-law seduces (seeks to seduce) sister-in-law T425. (28); (121); (123); mother-in-law seduces son-in-law T417.1. (109); transformation of sex to seduce D658.3. (116); (117); (118).

SEDUCTION by impostor K1315. (57); by man disguising as woman K1321. (116); (117); (118); by masking as woman's husband K1311. (35).

SEE. — Journey to see deity F12. (37); person sees equally well by night or day F642.4. (132).

SEED. — Origin of seed A1425. (8); (24).

SEEDS. — Hoarded seeds A1425.0.1. (26).

SEEING. — Tabu: seeing supernatural creatures C311.1. (124).

SEEK. — Brother-in-law seduces (seeks to seduce) sister-in-law T425. (28); (121); (123); gods teach how to seek and prepare food A1420.2. (11); (39); (41).

SEEM. — Absent person seems to be present K1881. (146).

SEIZED. — Dupe persuaded to relax vigilance: seized K827. (93).

SELF-mutilation S160.1. (89); (90); -opening tree-trunk D1556. (100); -returning magic object D1602. (28); -returning sandal D1602.+. (123). — Accidental self-injury N397. (89); (90); culture hero can transform self A527.3.1. (42).

SERIES of upper worlds A651.1. (7).

SERPENT swallows man F911.7. (107); (108); (109); (110). — Creation of snake (serpent) A2145. (105); (106); devastating (man-eating) sea-monster (serpent) B16.5.1.2. (107); (108); (109); (110); giant serpent B875.1. (107); (108); (109); (110); helpful serpent B491.1. (108).

SERVED. — Child recognizes relative's flesh when it is served to be eaten G61.1. (63); (129).

SEVERAL. — New race from single pair (or several) after world calamity A1006.1. (16); (20).

SEX. — Mutilation: sex organs cut off S176. (63); transformation of sex to seduce D658.3. (116); (117); (118).

SEXUAL relations between man and demons G302.7.1. (83). — Long distance sexual intercourse K1391. (116); (120); origin of sexual intercourse A1352. (13).

SHADOW mistaken for substance J1790. (130).

SHAGGY. — Giants with shaggy hair on their bodies F531.1.6.3. (124).

SHAM. — Thief shams sickness and steals K341.2.2. (26).

SHAMAN. — Tapir as shaman's spirit helper F403.2.2.1.+. (82).

SHAMANISM. — Origin of priesthood (shamanism, etc.) A1654. (37); (58).

SHARP. — Deer's means of defense: sharp hearing A2461.+. (69); origin of deer's sharp hearing A2428.+. (69).

SHARPENED. — Ogre with sharpened leg G341.1. (89); (90); the sharpened leg J2424. (89); (90).

SHELL. — Origin of knots on armadillo's shell A2312.+. (26).

SHORT pregnancy T573. (13); (39); (42). — Why hawk's neck feathers are short A2313.+. (106).

SHOT. — One arrow shot into end of last one to make rope of arrows F661.7.3. (115).

SICKNESS. — Thief shams sickness and steals K341.2.2. (26).

SINGEING. — Animal characteristics from burning or singeing A2218. (69); (70); (71); (106).

SINGING. — Knowledge from singing D1781.+. (103); song duel. Contest in singing H503.1. (89).

SINGLE. — New race from single pair (or several) after world calamity A1006.1. (16); (20).

SINK. — Man sinks into earth F942. (18); (64).

SISTER. — Brother-in-law marries sister-in-law T425.+. (42); brother-in-law seduces (seeks to seduce) sister-in-law T425. (28); (121); (123); brother-sister incest T415. (22); brother-sister marriage T415.5. (22); punishment for man who makes advances to sister-in-law Q242.3. (28).

SITUATION. — Transformation to escape difficult situation D642. (61).

SIZE of object changed at will D631.3. (8).

SKILLFUL hunter F679.5. (83); (100); marksman F661. (83).

SKUNK. — Helpful skunk B430.+. (147).

SKY lowers on people F791.1. (18); -rope F51. (10); (12); (13); (14); speaks D1619.+. (18). — Animals drop from sky A1795.+. (68); ascent to stars. People or animals ascend to the sky and become stars A761. (3); (5); (6); bird ogre lives in sky G630.+. (100); (101); creation of the sky A701. (24); creator goes to sky A81. (24); first man descends from sky A1231. (16); first woman descends from sky A1231.+. (12); (13); jaguar drops from sky A1795.+. (74); ogre lives in sky G630.+. (93); old man from sky as creator A21.2. (11); woman from sky-world marries mortal man T111.2. (136); (137); (138); (139); (140); women live in the sky F167.+. (12); (13).

SLAIN. — Animals from body of slain person A1724.1. (67); bird from body of slain person A1724.1.+. (89); (90); (91); (92); (95); (97); (98); birds from body of slain monster A1724.1.+. (64); parts of slain animals as token of slaying H105. (100); plants from body of slain person or animal A2611. (61); (62); (63); (64); (65); (66).

SLAYING. — Parts of slain animals as token of slaying H105. (100);

penis of monster as token (proof) of slaying H105.4.+. (67); tail of monster as token (proof) of slaying H105.4.+. (64); (65); (66).

SLEEP feigned to kill enemy K911.3. (128). — Deception by feigned death (sleep) K1860. (121); deception by pretending sleep K1868. (45); (128); murder in one's sleep K959.2. (122); (138).

SLEEPING. — Intercourse with sleeping girl T475.2.1. (118); the sleeping guard N396. (13).

SMALL animal overcomes large L315. (146); earth made to grow large D489.+. (8). — Giants large or small at will F531.6.5.2. (118); very small hero L112.2. (115).

SMELL. — Recognition by smell H30.+. (35); (57).

SNAKE as ogre G354.1. (107); (108); (109); (110). — Creation of snake (serpent) A2145. (105); (106); victim persuaded to hold out his tongue: bit by snake K825.+. (100); woman gives birth to a snake T554.7. (105); (106).

SNAKES. — How snakes received their names A2571.+. (106); why snakes are venomous A2532.1. (106); why some snakes are harmless A2531.+. (106).

SNAKESKIN. — Conception from snakeskin in vagina T532.1.+. (105); (106).

SOFT. — Swallowed person becomes soft F921.1.+. (108).

SOIL. — Magic control of soil and crops D2157. (64).

SON. — Animal son eats human mother G71.+. (131); cruel son S21. (131); father's consent to son's (daughter's) marriage necessary T131.1.2. (33); mother-in-law seduces son-in-law T417.1. (109).

SONG duel. Contest in singing H503.1. (89). — Magic healing song D1500.1.24. (58).

SOUL (life) in the heart E714.4. (63); journeys from the body E721. (107). — Deity provides man with soul A185.12. (11); demons carry off man's soul F402.1.5.1.+. (83).

SOUNDS. — Illusory sounds K1887. (147); other sounds misunderstood J1812. (147); recognition by sounds H30.+. (67).

SOWING. — Origin of sowing and planting A1441.4. (33); (37).

SPEAK. — Sky speaks D1619.+. (18).

SPEAKING bird B211.3. (104); tree D1610.2. (100).

SPEEDY. — Miraculous speedy growth of a tree D2157.4. (26).

SPIRIT causes death F402.1.11. (83); gives warning F403.2.3.2. (83); pursues person F402.1.10. (83). — Familiar spirit in animal form F403.2.2.1. (127); invisible spirit laughs F412.1.+. (83); tabu: offending wood-spirit C43. (124); tapir as shaman's spirit helper F403.2.2.1.+. (82); wood-spirit F441. (64); (124); wood-spirit gigantic F441.5.2. (124).

SPIRITOUS. — Acquisition of spiritous liquors A1427. (58); (59).

SPIRITS help mortal F403.2. (11); (58); live in caves F402.6.4.1. (83). —
Cannibalistic spirits G11.10. (124); evil spirits F402. (59).

SPITTING. — Transformation by spitting D560.+. (139); (140).

SPOT. — Achilles heel. Invulnerability except in one spot Z311. (113);
(114); eyes only vulnerable spot Z310.+. (61); ogress at a spot along
the road takes toll of lives G321.2. (95); why woodpecker has white
spot on its head A2412.2.+. (148).

SPRINKLING. — Resuscitation by sprinkling earth E50.+. (15); (136);
(137); (138); (139); (140).

SQUEEZING. — Ogre kills by squeezing testicles G310.+. (63).

STABBING. — Murder by stabbing S115. (89); (90).

STAFF stuck in river bed stops water D1549.3.8.+. (42). — Magic staff
D1254. (42); river where culture hero drags his staff A934.4.+. (42).

STAR descends as human being A762. (9); (10); (136); (137); (138);
(139); (140). — Mortal marries star-girl A762.2. (136); (137); (138);
(139); (140); transformation: man to star D293. (5); (6); transformation: star to bird D440.+. (137); transformation: star to person
D439.5.2. (136); (137); (138); (139); (140); transformation: woman
to star D293.+. (3); visit to star-world F15. (68); (137); (138);
wish for star wife realized C15.1.1. (136); (137); (138); (139).

STARS are women A761.6.+. (137); as birds A760.+. (88); as children
of the moon A764.1. (137); descend as birds A762.+. (88); thought
of as living beings A761.6. (88). — Ascent to stars. People or
animals ascend to the sky and become stars A761. (3); (5); (6).

STATEMENTS. — Enigmatic statements H580. (109).

STAYING. — Contest: staying awake H1540.+. (90).

STEAL. — Thief shams sickness and steals K341.2.2. (26); transformation to steal D657. (41).

STERILE. — Land made magically sterile D2081. (33).

STINGINESS W152. (51); (52); (53).

STOLEN. — Eaters of stolen food detected J1144. (12); (13); (14);
owner's interest distracted while goods are stolen K341. (146); quest
for lost (stolen) family H1385.9. (123).

STONES. — Extraordinary rocks and stones F800. (91); (92).

STOP. — Staff stuck in river bed stops water D1549.3.8.+. (42); why
deer run, stop, and run on again A2461.4. (69).

STOPPED. — Punishment: bodily orifices stopped up Q450.+. (144).

STRANGLING. — Punishment: strangling Q424. (85).

STRATEGY. — Animals overcome man's adversary by strategy B524.2.
(105); (106); (114); (132); murder by strategy K910. (64); (65); (66);
(67); (89); (90); (91); (92); (100); (101); (105); (106).

STREAMS. — Origin of streams A930. (41); (42); (43).

STRENGTH. — Chief chosen on basis of strength P11.4.+. (112); magic strength D1830. (112); magic strength-giving drink D1335.2. (112); test of strength H1562. (79).

STRIKE. — Escaping before enemy can strike J641. (57); (64); (65); (66); (67); (77); (87); (115); (132).

STRIKING. — Ogre killed by striking G512.8. (63); (104); (113); (114); (128); ogre killed by striking with club G512.8.1. (102).

STRONG. — Remarkably strong man F610. (112); why certain armadillo is strong A2528.+. (80); wise fear of the weak for the strong J613. (64); (65); (66); (67); (108); (113); (114); (115); (125); (130); (131).

STRUCK. — Animal characteristics from being struck A2213.5. (14); (79).

STUCK. — Staff stuck in river bed stops water D1549.3.8.+. (42).

STUNG. — Punishment: being stung by wasps Q453.+. (121).

SUBSTANCE. — Shadow mistaken for substance J1790. (130).

SUBSTITUTED eyes. Lost eyes are replaced by those of another person or animal E781.1. (137).

SUCCESSFULLY. — Eyes successfully replaced E781. (136); (137).

SUFFOCATION. — Murder by suffocation S113.2. (98).

SUITORS ill-treated T75.0.1. (139); (140); (141); (142). — Demon suitors of boy F402.1.15.+. (83).

SUN as human being A736. (72); creates useful animals A1703.+. (72); -god as creator A1.1. (72); hot A733.+. (1); (2). — Contest between sun and moon A736.11. (1); (2); eclipse caused by monster devouring sun or moon A737.1. (4).

SUPERNATURAL growth T615. (42); (131); helpers N810. (122). — Marriage of mortal and supernatural being T111. (41); (42); resuscitation by supernatural person E121. (136); (137); (138); (139); (140); tabu: offending supernatural relative C30. (136); (137); (138); (139); (140); tabu: seeing supernatural creatures C311.1. (124).

SUPPLIED. — Food supplied by magic D1030.1. (44); (48).

SUPPLY. — Acquisition of food supply — miscellaneous A1429. (26); (27); magic food-basket (vessel) supplies food D1472.1.19. (44).

SUPPORTED. — Earth supported by roots A840.+. (21).

SURPRISE capture R4. (12); (13); (14).

SURVIVE. — Marvelous tree survives world-fire A1029.1.+. (24).

SURVIVOR. — Unique survivor Z356. (18); (61); (98).

SWALLOW. — Serpent swallows man F911.7. (107); (108); (109); (110).

SWALLOWED person becomes bald F921. (108); (110); person becomes soft F921.1.+. (108). — Person (animal) swallowed without killing F911. (107); (108); (109); (110).

SWALLOWER. — Victim kills swallower from within by cutting F912.2. (107); (108); (109); (110).

SWEAT. — Man to earn bread by sweat of his brow A1346. (33); (34).

SWIFT. — Why certain armadillo is swift A2555. +. (80).

TABU: going forth during menses C141. (106); killing certain fish C841.9. (47); looking around C332. (20); looking at certain person or thing C310. (48); looking back C331. (33); looking in certain direction C330. (21); offending supernatural relative C30. (136); (137); (138); (139); (140); offending wood-spirit C43. (124); seeing supernatural creatures C311.1. (124); widow not to go outside C898. +. (106). — Death by drowning for breaking tabu C923. (47); flood as punishment for breaking tabu A1018.1. (47); immediate death for breaking tabu C921. (136); (137); (138); (139); (140); laughing tabu C460. (124); loss of wife (husband) for breaking tabu C932. (136); (139).

TAIL of monster as token (proof) of slaying H105.4. +. (64); (65); (66). — Why anteater has tail A2378.1. +. (69).

TAILS. — Persons with tails F518. (62); (64); (65); (66).

TAKE. — Ogress at a spot along the road takes toll of lives G321.2. (95).

TAKEN. — Head of murdered man taken along as trophy S139.2.1.1. (112); (113).

TAPIETE. — Origin of the Tapiete A1611. +. (9).

TAPIR as shaman's spirit helper F403.2.2.1. +. (82). — Food of tapir A2435. +. (69); tapir's habitual bodily movements A2470. +. (69); why tapir has long nose A2335.3.2. (79); why tapir is nocturnal A2491. +. (69); why tapir is pugnacious A2524. +. (69); (70); (71).

TAPIRS. — Chief of tapirs B241.2. +. (79); (82).

TASTE of human flesh leads to habitual cannibalism G36. (89).

TEACH. — Culture hero teaches arts and crafts A541. (43); deity teaches mortal A185.3. (11); (33); (37); (56); gods teach how to seek and prepare food A1420.2. (11); (39); (41).

TEETH. — Large teeth F544.3. +. (64); recognition by teeth H50. +. (57); remarkably long teeth F544.3.5. (62).

TEST of strength H1562. (79). — Cold test H1512. (1); (2); heat test. Attempt to kill hero by burning him in fire H1511. (1); (2).

TESTICLES. — Ogre kills by squeezing testicles G310. +. (63).

TESTS of endurance H1500. (1); (2).

THEFT of fire by bird A1415.2.1. (50); (51); (52); (53); (54); punished Q212. (33); (121). — Vain attempts to circumvent theft of fire A1415.4. (52); (53); (54).

THEFTS and cheats — general K300. (12); (13); (14).

THIEF climbing rope discovered and rope cut K1622. (12); (13); (14); escapes detection K400. (13); (14); shams sickness and steals K341.2.2. (26).

THORNS on plants A2752. (29).

THOUGHT. — Reflection in water thought to be the original of the thing reflected J1791. (147); stars thought of as living beings A761.6. (88).

THOUGHTS. — Magic knowledge of another's thoughts D1819.1. (136).

THROWING. — Murder by throwing earth over victim D2061.2.+. (63).

THUNDER. — Origin of thunder A1142. (7).

TIED. — Animal allows himself to be tied to another for safety K713.1.1. (147).

TIME. — In time of plenty provide for want J711. (69); man goes to heaven for limited time F11.3. (68); (137); (138).

TINY amount of food magically satisfies D1349.1.6. (32).

TOAD drops from clouds A1795.+. (84). — Punishment: transformation into toad Q551.3.2.3.+. (38).

TOBA. — Origin of the Toba A1611.+. (9).

TOBACCO from ashes of bad woman A2611.2.+. (61); (62); (64); (65); (66); from grave of bad woman A2611.2. (63). — Origin of tobacco A2691.2. (61); (62); (63); (64); (65); (66); reincarnation as tobacco plant E631.5.1. (62).

TOKEN. — Parts of slain animals as token of slaying H105. (100); penis of monster as token (proof) of slaying H105.4.+. (67); tail of monster as token (proof) of slaying H105.4.+. (64); (65); (66); victim lured into approach by false token K839.2. (64); (89); (90).

TOKENS of exploits H84. (64); (65); (66); (67); (100).

TOLL. — Ogress at a spot along the road takes toll of lives G321.2. (95).

TONGUE. — Victim persuaded to hold out his tongue: bit by snake K825.+. (100); victim persuaded to hold out his tongue: cut off K825. (101).

TOP. — Sea released from tree-top A924.3. (42).

TORN. — Eyes torn out magically replaced D2161.3.1.1. (136); (137).

TOUCHING. — Conception from touching another's garment T532.5.1. (119).

TRANSFORM. — Culture hero can transform self A527.3.1. (42).

TRANSFORMATION: ashes into birds D441.6.1.+. (89); (90); (91); (92); (95); (96); (97); (98); by being burned D576. (69); (70); (71); by calling out D520.+. (94); by eating ashes D551.+. (134); by spitting D560.+. (139); (140); flight D671. (100); intestines to lianas D457.+. (28); intestines to person D437.+. (28); leaf to beans D451.8.+. (139); (140); maize to brushwood D451.+. (33); man to animal D100. (11); (20); (24); (69); (124); man to armadillo D100.+. (116); (117); (121); man to bird D150. (18); (21); (22); (87); (99); (100); (134); man to butterfly D186.1. (100); man to deer D114.1.1. (127); man to dog D141. (41); man to eagle D152.2. (102); man to eel D173. (61); man to iguana D197.1. (18); (76); man to ogre D94. (62); man to peccary D114.3.1. (18); (70); (77); (78); man to star D293. (5); (6); man to tree D215. (42); man to woman D12. (116); (117); (118); man (woman) to flower D212. (100); normal man to cannibal D91. (62); (67); of sex to seduce D658.3. (116); (117); (118); parakeet to person D350.+. (15); part of animal or person to person D437. (123); star to bird D440.+. (137); star to person D439.5.2. (136); (137); (138); (139); (140); to elude pursuers D642.7. (127); to escape death D642.2. (87); (89); (100); (124); to escape difficult situation D642. (61); to escape from captivity D642.1. (124); to escape notice D642.5. (89); to kill enemy D651.1. (102); to receive food D655. (41); to steal D657. (41); vizcacha to capybara D410.+. (81); wasp to person D380.+. (111); woman to anteater D100.+. (22); woman to bat D100.+. (106); woman to bird D150.+. (94); woman to star D293.+. (3). — Creation of animals through transformation A1710. (69); (70); (71); (106); creation of birds through transformation A1710.+. (99); creation of plants by transformation A2610. (28); gradual transformation D681. (81); partial transformation D682. (41); partial transformation — color changed D682.4. (110); punishment: transformation into frog Q551.3.2.3. (38); punishment: transformation into toad Q551.3.2.3.+. (38); repeated transformation D610. (124).

TRANSFORMATIONS. — Animals from transformations after deluge or world calamity A1711. (18); (20).

TRANSFORMED. — Bird from transformed man A1715.+. (87); parts of human or animal body transformed into plants A2611.0.5. (28); (123); person transformed to moon A747. (3); (56).

TRAP. — Ogre traps victim G421. (97); (98).

TRAPPED. — Victim trapped K730. (12); (13); (14); (15); (64); (67); (114); (134).

TRAVEL. — Object travels by itself D1643. (28); (121).

TREACHEROUS bird K2295.+. (136); (138); brother K2211. (28); fox K2295.+. (144); (147); murder of enemy's children or charges K930. (100); (101); partner K2296. (147).

TREATED. — Suitors ill-treated T75.0.1. (139); (140); (141); (142).

TREE as repository of fire A1414.7.1. (19); (51); containing water and fish F811.+. (39); (42); (49); opens and conceals fugitive D1393.1. (100); (plant) protects D1380.2. (100); refuge R311. (42); (44); (45); (46); (47); (70); (87); (100); (101); (131); (135); to upper world F54. (15); (24). — Bleeding tree F811.20. (42); escape from deluge on tree A1023. (42); (44); (45); (46); (47); extraordinary tree F811. (15); (26); (39); (42); (49); fish-producing tree F811.5.3. (39); (42); (49); magic tree D950. (100); marvelous tree survives world-fire A1029.1.+. (24); miraculous speedy growth of a tree D2157.4. (26); origin of algarrobo tree A2681.+. (26); (27); sea released from tree-top A924.3. (42); self-opening tree-trunk D1556. (100); speaking tree D1610.2. (100); transformation: man to tree D215. (42).

TREES. — Ogres live in trees G637. (95); origin of trees A2681. (24); (25); why jaguar scratches trees A2540.+. (69).

TRIBES. — Distribution of tribes A1620. (21); origin of particular tribes A1611. (22); origin of tribes from choices made A1614.4. (55).

TRICK. — Entrance into girl's (man's) room (bed) by trick K1340. (117); (118).

TRICKSTER. — Bird as trickster J1117.+. (53); (146); culture hero as dupe or trickster A521. (42); diving match: trickster eats food while dupe is under water K16.2. (146); fatal deception into trickster's power K810. (89); (90); (91); (92); (93); (97); (132); (134); fox as trickster J1117.+. (26); (29); (33); (34); (35); (42); (44); (45); (46); (47); (48); (49); (57); (144); (145); (147); iguana as trickster J1117.+. (148); lamb as trickster J1117.+. (150); victim lured by kind words approaches trickster and is killed K815. (93); (98).

TROPHY. — Head of murdered man taken along as trophy S139.2.1.1. (112); (113).

TRUNK. — Self-opening tree-trunk D1556. (100).

TRUTH given in vision D1810.8.1. (107).

TRY. — Foolish imitation by an animal. Tries to go beyond his powers J2413. (147); (149); (150).

UGLINESS. — Extraordinary ugliness F576. (139); (140); (141); (142).

UGLY man becomes handsome D52.2. (141); (142).

UNDER. — Contest in remaining under water H1543. (146); diving match: trickster eats food while dupe is under water K16.2. (146).

UNDERGROUND passages F721.1. (39). — Ogre lives underground G630.+. (66).

UNDERWORLD. — God of the underworld A300. (30); (31); (58); (64).

UNEQUAL marriage T121. (41).

UNIQUE survivor Z356. (18); (61); (98); vulnerability Z310. (63).

UNKINDNESS punished Q280. (100); (101); (142); (143).

UNKNOWN (clandestine) paramour T475. (39); (139). — Infant picks out his unknown father H481. (39); (40).

UNNATURAL mother eats children G72.+. (113); (114).

UNSUCCESSFUL. — Animals created after initial unsuccessful experiment A630.+. (69); (70); (71).

UNWITTING marriage to cannibal G81. (63).

UPPER. — Ascent to upper world on arrow chain F53. (115); birds carry person from upper world F62.2. (138); inhabitant of upper world visits earth F30. (7); (9); (10); (12); (13); (14); (15); (56); (72); (93); journey to upper world F10. (17); (37); (68); (135); (136); (137); (138); (141); rain from sea in upper world A1131.3. (7); refuge in upper world R323. (24); (115); (135); return from upper world F10.1. (68); (137); (138); (141); series of upper worlds A651.1. (7); tree to upper world F54. (15); (24); women live in upper world F167.+. (14).

URINE. — Crystals from urine D1454.+. (136); jewels from urine D1454.+. (137); (138); magic urine D1002.1. (136); (137); (138).

USE. — Jaguar uses fire B200.+. (129); origin of the use of the rattle A1461.4. (58).

USEFUL. — Sun creates useful animals A1703.+. (72).

VAGINA. — Conception from sand in vagina T532.+. (10); conception from snakeskin in vagina T532.1.+. (105); (106).

VAIN attempts to circumvent theft of fire A1415.4. (52); (53); (54).

VANISHED. — Quest for vanished wife (mistress) H1385.3. (28); (136); (137); (138).

VEGETABLES produced by magic D2178.+. (136); (139); (140).

VENOMOUS. — Why snakes are venomous A2532.1. (106).

VESSEL. — Inexhaustible vessel D1652.5. (44); (133); magic food-basket (vessel) supplies food D1472.1.19. (44); magic vessel D1171. (44).

VICTIM burned in his own house (or hiding place) K812. (96); (97); (98); kills swallower from within by cutting F912.2. (107); (108); (109); (110); lured by kind words approaches trickster and is killed K815. (93); (98); lured into approach by false token K839.2. (64); (89); (90); persuaded to hold out his tongue: bit by snake K825.+. (100); persuaded to hold out his tongue: cut off K825. (101); trapped K730. (12); (13); (14); (15); (64); (67); (114); (134). — Cutting rope to kill ogre who is climbing the rope to kill his victim K678. (115); murder by throwing earth over victim D2061.2.+. (63); ogre traps victim G421. (97); (98); rope cut and victim dropped K963. (12); (13); (115).

VICTIMS. — Bones of victims in front of ogre's house G691.+. (100); (104).
VIGILANCE. — Dupe persuaded to relax vigilance: seized K827. (93).
VISION. — Truth given in vision D1810.8.1. (107).
VISIONS. — Non-religious visions V514. (107).
VISIT to land of moon F16. (32); (37); (141); (142); (143); to star-world F15. (68); (137); (138). — Inhabitant of upper world visits earth F30. (7); (9); (10); (12); (13); (14); (15); (56); (72); (93).
VITAL bodily members E780. (28).
VIVIFIED. — Man made from clay image and vivified A1241.3. (9).
VIZCACHA. — Transformation: vizcacha to capybara D410.+. (81).
VIZCACHAS. — Chief of vizcachas B241.2.+. (81).
VOICE. — Man with marvelous voice F688. (89).
VULNERABILITY. — Unique vulnerability Z310. (63).
VULNERABLE. — Eyes only vulnerable spot Z310.+. (61).
VULTURE. — Creation of vulture A1931. (91); (92).
WALK. — Cause of bird's walk A2441.2. (94).
WANT. — In time of plenty provide for want J711. (69).
WARN. — Animals warn against attack B521.3. (98); dream warns of danger which will happen in near future D1810.8.3.2. (78); dream warns of illness or injury D1810.8.3.1.1. (78).
WARNING in dreams D1810.8.3. (78); (120). — Bird gives warning B143.1. (98); (108); (123); spirit gives warning F403.2.3.2. (83).
WARNINGS. — Attention to warnings J1050. (30); (78); inattention to warnings J652. (13); (46); (47); (48); (100); (108); (124); (138).
WASP as ogre G350.+. (111). — Devastating wasp B16.6.+. (111); transformation: wasp to person D380.+. (111).
WASPS. — Punishment: being stung by wasps Q453.+. (121).
WATER. — Contest in remaining under water H1543. (146); diving match: trickster eats food while dupe is under water K16.2. (146); owner of water A420.+. (46); reflection in water thought to be the original of the thing reflected J1791. (147); staff stuck in river bed stops water D1549.3.8.+. (42); tree containing water and fish F811.+. (39); (42); (49); why capybara lives in the water A2433.2.2.+. (81).
WATERMELON. — Origin of watermelon A2687.+. (32).
WATERS made to dry up D2151.0.2. (107); (108). — Magic control of waters D2151. (45); (47); (48).
WATERSNAKES. — Queen of watersnakes B244.1.1. (108).
WEAK. — Wise fear of the weak for the strong J613. (64); (65); (66); (67); (108); (113); (114); (115); (125); (130); (131).
WEAPON. — Giant with club as weapon F531.4.5.1.+. (122).

WHITE. — Demon in form of white woman G302.3.3.+. (83); origin of white man A1614.9. (24); why woodpecker has white spot on its head A2412.2.+. (148).

WHOLE. — Partially eaten fruit made whole again D2150.+. (32); (37).

WIDOW. — Tabu: widow not to go outside C898.+. (106).

WIFE flees from animal husband R227.1. (129). — Creator's wife A32.3. (11); cruel wife S60.+. (87); help from ogre's wife (mistress) G530.1. (100); loss of wife (husband) for breaking tabu C932. (136); (139); quest for vanished wife (mistress) H1385.3. (28); (136); (137); (138); wish for star wife realized C15.1.1. (136); (137); (138); (139).

WILD. — Origin of wild boar A1871.1. (85); why wild boar is fierce A2524.+. (69); why wild boar lives in woods A2433.2.1.+. (69).

WILDCAT. — Food of wildcat A2435.3.2.+. (69); (70); (71); why wildcat is nocturnal A2491.+. (69); wildcat's dwelling A2432.+. (69).

WILL. — Giants large or small at will F531.6.5.2. (118); person changes appearance at will D631.1.1. (61); (100); (116); (117); (121); (124); (127); (128); (134); size of object changed at will D631.3. (8).

WIND produced by magic D2142.1. (67); (100). — Burning intestinal wind F1041.+. (108); (109); magic intestinal wind causes disease D1500.4.+. (132); magic wind D906. (108).

WINGS. — Flight on artificial wings F1021.1. (135); (149).

WISDOM (knowledge) from dream J157. (11); (120); (128); of caution J580. (20); (21); (42); (62); (78); (93); (104); (105); (106).

WISE fear of the weak for the strong J613. (64); (65); (66); (67); (108); (113); (114); (115); (125); (130); (131).

WISH for star wife realized C15.1.1. (136); (137); (138); (139). — Overheard wish is realized N699.6. (137); (138); (139).

WITHIN. — Animal (monster) killed from within K952. (107); (108); (109); (110); victim kills swallower from within by cutting F912.2. (107); (108); (109); (110).

WOMAN devours her husband G11.6.4. (113); (114); from sky-world marries mortal man T111.2. (136); (137); (138); (139); (140); gives birth to a snake T554.7. (105); (106); plans to eat her children G72.1. (63). — Attempted rape of man disguised as woman J1820.+. (118); condition of first man (woman) A1281. (12); (13); (15); creation of first man's (woman's) mate A1275. (9); demon in form of white woman G302.3.3.+. (83); first man (woman) A1280. (9); (10); (12); (13); (15); (16); first woman descends from sky A1231.+. (12); (13); man-eating woman G11.6. (61); (62); (63); (64); (66); (113); (114); old woman as creator A15.1.1. (11); remarkably beautiful woman F575.1. (39); (40); (41); (106); seduction by man disguising as woman K1321. (116); (117); (118); seduction by masking as woman's husband K1311. (35); tobacco from ashes of bad woman A2611.2.+. (61); (62); (64); (65); (66); tobacco from grave of bad woman A2611.2. (63); transformation: man (woman) to flower D212. (100); transformation: man to woman D12. (116); (117); (118); transformation: woman to anteater D100.+. (22); transformation: woman to bat D100.+. (106); transformation: woman to bird D150.+. (94); transformation: woman to star D293.+. (3).

WOMEN live in the sky F167.+. (12); (13); live in upper world F167.+. (14). — Journey to land of women F112. (145); stars are women A761.6.+. (137).

WON. — Endurance contest won by deception K50. (148); race won by deception K11. (150).

WOOD-spirit F441. (64); (124); -spirit gigantic F441.5.2. (124). — Tabu: offending wood-spirit C43. (124).

WOODPECKER. — Color of woodpecker A2411.2.4.1. (148); helpful woodpecker B461.1. (108); (148); why woodpecker has white spot on its head A2412.2.+. (148).

WOODS. — Why anteater lives in woods A2433.2.1.+. (75); why iguana lives in woods A2433.2.1.+. (76); why peccary lives in woods A2433.2.1.+. (69); (77); why wild boar lives in woods A2433.2.1.+. (69).

WOOER. — Girl as wooer T55. (33); (57); (119).

WOOING by emissary T51. (41); (57).

WORDS. — Victim lured by kind words approaches trickster and is killed K815. (93); (98).

WORLD-fire A1030. (19); (20); (21); (23); (24); (25). — Animals from transformations after deluge or world calamity A1711. (18); (20); ascent to upper world on arrow chain F53. (115); birds carry person from upper world F62.2. (138); earth-disturbances at end of world A1060. (18); earthquakes at the end of the world A1061.1. (18); inhabitant of upper world visits earth F30. (7); (9); (10); (12); (13); (14); (15); (56); (72); (93); journey to lower world F80. (21); journey to upper world F10. (17); (37); (68); (135); (136); (137); (138); (141); marvelous tree survives world-fire A1029.1.+. (24); men hide from world-fire and renew race A1038. (19); (20); (21); new race from single pair (or several) after world calamity A1006.1. (16); (20); preservation of life during world calamity A1005. (17);

(18); (19); (20); (21); (23); quest for the world's end H1371.1. (21); rain from sea in upper world A1131.3. (7); refuge in lower world R323.+. (21); refuge in upper world R323. (24); (115); (135); renewal of world after world calamity A1006. (16); (18); (21); (23); (24); (25); return from upper world F10.1. (68); (137); (138); (141); tree to upper world F54. (15); (24); visit to star-world F15. (68); (137); (138); woman from sky-world marries mortal man T111.2. (136); (137); (138); (139); (140); women live in upper world F167.+. (14).

WORLDS above and below A651.3. (12); (13); (14); (15); (21). — Series of upper worlds A651.1. (7).

WOULD-be killers killed K1626. (89); (90); (91); (92).

YOUNG. — Foolish marriage of old man and young girl J445.2. (87).

YOUNGER. — Elder brother rescues younger R155.2. (107); (108); elder children to protect younger P250.1. (6).

YOUTH. — Age and youth in love T91.4. (41).

Motif Distribution by Motif Group

The Thompson category with by far the largest number of motifs is the one relating to MYTHOLOGY. It contains 481 motifs (26%), more than a quarter of the total number. The second largest category, MAGIC, contains only about half as many motifs, 247 (13%). These are followed by MARVELS (189 = 10%), and four categories each containing 7% of the total.

Of the subcategories, the four largest all cluster around 5%: *Creation and ordering of human life* (108 motifs), *Transformation* (106), *Animal characteristics* (103), and *Magic powers and manifestations* (101). Not surprisingly, all four belong to the two numerically dominant categories.

Motif group	Motif subgroup	Number of motifs
MYTHOLOGICAL MOTIFS	Creator	10
	Gods	18
	Demigods and culture heroes	18
	Cosmogony and cosmology	59
	Topographical features of the earth	8
	World calamities	46
	Establishment of natural order	10
	Creation and ordering of human life	108
	Creation of animal life	54
	Animal characteristics	103
	Origin of trees and plants	42
	Origin of plant characteristics	5
	Subtotal motifs	481

Motif group	Motif subgroup	Number of motifs
ANIMALS	Mythical animals	32
	Magic animals	7
	Animals with human traits	33
	Friendly animals	57
	Marriage of person to animal	4
	Fanciful traits of animals	3
	Miscellaneous animal motifs	6
	Subtotal motifs	142
TABU	Tabu connected with supernatural beings	10
	Sex tabu	1
	Looking tabu	5
	Speaking tabu	1
	Miscellaneous tabus	2
	Punishment for breaking tabu	8
	Subtotal motifs	27
MAGIC	Transformation	106
	Magic objects	40
	Magic powers and manifestations	101
	Subtotal motifs	247
THE DEAD	Resuscitation	41
	Ghosts and other revenants	1
	Reincarnation	1
	The Soul	8
	Subtotal motifs	51
MARVELS	Otherworld journeys	57
	Marvelous creatures	65
	Extraordinary places and things	29
	Extraordinary occurrences	38
	Subtotal motifs	189

Motif group	Motif subgroup	Number of motifs
OGRES	Kinds of ogres	90
	Falling into ogre's power	2
	Ogre defeated	34
	Other ogre motifs	7
	Subtotal motifs	133
TESTS	Identity tests: recognition	16
	Marriage tests	2
	Tests of cleverness	2
	Tests of prowess: quests	16
	Other tests	15
	Subtotal motifs	51
THE WISE AND THE FOOLISH	Acquisition and possession of wisdom (knowledge)	3
	Wise and unwise conduct	67
	Cleverness	46
	Fools (and other unwise persons)	28
	Subtotal motifs	144
DECEPTIONS	Contests won by deception	4
	Thefts and cheats	10
	Escape by deception	9
	Capture by deception	18
	Fatal deception	55
	Deception into self-injury	4
	Deception into humiliating position	1
	Seduction or deceptive marriage	9
	Dupe's property destroyed	1
	Deceiver falls into own trap	7
	Deception through shams	11
	Villains and traitors	6
	Subtotal motifs	135

Motif group	*Motif subgroup*	*Number of motifs*
REVERSAL OF FORTUNE	Unpromising hero (heroine)	1
	Triumph of the weak	1
	Subtotal motifs	2
CHANCE AND FATE	Unlucky accidents	3
	Lucky accidents	11
	Helpers	20
	Subtotal motifs	34
SOCIETY	Royalty and nobility	1
	The family	4
	Customs	2
	Subtotal motifs	7
REWARDS AND PUNISHMENTS	Deeds punished	10
	Kinds of punishment	42
	Subtotal motifs	52
CAPTIVES AND FUGITIVES	Captivity	9
	Rescues	3
	Escapes and pursuits	3
	Refuges and recapture	16
	Subtotal motifs	31
UNNATURAL CRUELTY	Cruel relatives	12
	Revolting murders or mutilations	16
	Abandoned or murdered children	1
	Subtotal motifs	29

Motif group	Motif subgroup	Number of motifs
SEX	Love	10
	Marriage	17
	Illicit sexual relations	19
	Conception and birth	19
	Care of children	5
	Subtotal motifs	70
THE NATURE OF LIFE	Nature of life—miscellaneous	1
	Subtotal motifs	1
RELIGION	Religious motifs—miscellaneous	1
	Subtotal motifs	1
TRAITS OF CHARACTER	Favorable traits of character	1
	Unfavorable traits of character	5
	Subtotal motifs	6
MISCELLANEOUS GROUPS OF MOTIFS	Unique exceptions	7
	Subtotal motifs	7
21 MOTIF GROUPS	88 SUBGROUPS	
	TOTAL NUMBER OF MOTIFS	1840

Glossary

Agouti	Rodent of the genus *Dasyprocta*, about the size of a rabbit.
Ahláta	Boa constrictor.
Akoié	Rosy-billed pochard, *Netta peposaca;* a duck.
Alawó	Black aquatic bird, shamanic tutelary spirit who produces loud thunder claps.
Algarroba	Fruit of the algarrobo, the carob tree (*Prosopris nigra* H.). Fruit has sweet pulpy edible pods.
Algarrobo	Carob tree (*Prosopis nigra* H.).
Aloja	Fermented drink.
Anaconda	A large arboreal snake, *Eunectes marinus*, of the boa family of tropical South America.
Añapa	Unfermented drink made of ground fruit and water.
Anco	Squash.
Anteater	*See* Okosa.
Armadillo	*See* Gualacate.
Armadillo	*See* Ithlió.
Armadillo	*See* Kasókchi.
Aséta	*See* Gualacate.
Atá	Coragyps atratus; vulture.
Athlu	Iguana, *Tupinambis tegixiu.*
Ausá	White-lipped peccary, *Tayassu pecari albirostris.*
Black-and-chestnut eagle	*Oroaetus isidori.*
Bola verde	*Capparis speciosa.*
Bottle tree	*Chorisia insignis*, the palo boracho or yuchan tree with a bulbous extended trunk.
Burrowing owl	*Speotyto cunicularia.*
Canary-winged parakeet	*Protogeris versicolorus.*
Canauba	Palm, *Copernicia cerifera.*

Caracara	*Polyborus vulgaris,* large hawk of vulturelike habits with long legs and able to run well on the ground. Common in the Chaco region.
Caraguata	*Bromelia argentina* of Argentina and Paraguay. Plant with leaves that yield a long silky fiber. Used as basic cordage material. Its fruit is edible.
Cata	*See* Canary-winged parakeet.
Chachalaca	*See* Charata.
Chaguar	Vegetable fiber of caraguata (*Bromelia argentina*). *See* Caraguata.
Chalk-browed mockingbird	*Mimus saturninus.*
Chancho rosillo	Peccary, *Dicotyles tajacu.*
Charata	Chaco chachalaca (*Ortalis canicollis*). Lives in trees with thick scrub below.
Chicha	Fermented beverage.
Chunga	*Chunga burmeisteri,* a cariama of northern Argentina that is smaller and darker than the crested cariama, has a shorter crest, and frequents more wooded terrain.
Condor	*Sarcoramphus papa,* king vulture.
Creamy-bellied thrush	*Turdus amaurochalinus.*
Dark-billed cuckoo	*Coccyzus melacoryphus.*
Deer	*Mazama americana.*
Dorado	*Salminus maxillosus,* large golden characin of the Río de la Plata drainage and related species that resemble salmons and are outstanding food fishes.
Echéie	Vampire, *Desmodus rotundus.*
Fox	*Cerdocyon thons.*
Great Kiskadee	*See* Pétohi.
Gualacate	White-brisked hairy armadillo, *Chaetophractus villosus.*
Honey bear	*Tamandua tetradactyla.*
Iguana	*See* Athlu.
Ithlió	*Tolypeutes matacus.*
Ixñéni	Plumbeous ibis, *Harpiprion caerulescens;* a marsh bird.
Kaláwon	*See* Alawó.
Kasókchi	Nine-banded armadillo, *Dasypus novemcinctus.*
Kíxnie	Collared peccary, *Dicotyles tajacu tajacu.*

Laughing falcon	*Herpetotheres cachinnans.*
Lignum vitae	Tree, *Caesalpinia melanocarpa.*
Mahsas	Bees, *Trigona sp.*
Maize parrot	*Pionus maximilianus.*
Mistol tree	*Zizyphus mistol,* useful tree with edible fruit.
Mojarra	Generic name for freshwater fish.
Molle	General term in Argentina for a variety of plants.
Moro moro	Hone-producing bee, *Melipona.*
Okosa	Giant anteater, *Priodontes maximus.*
Palo santo	*Bulnesia sarmienti* L. of the family Zygophyllaceae; occurs in the dry hinterlands of Argentina and Paraguay and has a resinous heartwood.
Pasá	A large stork of tropical America, *Jabiru mycteria.*
Peccary	Several species of more or less nocturnal gregarious wild boar of the genus *Tayassu.*
Peccary	*See* Ausá.
Peccary	*See* Chancho rosillo.
Peccary	*See* Kíxnie.
Peccary	*See* Quimilero.
Pétohi	The great kiskadee, *Pitangus sulphuratus;* tyrant-flycatcher.
Pez armado	Armored catfish.
Plumbeous ibis	*Harpiprion caerulescens. See* Ixñéni.
Quebracho blanco	*Aspidosperma quebracho (Aspidosperma blanco Sch.),* tree of Argentina and Chile with notably hard wood that yields quebracho bark as a source of tannin.
Quimilero	Four species of peccary.
Red-headed vulture	*Cathartes aura.*
Rhea	*Rhea americana,* a large flightless bird that resembles but is smaller than the African ostrich.
Rosy-billed pochard	*See* Akoié.
Rufous ovenbird	*Funarius rufus,* passerine bird which derives its name from the shape of its nest.
Sachasandia	*Capparis salicifolia.*
See	Martinete, heron-like bird with a tuft of white feathers.
Sparrow hawk	*Accipiter* sp.
Striped cuckoo	*Tapera naevia.*
Tala tree	*Celtis tala,* timber tree of Argentina.
Tséxmataki	Mythical personnage, incarnation of cannibalism.

Tuco-tuco	South American hystricomorph burrowing rodent of the genus *Ctenomys*.
Tusca	*Acacia moniliformis,* a scrubwood.
Ucle	Kind of cactus.
Vizcacha	*Also* viscacha, viscache, or biscacha. Burrowing rodent closely related to the chinchilla. Sometimes referred to as rabbit by Europeans.
Woodcreeper	Bird belonging to the Dendrocolaptidae family.

Bibliography

Bartolomé, Miguel Alberto
  1972   "Indian Groups in Argentina: The Chaco Area and Mi-
          siones Province." In *The Situation of the Indian in South
          America*, W. Dostal, ed., 430–432. Geneva: World Coun-
          cil of Churches.
Bejarano, Ramón César
  1977   *Parcialidades indígenas actuales.* Private edition.
Bórmida, Marcelo
  1969–1970a "Mito y cultura." *Runa* 11 (1–2):9–52.
  1969–1970b "Problemas de heurística mitográfica." *Runa* 11(1–2):53–55.
Brinton, Daniel Garrison
  1891   *The American Race: A Linguistic Classification and Ethno-
          graphic Description of the Native Tribes of North and
          South America.* New York.
Canals Frau, Salvador
  1953   *Las poblaciones indígenas de la Argentina.* Buenos Aires.
Chase-Sardi, Miguel
  1972   *La situación actual de los indígenas en el Paraguay.* Centro
          de Estudios Antropológicos, Universidad Católica Nuestra
          Señora de la Asunción. Asunción del Paraguay.
Chervin, Arthur
  1907–1908 *Anthropologie Bolivienne: Mission Scientifique G. de
          Créqui-Montfort et E. Senéchal de la Grange.* 3 vols. Paris.
Comajuncosa, A., and A. Corrado
  1884   *El colegio franciscano de Tarija y sus misiones.* Noticias
          Históricas Recogidas por los Misioneros del Mismo Cole-
          gio. Quaracchi.
Cordeu, Edgardo J.
  1967   *Cambio cultural y configuración ocupacional en una co-
          munidad toba: Miraflores-Chaco.* Informe Preliminar.
          Publicación No. 123J. Buenos Aires: Comisión Nacional
          del Río Bermejo.

1969   "La comunidad toba de Miraflores: materiales para el
              estudio de un proceso de cambio." Buenos Aires: Comisión
              Nacional de la Cuenca del Plata.
1969–1970 "Aproximación al horizonte mítico de los Tobas." *Runa*
              12(1–2):67–176.
1973*a*   "Textos míticos de los angaite (chena nesma) y sanapana."
              Scripta Ethnologica 1(1):199–234.
1973*b*   "Algunos personajes y nociones míticos de los angaite o
              chenanesma." *Scripta Ethnologica* 1(1):237–248.
1980   "Aishtuwente: la idea de deidad en la religiosidad chama-
              coco." Doctoral thesis, Universidad de Buenos Aires.
1984   "Categorías básicas, principios lógicos y redes simbólicas
              de la cosmovisión de los indios Ishír." *Journal of Latin
              American Lore* 10(2):189–276.
Ms.   "Mitos y relatos de los Ishír: literatura oral de los indios
              Chamacoco del Chaco Boreal."
Cordeu, Edgardo J., and Alejandra Siffredi
1978   "La expresión de lo numinoso en dos mitologías del Gran
              Chaco: apuntes sobre el mito y la intuición de la potencia
              entre los Chamacoco y los Chorote." *Revista del Instituto
              de Antropología* (Universidad Nacional de Córdoba)6:
              159–196.
Gerzenstein, A.
1978   "Lengua chorote: Instituto de Lingüística." *Archivo de
              Lenguas Precolombianas*, 2 vols. Facultad de Filosofía y
              Letras, Universidad de Buenos Aires.
Haekel, Josef
1959   "Purá und Hochgott: Probleme der südamerikanischen
              Religionsethnologie." *Archiv für Völkerkunde*, vol. 13.
              Vienna.
Hunt, Richard James
1915   "El choroti o yofuaha." *Revista del Museo de La Plata*
              (Liverpool), vol. 23.
Karsten, Rafael
1932   *Indian Tribes of the Argentine and Bolivian Chaco*. Socie-
              tas Scientiarum Fennica, vol. 4. Helsinki.
Key, Harold, and Mary Key
1967   *Bolivian Indian Tribes: Classification, Bibliography, and
              Map of Present Language Distribution*. Norman: Summer
              Institute of Linguistics, University of Oklahoma.
Loukotka, Čestmír
1968   *Classification of South American Indian Languages*. Los

Angeles: UCLA Latin American Center Publications, University of California.

Lozano, Pedro
1941   *Descripción corográfica del Gran Chaco Gualamba.* Universidad Nacional Tucumán, no. 283. Tucumán.

Mashnshnek, Celia Olga
1972   "Algunos personajes de la mitología chorote." *Relaciones* (n.s.) 6:109–143.
1973*a*   "Seres potentes y héroes míticos de los Mataco del Chaco central." *Scripta Ethnologica* 1(1):105–154.
1973*b*   "La economía de los Chorote del Chaco central: algunos aspectos mítico-religiosos de la producción." *Relaciones* (n.s.) 7:57–63.
1974   "La economía de los Mataco del Chaco Argentino." *Cuadernos Franciscanos* 35:26–32.
1975   "Textos míticos de los Chulupí del Chaco central." *Scripta Ethnologica* 3(1):151–189.
1976   "El mito en la vida de los aborígenes del Chaco central: presencia y actuación de las teofanías." *Scripta Ethnologica* 4(1):7–27.
1978   "Aspectos mítico-religiosos en la economía de los Mataco del Chaco central." *Revista Española de Antropología Americana* 78:181–202.

Nivel, E. van
1845   "Informe de la expedición de 1844." *La Gaceta Mercantil,* no. 6419 (March 14, 1845). Buenos Aires.

von Nordenskiöld, Erland
1912   La vie des Indiens dans le Chaco. *Revue de Géographie* 6:3.
1926   *Indianliv.* Stockholm: Åhlén and Åkerlund.

von Rosen, Eric
1904   "The Chorotes, Indians of the Bolivian Chaco." *Proceedings of the International Congress of Americanists* 14(2): 649–658.
1924   *Ethnographical Research During the Swedish Chaco-Cordillera Expedition 1901–1902.* Fritu: Stockholm.

Siffredi, Alejandra
1973   "La autoconciencia de las relaciones sociales entre los Yojwáha-Chorote." *Scripta Ethnologica* 1(1):71–103.
1974   "La vida social de los Chorote: informe preliminar." *Cuadernos Franciscanos* (Salta), no. 35:38–50.
1976   "El papel de la polaridad en la intuición de la potencia."

Scripta Ethnologica 4(1):147–155.

1979   "La noción de reciprocidad entre los Yohwaha-Chorote."
          Scripta Ethnologica 3(1):41–70.

1982   "Temporalidad y espacio en la cosmovisión Chorote Mon-
          taraz." Doctoral thesis, Universidad de Buenos Aires.

1984   "Los niveles semánticos de la cosmovisión Chorote."
          Journal of Latin American Lore 10(1):87–110.

Smith, Robert Jerome

Ms.   "Ethnological Research in Paraguay, 1975–1976."

Susnik, B.

1972   "Dimensiones migratorias y pautas culturales de los pueb-
          los del Gran Chaco y su periferia. (Enfoque etnológico)."
          Suplemento Antropológico 7(1–2). Asunción del Paraguay.

Thompson, Stith

1955–1958 *Motif-Index of Folk Literature.* 6 vols. Bloomington: Indi-
          ana University Press.

Wassén, Henry

1966–1967 "Four Swedish Anthropologists in Argentina in the First
          Decades of the 20th Century: Bio-Bibliographical Notes."
          Folk 8–9:343–350.

Zerries, Otto

1969   "Entstehung oder Erwerb der Kulturpflanzen und Begin
          des Bodenbaues im Mythos der Indianer Südamerikas."
          Paideuma 15:64–124.